Introducing
Social Work

Sara Miller McCune founded SAGE Publishing in 1965 to support the dissemination of usable knowledge and educate a global community. SAGE publishes more than 1000 journals and over 800 new books each year, spanning a wide range of subject areas. Our growing selection of library products includes archives, data, case studies and video. SAGE remains majority owned by our founder and after her lifetime will become owned by a charitable trust that secures the company's continued independence.

Los Angeles | London | New Delhi | Singapore | Washington DC | Melbourne

Introducing Social Work

Edited by
Jonathan Parker

Learning Matters
A SAGE Publishing Company
1 Oliver's Yard
55 City Road
London EC1Y 1SP

SAGE Publications Inc.
2455 Teller Road
Thousand Oaks, California 91320

SAGE Publications India Pvt Ltd
B 1/I 1 Mohan Cooperative Industrial Area
Mathura Road
New Delhi 110 044

SAGE Publications Asia-Pacific Pte Ltd
3 Church Street
#10-04 Samsung Hub
Singapore 049483

Editor: Kate Keers/Catriona McMullen
Development editor: Sarah Turpie
Senior project editor: Chris Marke
Project management: Swales & Willis Ltd, Exeter, Devon
Marketing manager: Camille Richmond
Cover design: Wendy Scott
Typeset by: C&M Digitals (P) Ltd, Chennai, India
Printed in the UK

Library of Congress Control Number: 2020930947

British Library Cataloguing in Publication Data

A catalogue record for this book is available from the
British Library

ISBN 978-1-5264-6335-7
ISBN 978-1-5264-6336-4 (pbk)

At SAGE we take sustainability seriously. Most of our products are printed in the UK using responsibly sourced papers and
boards. When we print overseas we ensure sustainable papers are used as measured by the PREPS grading system. We
undertake an annual audit to monitor our sustainability.

Contents

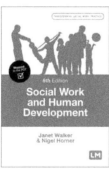

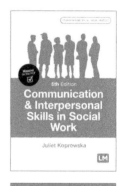

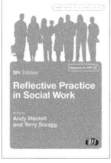

Acknowledgements

Drawing together a compendium such as this is a complex, lengthy and often fraught task. As such it could not have been possible without the unstinting commitment and input of the chapter authors, to whom my grateful thanks must go. It is also important to acknowledge that the many students I have had the privilege to teach over the years have provided me with thoughts and questions that need to be explored. I hope this book goes some way to providing a forum to air such questions for future students. My thanks must also go to Kate Keers, who first explored the idea with me for this book some years ago, and to Cat McMullen, who stepped into Kate's shoes at Sage. The two of you have been continually supportive and encouraging and able to ensure I stay on track! The steady hand of Sarah Turpie as freelance editor has helped me enormously with the task of drawing everything together. Finally, I must say a big thank you to my wonderful wife, Sara Ashencaen Crabtree, who has put up with my hermit-like existence as the book came into shape, while having to finish books of her own! Without you all this book would still be at the 'thinking' stage.

About the authors

Jonathan Parker is Professor of Society and Social Welfare at Bournemouth University and a Fellow of the Academy of Social Sciences. He is Visiting Professor at the Tasik Chini Research Centre Universiti Kebangsaan Malaysia, Universiti Sains Malaysia and member of the academic team for the social work doctoral programme at Università del Sacro Cuore, Milan. He was one of the founders and director of the Family Assessment and Support Unit, a placement agency attached to the University of Hull.

Lucille Allain is Associate Professor in Social Work and Director of Programmes for the social work pre-qualifying programmes at Middlesex University. She has 18 years of child and family social work experience in child protection, looked after children and disabled children. Her experience spans working as a social worker, as a manager and in commissioning and developing new services. Her current research focuses on social work practice and young people leaving care.

Ann Anka is a Lecturer in Social Work at the University of East Anglia. She is a registered social worker and her specialist areas of practice include working with older people and palliative care. Her research interests are in the involvement of people who use services in the assessments of students, and working with those deemed as marginal or failing students.

Toby Berman-Rossi was a Professor of Social Work at Barry University who died in 2004. Her areas of expertise were social work with groups and social work practice with older people. Her work with Timothy B. Kelly formed the basis for the chapter.

Toby Brandon is a Lecturer within the Department of Social Work, Education and Community Wellbeing at Northumbria University. He lectures extensively within Disability and Mad Studies, and his interests lie in inclusion and engagement, disablist hate crime, advocacy and mental health recovery.

Sean Creaney is a Lecturer in Psychosocial Analysis of Offending Behaviour at Edge Hill University. He was previously a Trustee of the National Association for Youth Justice, where he advocated for the establishment of a rights-based statutory framework, and is currently an adviser at social justice charity Peer Power.

Emma Evans is a Learning and Organisational Development Advisor with Dorset County Council adult services team.

Jo Finch is Programme Leader for the Professional Doctorate in Social Work and Deputy Director of the Centre for Social Work Research at the University of East London. She has previously worked as a children and families social worker in both the voluntary and statutory sectors.

Nick Frost is Professor of Social Work (Childhood, Children and Families) at Leeds Beckett University. He researches and writes widely in relation to childhood, multi-disciplinary work, children in care, family support and safeguarding. He has been the Independent Chair of Bradford Safeguarding Children Board since 2010, and has been a keynote speaker at regional, national and international conferences on child welfare and professional learning.

Helen Guizani is an Assistant Team Manager of the Child Asylum and 16+ Team within Solihull Children's Services, and currently works in the Aspire Through Care Team, supporting looked after children and young people within the authority. She also manages and mentors a number of both newly qualified practitioners and social work students.

Deborah Hadwin is a Senior Lecturer in Social Work at De Montfort University and is a PhD student at Coventry researching local authority responses to unaccompanied refugee minors as they reach adulthood. Prior to entering academia she worked in local authorities for 18 years, seven of those years as a manager working with unaccompanied refugee minors.

Trish Hafford-Letchfield is Professor of Social Work and Social Policy at the University of Strathclyde. A qualified social worker, she has several years' experience of managing statutory social work services for adults. She has written textbooks on leadership, management and organisational development and has a particular interest in the experiences of ageing in marginalised communities.

Orlanda Harvey is a PhD student at Bournemouth University, undertaking a mixed methods study in androgenic anabolic steroid use. She qualified as a social worker in 2016 and has worked in the addiction and adult social work fields and organisational development.

Robert Johns teaches at the University of East London, where he has been Head of Social Work and programme leader for the qualifying MA offered in conjunction with the Tavistock and Portman NHS Foundation Trust. He is the author of *Using the Law in Social Work*, now in its eighth edition, *Social Work, Social Policy and Older People* and, most recently, *Capacity and Autonomy*.

Nancy Kelly is Professor and Head of Social Work at Northumbria University. Nancy is a social psychologist specialising in children and families' social work and child safeguarding.

Timothy B. Kelly is Dean of the School of Education and Social Work, and Professor of Social Work at the University of Dundee. His research interests include the care of older people in health and social care settings, supporting carers, groupwork practice and improving professional social work education.

Juliet Koprowska is a Lecturer at the University of York and has taught both interviewing skills and mental health for many years. She was a key participant in the creation of models for teaching interviewing skills and for undertaking direct observation, both of which have been widely adopted, and is currently co-running a project on interprofessional learning in mental health.

Sally Lee is a Lecturer in Social Work at Bournemouth University. Her research interests include safeguarding adults, the impact on practice of the Care Act 2014, wellbeing focused theory and practice and sexual wellbeing and disability.

Allan Norman qualified as a social worker in 1990, and as a solicitor 10 years later. In addition to maintaining an independent social work practice, Celtic Knot, Allan trains and lectures on social work law, including contributing to qualifying and post-qualifying courses at the Universities of Birmingham and Sheffield.

Steve O'Driscoll is a service user who now works for ReCoCo (the Recover College Collective) working with service users with mental ill-health.

Sioban O'Farrell-Pearce is Associate Lecturer in Social Work at Middlesex University.

Keith Popple is Emeritus Professor and formerly Head of Social Work at London South Bank University. Previously a fieldworker, he is Visiting Professor at a number of UK universities. Keith has for many years written widely in the area of social work, social policy and community development.

Lucy Rai is Director of the Scholarship and Innovation Centre (PRAXIS) for the Faculty of Wellbeing, Education and Language Studies and Senior Lecturer in Social Work at the Open University. Lucy is an editor for *Open Learning: Journal of Open, Distance and eLearning.* She has been researching and publishing on academic and professional writing since 2012.

Joanna Rawles is a Senior Lecturer and Head of Social Work (England) at the Open University. Her research interests include the development of critical thinking and professional decision making skills.

Kim Robinson is Senior Lecturer in Social Work at Deakin University. She has been a social work practitioner and manager in community health and refugee services for over 15 years in both the UK and Australia. Her research interests are in the fields of trauma and human rights, with a focus on domestic violence, refugees and asylum seekers and unaccompanied asylum seekers leaving care.

Steven M. Shardlow is Emeritus Professor of Social Work at Keele University, a Fellow of the Academy of Social Sciences (UK) and a Fellow of the Higher Education Academy. He is also Editor-in-Chief of the *Journal of Social Work* and an Honorary Professor in Social Work at the Polytechnic University of Hong Kong.

Gurnam Singh is Honorary Associate Professor of Sociology, University of Warwick and Visiting Professor of Social Work, University of Chester. In 2009, he was awarded a National Teaching Fellowship from the UK Higher Education Academy for his contribution to Higher Education.

Roger Smith is Professor of Social Work and Director of the Master's in Social Work at Durham University. He has researched and published widely on young people and crime, and his current areas of interest include participatory models of practice in youth justice;

models of evaluation in interprofessional education; power, networks and their implications for social work; and innovations in social work education.

Carole Southall is a Lecturer in Social Work at Northumbria University with a particular interest in adult social work and participation.

Sue Taplin is a Lecturer in Social Work at the University of Leeds. Sue is registered as a social worker with practice and research experience in palliative care and interprofessional practice education.

Brian J. Taylor is Senior Lecturer in Social Work at the University of Ulster where he had the lead role for post-qualifying education and training. His research and teaching interests are in decision making, assessment, risk and evidence based practice and he has had a lead role in developing the Northern Ireland Single Assessment Tool for the health and social care of older people.

Barbra Teater is Professor of Social Work at the College of Staten Island, City University of New York, where she is director of the Master of Social Work (MSW) program and is affiliated with the PhD in Social Welfare at The Graduate Center. Her research focuses on social workers' use of theories and methods, research methods for social workers, and ageism and social work practice with older adults.

Prospera Tedam is Assistant Professor in Social Work at United Arab Emirates University in Al Ain and has previously taught social work at the Open University, University of Northampton and Anglia Ruskin University in the United Kingdom. She is an associate editor for *Child Abuse Review* and has research interests in social work with Black and Minority Ethnic families, anti-oppressive and anti-racist social work and relationship based practice.

Janet Walker is Associate Professor and Deputy Head in the School of Health and Social Care at the University of Lincoln. She has experience of research and support for teaching and learning in England, Europe, and is currently engaged in a project to support the development of social work education in Malawi. Janet also has considerable experience of working in children's services as a social worker and a manager.

Melanie Watts is a Senior Lecturer in Social Work at Leeds Beckett University. Before commencing her academic career, Melanie was a social worker in the practice area of children and families and looked after children working in the statutory sector for nine years. Her research interests are improving outcomes for children in care, therapeutic work with children and young people and decision making in child protection practice.

Series editor's preface

During recent teaching sessions for student social workers I have been struck keenly by the changes permeating our contemporary world. Values and ethics lie at the heart of social work, and social work education, and we address these throughout all the books in the series. The positions that we take in terms of values and ethics is, to an extent, determined by context, time and experience and these are expressed in different ways by students coming into social work education today and, of course, by the different routes students take through their educational experience.

Since the turn of this century we have witnessed shifts and challenges as the marketised neoliberal landscape of politics, economy and social life may attract little comment or contest from some and even the acceptance of populist right wing positions. We have also observed the political machinery directing much of statutory social work towards a focus on individuals apart from their environment. However, on a more positive note, we have also seen a new turn to the social in the #MeToo campaign where unquestioned entitlement to women's bodies and psychology is exposed and resisted. We have seen defiance of those perpetuating social injustices that see long-term migrant residents alongside today's new arrivals abused and shunned by society, institutions as well as individuals.

It is likely that, as a student of social work, you will lay bare and face many previously unquestioned assumptions, which can be very perplexing and uncover needs for learning, support and understanding. This series of books acts as an aid as you make these steps. Each book stands in a long and international tradition of social work that promotes social justice and human rights, introducing you to the importance of sometimes new and difficult concepts, and inculcating the importance of close questioning of yourself as you make your journey towards becoming part of that tradition.

There are numerous contemporary challenges for the wider world, and for all four countries of the UK. These include political shifts to the 'popular' Right, a growing antipathy to care and support, and dealing with lies and 'alternative truths' in our daily lives. Alongside this is the need to address the impact of an increasingly ageing population with its attendant social care needs and working with the financial implications that such a changing demography brings. At the other end of the lifespan the need for high-quality childcare, welfare and safeguarding services has been highlighted as society develops and responds to the changing complexion. As demand rises so do the costs and the unquestioned assumption that austerity measures are necessary continues to create tensions and restrictions in services, policies and expectations.

As a social worker you will work with a diverse range of people throughout your career, many of whom have experienced significant, even traumatic, events that require a professional and caring response. As well as working with individuals, however, you may be required to respond to the needs of a particular community disadvantaged by local, national or world events or groups excluded within their local communities because of assumptions made about them.

The importance of high-quality social work education remains if we are adequately to address the complexities of modern life. We should continually strive for excellence in education as this allows us to focus clearly on what knowledge it is useful to engage with when learning to be a social worker. Questioning everything, especially from a position of knowledge, is central to being a social worker.

The books in this series respond to the agendas driven by changes brought about by professional bodies, governments and disciplinary reviews. They aim to build on and offer introductory texts based on up-to-date knowledge and to help communicate this in an accessible way, so preparing the ground for future study and for encouraging good practice as you develop your social work career. Each book in the series is written by academics and practitioners who are passionate about social work and social services and aim to instil that passion in others.

This volume introduces you to the range of fields, processes and practices involved in beginning social work practice. It is a compendium volume to the series as a whole and sets the scene for exploring more specialised areas of practice through other books in the series and providing you with a grounding from which to enhance your learning through research and other contemporary scholarship.

Professor Jonathan Parker

December 2019

Introduction

Achieving a social work degree

This book will help you to develop social work capabilities from the Professional Capabilities Framework (PCF) (BASW, 2018), which sets out the values, knowledge and skills that social workers should command at different levels of experience including student social workers and those who are newly qualified. There are nine professional domains included in the PCF and these are addressed and supported throughout the chapters contained in this book:

1. *Professionalism*

Identify and behave as a professional social worker, committed to professional development.

2. *Values and ethics*

Apply social work ethical principles and value to guide professional practices.

3. *Diversity and equality*

Recognise diversity and apply anti-discriminatory and anti-oppressive principles in practice.

4. *Rights, justice and economic wellbeing*

Advance human rights and promote social justice and economic wellbeing.

5. *Knowledge*

Develop and apply relevant knowledge from social work practice and research, social sciences, law, other professional and relevant fields and from the experience of people who use services.

6. *Critical reflection and analysis*

Apply critical reflection and analysis to inform and provide a rationale for professional decision making.

(Continued)

(Continued)

7. _Skills and interventions_

Use judgement, knowledge and authority to intervene with individuals, families and communities to promote independence, provide support, prevent harm and enable progress.

8. _Contexts and organisations_

Engage with, inform and adapt to changing organisational contexts, and the social and policy environments that shape practice. Operate effectively within and contribute to the development of organisations and services, including multi-agency and interprofessional settings.

9. _Professional leadership_

Promote the profession and good social work practice. Take responsibility for the professional learning and development of others. Develop personal influence and be part of the collective leadership and impact of the profession.

See Appendix 1 for the Professional Capabilities Framework Fan and a description of the nine domains.

This book will also introduce you to the academic standards in the 2019 social work benchmark statement (see Appendix 2).

This book represents a comprehensive distillation of key subjects within the social work qualifying curriculum in England and the UK in particular. It will also have reach as an introductory text across other countries and we have included a number of chapters from social work academics in other countries that demonstrate the transferability of concepts, knowledge, skills and values. The book acts primarily as both an introduction to the key elements of contemporary social work and as a pathway into other books within the Transforming Social Work Practice series, guiding you to texts in more depth and covering the essential elements of the curriculum.

There are three parts to the book. A metaphor from geology outlines the layers which build the book, ranging from bedrock (the solid foundation), soil and subsoil (the fertile element), to the organic growth sprouting from and supported by the other two elements (diverse ecosystems). Each part is interdependent with the other, forming a guide to the complexities of modern day social work.

Part I: Social work theory and methods

The first part of the book introduces key theories and models for, about and developed from social work. This section forms the bedrock upon which readers can further enhance their knowledge, and from which they can explore the skills and approaches used in various areas of contemporary practice. Each chapter in Part I will set out the key points of focus, introducing the thoughts and work of key seminal writers, include up-to-date research, and pose critical questions for readers to explore.

In **Chapter 1,** Jo Finch and Jonathan Parker introduce the history and context of contemporary social work and set this within an international context that shows some of the complexities of the profession. This leads, in **Chapter 2**, to Steven M. Shardlow exploring the central place of values and ethics in social work. Having a clear and explicit sense of professional values is fundamental to practising while using different theories and methods in social work practice with people. Barbra Teater introduces key theories and methods for practice in **Chapter 3**. In turn, all social work requires a foundation from which to employ those theories and in **Chapter 4** Robert Johns provides an overview of the broad ever-changing legislation underpinning the profession. The latter two chapters in this part of the book concern important aspects of those people with whom social workers practise and the professional relationship. In **Chapter 5** Janet Walker examines the different models and theories that help social workers understand the complexities of human growth and development and, in **Chapter 6**, Jonathan Parker takes a tour through the processes of social work introducing a critical model for understanding this, which leads us to Part II.

Part II: Social work skills

Social work integrates theory and practice, or knowledge and skills (the substratum and soil of our geological metaphor). In the second section of this compendium a range of core skills are discussed, stemming from the administrative to the interpersonal, cognitive, affective and creative aspects of social work. The chapters in this section will introduce important skills and situate these in the context of contemporary practice. Key thinkers, important research and examples of these core skills will be introduced. The advantages and limitations will be identified in a critical presentation of these skills.

As a crucial starting point in **Chapter 7**, Prospera Tedam offers a clear model for developing skills in anti-oppressive practice. This is followed in **Chapter 8** by Lucy Rai exploring the field of writing in social work and problematising the concept of writing as a discrete 'skill' and suggesting it would be better seen as an integral part of the social work role. Joanna Rawles explores, in **Chapter 9**, two related issues that are often found so taxing: critical thinking and reflective practice.

In **Chapter 10**, Juliet Koprowska considers the relational aspects of social work through an overview of communication and interpersonal skills. These are fundamental to taking up one's role in the courtroom and this is the subject of the subsequent **Chapter 11**, by Allan Norman. Of course, it is not just communication on a one-to-one basis that frames social work practice, as Tim Kelly relates in **Chapter 12** where he outlines the key skills in groupwork, an important if much ignored area of practice in the UK. As one progresses as a social worker it is likely that you will assume a management or leadership role; however, as Trish Hafford-Letchfield points out in **Chapter 13**, you are taking various forms of leadership and managing yourself and your case load throughout your career as a social worker, including when you are a student.

Social work is an academic as well as a practical profession and relies on its research base to understand and negotiate the complex and diverse lives of people that it services. In **Chapter 14**, Brian J. Taylor considers the ways in which research can be used and understood to aid practice. In **Chapter 15**, Jo Finch looks at the important area of looking after yourself. Sometimes we spend our time looking outwards to the support of others, forgetting that we can only do so well when we also consider our own needs. Finally in this section of the book, in **Chapter 16** Jonathan Parker explores some of the creative and playful approaches that we might take in social work practice that make it more meaningful and powerful in including people in demanding change.

Part III: Social work interventions in practice

The final section of the book brings together 13 chapters dealing with specific fields of practice which represent the complex 'ecosystem' of contemporary social work. Each chapter will introduce and outline the central elements of practice in these areas, the challenges and ways of working alongside people in these contexts. As with the other sections, key writers and thinkers will be discussed, and up-to-date research presented. Critical questions for improving understanding and practice are included within these chapters.

In **Chapter 17**, Nancy Kelly explores the world of child safeguarding and the key elements social workers need to keep in mind as they work in this fraught area of practice. Following on from this, Melanie Watts and Nick Frost, in **Chapter 18**, consider families and children in need. A specific and contemporary area of work with children and families concerns work with unaccompanied refugee minors. This is taken up in **Chapter 19** by Deborah Hadwin, Helen Guizani and Gurnam Singh, who show the fundamentally political nature of social work practice. In **Chapter 20**, Sean Creaney and Roger Smith examine a further focus in children and young people's social work, that of youth justice.

Chapter 21 presents issues in mental health and the implications for social work practice. Toby Brandon, Carole Southall and Steve O'Driscoll explore the impacts of mental illness and the social work role in working with people at various stages in the lifespan. Following this, Sally Lee examines disability across the lifespan in **Chapter 22** and, in **Chapter 23**, Emma Evans and Sally Lee focus on learning disabilities and the social work role. Fostering and adoption work in social work concerns all aspects of the life course as well, since it is not only the children and young people but the adults too who are involved in the process. Lucille Allain and Sioban O'Farrell-Pearce explore the area in **Chapter 24**. Complementing the earlier focus on unaccompanied refugee minors, Kim Robinson looks at social work with refugees and asylum seekers in **Chapter 25**, drawing on her experience in Australia.

In **Chapter 26** Orlanda Harvey covers the vast scope of social work with substance use, outlining the complex area in subject matter, law and practice. Social work with older people is equally broad and Ann Anka introduces this in **Chapter 27**. In **Chapter 28**, Sue Taplin discusses the social work role with people who are dying and those who are bereaved. Finally in this volume, in **Chapter 29**, the importance of communities is brought clearly into the picture by Keith Popple.

How to use the book

The book can be read as a whole for you to gain information on a range of areas and to introduce you in general terms to contemporary social work practice. You may also read specific chapters in any order to guide you into a particular subject area and to gain pointers to aid further in-depth study of it.

All chapters are interactive and include case studies, activities and research summaries to help you engage with the material and to develop a critical thinking approach to the areas under discussion.

The book is a 'taster'. It introduces you to many of the wide-ranging areas of social work practice and provides you with suggestions for further reading and study. Social work is a complex, volatile profession that often treads an uncomfortable path between two worlds – the societal and normative and that of marginalisation and deviance. As such you are called on to reflect deeply on what it is you are doing, thinking and why. This book provides an introduction and, hopefully, some of the questions to begin that process.

Part One

Social work theory and methods

1

The history and context of contemporary social work (including global social work)

Jo Finch and Jonathan Parker

Chapter objectives

By reading this chapter you should be able to:

- chart the history and development of social work in the UK;
- examine how economic, historical, political and social forces interact to influence policy and practice development in social work;
- set social work in a global perspective.

Introduction

A historical perspective and appreciation of the profession's early roots and subsequent development of social work is an important first step in critically understanding the current social work role, its challenges and contradictions, and provides a useful foundation for critically exploring these. The history of social work shows it is a product of political, social and economic forces within society. The development of social work since the nineteenth century is a product of industrialisation and urbanisation. Its contradictory aims, maintaining the social order as well as promoting social justice (or care versus control), represent a dilemma that has not gone away. A holistic and historical understanding of how the profession got to where it is now is central to a profession which remains much maligned and subject to intense media, public and political hostility when things go tragically wrong. So, as you read this chapter, reflect on how the early beginnings of social work continue to influence contemporary social work policy and practice.

Throughout the chapter we explore the early beginnings of what we now call social work, its development through history and underpinning legislation that moulds it. In the final part, we consider globalisation and its impact on social work in the UK and wider considerations of social work as a global profession, as well as considerations of what international social work is.

Early beginnings

It is often believed that social work 'began' in the UK when the post-Second World War welfare state was introduced in 1948. The introduction of the welfare state in the UK was certainly a significant one for the profession, as will be explored later on in this chapter, but the profession's early beginnings and roots can be argued to have gone back much further in history. Hill et al. (2019) argue that whilst social work as a professional role with a set of distinct practices and activities did not exist until the late eighteenth century, social work type activities have been practised for centuries. In other words, activities and practices, albeit informal and formal, providing care, compassion and concern for others have historically been a feature of many societies (Horner, 2006). Many of the world's major religions have traditionally promoted the virtues and necessity of charity, duty and responsibility to others in less fortunate situations, as well as kindness and empathy (Finkel, 2018). Payne (2005) notes further that throughout the ancient and Mediterranean worlds, for example, such societies were managing complex social issues, many of which we can still recognise today as social problems. Such ancient societies, therefore, were providing charity and philanthropy via religious institutions, the state as well as private individuals; again, similar to today.

Historically, churches and monasteries in the UK played a significant part in assisting the poor, the sick and those deemed destitute. As Horner (2006) notes, whilst the very early beginnings of social work can be contested, what is less contestable are the enactments, legislative measures of the state that have served to assist, control or regulate people. Here we can see the very earliest beginnings of significant questions about the role of 'social workers', as enforcers of regulatory government policy, or critical care givers.

The Elizabethan Poor Law (1601)

There has been longstanding legislation aimed at addressing societal problems and concerns (Slack, 1990; Charlesworth, 2010). For example, legislation was enacted in 1383 to manage the 'problem' of beggars and vagabonds (Ridley, 2002; Charlesworth, 2010). The Elizabethan Poor Law of 1601 replaced earlier iterations of the Act in 1536 and 1598. There was concern about rising levels of public destitution, possible social disorder and the need to protect private property (Horner, 2006). The Act was also needed to address wider societal changes such as the breakdown of feudalism, the dissolution of the monasteries and concern about the decline of religious moral values, poor harvests and population increases. The 1601 Poor Law Act therefore was a significant and important piece of legislation which was not amended until 1834, and its underpinning assumptions and values, as will be explored next, can be argued to continue to this day.

The 1601 Act importantly changed the system from one of localised relief to a national system of welfare based on parishes (a defined administrative area, like a council), provision, responsibilities and duties. The Act required parishes to provide both 'outdoor relief' and 'indoor relief' and to:

- levy a compulsory poor rate (i.e. a tax that everyone with means had to pay for the provision of 'relief');
- provide 'outdoor relief' to the working poor in the form of money, clothes or food, or indeed provide workers with tools;
- apprentice orphaned children, or children whose parents could not provide for them;
- provide alms-houses.

The underpinning assumptions in this Act were that people were required to work if they could work and that if they were unable to work it was the responsibility of the family to provide care and support. If people did not have family to take care of their immediate needs, or the family did not have the means to assist, then the parish had responsibilities to those deemed 'impotent poor' – children, older people or those who were sick or disabled – but not those deemed 'able-bodied'. The deserving poor might also be offered either outdoor relief (in the forms of money, clothing, food or working tools) or indoor relief, in alms-houses. However, those deemed undeserving were sent to correctional houses. There were also rules about who could claim relief from the parish in terms of residency – those seeking support who came from other parishes were refused (Dickens, 2016). Those that administered the system of relief (and assessing need) were known as 'Overseers of the Poor' (Hill et al., 2019, p16). We can detect in this Act the early beginnings of questions about how the state should intervene with orphaned children, or children whose parents could not provide for them, questions about those deemed deserving and undeserving of state assistance, the moral obligation to work if you can, and issues around eligibility criteria – all of which remain very much contemporary concerns. What we can also detect is the firm link that has developed between social welfare provisions and issues around morality and the characteristics of individuals. This is a political position, a classical liberal (now neo-liberal) view that individuals are responsible for being in poverty, set against a contemporary social work value position that acknowledges the potential negative impact of the structure on individuals (how society is formed and issues around inequality). The fundamental tenets of a process of assessment to decide who is eligible or not and who is deserving or not have, however, remained a key aspect of the social work role.

Activity 1.1

Do you think notions of deserving and undeserving poor still exist? If so, write down what groups of people might, today, be deemed deserving or undeserving. Reflect on reasons for a group or an individual being labelled deserving or undeserving.

Think back to the introduction. How do the above very early beginnings of social work activity continue to shape contemporary social work policy and practice?

The Poor Law Amendment Act (1834)

The Victorian era (1837–1901) saw huge societal changes, with the move from a largely rural society to an urban one, massive rapid industrialisation, and accompanying changes to the types of work people undertook, which, it could be argued, precluded some people from being able to undertake the type of work that was now required. Given such huge societal changes, there was increasing unease that the 1601 Poor Law was unable to cope with the increase in demands (Green and Clarke, 2016). Accompanying political changes was a growing acceptance that the state should intervene more readily in people lives (Heywood, 2007), with the same dual aim of managing potential social unrest alongside humanitarian action to address issues of poverty and need (Green and Clarke, 2016).

In 1832, a Royal Commission was established to lay down policies and procedures in a revised law (Dickens, 2016). One of its major aims was to ensure that a system of relief would encourage and not be a disincentive to work, similarly to today's debates. The amended Poor Law Act (1834) aimed to stop the provision of 'outdoor' relief – provision of money, clothes and working tools – and provide only 'indoor relief' in the form of workhouses. The Act heralded the term 'less eligibility criteria' which meant that those deemed able-bodied who were dependent on poor relief could not be better off than those of the lowest pay living outside of the workhouse (Bloy, 2002).

The workhouses were run by a board of guardians and conditions were very harsh and strict. Women, men and children were segregated and were required to undertake work. Entering the workhouse was very much seen as a last resort and some of the stigma and shame associated with entering a workhouse still exists today, in terms of the shame and stigma of being a welfare recipient (Fothergill, 2002; Pellissery et al., 2014). From generic workhouses, one can also see the development of specialist institutional provision, such as charitable hospitals for the sick, asylums for those with disabilities and mental ill health, and educational institutions.

The underpinning philosophy of such an approach to managing poverty was one that centred on the moral obligation to work if one was capable. The belief continued (as from medieval times) that a distinction could be made between those who could be classed (later assessed by charity workers) as deserving poor because of incidents that were outside of the individual's control such as disability, misfortune, injury or old age and infirmity. Those who were deemed capable of work but in destitution were viewed as being responsible for their plight and, like now, moral judgements were applied. The 'undeserving' poor therefore were labelled as feckless, lazy, idle and immoral (Morrison, 2019).

Activity 1.2

Think about the ways in which people who receive 'welfare' are depicted in the media and identify some of the terms used to describe people in receipt of welfare.

Having done so, read again the previous section and check your thoughts against that discussion.

The emergence of social problems

A further impact of rapid industrialisation and urbanisation was that poverty (and other social problems such as drunkenness, prostitution, crime, child neglect and poor and dangerous working conditions) became much more 'visible' and offended Victorian sensibilities. An evocative account of the lives of London's working poor was written by Henry Mayhew around 1851. Mayhew was a journalist, playwright and social reformer and the full title of his very long work was: *London labour and the London poor; a cyclopædia of the condition and earnings of those that will work, those that cannot work, and those that will not work* (British Library, exact date unknown). This long work, however, contributed to bringing the plight of impoverished people to wider public and political attention. In one section of the book, for example, Mayhew describes his encounter with a 'neglected child' (Mayhew, 1851, p481). Other writers of the day – Arthur Morrison, Charles Dickens, and poet William Blake – also brought the significant social problems into the wider public and political consciousness. Concern also began to arise about the very poor conditions people lived in, including poor sanitation and health, which resulted in serious epidemics such as cholera. These also began to affect the middle classes (Hill et al., 2019).

Social reform

In this period a number of industrialists engaged in philanthropy and charitable activities and some promoted a degree of social reform. For example, the Quaker confectionary manufacturers, Cadbury and Rowntree, provided good quality accommodation for their workers, provided schools for the workers' children and provided health benefits. Concern began to be voiced about dangerous working conditions which could cause short-term or long-term serious injury to workers. Legislation therefore began to be introduced to make working in factories safer. The 1833 Factory Act, for example, saw measures being introduced to protect child workers in England and Wales. Indeed, the Act required factories to:

- not employ child workers under nine years of age;
- have age certificates for their child workers;
- restrict the hours of children aged nine to 13 to no more than nine hours a day;
- restrict the hours of children aged 13 to 18 to no more than 12 hours a day;
- not allow children to work at night;
- provide two hours' schooling each day for children.

(Adapted from the National Archives, date unknown)

Notions of childhood began to change significantly during this time, with the move from viewing children as small adults to viewing children as in need of protection, with distinct rights, rather than merely being the chattels (the property) of their fathers (Finch, 2020). With this changing notion of what a child was, compulsory schooling was introduced in 1870 (followed by further education legislation in 1893). The Act required that:

- local education boards should inspect schools to ensure there were sufficient places;
- elementary education must be provided for children aged between five and 13;
- schools should be publicly funded;
- parents had to pay for their children's education, unless they could not afford to;
- attendance should be compulsory;
- religious teaching should be non-denominational, and that parents could withdraw their children from religious education;
- schools should be regularly inspected to maintain the standard of education.

(Adapted from British Library archive, date unknown)

Further social reform focused on sanitation and housing, i.e. introducing minimum standards, campaigns for universal franchise, workers' rights and prisoner conditions and rights to name but a few. Famous social reformers during this period included Elizabeth Fry (married to the nephew of J.S. Fry, another Quaker confectionary manufacturer), who is largely known for her work in campaigning for prison reform in the early part of the eighteenth century, but also set up the first District Visiting service, sending volunteers into people's homes to assist those with medical needs, setting up a refuge for young women recently released from prison and working with the homeless in London. Other well-known social reformers included Charles Booth of the Salvation Army, who focused on homelessness issues, Octavia Hill, who championed housing projects for the working poor and Edwin Chadwick, who campaigned for improvements to health and sanitation (Englander, 1998).

There was significant growth in the charity sector, including the Charity Organisation Society. Octavia Hill and Thomas Barnardo set up orphanages and charities that are still in existence today (the National Society for Prevention of Cruelty to Children (NSPCC) and Action for Children – formerly National Children's Homes). Alongside this growth of charity, government legislation, philanthropy by industrialists, the work of religious organisations and both religiously inspired and non-religious social reformers campaigned for a wide range of solutions to address a myriad of social problems. Alongside this, concerns began to grow for the development of social welfare provision. There were social activists, like the Chartists campaigning for workers' rights and democracy and the Settlement movement which campaigned for rich and poor people to live in close proximity to one another (Lymbery, 2005).

In this, we can see the more formal beginnings of social work, such as the direct provision of services to those in need via charities, religious institutions or through industrialists, as well as the associated social reform campaigners and political activists. There was a lot of potential welfare/charitable provision and concern began to be raised about the lack of coordination between the various charities and that people were often in receipt of multiple charitable offerings.

The Charity Organisation Societies

The London Charity Organisation Society (COS), led by Helen Bosanquet and Octavia Hill, was established in 1869 and was referred to originally as the Society of Charitable Relief and Repressing Mendicity (Idleness) (Payne, 2005). The aim was to develop principles of charitable giving and to act as a coordinator of all the various relief and charity activities. District organisations were thus developed, bringing together multiple local/district charities. The COS formalised the notion of assessing entitlement and extent of need. This developed the approach of social casework as the method to assess need. The COS workers promoted self-help and aimed to promote self-resilience. A key role was to administer the workhouse's 'less eligibility' test and to engage in what was termed 'scientific charity'. The COS volunteer workers were largely middle class women, who had the financial means not to have to engage in paid employment. As Horner (2006) argues, the late eighteenth century saw fault lines developing. The COS focused on the threat to social order posed by poverty and the solution was to promote self-help among the poor. State intervention, in such a view, would promulgate further poverty, create dependency and not promote the incentive to work. On the other hand, social reformers such as Beatrice and Sydney Webb and the Fabians argued for a more structural perspective on the causes of poverty and inequality and claimed that the state had a duty to intervene to address such issues.

The late eighteenth century and early nineteenth century saw the first formalised beginnings of social work education, with London COS volunteers, for example, undertaking a series of lectures in 1903 at what is now the London School of Economics. Similar lecture series were set up in other parts of the country, such as Liverpool and Birmingham.

In 1905–09, a Royal Commission on the Poor Laws was set up. Many of the social reformers were on the commission and the COS leaders advocated the maintenance of the Poor Law with some amendments. This was known as the Majority Report. Beatrice Webb and her supporters, on the other hand, argued for the Poor Laws to be abolished and replaced by a state run service for health, education and employment. This was known as the Minority Report.

The Poor Law to 1948

During this period, more protective legislation was enacted and the early beginnings of a welfare state began to be implemented. Measures included the introduction of an old age pension, and national security contributions to pay for unemployment and medical care.

Health services improved with the introduction of maternal and child clinics. The influence of the Labour Party also grew.

A significant event that changed society was the First World War. Working, middle and upper class soldiers began to be in more direct contact with one another, and working class soldiers eventually became senior military leaders – formerly this was the preserve of the middle and upper classes. The war also brought issues of injury to soldiers, both physical and mental, to the forefront. The post-war world depression, followed by the Second World War, gave support for the development of a welfare state. Indeed, in 1942, William Beveridge wrote his famous report which identified the five evil giants: want (poverty), disease (ill health), ignorance (education), idleness (unemployment) and squalor (homelessness and poor housing) (Horner, 2006). In 1948, therefore, whilst philanthropy, charities, friendly societies and trade unions did not disappear, the state became the main source of the funding and the provision of welfare support. Horner (2006) argues that personal social services were more an 'afterthought' (2006, p13) in Beveridge's welfare state plans, but the 1948 Children Act (in part a response to the tragic death in 1945 of Dennis O'Neil, a child sent to work on a farm) made local authorities responsible for children whose parents were assessed as 'unfit'. Three areas of social work thus began to emerge: (1) children's departments; (2) departments working with the 'elderly', those with disabilities and homeless people; and (3) more health orientated services that worked with people with mental ill health and those with learning disabilities. Various other major reforms ensued. The Seebohm Committee was established in 1965 with a focus on social work and recommended the establishment of a social service department in each local authority whose remit was generic, and required qualified social workers to undertake this work. Since this time, social work policy, practice and education have appeared to be in constant flux and change and we do not aim to discuss recent history here. Rather, of relevance to this chapter is the question about the extent to which the early beginnings of social work continue to influence contemporary practice. It is also relevant to note that society has changed considerably, not least due to the impact of globalisation, and so the extent to which contemporary social work practice has responded adequately (or not) to such changes remains debatable. The following case study helps to illustrate this.

Case study 1.1

Mercy was a social work student at an English university in a large cosmopolitan urban city. She had worked as a teaching assistant in a local school before coming to university. When she arrived at university she was surprised at the range of teaching, the different service user groups discussed and at some of the roles and interventions being covered in the curriculum. She had thought that social work was concerned with helping families with children to cope with low income, inadequate accommodation and parenting skills. She had not paid much attention to statutory roles nor to working with people in other settings – older people, people with disabilities and those with mental ill health or substance use problems. This made her re-evaluate why she was studying social work and what she wanted to do in her career.

Just like Mercy, we all enter social work with preconceived ideas, some right and some less so, and we all benefit from seeing social work in its historical and global context. We now turn briefly to consider the international aspects of social work.

Social work as an international profession

In the twenty-first century we talk increasingly of internationalisation and global issues, but international connections have been part of social work for many years. The Charity Organisation Society and later the Settlement movement were quickly adopted in the US (Payne, 2005). Also, as Frampton (2019) points out, the COS model drew on an earlier German welfare charity, the *Elberfelder System*. The early twentieth century saw a rise in those connections and the beginnings of an international movement through the work of Alice Salomon, a German social worker who travelled extensively and founded the International Association of Schools of Social Work, Mary Richmond's development of social casework in the US which drew on the assessment and case management method of the COS, and Jane Addams' development of Settlement and the recognition of structural influences on people's lives (Oakley, 2019). However, we must ask ourselves whether there is such a thing as international social work. This is especially important in contemporary social work in the UK which is being redefined as a residual and statutory safeguarding profession (Parker, 2018; 2019a).

Over time we have developed internationally accepted definitions of social work, but these remain to some extent contested and are necessarily interpreted differently in different country contexts. The International Federation of Social Workers (IFSW) definition of social work globally is as follows:

Social work is a practice-based profession and an academic discipline that promotes social change and development, social cohesion, and the empowerment and liberation of people. Principles of social justice, human rights, collective responsibility and respect for diversities are central to social work. Underpinned by theories of social work, social sciences, humanities and indigenous knowledge, social work engages people and structures to address life challenges and enhance wellbeing. The above definition may be amplified at national and/or regional levels.

(IFSW, 2014)

The question is perhaps whether there is a single international profession called social work or whether there are core elements, practised locally, which reflect a set of principles and practices that may be seen as international social work. The influence of social work has extended to other countries through the medium of colonialism which is rightly critiqued now as inappropriate (Parker, 2019a). There is a danger that we may each fall into the trap of seeing our own social work perspective through a normative lens, thinking it is *the* way to do social work and the potential for a neo-colonial approach to international social work remains. However, this is not the only way to understand international perspectives.

Healy (2008) describes international social work as the capacity the profession has to undertake practice actions that are international; this might include development activities and aid programmes or international exchanges but may also concern working with challenging global issues such as migration and family reunion or sharing practice examples, views and values. It is also important to recognise, in an increasingly insular UK, that social work globally has influenced policy and practice development in the United Nations that carries international implications. Similarly, Hugman (2010) suggests that international social work concerns the social worker practising locally in situations that result from global actions. For instance, this may include working with people affected by the climate crisis. Should they live in the Global South (low and middle income countries) their predicaments may result from the actions of the Global North (high income countries). It may also be the case that a migrant family you are working with in the UK is affected by civil war and oppression of family members in their country of origin. Thus social work has an international perspective in respect to practice, even if practice differs from country to country.

However the question of international social work is resolved, we would stress that it is important for your practice as a social worker to be international in outlook, to learn from and share with others in different countries, to read about other countries' approaches to social work, and especially to be able to negotiate the complex, interconnected global world that we inhabit. Without recognition of the centrality of international issues we become insular in outlook, normative in thinking and rigid and inappropriate in practice.

Key points summary

- The historical development of social work is important background to understanding contemporary social work practice in the UK.
- Historical developments in social policy, welfare and social work continue to exert a significant influence on social work today.
- Social work and its historical development cannot be seen apart from its place within an international context.
- Understanding the history and context of UK and global social work gives you a professional literacy important to your future development.

Suggested further reading

Payne, M. (2005) *The Origins of Social Work: Continuity and Change*. Basingstoke: Palgrave Macmillan.

Green, L. and Clarke, K. (2016) *Social Policy for Social Work*. Bristol: Policy Press.

Finkel, A. (2019) *Compassion: A Global History of Social Policy*. London: Macmillan International.

Useful resources

https://historyofsocialwork.org/eng/reacties.php

This contains information on key social reformers from 1817 to 2001.

http://www.socialwork.ed.ac.uk/centenary/timeline

A history of major policy developments and the history of social work education.

http://www.open.ac.uk/health-and-social-care/research/shld/timeline-learning-disability-history

Timeline of learning disability history.

2

Social work values and ethics

Steven M. Shardlow

Chapter objectives

By reading this chapter you will understand:

- the parameters of the terms 'values' and 'ethics' when used in the context of social work;
- some of the different ethical approaches that have been proposed to assist people to behave ethically;
- the type and nature of guidance that has been provided to social workers to enable them to behave ethically.

Introduction

Not only in our personal interactions with others but also our professional lives one of the most incessant questions to confront us is how we should behave towards other people.

Leaving aside the personal for the professional, as we must in this chapter, the unrelenting challenges found in each new situation that we experience demand careful and exacting reflection about how we ought to behave as a *professional social worker*. We may legitimately ask if there are differences between the way in which we should behave as *citizen* and as a *professional social worker* and, if so, what justifies these differences? Questions about how to behave towards others lie at the core of discussion about values and ethics in social work. While there have been differing views about what to include in the notion of social work ethics and values, here the notion of ethics and values is bounded by consideration of issues that govern behaviour as a professional social worker.

Each of the three chapter objectives forms a separate subsection of the chapter, in which we will explore how social workers should behave, *if* their actions are to be judged ethical. There have been many ways suggested to both *understand* questions about how we ought to behave and also to *answer* those questions. Here we will explore three different types of answer. First, we discuss systems based on fundamental ethical principles that are applicable to behaviour generally. Second, we consider guidance which may be specific to social work but equally may have more general applicability. Third, we look at professional values that derive both from ethical systems and from professional guidance. Examples are given of the type of challenges that confront social workers seeking to behave ethically.

Ethics and values?

'Ethics' is the branch of philosophy concerned with questions about how we ought to behave. In Western thought, the first systematic approach to such questions is usually taken to have emerged during the fifth century BCE in Athens, since when many approaches have developed.

In this chapter, to illuminate how social workers *ought* to behave, our spotlight falls upon 'normative ethics'. Using the word 'normative' implies the existence of a set of 'norms', standards or requirements about how we ought to behave; we will explore a little later to what extent this is the case for social work.

'Values' can be taken to be those rules, statements or principles that are held dear, either by an individual or by professional social work bodies. The term *values* has been used in various ways in social work (Timms, 1983, p107). For example, the term *values* may imply the existence of a defined set of social work values, found in the phrase *the value-base* of social work. It is a phrase commonly heard, which implies not only the existence of a universal set of values, nationally or internationally pertinent, but also that these values are fundamental to social work. The existence of universal and fundamental values should not be presumed; these must be demonstrated to exist.

Once the scope of 'ethical' and 'value' questions about how we ought to behave as social workers is established, then two other questions arise: 'What guidance is available to help social workers determine how to behave?' and 'What are recognised by social workers as the values of the profession?' Before we can examine the guidance available for social work and the values of the profession, it is helpful to review some ethical approaches.

Ethical approaches

Given the large number of approaches developed in Western thought since the emergence of ethics 2500 years ago about how to behave towards others, only the most significant have been discussed here. Non-Western approaches about how to behave towards others have distinct approaches. For example, in China, Confucianism emphasises the importance of: harmony between individuals; avoidance of conflict; subjugation of desire to performance of role expectations, exemplified by traditional *filial piety*, which combines notions of respect for elders with expectations that adult children care for their older parents. There are four major branches of Western *normative ethics*, i.e. ethical systems that specify how we ought to behave, which have particular relevance for social work. These are *deontological, consequentialist, virtue* ethics and the ethics of *care*. Two of these approaches, deontological and consequentialist, were grounded in the Enlightenment: key was the attempt to understand the world through the lens of reason and rationality. The third, virtue ethics, has older roots derived from the world before the Common Era. The fourth, the ethics of care, is a more recent development and derives from feminist thought.

Principle, consequence, virtue or care?

Systems of morality based on rules about how to behave, deontological (derived from the ancient Greek for obligation or duty) theories are grounded in the notion that if you follow the rules required then you will perform the right action and behave morally. In this respect, these types of moral theory have some similarity to religious codes, which prescribe a set of acceptable and unacceptable behaviours; for example, the revelation of the Ten Commandments to Moses (in Judeo-Christian tradition) or the development of Sharia Law (interpretations of the teachings of the Prophet Muhammad). Adherence to faith-based codes depends upon belief in a deity, and that breaching these codes may have consequences for the individual, not only in the current corporeal world, but also more importantly for many believers in a perpetual afterlife. So, the question that confronts any proponent of a rule-based system of ethics is how to ground the ethical system in a justification that commands respect and requires adherence. The most notable, possibly the first, person to propose such a system of deontological ethics was Immanuel Kant (1724–1804).

How did Kant ground his ethical system without reliance on an external deity? For Kant it was a requirement that any system of ethics should be universal, i.e. it would apply in all circumstances. It is difficult to imagine a non-universal ethical system, one in which we could pick and choose which rules to apply according to circumstance; such a system would fail the test of universality. Kant's ethical approach rests on the assumptions that people are rational beings, and that rational beings would adhere to a universal principle because this would be in their interests. For example, imagine a principle that a person should not kill another person; rational individuals would follow this principle, as if all followed this principle, each person would be safe from being killed. Kant termed this type of principle, one that all rational beings would follow, a *categorical imperative* – a rule that must be followed.

Key thinkers and theorists

Kant's categorical imperative has been variously stated; the key elements are:

I ought never to act except in such a way that I can also will that my maxim should become a universal law

(Kant, 1785, p67)

and

Act in such a way that you always treat humanity whether in your own person or in the person of any other, never simply as a means but always at the same time as an end

(Kant, 1785, p91)

A colloquial phrasing of the categorical imperative would resemble the traditional folk maxim, 'do as you would be done by'. This phrase sums up the essence of Kantian ethics: *act towards others as you would wish them to act towards you*. The key difficulty with this type of deontological theory is the assumption that individuals are rational and that by virtue of rationality would think in similar ways to one another and would accept the same categorial imperatives; in the real diverse world, a key issue for social work, they may not.

A different approach from deontological ethics is found in consequential ethical systems. As the name suggests, in consequentialist theories the rightness or wrongness of an action is determined by the outcome of that action, i.e. by its consequences. The most well-known consequentialist ethical theory is utilitarianism, developed initially by Jeremy Bentham (1784–1832) and elaborated on subsequently by John Stuart Mill (1806–1873). According to the tenets of utilitarianism, to determine the ethical value of action it would be necessary to calculate the extent to which the action increased or decreased the sum of human happiness – the so-called *principle of utility*. Actions that produce a greater increase in the sum of happiness are to be preferred over those that generate a lesser increase or lead to a reduction in the total level of human happiness. For Bentham, happiness was not a differentiated commodity – all activities leading to human happiness were of equal value; to that end pushpin was to be valued as much as poetry, provided the quotient of happiness generated by each activity was the same. Whereas for Mill, some activities were of higher value than others; famously Mill would have preferred to be Socrates (fifth century BCE Athenian philosopher) and dissatisfied than a pig and satisfied. As with deontological approaches, in fact for any ethical system, the real challenge is to provide a convincing justification. Mill offered a justification for the adoption of utilitarianism based on apparent empirical evidence that people desire happiness.

Key thinkers and theorists

Mill's proof:

The only proof capable of being given that an object is visible is that people actually see it. The only proof that a sound is audible is that people hear it. In like manner ... the sole evidence ... that anything is desirable, is that people do actually desire it ... No reason can be given why the general happiness is desirable, except that each person ... desires his own happiness ... each person's happiness is a good to that person and general happiness is a good to the aggregate of persons.

(Mill, 1861 (1970 edition), pp32–33)

There are a number of well-established difficulties with utilitarianism, notably the 'justice problem' and the 'keeping promises' problem. The justice problem refers to the situation in which punishing someone for a crime that they did not commit may make the population feel happy that the criminal has been caught. In like manner, whether or not to keep a promise is dependent on the consequences. There are ways around these difficulties, which to a large degree centre on whether individual acts are being evaluated (act utilitarianism) or classes of acts (rule utilitarianism).

One of the earliest approaches to ethical theory, virtue ethics – originally associated with Aristotle (384–322 BCE; see Kenny, 2011) in Western thought and Confucius in Eastern thought – has experienced a revival since the last quarter of the twentieth century (see a notable exponent, Hursthouse, 1999). In original Aristotelean form, for a person to behave ethically they would cultivate virtues such as courage, kindness and trustworthiness. The cultivation of these virtues by an individual would lead to a sense of wellbeing (eudemonia). To attain this sense of wellbeing the individual had to follow the *golden rule*, which required the acquisition of virtues through pursuit of moderation. For example, too much courage leads to reckless behaviour; too little to cowardice. The importance of courage as a virtue on an ancient Greek battlefield is clear. At first glance it may be a little less easy to see the relevance to current social work practice. Yet there are occasions when a social worker must demonstrate courage; for example, when advocating for a service user against an intransigent organisation – perhaps not the same magnitude as battlefield fighting.

Activity 2.1

- List as many virtues as you can that would be desirable for the modern-day social worker to possess.
- What would be the consequence of having too *much* of each of these virtues?
- What would be the consequence of having too *little* of each of these virtues?

	Name of virtue	Consequence of having too *much* of this virtue	Consequence of having too *little* of this virtue
1			
2			
3			
4			
5			
6			

- Can you give an example from your own practice where you have used these virtues (if not from practice then other areas of your life)?

The revival of virtue ethics has emphasised the importance of *agent* and *motivation*. Consider the following statement: according to the principles of virtue ethics to act ethically, it is only necessary to ask how the virtuous person would behave in a particular situation and to act as would the virtuous person. Is it sufficient for the agent (the person doing the action) to follow a virtuous example of an action even if it is for the wrong reasons, so that the act would be ethical but the motivation would not be virtuous? Alternatively, is it necessary for an agent to act from a virtuous motive for an action to be virtuous? There is no unequivocal answer to such questions.

Since the 1980s, the *ethics of care*, an approach to ethics with some similarities to virtue ethics, has emerged. The ethics of care is a feminist approach to ethics that first appeared in an influential work, *In a Different Voice* by Carol Gilligan (1982). In this book, Gilligan argued that notions of moral development overemphasised male experience and that female experiences had been given less emphasis or ignored. From this starting point Gilligan argued that men and women tend to approach moral problems differently. A concern for justice to regulate competing interests of autonomous individuals is perhaps more typical of males, as independence is highly prized, whereas a concern for the connections with others through relationships is perhaps a more typical female approach with an emphasis on moral decision making grounded in caring for others.

While deontological, consequentialist, virtue or ethics of care theories have been influential in shaping ideas about moral philosophy, we may ask: to what extent have they influenced the theory and practice of social work? These approaches to ethics are important because they have provided and continue to provide, albeit at a very general level, guidance about how to behave both in day-to-day life and also as a social work professional and can be used when making decisions. For example, when making decisions about policy, consequentialist theories can enable policy makers to consider which of several possible actions will lead to the best outcomes, e.g. the greatest happiness for the population, provided minorities are not penalised. When making decisions at a more individual level, deontological theories, virtue-based theories or approaches based on the ethics of care may be helpful to the social worker.

Case study 2.1

Blossom, an older woman (82) of mixed Spanish and Caribbean heritage, lives alone in a modest first-floor apartment. Her family live in other countries; a son in the USA contacts her regularly by phone. Recently, she fell and broke her hip; she now has limited mobility; there is considerable evidence that she is not caring for herself. She hoards items and her flat is a health and safety hazard. How would you balance your concern for her safety with her rights to live independently?

What guidance do we have about how to behave as social workers?

Since 2005, *social worker* has been a protected title under Article 39(1) of the Health and Social Care Professionals Act 2005. From that date, to be able to use the title *social worker* professionals were required to be registered with the regulatory body for the respective UK country (in England, Social Work England – until 2 December 2018 it was Health and Care Professions Council (HCPC); in Northern Ireland, Northern Ireland Social Care Council (NISCC); in Scotland, Scottish Social Services Council (SSSC); and in Wales, Social Care Wales). Registration required a specified level of social work qualification, adherence to a code of practice (slightly different in each country) and made registrants subject to a disciplinary regime that could remove an individual from the register and thus remove that individual's licence to practice as a social worker. These codes of practice were designed both to make clear to those using social work services the standards they could expect and also to give guidance to social workers about to behave. Approaches to regulation and provision of guidance for social workers vary in different countries; not all have a registration process or protect the title of social work. These codes of practice provide one form of guidance for social workers, who must also follow the requirements of statutes and governmental regulation, for example Working Together to Safeguard Children (HM Government, 2018).

Activity 2.2

The codes of practice for each country in the United Kingdom can be found at the web addresses below. Read these codes and see if you can identify any differences. What could be the implications of any differences for social workers and service users and how important might they be? (If you are reading this chapter in a country other than the United Kingdom, compare one of these codes with the code for your country).

England: **https://socialworkengland.org.uk/professional-standards**

Northern Ireland: **https://niscc.info/registration-standards/standards-of-conduct-and-practice**

Scotland: **https://www.sssc.uk.com/knowledgebase/article/KA-02412/en-us**

Wales: **https://socialcare.wales/fitness-to-practise/codes-of-practice-and-guidance**

One difference that you may have noticed is that each of these codes has a different title; what might be the significance of these titles?

Although claims have often been made that social work is a global profession with a universal set of professional values (IFSW, 2014), close inspection of ethical guidance used in countries around the world reveals a surprising number of differences as well as similarities. For example, the codes of ethics used in the United States (NASW, 2018) contain guidance about charges for social work, social work and dual relationships with service users and social work and research, which are not found in the UK codes.

In the various codes of ethics, sets of professional standards and writings about social work ethics a number of common professional values can be found: ideas about values that social workers ought to maintain and demonstrate as fundamental components of day-to-day social work practice. Some of the most important of these values are explored below.

Diversity and relativism

A fundamental tenet of social work has been the recognition that we live in societies characterised by diversity and that the experiences of individuals in those societies, their sense of inclusion and exclusion, are to a large extent shaped by these various forms of diversity found in respect to gender, race, class, disability, sexual orientation, health, religion and nationality. One of the earliest ways in which diversity was encapsulated within social work values was through the notion of *respect for persons*. Embedded within this notion was the core idea that all persons should be treated with respect and dignity – to be achieved by separating the person from any act that they may have committed, for example the paedophile; while the crime may be abhorrent the person still deserves to be treated as a person. This is similar to ideas found in Christian teachings. The gradual recognition that many groups in society experience discrimination and structural oppression has led to the value position that it is the responsibility of social workers to challenge structural oppression through anti-oppressive practice and to develop cultural competence. We should be cautious as social workers about making too many claims about our exceptionalism, i.e. about the way in which we treat others as compared to other professions. Ideals we have but, like many other occupational and professional groups, we should recognise that we sometimes fall short of those noble ideals.

Accountability

In the second half of the twentieth century, academic debate and professional discussion about social work posed questions about the nature of social work. Was it or was it not a

21

profession? Whilst this may now appear to be something of a sterile debate, there was one kernel of importance in the discussion. As *ideal types*, typically, professions are held to be accountable to the people for whom they provide services, a relationship usually mediated through state licensed national professional associations. Occupations that are not professions are usually seen to be accountable through employer organisations. Social workers have a complex set of accountability relationships that cannot easily be characterised as one of these simple ideal types. Doubtless, most social workers would wish to see themselves directly accountable to the people who use social work services. However, there is generally no cash-nexus, the usual mechanism to establish direct accountability, between the social worker and the citizen using their services (except for a few in private practice). The social worker is accountable both through the competent regulatory body (see above) and also through their employer. This shared accountability is not without complexity. For example, prior to 2 December 2019, in England social workers had a responsibility, according to the regulatory code of practice, to report circumstances where lack of resources might lead to unsafe practice. Currently, they do not have this responsibility (now removed from the code of practice), in effect making social workers less independent, less accountable to the citizens using services and more beholden to their employer.

Power, participation and control

If debates about accountability tend to be framed in terms of the delivery of service by the professional to the citizen, then debates about the power of professional social workers are frequently couched in ways that acknowledge the lack of equality between citizen and social worker. There have been shifts in the distribution of power for *some* citizens vis-à-vis social workers in recent years. The growth of citizen participation in service delivery and planning has enabled some citizens to have more control. This can be seen most strongly in the field of social work with adults through, for example, the provision of direct payments to citizens who are thereby enabled to make their own decisions about the purchase of services. Such initiatives have the potential to change the nature of the relationship between the citizen and the social worker such that the social worker becomes an adviser rather than a gatekeeper who controls resources. The empowerment of citizens using services is very much a work-in-progress.

Autonomy and self-realisation

To many it may seem axiomatic that individuals should have a freedom to pursue their interests, provided that the pursuit of those interests does not curtail the ability of others to pursue their interests. This view is the classic view of freedom or liberty found in post-enlightenment Western thought; it is the freedom from restraint. While this is for many a noble aim – to be a fully autonomous individual – as an approach it does not fully take account of the interconnectedness of human beings. For example, as a parent I have duties to care for my children, and as an adult I may have a duty to care for my parents (filial piety). These duties may entail a curtailment of my autonomy; for example I may have to be able to care for relatives at certain times of the day, and at those times I am not free to do as I choose. Of course, I can ignore my responsibilities but that may imperil others. From early in the history of the profession, writings about social work have employed the notion of *self-determination* which rather ingeniously sidesteps the conundrum of having to balance the individual's sense of autonomy with responsibilities to others. The individual can determine for themselves (i.e. be self-determining) whether to give priority to their own autonomy or to their responsibilities to others, if these ideas are in conflict.

Privacy and confidentiality

When citizens become involved with professional social work, they should be able to have confidence that any information that they give to the social worker is treated in confidence and their privacy respected. This is best practice if the citizen *chooses* to become involved with social work; however, if the engagement with social work is involuntary and duly required by law then information about the citizen may be shared across a number of agencies. The protection and proper use of information about citizens is a complex matter, made even more so by the existence of social media. Not that social workers should be posting information about citizens using social work on social media, but others may do so. In all circumstances, citizens should be clear about how information that they provide or about them will be used by social workers and employing agencies.

Research summary

The extent of empirical research about social work ethics and values has not been vast; nonetheless, several different research strands are discernable. One strand concerns the outcomes, fairness and experiences of social workers subject to disciplinary procedures; Worsley, McLaughlin and Leigh (2017) explored the emotional toll and costs of a disciplinary process. A second strand has examined the challenges social workers face when practising in accord with professional values: challenges frequently relate to organisational constraints. Fenton (2014) studied Scottish criminal justice social work and found that managerial risk-averse work environments can engender ethical stress. A third strand notes that social workers may be conflicted in their role due to: incompatibility between different values or principles; dual relationships with service users (different types of professional relationship with a single service user); and conflicts between a social worker's personal and professional values. A fourth strand relates to ethical issues implicit in new developments in social work; for example, Bowles et al.'s (2018) comparative analysis of three countries' Codes of Ethics which explored the extent of respect for environmental issues.

Conclusion

The practice of social work could well be described as *practical ethics* or *ethics in action*. The very idea of 'social work' contains a fundamental ethical notion, i.e. that a group or groups of people in society are deserving of or need help. The decision to help those individuals is fundamentally a moral decision (notwithstanding the cynical view that social work is part of the functional machinery of society necessary to preserve social order). Decisions about whom to help, how much help they should receive and what kind of help they should have all then follow in swift succession. The various moral theories outlined in this chapter may help in exploring the implications of such questions, just as they may provide some guidance about how to behave and make decisions about day-to-day practice. Similarly, the professional values outlined in this chapter are beacons to which we should all strive in the performance of social work.

Key points summary

- Ethics is a branch of moral philosophy concerned with how we ought to live a good life, and by implication how we ought to behave as social workers engaged in professional practice that is moral in character.
- Our professional values are those principles or guides to how we should practice social work that have received the official imprimatur of professional associations, regulatory bodies, governmental bodies and the social work academe.
- A number of different ethical approaches have been developed. Some of the most influential in social work have been: deontological theories, based on the desire of the individual to perform good acts; consequentialist theories, where the outcome of an action determines the value of the act; virtue-based theories, where individuals should cultivate specific virtues in themselves and act in accord with these virtues; and ethics of care, which takes account of both the relationships and networks to which an individual belongs and the different approaches that men and women tend to take in their approach to ethical issues.
- These different types of ethical theory have been used both to inform the development of professional ethical codes and also to provide moral guidance for social workers in their decision making and day-to-day professional practice.
- Since the birth of modern social work in the final quarter of the nineteenth century, a number of core values have become embedded within the *idea of social work*. These are focused around: diversity and relativism; autonomy and self-realisation; power, participation and control; and privacy and confidentiality.

Suggested further reading

Parrott, L. (2014) *Values and Ethics in Social Work Practice* (3rd ed). London: Sage.

Beckett, C., Maynard, A. and Jordan, P. (2017) *Values and Ethics in Social Work* (2nd ed). London: Sage.

Bell, L. and Hafford-Letchfield, T. (eds) (2015) *Ethics, Values and Social Work Practice*. Milton Keynes: Open University Press.

Gray, M. and Webb, S. A. (eds) (2010) *Ethics and Value Perspectives in Social Work*. London: Red Globe Press.

Reamer, F. G. (2018) *Social Work Values and Ethics* (5th ed). New York: Columbia University Press.

3

Theories and methods of social work practice

Barbra Teater

Chapter objectives

By reading this chapter you should be able to:

- explain the difference between a theory and a method and specify the role of each in social work practice;
- ascertain the importance of applying theories and methods to social work practice;
- identify key social work theories and methods applicable to social work practice;
- reflect on how social work theories and methods can be applied to your practice.

Introduction

Theory is essential to social work practice as it provides the foundation, or bedrock, on which social work interventions, or methods, are based. Theories provide social workers with an understanding, explanation and/or prediction of human functioning and behaviour, social interactions and social structures, and point social workers to specific methods to employ when intervening with individual service users, families, groups, communities and organisations. This chapter will outline the definitions of theory and method and detail their relationship with each other and their importance to social work practice. The chapter will then provide an overview of the different types of theories that influence social work practice along with the practice methods informed by such theories. The reader is encouraged to reflect on how they make practice decisions and what theories influence their choice of practice methods. Further readings are provided to encourage the reader to explore specific theories and methods in more depth.

Theory, method, and social work practice

The global definition of social work practice emphasises the importance of theory in practice by stating:

Underpinned by theories of social work, social sciences, humanities, and indigenous knowledges, social work engages people and structures to address life challenges and enhance wellbeing.

(International Federation of Social Workers [IFSW], 2014)

As the definition states, in achieving the aims of social work practice, social workers must use theory to guide their practice through the stages of engagement, assessment, intervention and evaluation. A theory consists of a set of assumptions, beliefs or ideas about particular phenomena in the world, which could be assumptions of human behaviour, human growth and development, psychological and social functioning, the construction of social order and the ideas of social justice (Teater, 2015). Theory is synonymous with hypothesis, premise, presumption, speculation and assumption, and established theories provide social workers with an explanation or prediction about what can or might happen in a certain situation given specific circumstances. Theories in social work practice are often drawn from other disciplines, such as psychology, sociology and philosophy, and are continually evolving as new knowledge is gained from changes in the social structures and social order and from individuals adapting and changing to their surroundings.

Theory is important to social work as it helps the social worker to explain or speculate what might be occurring with a service user, which then informs the social worker on how best to intervene in order to alleviate problems or difficulties and promote human growth and wellbeing. In this sense, theories serve as the knowledge (or assumptions) about what is occurring, why, and how best to address or alleviate problems or difficulties. The theory the social worker applies to a specific situation will then influence the type of method, or intervention, the social worker will employ to alleviate problems and promote wellbeing. A method is a set of techniques or skills that a social worker utilises in order to accomplish tasks and reach goals. Method is synonymous with intervention, practice, approach, technique or mode. In summary, theories and methods are both independent and interrelated in that theories explain for social workers what might be happening or what might occur in the future and based on the information the theory or theories provide, social workers will select a specific method or combination of methods to alleviate problems, achieve goals and promote wellbeing.

In addition to 'theory' and 'method', social workers might come across concepts such as perspective and model, which are also used to inform social work practice. A perspective is a particular value base that informs the way in which social workers view or see the world. A model is a structured and organised description, usually depicted logically and/or graphically, of what and how something happens. Theories are generally developed based on a particular perspective, and, likewise, the general perspective of social workers will often inform the type of theory they choose to apply to their practice. Additionally, theories help to inform what methods to use in practice, and theories and methods can often be depicted through models.

Case study 3.1

An example of the ways in which theories and methods can influence practice is seen in the case of eight-year-old Sam. Sam has been described as being disruptive in her school classroom, which has impacted her own learning as well as the learning environment for the other students.

A social worker who generally views human behaviour from a social learning perspective, which assumes that behaviours are learned through modelling and positive and negative consequences to behaviours (e.g. reactions, punishments and/or rewards), will most likely look to behavioural theories (i.e. cognitive theory; behavioural theory; social learning theory) to help explain and predict why Sam is behaving in this way and will approach the intervention with Sam by using behavioural techniques, such as structured consequences for her behaviours in an attempt to condition Sam to behave in a specific way. Alternatively, a social worker coming from a social constructivist perspective may work with Sam to illicit her interpretation of what is happening in the classroom and identify Sam's strengths and goals. The work together might involve utilising solution-focused practice where Sam and the social worker focus on times when things are going well for Sam in the classroom and attempt to do more of what has been going well. Finally, a social worker coming from a systems perspective may conduct a holistic assessment of Sam and determine that the presenting problem of her behaviour in the classroom might actually be a response to difficulties in the home environment and the social worker may utilise elements of task-centred social work and/or family therapy to work with the family, versus Sam alone, to alleviate distress at home that may, in turn, alleviate Sam's difficulties in the classroom.

In summary, the use of theories and methods in social work practice enables social workers to make best practice decisions. If social workers fail to use theories and methods, then they are practising carelessly as there is no rationale or bedrock on which the choice of practice methods are based.

Activity 3.1

What influences your practice decisions?

Consider your social work placement or professional practice experience and answer the following questions:

- How do you know how to approach a service user? (engagement)
- How do you know what questions to ask to identify the service user's reasons for social work involvement? (assessment)
- How do you know what to do after you have identified the service user's reasons for social work involvement and his/her goals for the work together? (intervention)
- How do you know if your work with the service user is effective? (evaluation)

Theories and methods of social work practice

Table 3.1 presents a summary of the prominent theories and methods used in social work practice. The table provides specific theories listed under each heading, the theorists responsible for the development of such theories, and the different practice methods that might be used in social work practice based on the theory. The theories were predominantly developed within the professions and/or academic disciplines of psychology, psychiatry, sociology, psychology and counselling, and range from explaining: human functioning and development at the micro level through individual biological, psychological and social development; psychological functioning at the mezzo level through relationships and social interactions; to societal influences on social order, construction of rules and norms, and explanations of inequalities and disadvantage at the macro level (Teater, 2015). Each of the seven main theories is described below including the relevant practice methods.

Table 3.1 Theories used in social work practice

Theory	Theorists	Practice method
Developmental theories Includes: Cognitive development Attachment theories Life stage theories Theories of need Faith and moral reasoning	Piaget; Vygotsky; Havighurst; Bowlby; Ainsworth; Erikson; Maslow; Fowler; Kohlberg	Assessment
Psychodynamic theories Includes: Psychoanalytic theory Ego psychology Object relations theory Self-psychology Crisis theory	S. Freud; A. Freud; Jung; Adler; Klein; Kohut; Horney Kernberg; Mahler	Psychodynamic therapy Psychoanalytic therapy Psychotherapy Jungian analysis Transactional analysis Crisis intervention Task-centred social work Relational, or relationship-based, social work Counselling

Behavioural and social learning theories	Pavlov; Watson; Skinner; Thorndike; Bandura; Beck; Ellis	Behavioural therapy
Includes: Behavioural theory Social learning theory Cognitive theory Social cognitive theory Group work theory		Cognitive therapy Cognitive behavioural therapy Cognitive based transactional analysis Task-centred social work Groupwork
Humanistic theories	Maslow; Rogers; May; Frankl	Person centred therapy
Includes: Phenomenology Existentialism Humanistic person-centred Strengths-based		Existential therapy Counselling Gestalt therapy Hypnosis and meditation Mindfulness Motivational interviewing Advocacy Strengths-based
Social constructivist theories	Foucault; Vygotsky; Berger & Luckmann; Gergen; Mead; Blumer; Cooley; Goffman	Narrative therapy
Includes: Symbolic interactionism Communication theory Role theory		Social constructivist approach Solution focused brief therapy Anti-oppressive, racist and discriminatory practice Cultural competency Advocacy Strengths-based
Systems theories	Pincus & Minahan; Goldstein; Specht & Vickery; Gitterman & Germain; Minuchin; Parons; Bowen; Satir; Merton; Dominell; Bronfenbrenner	Assessment
Includes: General systems theory Life model Family systems theory Ecological systems theory		Couple and family therapy Family systems therapy Community development Community practice Task-centred social work Ecological and green practice
Critical theories	Marx; Habermas; Weber; Solomon; Mancoske & Hunzeker; Bern; Miller; Jordan; Dominelli; Thompson; Dalrymple & Burke; Fook; Healy; McRuer; Bell; Freeman; Delgado; de Lauretis	Advocacy
Includes: Critical social work theory Conflict theory Empowerment theory Feminist theory Anti-oppressive, racist and discriminatory theory Critical race theory Crip theory Queer theory		Empowerment approach Anti-oppressive, racist and discriminatory practice Cultural competency Consciousness-raising Community practice Community development Task-centred social work

Adapted from Teater (2015)

Developmental theories

Developmental theories are concerned with describing and predicting how individuals grow and develop biologically, psychologically, socially and emotionally. Developmental theories can focus on a specific stage in the lifespan, such as childhood, or they may span across the entire lifespan. For example, Bowlby's (1988) theory of attachment is concerned with the type of attachment (secure; insecure, ambivalent; insecure, avoidant;

disorganised) a child experienced with her/his main caregiver, which can then explain how a child develops socially and emotionally and her/his ability or inability to develop relationships with others in the future. Other developmental theories focus on changes across the lifespan. For example, Erikson's stages of psychosocial development consist of eight stages individuals can progress through from infancy to older adults that range from trust versus mistrust (infant–18 months) to ego integrity versus despair (65 years and older) (Crain, 2011). The individual is theorised to experience tension or a crisis in each stage between the two extremes (e.g. trust versus mistrust) and must work through each stage in order to have a healthy psychosocial development. Social work intervention may assist a service user who is stuck or struggling to work through a particular stage and progress their psychosocial development.

Developmental theories are helpful to social workers by assisting in assessing the service user's current level of development and functioning against the stages or levels of the developmental theory. The assessment of the current stage or level can help to explain the service user's situation or behaviour, and can assist in determining the most appropriate method to use in practice.

Psychodynamic theories

Psychodynamic theories, originally based in Sigmund Freud's psychoanalysis, aim to explain human behaviour and personality by focusing on the psychological drives and forces within the individual and how past experiences shape current behaviour, functioning and relationships. The originating psychodynamic theories, such as Freud's Drive Theory (explaining the id, ego and superego), focused on the role of the unconscious mind in shaping an individual's personality and behaviour. Such theories are concerned with childhood experiences as critical in the development of the behaviour, psychological thinking and the personality of the individual as they age and, in particular, any difficulties or traumas experienced in childhood are viewed as leading to psychological distress and dysfunction in later life. Psychological distress and dysfunction are addressed through psychoanalytic therapy, which aims to bring the unresolved issues or repressed trauma buried within the unconscious to the conscious mind where the service user can address the unresolved and underlying problems (Sharf, 2016).

Other common terms within psychodynamic theories include defence mechanisms, transference and countertransference. Defence mechanisms, such as denial, disassociation, regression, acting out, projection or displacement, are tools used by the unconscious mind to react to situations that may cause anxiety or distress (Sharf, 2016). The defence mechanisms protect the individual by distancing her/himself from reality. Transference is the idea that we unconsciously transfer thoughts, feelings and experiences from our previous relationships to current relationships; for example, a service user reacting to a social worker as if she/he were a parental figure. Countertransference occurs when the social worker picks up on the unconscious signals from the service user and begins to act out the particular role (e.g. parental role).

Psychodynamic theories have evolved since Freud by shifting the attention away from the role of the unconscious and focusing more on how people cope with stress and trauma and on the importance of relationships. For example, crisis theory focuses on how individuals cope in a crisis or traumatic situation, which often results in psychological and physiological distress, and how such experiences enable them to grow and develop (Caplan, 1964). Klein's object relations theory describes how relationships developed in childhood form the focus of individuals' personality, drives, views of themselves and others, and influences how they interact in interpersonal relationships (Sharf, 2016). Relational social work focuses on the therapeutic relationship within a social work interaction as the most important factor in facilitating change (Ruch et al., 2018); the acts of transference and countertransference are important to recognise as key features in relational social work.

Psychodynamic theories are useful to social workers by enabling the worker to explore a service user's past experiences and hypothesise about how such experiences are contributing to or sustaining the presenting problem. Based on the assessment, psychodynamic theories point the social worker towards interventions such as psychotherapy, crisis intervention or transactional analysis, which aim to explore and tackle defence mechanisms, identify and build on coping skills, and/or explore past or current relationships.

Behavioural, cognitive, and social learning theories

Behavioural, cognitive, and social learning theories were developed as a backlash to the psychodynamic theories. Behavioural and cognitive theorists departed from the focus on the unconscious and instead explained human behaviour and cognitive and emotional processing as a product of learning from and responding to the cues received from the interactions with the social environment. Behavioural theorists, such as Pavlov, Watson, Thorndike and Skinner, believed that behaviours were learned through a process of conditioning and, therefore, could be unlearned. In particular, behavioural theorists focused on classical and respondent conditioning, which describes how an individual's behaviour is a result of prior learning, and operant or instrumental conditioning, which describes how behaviours can be learned by providing positive or negative consequences in response to behaviours; positive reinforcers will lead to an increase in the behaviour and negative consequences will lead to a decrease in the behaviour. Cognitive theorists, such as Beck and Ellis, focused on how individuals, as thinking creatures, do not automatically respond with particular behaviours to situations but, rather, process the situation through their cognition which then affects their behavioural response; the focus is on how thinking (cognition) mediates the behaviour (e.g. the A-B-C model). Finally, social learning theory focuses on how behaviours are learned through positive and negative reinforcers, but also through observing and then modelling the actions of others (e.g. parents; teachers). For example, an individual may observe the behaviours and actions of a parental figure, imitate the behaviours, and then receive positive or negative reinforcement for such modelled behaviours which influences whether the behaviour becomes a part of the individual in the future.

Behavioural, cognitive, and social learning theories can assist a social worker in exploring how behaviours have been learned through the service user's interactions with the social environment, her/his receipt of positive or negative reinforcers, and/or how the service user's cognition and belief systems can be contributing to the problematic behaviour. If behaviours or cognitions are problematic for the service user, then the focus of social work intervention is to unlearn such behaviours or cognitions, for example through the use of cognitive behavioural therapy (CBT) or task-centred social work, and develop new healthy ones that reduce distress and dysfunction and contribute to the service user's wellbeing.

Humanistic theories

Humanistic theories, based in humanistic psychology, were developed in rejection to both psychodynamic theories and behavioural theories, which focused on the unconscious or positive or negative reinforcers in determining behaviours. Instead, humanistic theory views individuals as conscious, meaning-making and purposeful. Humanistic theories consist of the following five core values: (1) human beings supersede the sum of their parts; (2) human beings have their existence in a uniquely human context, as well as in a cosmic ecology; (3) human beings are conscious: they are aware and aware of being aware both of oneself and in the context of other people; (4) human beings have some choice and, thus, responsibility; and (5) human beings are intentional, aim at goals, are aware that they cause future events, and seek meaning, value and creativity (Greening, 2006, p. 239). The focus of humanistic theories is to see the good in humans and their potential, creativity, hope, health, connection, meaning, purpose, and ability to achieve their full potential (Crain, 2011). Theories such as phenomenology and existentialism focus on the lived subjective and conscious experiences of individuals, how individuals make sense of their lives and their place and meaning within the world, and how they attribute meaning to the phenomena they encounter (Sharf, 2016).

Applying humanistic theories to social work practice involves taking a person-centred approach (Rogers, 1959) where the social worker is empathic, has unconditional positive regard for the service user, and is genuine in the interaction with the service user in order to establish a relationship that will lead to personality and behavioural change. The focus of the work together is on exploring the experiences of the service user and the meanings they attribute to such experiences. Interventions will explore the service user's experiences, meaning, hopes and aspirations and could include such practice methods of the person-centred approach; existential therapy; counselling; gestalt therapy; hypnosis; meditation; motivational interviewing; and advocacy.

Social constructivist theories

Social constructivist theories focus on how each individual has a unique reality and view of the world. Based in the theory of social constructionism by Berger and Luckmann (1966), social constructivism aims to explore reality creation and the ways in which individuals give meaning based on their lived experiences, and societal and cultural rules, norms and expectations. The basic premises of social constructivist theories consist of the following: (1) each individual has her/his own reality and way of viewing the world that cannot be fully understood by another person; (2) an individual's reality is based on societal rules and norms, culture, history and the person's interactions within these structures and forces; (3) the meaning of such interactions and societal forces are processed through one's cognition, which forms her/his reality; (4) the only way to attempt to understand another person's reality is through the use of communication; and (5) there is no one reality or one truth (Teater, 2020).

Social constructivist theories focus on how individuals give meaning to experiences, interactions and relationships. For example, role theory explores how individuals take on socially defined roles (e.g. mother, daughter, partner, professional) and the ways in which they make sense of such roles and are able to adhere to societal expectations of how each role should be performed (DeLamater and Collett, 2019), and communication theory proposes that people cannot *not* communicate, which affects how people interact and make sense of their world (Watzlawick et al., 1967). Social constructivist theories require social workers to take a position of curiosity with service users, use the language of service users in an attempt to understand their reality and view of the world, and acknowledge that no two service users will have the same reality or view of the world despite having similar lived experiences (Teater, 2020). Social constructivist interventions, such as narrative therapy, solution-focused brief therapy, anti-oppressive, racist and discriminatory practices, and advocacy, will aim to explore service users' experiences and meanings and will work to reframe problematic thoughts and views and/or challenge societal assumptions or social constructs that are preventing the service user from growing and developing.

Systems theories

System theories focus on the interaction and relationship between two or more systems and how they affect each other. A system is defined as a complex set of elements that interact together to make a functional whole. Examples of systems include individuals, couples, families, groups, communities, organisations, society and the world. Systems theory, derived from general systems theory, aims to assess how individuals (or other systems) operate and the extent to which they are able to grow develop, evolve and function through their interactions with the physical and social environment. For example, when working with individual service users, social workers may conduct a bio-psycho-social-spiritual assessment to assess how these different systems of the individual are functioning as well as assess for how other larger systems, such as the environment and social policies and structures, are helping or hindering the individual's functioning.

Systems theory enables the social worker to see beyond functioning at an individual level, such as psychodynamic and developmental theories, to how other larger systems may be impacting the extent to which a service user is able to function, grow and develop. Based on a holistic assessment of the systems within a service user's life, the social worker is able to determine where to focus the intervention, which could include practice methods such as: couple and family therapy; family systems therapy; community development; community practice; and ecological and green practice. The intervention may be with a system other than the individual (e.g. family; community; organisation; policy; society; environment). For example, a child's 'behavioural problems' may not be a result of a problem with the child but, rather, difficulties within the parental system to which the child is reacting. Focusing on the child would not solve the problem, but focusing on the parental system, through couples or family therapy, may best resolve the problem.

Critical theories

Critical theories examine and critique the social and political structures and the ways in which they affect individuals, families, groups and/or communities. The theories highlight the inequalities, disadvantage and social injustice in society and how they are sustained through social and political structures. For example, conflict theory, based on the works of Karl Marx and Max Weber, explores inequalities in wealth, power and class and how such inequalities impact on individuals and create conflict between and within social groups. Other theories, such as critical race theory, developed by Bell, Freeman and Delgado, examine the social construction of 'race' and the ways in which this construction sustains white supremacy, white privilege, racial power and institutional oppression, and crip theory, developed by McRuer, explores the construction of 'able-bodiedness' and the ways in which bodies are identified as 'normal' or as 'abject'. The aim of critical theories is to acknowledge inequalities, disadvantage and social injustice and challenge the societal and political structures that are sustaining them.

Critical theories are useful to social work practice by providing a theoretical basis for assessing the service user within her/his environment and examining the social and political structures that may be oppressing the service user. The assessment will point the social worker to the appropriate practice method to tackle structural oppression and discrimination, which can include: advocacy, the empowerment approach, anti-oppressive, anti-racist and anti-discriminatory practice, consciousness-raising, community practice, and community development.

Research summary

As with any helping profession working with service users in need and/or in vulnerable situations, social workers must apply the necessary knowledge and research evidence to their assessment of service user problems and to their choice of intervention. They must ensure their assessments of practice situations and choice of practice methods are grounded in established theories and are deemed appropriate (often established through research) for the specific situation. This often involves an exploration of the research base for a theory or method, which is varied based on the particular approach. For example, behavioural theories are well researched demonstrating effectiveness across a variety of populations and service user needs, yet other theories, such as psychodynamic theories, have a limited body of research to demonstrate effectiveness (Teater, 2020).

As individuals and situations are variable, social workers must continually evaluate their practice to explore what works with specific service user problems in different situations and settings given the service user's characteristics or demographics. Simply stated, no single approach to social work practice will fit all practice situations. The task of the social worker is to fully assess the service user situation, the surrounding environment influencing the service user, and the practice setting to determine the best course of action (intervention or method) that will meet the needs of the service user.

Social workers should continually evaluate their use of theories and methods with service users, which could be through feedback from the service user and/or through the process of critical reflection where social workers could ask themselves the following questions during their social work practice:

1. What went well?
2. What did not go so well?
3. What would I do the same or different in the future, and why?

In answering these questions, the social worker should provide specific examples for the first two questions by considering how they worked in engaging and interacting with the service user, the assessment tools and process with the service user, and the implementation of the specific practice method with the service user. Participating in the process of critical reflection on one's practice will build the social worker's practice wisdom, which can assist in quickly and accurately deciding what specific theories and methods tend to be effective in different situations with service users of differing characteristics and demographics.

Activity 3.2

Reflecting on your use of theories and methods in practice

Review the theories and practice methods in Table 3.1 and consider the following:

- Which theories and methods will you learn more about after reading this chapter?
- Which theories and practice methods are most applicable to the service user population with whom you work? Reflect on why you believe these theories and methods are the most appropriate.
- Which theory or theories most resonate with your professional perspective (i.e. approach to social work practice)? In what ways (if any) could you approach your social work practice from a different theoretical perspective?

Conclusion

This chapter has explored the definition and role of theories and methods in social work practice. Theories serve as the foundation of social work practice by guiding the social worker in how to assess service users' development, functioning and social situations, which will determine the best course of action and choice of methods to apply in order to alleviate service user problems and promote growth and development. This chapter provided a brief overview of seven general types of theories often used in social work practice and the practice methods selected in the intervention stage based on the theory applied. Social workers are encouraged to become familiar with the different types of theories and practice methods to enable them to make the best practice decisions with working with service users. Additionally, social workers should continually evaluate their practice to determine their effectiveness and further build their knowledge and skills for future social work practice.

Key points summary

- Theory serves as the foundation to social work practice by providing a set of assumptions, beliefs or ideas about particular phenomena in the world, which could be assumptions of human behaviour, human growth and development, psychological and social functioning, the construction of social order, and the ideas of social justice.
- Theories help the social worker to determine the most appropriate method, or intervention, to employ in practice to alleviate problems and promote human growth and wellbeing.
- A method is a set of techniques or skills that a social worker utilises in order to accomplish tasks and reach goals.
- In practising responsibly and effectively, social workers must ensure their assessments of practice situations and choice of practice methods are grounded in established theories, and are deemed appropriate given the specific service user's characteristics, situations, values and wishes.

Suggested further reading

Deacon, L. and Macdonald, S. J. (eds) (2017) *Social Work Theory and Practice*. London: Sage.

Payne, M. (2016) *Modern Social Work Theory* (4th ed). Oxford: Oxford University Press.

Teater, B. (2020) *An Introduction to Social Work Theories and Methods* (3rd ed). London: Open University Press.

Turner, F. J. (ed) (2017) *Social Work Treatment: Interlocking Theoretical Approaches* (6th ed). New York: Oxford University Press.

4

Social work and the law

Robert Johns

Chapter objectives

The aims of this chapter are:

- to set out exactly why law is a cornerstone of social work practice in the UK;
- to explain how and why law really matters to social work service users and practitioners;
- to offer some examples of key areas in which social workers must know in some detail what the law says about what they can, may or cannot do.

Introduction

This chapter begins with an exploration of the general relevance of law in people's everyday lives before going on to consider different facets of law and how the law became of great importance in social work. Relating this to the development of social work as an intrinsic part of the welfare state, the discussion then proceeds to itemise a number of significant ways in which the law plays a key role in social work practice. Part of this concerns the protection and reassurance offered to service users so it is important to set out how the law does this. Having focused on service users, the discussion turns to contemporary social work practice. Here the chapter will summarise, briefly, how key legal principles and legislation provide an essential framework for practice, noting in passing some differences in substantive law between the four constituent countries of the UK. This part of the chapter utilises fictional but realistic case examples. Finally, the chapter asks readers to reflect on how a knowledge of law might inform their future practice, offering guidance on further reading in this area.

What's your experience of the law?

Too embarrassed to say? Skeletons in the cupboard, are there? Tempted to skip this chapter and move on to the next? Don't. Now relax. The question is not really asking you to confess your adolescent, or even indeed adult, misdemeanours. If you are feeling a bit sheepish, then that is because you are interpreting the question in a very specific way. You are looking at law as sets of rules of behaviour that, if broken, result in some kind of sanction or punishment (in legal jargon, a sentence). Law is more than just that. How much more? Let's ask another question: do you have any direct, first-hand personal experience of the weather? Silly question, you may be thinking. It's like asking if you have any experience of breathing. Of course you have; air is all around us. Likewise, there is always weather, so inevitably we all experience it. Law is exactly the same.

> **Case study 4.1**
>
> Let us take a simple example of Surinder's journey. After getting up, getting dressed and getting herself ready, Surinder leaves her flat and begins to make her way to the station. She walks along the pavement and crosses two streets, in both cases using the pedestrian crossing. When she arrives at the station she buys a ticket to travel on the train, and when this gets to her destination, she walks through the shopping centre to the university where she is studying social work. At the entrance to the campus she shows her student card in order to gain entry and then finds her way to the social work law lecture. She greets her fellow students, the lecturer arrives promptly, and then the lecture begins.
>
> How many laws apply? If you think the answer is none, think again. There are all sorts of other ways in which the law regulates the way people behave, and we are not just talking about law relating to offences, the criminal law. Let us take the case study in stages.
>
> 1. *Surinder gets dressed and walks along the pavement.*
>   - *Wearing clothes is more than just a practical necessity; failing to do so risks causing offence and can result in legal action. Insisting on the right to walk*

> *stark naked in public will get nowhere, as demonstrated by an unsuccessful attempt to claim that repeated imprisonment for persistently breaking the law prohibiting public nudity in Scotland was a breach of fundamental human rights (Gough v United Kingdom, 2014). In walking along the pavements, Surinder is entitled to do so freely without being obstructed; deliberately getting in her way would be a criminal offence, and even assaulting someone accidentally by doing something careless could theoretically result in a civil action – that is, a claim for compensation could be made.*

2. **She crosses the street.**

   - *Surinder is entitled to make assumptions about her safety on the pavement and the predictability of the traffic. Traffic must keep to the left, and drivers must stop at traffic lights and pedestrian crossings; breaching these laws risks prosecution.*

3. **She buys a ticket to use the train.**

   - *She thereby enters into a contract with the rail company, and all sorts of additional regulations apply to that specific contract, for example compensation for delays. The key point here is that any transaction like this is an invitation to enter into a legal contract.*

4. **She walks through a shopping centre.**

   - *While generally people have the right to go wherever they want, simply because there is no law that stops them, this may not be true here since the shopping centre could be privately owned and admission permitted only when the shops are open. Ownership accords legal rights. Surinder may not have a right to go through the shopping centre.*

5. **At the entrance to the campus she shows her student card in order to gain entry.**

   - *Surinder knows she only has the right to enter university premises because she has entered into a contract with the university: she has paid her fees and in return the university permits access to facilities. This is a contract and it has obligations on both sides.*

6. **The lecturer arrives promptly and the lecture begins.**

   - *So the university's part of the contract is now being fulfilled; tuition is being offered at the time stipulated, and the university is entitled make additional rules such as not allowing people to be admitted to lectures if they arrive late. We shall firmly and resolutely ignore the issue of what happens if lecturers are not punctual!*

These answers are not necessarily conclusive; indeed there are a number of other ways in which the law operates. For example, there is an underlying assumption of equality of entitlement. By this we mean that no one could refuse to enter into a contract, such as selling a ticket or goods or services, simply on the grounds of race or gender. Universities no longer discriminate against women, so Surinder is as entitled as anyone else to apply for admission; indeed to refuse to consider her would be a breach of equality legislation. However, prior to 1868, when the first nine women were admitted to the University of London, it was standard practice in the UK for all universities to admit only men.

Equality legislation has raised expectations of fair dealing, but in historical terms this is comparatively recent. It has to be conceded that law can be disempowering, and indeed oppressive. In the past, for example, people have found themselves enslaved, or lost property to which they were hitherto entitled, or have been victimised because of their beliefs or sexuality. There was no 'natural' law prohibiting slavery in Britain, so this form of extreme oppression was tolerated until specific laws were introduced to prohibit it. Likewise, during the eighteenth century a whole welter of 'enclosure' legislation was introduced specifically with the intention of depriving people of property to which they thought they were entitled – the so-called 'common' land was taken away from them and fenced off so that people were effectively deprived of their livelihood. In this way the law was used by those in power in order to acquire property and much hardship was the result. There is a long history of discrimination against atheists, the law taking the form of prohibition of blasphemy. This and homophobia resulted in a successful private prosecution of *Gay News* (Whitehouse v Lemon, 1979). In 2013, an international survey revealed that convictions for blasphemy still result in mandatory imprisonment in 39 countries and possible death sentence in 13 (Cherry, 2013).

So law can be both empowering and disempowering. It also changes over time. The expansion of human rights law is probably the most significant change over the last 70 years or so, beginning in 1948 with the United Nations Declaration followed by the European Convention in 1950. These represent international determination to avoid repeating Second World War atrocities. Do note, though, that a significant difference between them is that while the European Convention on Human Rights (Council of Europe, 2013) is enshrined in UK legislation through the Human Rights Act 1998, the United Nations Declaration (United Nations, 2015) is not, although the latter is highly influential.

Different facets of law

This brief survey indicates that law is not set in tablets of stone and is not neutral. Sometimes law is empowering, sometimes it is disempowering. It is not all about penalising certain actions, it can be about according entitlement. Law can be a vehicle for promoting and securing positive rights.

There may be a dichotomy here: law is a vehicle for justice, yet is also judgemental. Sometimes, in cases involving social workers, there can be a simultaneous conflict between these two aspects (Dickens, 2017). Note that by justice here we essentially mean social justice, legal mechanisms for creating a more equal and just society. This last ambition is founded on key ethical principles underpinning the role of law, the key principle being that it is the duty of the state to pass legislation that enables people to participate as fully as possible in society. Why, and to what extent, should the state do this?

Activity 4.1

Why should the law promote social justice?

This is a point at which values and ethics meet law and social policy (Braye and Preston-Shoot, 2016). The best way to answer this question is to draw on the social sciences and philosophy. Political theorists differ markedly in their answers depending on their interpretation of the legitimate role of the state. Some say the state has no overall obligation to social justice at all: people are entitled to what they are paid, no matter how unfair those earnings appear to others in a free market and there is no moral obligation to redistribute wealth (Nozick, 1974). In social justice terms, redistribution of wealth includes providing services and support to those who are disadvantaged in a free-market society, distribution in accordance with need. This conflicts with other aspects of justice, distribution in accordance with rights and desert (Miller, 1979). Rawls, who exercised a significant influence on social work thinking, argues that only when people's basic needs are met can they effectively exercise their other rights and liberties (Rawls, 1999, p7).

As to practicality, and what developments in social justice mean for social work, readers need to look to the discipline of social policy and its connections with social work.

As far as social work law is concerned, this social justice aspect of law is critical since fundamentally social work is about empowering people: assisting people to lead more fulfilling lives through being supported, being protected when vulnerable, and participating in decision-making (Adams, 2008; Banks, 2012; Beckett and Maynard, 2017; Gray and Webb, 2010). Social work law is thus essentially about enabling and facilitating, rather than preventing, constraining or restricting. Hence there is not a great deal of criminal law (law concerning offences and penalties) in social work law textbooks. Instead most social work law concerns itself with the duties laid on local authorities to provide services that enable people to lead more fulfilled lives, and associated service user rights.

In order to understand how this has come about and why law is of such prominence in social work, it will be beneficial to connect this to early developments of social work.

How did the law come to be so important in social work?

Several commentators trace the origins of contemporary social work to the Victorian Charity Organisation Society, whose task was to ensure that financial and material relief was directed to the worthiest recipients (Cunningham and Cunningham, 2017; Horner, 2019). Thus it was linked to the centralisation of poor relief. Conversely, social work also arose from social action attempts to integrate rich and poor: for example, the settlement movement with links to universities, such as the University of Glasgow settlement and Toynbee Hall in East London. A third aspect is the development of outreach projects into the community. On these three aspects it is possible to build an analysis of some of the tensions between law and social work (Beckett and Maynard, 2017).

A common feature of all these aspects is that they have now been incorporated into the role of government, central and local. Checking entitlements to welfare payments is primarily a responsibility of a central government department. Social action and outreach takes the form of social workers working in local communities, enabling people to access services that meet their needs, supporting those who have additional needs such as a disability, and addressing various kinds of problems which people encounter. These responsibilities developed piecemeal, primarily originating in the development of the welfare state (1945–1950). So, for example, the Children Act 1948 ordered every UK local authority to establish a department of social workers to help families look after their children, if necessary by providing foster care or places in children's homes. In the late 1960s various Acts extended social work responsibilities to the field of youth justice. Alongside workers with children and families, other social workers focused on mental health, whilst the third group of social workers acquired responsibilities under the National Assistance Act 1948, a UK-wide Act that conferred on local authorities a duty to provide care for older people and people with disabilities.

In the early 1970s various legislation combined all social work strands, resulting in a significant increase in demand for social work services, partly as a result of pressure from service users, and partly because of changes in the family in a more affluent society (Cunningham and Cunningham, 2014; Yuill and Gibson, 2011). Added to this was a growing awareness of issues such as child protection, domestic violence, substance use, and the desirability of moving people out of institutions and back into the community – the latter particularly in relation to mental health and learning disability. As a consequence, by the end of the 1970s it could be fairly stated that social work was predominately an activity carried out in statutory organisations, particularly local authorities, which were governed entirely by what the law permitted them to do.

So, in contrast to some other countries, social work grew in the UK as a result of legislative changes. Despite attempts to privatise or marketise parts of social work, most especially in residential and domiciliary care for older people, responsibilities have continued to grow, particularly in the field of child safeguarding. Here there has been tension between the role of the state and its responsibilities towards children, and the rights of families to bring up their own children in accordance with cultural norms and expectations. Consequently, there have been attempts to clarify the role of the state in line with policymakers' and legislators' requirements, service user expectations, and human rights parameters. The best example of this is the Cleveland Inquiry which focused on the crucial issue of accountability (Johns, 2017, chapter 1). This is a fundamental issue in social work law to which the discussion now turns.

Accountability

Activity 4.2

Can you think of some examples of where accountability is particularly important for service users?

Accountability is important for a number of reasons, all of which centre on the need for service users to have confidence in the integrity and quality of social work services, which naturally includes social workers themselves.

For many years, although social workers were primarily employed by local authorities empowered to intervene directly in service users' lives, anyone could call themselves a social worker. Consequently, not surprisingly, there were instances of devious individuals masquerading as social workers and preying on vulnerable people; children and adults. At the same time, there were also concerns about social workers' competence, emphasised in a number of inquiries into apparent 'failings' to protect children or vulnerable adults (Butler-Sloss, 1988; Clyde, 1992; Cornwall Adult Protection Committee, 2007; Coventry Safeguarding Board, 2013; DHSS, 1974; Haringey Safeguarding Board, 2009; Laming, 2003). To address this, regulatory bodies had been set up by government, empowered to set standards of training. The UK-wide Central Council for Education and Training in Social Work operated until 2001 when regulation of training was combined with enforced codes of conduct through the establishment of separate regulatory bodies in each of the four countries of the United Kingdom. Henceforth, 'social work' became a protected title and only registered social workers can now use it.

Legislation that set this up introduced compulsory registration of care homes and strengthened minimum standards of care enforced through an inspectorate. Exactly how this works varies between the four countries of the UK. Table 4.1 below clarifies exactly who does what.

Table 4.1   Registration of care homes

Country	Regulatory body	Registration and inspection authority
England	Social Work England	Children: Office for Standards in Education, Children's Services and Skills
		Adults: Care Quality Commission
Wales	Social Care Wales	Care Inspectorate Wales
Scotland	Scottish Social Services Council	The Care Inspectorate
Northern Ireland	Northern Ireland Social Care Council	Regulation and Quality Improvement Authority

In addition to accountability there are three other key interrelated areas in which the law is important to service users. In essence, these answer three critical questions:

- What can social workers offer; that is, what authority and power do they possess?
- What are the respective rights and duties of the state and service users?
- What is the process for enforcing people's rights especially when service users believe they have not received the service to which they thought they were entitled?

Authority and the power to assist

Service users and social workers themselves do need to know what the law actually says about what social workers can and cannot do. Here it is crucial to understand a fundamental principle governing all actions of everyone employed by a local authority: a local authority can only do what the law says it can do.

A local authority needs to be empowered by Parliament through a law that says either the local authority *must* or *may* do something, that is the action is *mandatory* or *permissive*. This is diametrically opposite to the position of individuals, who are free to do whatever they wish unless the law says that they may not. If local authorities step outside their powers they are acting *ultra vires* (meaning beyond powers) and liable to penalties. So it is vitally important to understand when and where a local authority can and cannot act, as the following examples will demonstrate.

Case study 4.2

If you have no previous knowledge of how social work actually operates in the UK, some of the answers to questions in this case study may surprise you.
  In each of the following case studies, consider

1. whether the request is one to which you think a local authority social worker has a responsibility to respond, and
2. if you think there is a duty or power to respond, can you say which law might apply?

(Note that as a consequence of devolution, the answer to the second question will vary in different countries of the UK, but after the exercise you will find some general answers to the questions.)

Table 4.2 Case studies

	Need	Local authority social worker's responsibility?
1	Abigail is finding that as she grows older living on her own she needs someone to help with everyday tasks	
2	Anton needs help filling in an income tax return	
3	Leanne, aged five, has been abused by her stepfather	
4	Glen, aged 14, is to appear in court having committed a third offence of shoplifting	
5	Diane desperately needs a larger house	
6	Fergus has lost money as the result of an email scam	
7	Tyrone has had several spells in a hospital psychiatric wing and needs support on discharge into the community	

8	Chloe, aged eight, is being looked after by friends of her parents while they work abroad for a couple of years
9	Gloria has lost the ability to manage her own financial affairs
10	Luke, aged 37, has recently been discharged from prison
11	Radoslaw, caring for his mother who has multiple disabilities, urgently needs a break for a few days
12	Clarice has problems preventing her teenage son mixing with a local gang
13	Corrine needs counselling as she was abused as a child and finds making relationships as an adult difficult
14	Harry was looked after by the local authority but is now coming up to 18 so needs to be more independent
15	Erica needs help with transport to get to and from work
16	Tom, aged 40, is homeless and appears to have no relatives
17	Grant is perpetually short of money and wants help with budgeting
18	Neville is no longer able to get up the stairs in his home, a house that he owns
19	Lorraine is frantic as for the third time her 12-year-old son has been excluded from school
20	Meera is overwhelmed by her problems, so much so that she wants someone else to look after her three-year-old child

It may be surprising to learn that in less than half of these cases a local authority social worker has a clear duty to assist. In the cases of Abigail, Radoslaw, and Neville (1, 11, and 18) this duty derives from adult care and carer legislation. Leanne and Chloe's cases (3 and 8) are examples of different kinds of child safeguarding, one being a private fostering arrangement. Glen (4) comes under youth justice whilst responsibility for Tyrone (7) derives from mental health legislation. Harry (14) is provided for by specific legislation concerning young people leaving care, whilst Meera's request to have her child looked after by someone else (20) is covered by more general children and family support legislation.

Under children and family support legislation, there is a power to assist by way of advice in the cases of Clarice and Lorraine (12 and 19), and there is a possibility of needing to use adult safeguarding legislation for Fergus and Gloria (6 and 9). Luke's case (10) is interesting in that this is a local authority social work obligation in Scotland but not in other parts of the UK, where the probation service will have responsibility. In all other cases, other agencies may be able to assist, but these places fall outside the ambit of local authority social work services.

Boundaries

Social work service users fall broadly into two categories: those who request services, and those who have social work imposed upon them. This latter kind of 'intervention' must derive from explicit legislation that accord social workers with the right to impose themselves on families, for example, where a child or a vulnerable adult needs protection or 'safeguarding'. Yet social workers cannot have unfettered powers to intervene where they believe it is right for them to do so, for in this role they are acting as agents of the 'state'. There must therefore be some clear demarcation between the obligations of the state to intervene in families where its agents (social workers) consider it necessary to do so, and the rights of people generally to live as they wish, in accordance with their own values.

This tension exists in every sphere of social work law: child safeguarding, adult care, domestic violence, mental health, mental capacity, youth justice, and adoption in particular. Each of these areas will have its own discrete area of legislation and court system, but such laws operate within the wider human rights context and all local authority actions must comply with the European Convention on Human Rights.

This Convention sets a benchmark for the formulation of statute law and for decision-making by courts. In short, laws passed by the UK Parliament and decisions made by UK courts should comply with the Convention, although there are exceptions, as most legal texts will explain. There are 14 'Articles' in the Convention. Of these, five potentially apply directly to social work practice:

- Article 2 – right to life
- Article 3 – prohibition of torture and inhuman or degrading treatment or punishment
- Article 5 – right to liberty
- Article 6 – right to fair trial, to reviews by courts or tribunals
- Article 8 – right to respect for privacy and family life

Activity 4.3

How might each of the following Articles apply to social work?

How well you are able to answer this question will inevitably depend on your experience of social work, but here are some examples of actual cases where these Articles have been engaged.

> The UK Supreme Court considered **Article 2** regarding whether a vulnerable person could be deprived of their liberty by social workers in Cheshire West and Chester v P [2014] UKSC 19.

> In Z and others v UK [2001] 2 FLR 612 a local authority's failure to intervene in a family so that children suffered inhuman treatment as a consequence was judged to be a breach of European Convention **Article 3**. **Article 6** was also considered since at that time the children did not have rights to challenge local authorities through an independent appeal body.

> **Article 5** was considered to have been breached in the case where a man was imprisoned for breaching a court order made in a domestic violence case (Hammerton v. the United Kingdom European Court Application 6287/10).

> In Re B (a child) [2013] UKSC 33 the Supreme Court had to weigh up the merits of a social work care plan for adoption in the light of a father's claim that he had a right under **Article 8** to resume care of his child.

Arbitration

The final area to consider is the process for reconsidering people's rights when service users are unhappy with social work action, or lack thereof. This does not just relate to the courts as already discussed, but also to tribunals and official arbitration services, such as the Ombudsman. However, there is an important rider that arbitration bodies will only intervene where there is evidence of unjust treatment, mistaken interpretation of the law, or maladministration. For example, in 2018 the relevant Ombudsman adjudicated that a local authority had failed to properly investigate safeguarding concerns which a service user had raised about the care family members were providing to her mother (Local Government and Social Care Ombudsman case 18 003 112).

So arbitration is the final area in which social work law is of particular importance, running alongside law relating to accountability, to social work authority and to the boundaries of intervention in service users' lives.

Conclusion

This chapter should have left readers in no doubt about why law is a cornerstone of social work practice in the UK, and why it matters to service users in particular. The exercises in the chapter have alerted you to the areas in which social workers must know about the law, although it was not intended to provide a guide to what the law actually says in each of these areas. That varies between individual countries of the UK and is covered in key social work law texts listed in the further reading guide.

Key points summary

- Law forms the backdrop to everyday life.
- Knowledge of the law is important for service users and social workers so people know what social workers may, can and cannot do.
- The law is complex, changeable and specific to countries.

Suggested further reading

Brammer, A. (2015) *Social Work Law* (4th ed). Harlow: Pearson.
Carr, H. and Goosey, D. (2019) *Law for Social Workers* (15th ed). Oxford: Oxford University Press.
Cunningham, J. and Cunningham, S. (2017) *Social Policy and Social Work* (2nd ed). London: Sage.
Horner, N. (2019) *What Is Social Work?* (5th ed). London: Sage.
Johns, R. (2020) *Using the Law in Social Work* (8th ed). London: Sage.

5

Human growth and development in social work

Janet Walker

Chapter objectives

The aims of this chapter are:

- to explore the importance of understanding human growth and development and the life course perspective for social work;
- to examine the 'staged' theories of human growth and development to highlight some of the different frameworks for thinking about human growth and development;
- to critique the impact of human growth and development and life course experiences, including economic and social inequalities, as the intersection of the influences of multiple interrelated systems;
- to highlight how people's experiences are structured by the consequences of inequalities;
- to reflect on the importance of life course perspectives on social work's role and responsibilities in 'making' sense of people's lives.

Introduction

In this chapter human growth refers to physical progress, the changes that happen in your body and appearance from birth to maturity across the lifespan. Human development refers to the complex and continuous changes that occur through our lifetime, and that are influenced by the conditions in which we live.

Activity 5.1

Given the definitions outlined above, why do you think it is important for social workers to understand human growth and to understand human development?

Explanations of human growth focus on the sequence of physical ('biological') changes that can be predicted or expected in relation to the human body. An understanding of human growth and the different expectations of physical changes that occur across the lifetime can support social workers to understand the developmental milestones that might normally be expected to be accomplished. Human development as a broader concept not only takes into account biological changes but also the behavioural expectations of changes in an individual. Further, it can be expanded to include the context in which a person develops and a consideration of the capabilities for a healthy life. An understanding of human development can support social workers to gain an understanding of the normal expectations of the interrelationships between the physiological and psychological expectations throughout the life course. It has a focus on directly enhancing human abilities, for example through the provision of a decent standard of living. It is also about creating the condition for human development; for example, this could include issues in relation to gender equality; participating in political and community life and so on.

A life course approach refers to a multidisciplinary, holistic and integrated way of understanding people's lives and the structural and social issues that have an impact upon them. It permits an array of different responses to support and enable people. This approach encompasses ideas and observations from an array of disciplines, notably history, sociology, demography, developmental psychology, biology and economics. In particular, it directs attention to the powerful connection between individual lives and the historical and socioeconomic context in which these lives unfold. As a concept, a life course is defined as *a sequence of socially defined events and roles that the individual enacts over time* (Giele and Elder, 1998, p22). A life course perspective is intended to support you in understanding a person's whole life context and experience from birth to death as a progressive and developmental path with opportunities for growth, adaptation and change across all aspects of their life.

Health warning!

- An understanding of human growth and development is central to knowledge and its application to practice for social workers.
- Understanding theories of human growth and development must recognise the importance of difference and diversity; understanding what would 'normally' be expected to be accomplished, underpinned by a critical appreciation of individual variation and issues in relation to, for example, delayed growth or development; the impact of cultural diversity.
- We need to recognise our own biases, attitudes, assumptions and values about the life course; for example, in considering the capacity and capabilities for the positive contribution that all citizens can make to society.
- We need to be aware of personal feelings; for example, recognising and appreciating the potential impact of our own life experiences on our responses to others.
- Theories can offer us explanations – but theories cannot explain everything! Theories have a focus on universal, predictable events and pathways. However, there are many different influences on a person's life. Not everybody grows and develops at the same stage and the same rate. Not every life event has the same impact and/or responses on every person in the same way.
- As social workers we need to recognise the potential influence of multiple events and experiences throughout the life course to recognise the influence on ourselves and, importantly, on the people we work with.

Case study 5.1

Liam (15) lives on a large estate of social housing on the edge of a city, the youngest in a family of two brothers and one sister. Neil, Liam's dad, works as a council worker. As a young man he was often in trouble with the police for car theft, influenced by a group of peers, and spent some time in a Youth Offender Institution. When not at work he prefers to spend this time in the company of other men, particularly at the local pub. Gill, Liam's mother, works part-time in a local supermarket. She suffers from depression and is an active drinker, saying, 'It helps me forget about things.'

Liam's older brothers are both in the army, coming home occasionally. Paige (20), his sister, has twin girls who are two years old and lives with her daughters' father nearby. Paige and her partner have become dependent on drugs and alcohol, with a number of 'friends' using their house to access drugs and alcohol. There is also a concern that Paige is the victim of violence from her partner, and that she has been made to prostitute herself in order to earn money for drugs. The twins have been very slow to walk and talk, with a poor diet. There is concern for the girls' neglected appearance and they are increasingly seen in the care of a number of the couple's friends.

Dorothy (68), Liam's maternal grandmother, lives in the next street and has been a major support in Liam's life, offering a place to stay when he is not happy or needs

(Continued)

(Continued)

support. Following the death of her partner four years ago, Dorothy has become 'disorganised', and she has been more forgetful. Liam is increasingly out at night, mixing with a group of friends who share an interest in cars. Recently he was arrested for joy-riding in a car stolen by some older boys. He is staying away from school more and more as he 'does not see the point of going. They just get on my case all the time.' He wants to join the army like his older brother but has been warned this may be unlikely because of his actions and behaviour.

This case study provides an example to support you in applying some of the theories, concepts and ideas as you work through this chapter. Acknowledging that this case study offers limited information, it may help you to reflect on your key concerns about Liam and his family. We will return to Liam and his family at the end of this chapter.

Theoretical models to aid understanding human growth and development

A person's life course from birth to death takes the individual through different stages in life, each consecutively associated with a specific age span, with its own characteristics, preoccupations and roles. The life course approach helps to further our understanding whilst recognising differences. While theorists (and societies) may differ as to how many stages there are, and exactly when they begin and end, there is general agreement that this is the pattern to be expected in life.

Development theories help to explain and analyse the life course and may enable us to predict outcomes. In this way, theories and researched evidence are important tools to help and guide practice, as they provide a framework to support our understanding and in seeking to make sense of human relationships and agency, an individual's capacity to determine and make meaning from their environment through purposive consciousness and reflective and creative action (Houston, 2010). They can support us in demonstrating how we have arrived at the decisions we make. Development theories can be conceptualised as a series of age-linked transitions that are embedded in social institutions, for example: family, schools, work, church, government; in a cultural context – as the integrated pattern of human behaviour that includes thoughts, behaviours, communications, actions, customs, beliefs, values, and institutions of a racial, ethnic, religious or social group; and imbedded in history – as conditions that influence the life course across time and place (Bengtson et al., 2012).

Physical and biological development across the lifespan

Physical development refers to the normal ways in which bodies grow, change and develop throughout a person's lifetime. Biological development, including genetics, nutrition and gender, can play a particularly important role in the course of early development.

These factors influence a child both in positive ways that can enhance their development and in negative ways that can compromise developmental outcomes.

Table 5.1 is intended to provide you with an understanding of the 'typical' expectations of physical growth across the life span. People's physical development can vary in many ways; and growth and development may not be sequential – people grow and develop at different rates, with a number of influences on our growth such as hereditary factors, gender and culture. However, understanding the broad expectations of physical development can help us to compare and contrast expectations with those of the people we are working with.

Table 5.1 Physical development

Stage	Normal physical development
Birth – Newborn (Neonate)	• Reflexes evident as automatic reactions to stimulation. For instance, babies automatically suck when presented with a nipple, and turn their heads when a parent speaks. • Near sighted, but visual acuity, or ability, develops quickly; attracted to objects of light-and-dark contrasts, such as the human face. • Respond to tastes, smells and sounds, especially the sound of the human voice. • Distinguish between the primary caregiver and others on the basis of sight, sound and smell.
Infancy (0–2)	• Period of rapid growth and change, with variations in height, weight, sensory capacities and other physical growth. • Development of gross and fine motor skills. • Milestones set for the development of the infant – sitting up, crawling, standing, cruising, walking, running.
Early Childhood (3–8 years)	• Time of relatively even growth. Height, weight, body proportions, body build, bones and muscles grow to make the child ready for adulthood. • Further develops gross and fine motor skills: for example, riding a tricycle, hopping on one foot, hops, skips and jumps confidently, turns pages of a book, buttons and unbuttons clothing, writes own name, joins up writing.
Late Childhood (8–12 years)	• Development of strength, speed and precision in the use of arms, legs and other body muscles. • Motor development takes place at a rapid pace from more generalised to more specialised form of activities.
Adolescence (12–18 years)	• Puberty – period of transition to adult life. • Legs and other muscles grow to size and strength sufficient for standing, talking and running to the maximum. • Development of primary and secondary sexual characteristics; the role of hormones in sexual maturity.
Early Adulthood (19–45 years)	• Reaches physical maturity. • Physical strength peaks. • Young adults have good strength and coordination skills (including fine motor skills), and quick reaction times. • Developing the ability to share intimacy, seeking to form relationships and find intimate love; people are at their sexual peak. • For women who choose to have children, motherhood and giving birth to a child is a very significant aspect of their physical development.

(Continued)

Table 5.1 (Continued)

Stage	Normal physical development
Middle Adulthood (46–65 years)	• Generally, experience good health and physical functioning. • Decreases in strength, coordination, reaction time, sensation (sight, hearing, taste, smell, touch) and fine motor skills. • Biopsychosocial changes that accompany midlife appear to be major turning points in terms of the decline that eventually typifies older adulthood.
Late Adulthood (65+)	• Skin continues to lose elasticity, reaction time slows further, and muscle strength diminishes. • Hearing and vision decline significantly. • Other senses, such as taste, touch and smell, less sensitive than they were in earlier years. • Immune system is weakened, more susceptible to illness. • A decrease in physical mobility

Biological-based theories focus on the individual in their environment, what we are born with ('nature') having greater influence than the family context in which we were born ('nurture'). Biological theories seek to explain behaviours through an examination of individual characteristics. The nature versus nurture debate involves the extent to which particular aspects of behaviour are a product of either inherited (genetic) or acquired (learned) influences.

Activity 5.2

Nature or nurture? How might 'nature' – the genetics you were born with – influence a person's life course? How might 'nurture' – your experiences of your upbringing and environment – influence a person's life course? What do you think has a greater influence on a person's early life course development – 'nature' or 'nurture'?

Inevitably there is a range of perspectives! Nature, as the biological basis of human growth and development, can indicate, for example, the colour of your eyes, which will probably have a limited or no influence on an individual's life course. However, it can also be used to justify and/or predict inherited characteristics and the influence on a person's life chances, for example your personality, intelligence, temperament, mental and physical health, and the potential for certain behaviours, for example, criminality. Nurture theory, whilst recognising the influence of genetics, suggests that environmental factors are the origins of a person's behaviour, for example our childhood experiences, how we are raised, social relationships, and the culture in which we are raised.

Table 5.2 Approaches to nature vs. nurture

Nature ⟵⟶ Nurture

Biological approaches	Psychoanalysis	Cognitive psychology	Humanism	Behaviourism
Focus on genetics, hormones and neurological explanations of behaviour. Example: Chomsky	Focus on the innate drives of sex and aggression (nature) and social upbringing during childhood (nurture). Example: Freud	Innate mental structures such as schema, perception and memory are constantly changed by the environment. Example: Piaget	Emphasis on basic physical needs and societal influence on self-concept. Example: Maslow	All behaviours are learned from the environment through conditioning. Examples: Skinner, Bandura

Psychological and sociological theories across the lifespan

Traditional approaches to understanding human growth and development across the life course often separate lives into discrete categories and stages. Psychologists and development researchers have proposed a number of different theories to describe and explain the process and stages that individuals go through as they develop. There are a number of different perspectives that can be taken to form an understanding of how we develop into who we are, broadly taken from the disciplines of biology, psychology and sociology. In brief:

- Psychological theories focus on people's 'biology', what goes on in people's minds, the development of their personality, emotional development and other related behaviours.
- Sociological theories emphasise social and environmental factors.

Psychological theories

One of the key theorists in understanding the development of children is Jean Piaget (1896–1980) (1936), who represents a psychological perspective, a consideration of how people develop across the life course by exploring their thoughts, feelings and behaviours. He believed that children seek to understand and adapt to their environment, and by doing so undertake certain actions as they move through progressive stages of development.

Table 5.3 Piaget's stages of cognitive development

Stage	Age	Major characteristics and development changes
Sensorimotor	0–2 years	Using senses and movement to understand the environment; learns about the world through basic actions such as sucking, grasping, looking and listening; realisation of object permanence; curiosity; realise actions can cause things to happen in the world around them; egocentric.

(Continued)

Table 5.3 (Continued)

Stage	Age	Major characteristics and development changes
Pre-operational	2–6 years	Begins to be able to use basic logic, but is not able to understand how other people might perceive the environment; symbolic functions and intuitive thoughts; learn to speak and learn that objects and images are symbols for something else; curious – asks questions; egocentric thinking, struggling to see the perspectives of others.
Concrete operations	7–12 years	Can now take account of different perspectives on the environment and is able to undertake more complex logical reasoning; develop cognitive inductive reasoning; concept of conservation; classify and build concrete operational structures. Thoughts and feelings are unique – can put ourselves in other people's shoes.
Formal operations	12 years +	Ability to imagine and speculate. Can conceive new ideas underpinned by reasoning, without the need for prior experience. Able to think more rationally about abstract concepts and hypothetical events; deeper understanding of our own identity and morality; can understand why people behave the way they behave. Deductive reasoning – to plan and think about thinking! Egocentric thought.

Piaget's theory of cognitive development helped add to our understanding of children's intellectual growth. It also stressed that children were not merely passive recipients of knowledge. Instead, children are constantly investigating and experimenting as they build their understanding of how the world works.

An understanding of attachment theory is an important aspect of the work of social workers, particularly with children in influencing the way that key relationships work. The original concept of 'attachment' has been attributed to the studies developed by John Bowlby (1907–1990) (1953, 1969, 1973, 1988). Mothers, whom Bowlby believed were the critical relationship in a child's early life, also had a biological need to be near and protect their children. Therefore 'attachment' is a primary motivational need. The impact of prolonged separation on children was viewed as 'maternal deprivation' – the temporary or permanent loss to a child of their mother's care and attention. However, what is apparent is that patterns of attachment can be affected by a variety of factors. The best predictor of a child's secure attachment is the attention and sensitivity of the primary caregiver.

> While rituals and behaviour may differ from one culture to another, all humans share a common set of attachment needs and goals – to have people who are close (primary caregivers) who act as a secure base and safe haven, with whom they want to spend time, and separation from whom provokes upset and protest.

(Shemmings, 2016, p8)

Experiences of attachment in childhood are seen to be carried on into adult life with significant influence on such things as the choice of partners, our relationships and our interaction with our community. As Howe (2011, p183) suggests: 'early loss, abuse or neglect and trauma, if unresolved have the power to seriously disturb thought and feeling across the lifecourse'.

Research summary

Attachment is central to infants' and children's social and emotional development as children need to feel secure in their relationships. Early relationships are seen as important as they are viewed by theorists as having a critical role in the person's emotional wellbeing throughout their life. Children use the people to whom they are attached as:

- a safe base from which to explore;
- a source of comfort; and
- a source of encouragement and guidance.

There are two parts to the development of attachment: an initial first part immediately after birth, referred to as 'bonding' (usually with the mother); and a second, more important part that develops during the early years of a baby's life.

Whilst the early days are not irrelevant, the first few months appear to be more crucial in developing a sense of attachment, particularly between parents and children.

Whilst Bowlby's research has had a significant impact, there have been criticisms of some of the early thinking on attachment theory. Children can make attachment relationships to other people, not just their mother. They can also form several attachments. Developing relationships with others is equally important, for example with fathers, siblings and other relatives. The key factor is that the person spends time with them building a relationship. Reliance on one 'exclusive' relationship can itself be damaging, as it does not allow for supportive, healthy relationships with others. Children need to experience stable, reliable relationships. Whilst early experience is important, the idea that this is the pattern for the rest of their lives denies the opportunity to potentially reverse the effect of negative early experiences. The child's outlook on the world depends on how distressing events are handled by others. Children's experiences and development also depend on what happens after the early years. Equally, positive experiences in early life do not make a child safe from later emotional damage.

Erik Erikson (1902–1994) believed that people continue to develop and grow well into older age. At each stage of development, a person faces a 'crisis' that they must master and mastering this crisis leads to the development of psychological virtue, a trait or quality which has meaning within a particular culture.

Table 5.4   Erikson's eight stages of development

Birth to one year	Trust versus mistrust, in which the child learns to trust others based upon the consistency of their caregiver(s).
One to three years	Autonomy vs shame and doubt, in which children begin to assert their independence.
Three to six years	Initiative vs guilt, in which children assert themselves more frequently.

(Continued)

Table 5.4 (Continued)

Six to eleven years	Industry vs inferiority, in which children begin to develop a sense of pride in their accomplishments.
Adolescence	Identity vs role confusion, in which children are becoming more independent, and begin to look at the future in terms of career, relationships, families and so on.
Young adulthood (20–30s)	Intimacy vs isolation, in which the person begins to share themselves more intimately with others, exploring relationships leading towards longer-term commitments with someone other than a family member.
Middle adulthood (40–60s)	Generativity vs stagnation. Careers are established, relationships are 'confirmed' and families are established. A feeling of contributing to society is achieved.
Late adulthood (ego integrity vs despair)	There is a tendency to slow down productivity and explore life as a retired person. Life and its accomplishments are explored and a person develops integrity if they are leading a successful life.

Erikson's model does not suggest that each 'stage' has to be completed before a person moves to the next, with the likelihood of unresolved issues. Each new stage of life does offer new challenges and opportunities to deal with unresolved issues.

Another model which explores the development of adults is Levinson's (1978) 'seasons of life' model. It states that adulthood involves distinct patterns or 'seasons of growth', and seeks to identify the psychological, social and cultural factors that influence development. In Levinson's model two key concepts always occur during 'seasons of change': the stable period, a time of consistency without much change in a person's life, and the transitional period, as the end of one period and the beginning of another, during which one's experience can vary.

Table 5.5 Levinson's seasons of life model

Age	Stage	Issues
17–22	Early Adult Transition	Forming a life structure – developing a sense of independence by separating from one's family and adopting a different lifestyle.
22–28	Entering the Adult World	Building a life structure: exploring and obtaining many adult roles that are needed to be happy and successful in one's career and relationship.
28–33	Adult World	Achieving the Dream: re-evaluating relationships formed in the 20s: establishes own role in society, pursues long-term plans and goals.
33–40		Settling Down: developing a sense of success in the major areas of one's life, primarily in career and relationships.

Early 40s–mid 40s		Evaluation of one's life goals and commitments. Can lead to 'mid-life crisis', with the potential to create a new life structure.
45–50	Middle Adulthood	Living with previous decisions; making choices about future choices and legacy.
Age 60+	Late Adulthood	Permanently settle down; reflection on life and the decisions made.

For Levinson (1978, p76), 'as long as life continues, no period marks the end of the opportunities, and the burdens of further development'.

The benefits of these 'staged' models are that they support theory building and conceptualisation of different stages and influences on people lives. They provide frameworks for understanding some of the common themes which have affected people through the ages and which affect individuals through the stages of their life.

Activity 5.3

What might be the critiques of staged theories?

Whilst the intention is not to negate the contribution of staged models of development, there is recognition of their limitations. Some of the issues you may have thought about include:

- the assumption that people move through each stage in sequence at certain ages; that their preoccupations, challenges and desired outcomes can be predicated by their stage of life course development; and that failure to progress satisfactorily through one stage will affect their wellbeing and success in later life;
- they are fixed and deterministic, making assumptions about progress through the different stages;
- they reinforce socially constructed expectations and structural oppressions;
- they fail to recognise the impact of life events such as redundancy, divorce and illness on the life course;
- they are dated. Most stage theories were written in the 1960s and 1970s by white, middle class, male academics and therefore do not reflect contemporary society;
- they do not take into account the context of contemporary society, for example, access to modern day toys and resources that can support cognitive and social development; access to early years projects and the support of professionals in supporting families and children; the impact of information technology and social media;
- there is no recognition of difference and diversity, for example, LGBTQ+ people, people with disabilities;
- they are Eurocentric/Western models of development, and do not reflect the differences of countries and different cultural identities.

However, as social workers it is important that, whilst understanding the potential limitations, we recognise that staged theories, some of which are described here, do provide a framework for understanding aspects of and the influence of life stages and life events on people.

Sociological influences across the lifespan

Whilst the focus thus far has been on an understanding of 'individual development' drawing on biological and psychological aspects of a person's life course, this section seeks to highlight the sociological aspects. Sociological aspects seek to identify different levels of influences of society on the different stages and the impact on behaviours, and lifestyles. As Green (2017, p26) states:

> *A sociology of the life course focuses on patterns, trends and change through individual lives, and how historical, societal and political norms, situations and transformations impact on them.*

One way of understanding this is through ecological theory. Ecological theory recognises that development – physical, social, emotional, language and cognitive – is an outcome of the interactions between the individual's biological factors and the environment in which the person is embedded. When physical, social and economic conditions demonstrate their ability to promote support and growth in the person they lead to successful outcomes. According to this theory, all systems are interrelated parts constituting an ordered whole and each subsystem influences other parts of the whole.

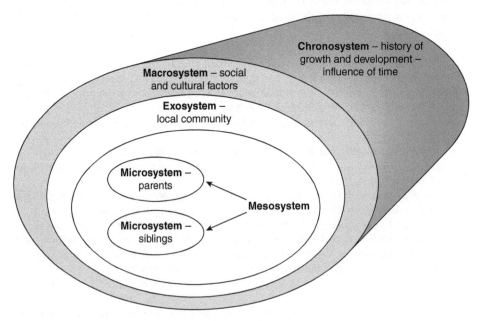

Figure 5.1   A diagram to represent ecological theory

Bronfenbrenner (1917–2005) (1979) examined the relationship between the environment and the individuals, as a set of nested structures. He identified four structures:

1. Microsystem – the immediate setting in which the individual finds themselves.
2. Mesosystem – the network of relationships which make up the individual's world.
3. Ecosystem – those factors that influence the person's life, even if the person is not present in them.
4. Macrosystem – the wider cultural context in which the smaller systems are embedded.

In addition, a fifth structure, the chronosystem, has been added to allow for examination of the different system over the life course of an individual.

Research summary

A lack of supportive, emotional and 'practical' structures that emphasise the importance of education can affect a child's positive experiences of school and their education attainment. Children's experience of disadvantage has an impact on the way most children experience school, with poorer children accepting at an early age that they are not going to have the same outcomes as better-off children; poverty can make children feel excluded, stigmatised and bullied because they cannot afford the same things as their peers (The Children's Commission on Poverty, 2014). Studies of experiences of poverty show that the age that young people leave school increases with family income; that is to say, youths from low income families tend to leave school earlier than those from high income families, and therefore may be less aspirational in, for example, accessing further education or work (Goodman and Gregg, 2010). This disadvantage has its roots in children's negative experience of school and the stigma they feel they experience, and the consequential emotional impact (The Children's Commission on Poverty, 2014; The Children's Society, 2015). These disadvantages persist across the life course and across generations (Goodman and Gregg, 2010). As the Joseph Rowntree Analysis Unit (2018, p5) identify:

> Living in poverty affects every aspect of people's lives and contributes to those on lower incomes experiencing poorer physical health and being more likely to have mental health issues.

Human growth and development is the process of progress from one stage to another stage of development embedded in multiple contexts and interacting with the social environment, embedded in a multi-layered social and cultural context (Bronfenbrenner, 1979).

Conclusions

The view that is presented in this chapter is that growth and development, change and opportunity are features of human development throughout the whole of life. Adopting a life course perspective allows us to take a view that is:

- multidimensional – lifelong and made up of biological, cognitive and social dimensions;
- multidirectional – not a single determined pathway, but can be characterised by growth, decline and loss;
- historical – influenced by the conditions in a given historical period and cultural, social and economic condition;
- a contextual approach – influenced by personal experiences, histories, environment and responses to it (Baltes, 1987).

This can help us in managing transitions in a person's life course and the potential impact on them. We need to recognise how social and environmental factors may impact on a personal life course, resulting in differing outcomes for people and what factors can mitigate any negative experiences.

Case study 5.2

Return to the case study of Liam and his family and the notes that you made. In what ways has an understanding of child development theories influenced your understanding of the issues? What areas can you identify that you need to know more about to influence your assessment of the case?

In thinking about this case, you may have considered the issues of physical growth. Whilst there is no indication that Liam did not meet his milestones, you will need more information to provide a fuller picture. Whilst adolescence is a complex time there are some concerns that his behaviours and actions may lead him into significant trouble. A detailed history of Liam's life course may provide valuable insights and opportunities to explore a positive way forward. His parents Neil and Gill, and their own life course history, may provide some indication of their life experiences on their past and current approach to parenting, and the challenges and strengths for supporting Liam in the future; for example, the impact of their dependence on alcohol and the impact of Gill's mental wellbeing on each of them and the wider family. In addition, the influence on Liam's life course of his siblings both in the past, currently and, potentially, into the future, is unclear. Dorothy, his grandmother, appears to be a significant figure in Liam's life and her influence could provide further impact. In addition, Dorothy appears to be experiencing her own life course issues and may need support. Paige's life course and those of her children present further challenges. There are indications that the twin girls are not meeting their developmental milestones, potentially through neglect by their parents. Attachment issues may need to be explored. The impact of Paige's (and her partner's) alcohol and drug use will need to be assessed, including their lifestyle and life choices; in addition, there is the concern about domestic harm. It is unclear how the wider family are and may be able to support Paige and her children.

Key points summary

- A life course approach emphasises a chronological and social perspective, looking back across an individual's life experiences or across generations to gain an understanding of past and current experiences and their impact on the individual and their family, for example to identify the underlying biological, behavioural and psychosocial processes that have shaped that persons across the life span.
- Growing evidence suggests that there are critical periods of growth and development, not just prior to birth and early infancy but also during childhood and adolescence, when environmental exposures do more damage to health and long-term health potential than they would at other times.
- There is also evidence of sensitive developmental stages in childhood and adolescence when social and cognitive skills, habits, coping strategies, attitudes and values are more easily acquired than at later ages. These abilities and skills strongly influence life course trajectories with implications for health in later life.
- Additionally, a life course approach considers the long-term health consequences of biological and social experiences in early and mid-adulthood, and whether these factors simply add additional risk or act interactively with early life biological and social factors, to attenuate or exacerbate long-term risks to health. Taking a life course perspective means to adopt an approach that considers the whole of a person's life as offering opportunities for growth, development and change.

Suggested further reading

Beckett, C. and Taylor, H. (2019) *Human Growth and Development* (4th ed). London: Sage.

Walker, J. (2020) *Social Work and Human Development* (6th ed). London: Sage/Learning Matters.

6

The social work process: assessment, planning, intervention and review

Jonathan Parker

Chapter objectives

By the end of the chapter you should be able to:

- explain why understanding social work as a process rather than a set of goals or outcomes is important;
- describe the core elements of the social work process;
- reflect on the ways in which contemporary social work and the relational process may create tension and how this may be overcome.

Introduction

In this chapter we will introduce the idea that social work is an active process that moves through various phases, all of which interlink with one another and allow a 'to-ing and fro-ing' between them as social work is undertaken. This concept fits well with the focus on relationships as the key feature of social work practice and acts as a corrective to an over-emphasis on hard, tangible outcomes that may not mean the same for all people. Outcomes are, of course, very important, but the way we achieve them is equally so. Social work, as a process, contains elements of skilled practice as both science or technicality, and artistry or wisdom. We will investigate how these two seemingly distinct concepts contribute to social work practice.

In this chapter we will explore four core elements of the social work process – assessment, planning, intervention, and review or evaluation. We will consider how these build together as social work with people to achieve changes or to maintain positions that are agreed by those involved.

Why is it important to see social work as a process?

Sometimes when you have a problem it can seem convenient to simply solve it. For instance, if you have a chest infection you would expect a doctor to diagnose it and to prescribe the treatment that is likely to cure it. Similarly, if someone has an on-going anxiety and depression they may feel they simply want it to go away and to stop. These are quite reasonable feelings. Thinking in these ways is, in this sense, outcome driven. However, social work practice concerns many such problems that interact together and may be better described as 'problems of living' and therefore not susceptible to the 'cures' and resolutions, or outcomes, that work everywhere, all of the time. Humans are complex entities who live alongside others in increasingly complex social circumstances and what might work for one person may not for another. Therefore, something more is needed in social work practice without dismissing the importance of a systematic approach that is based on the best 'evidence' and research that is available, taking all circumstances into account.

Social work as a process refers to what social workers do when working together with people who use their services, including those meetings and interactions with other professionals, agencies and people within their own organisations. What happens will differ according to each individual set of circumstances and from person to person or family to family. It will also differ depending on whether an assessment is being completed, plans for achieving goals are being discussed, work on those goals is being conducted or whether one is reviewing what has been accomplished. However, it is all part of social work practice.

Over the past 30 years or so, social work, along with other public institutions, has been the focus of increased scrutiny under the guise of promoting accountability, raising practice standards and protecting the public. This has seen a concomitant rise in so-called evidence-based practice which is an outcome-focused approach taken from bio-medicine that struggles in translation to the chaotic human world which social work inhabits. As a reaction to this depersonalised, target conscious approach to social work, practitioners and academics have once again raised the centrality of the person in the social work relationship. This relational dimension requires us to question and reflect on what we do in practice and how we do it, as well as on outcomes and resolutions. It is important to see social work as a process.

One way of addressing this is to envisage social work as both an art and a science that can hold together the human, the fluid and complex aspects of life alongside an appropriately theorised and regularised approach to practice (Parker, 2017). This is important because it acknowledges that what we do involves personal qualities, interpersonal skills alongside professional skill, expertise and knowledge. The former aspects also demand that we work alongside or with those citizens who use social services, which is an integral part of good social work practice.

Four core social work processes

Whilst the international definition of social work has been contested, in that it seems to privilege a model of social work promoted by the Global North (high income countries often with a colonial past), it provides a well-known reference point for considering social work processes. In its most recent iteration in 2014 (International Federation of Social Workers [IFSW], 2014), it also explicitly allows different countries to bring in local and indigenous understandings and interpretations. Thus, we will use the definition as a starting point for our debate.

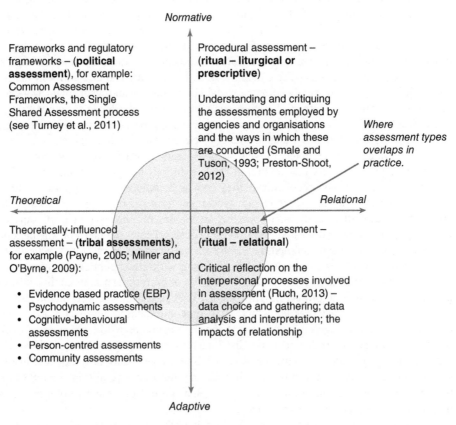

Figure 6.1 Assessment in daily social work practice

Parker et al., 2017b, originally Parker and Bradley, 2014.

Social work is a practice-based profession and an academic discipline that promotes social change and development, social cohesion, and the empowerment and liberation of people. Principles of social justice, human rights, collective responsibility and respect for diversities are central to social work. Underpinned by theories of social work, social sciences, humanities and indigenous knowledge, social work engages people and structures to address life challenges and enhance wellbeing. The above definition may be amplified at national and/or regional levels.

(IFSW, 2014)

The definition also helps us to see that social work is set within a social, cultural and political context which influences how it is seen, organised and practised. Elsewhere we have suggested a model for social work assessment that covers a range of 'types' or forms of assessment (see Figure 6.1; Parker et al., 2017). This model could be employed to consider the various aspects of the social work process which show its theoretical, political and socio-philosophical base (see Figure 6.2).

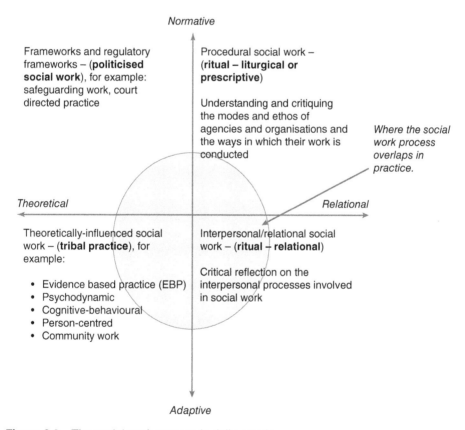

Figure 6.2 The social work process in daily practice

Adapted from Parker et al., 2017b; Parker and Bradley, 2014.

Activity 6.1

Why do you think it might be important to reflect on the underlying rationale for social work practices? Write down some of your ideas and consider them against the following discussion.

Social work represents a complex phenomenon that has developed in professional and organisational terms over the last 150 years or so. It is complex because it concerns ways in which people can be both helped and supported and also regulated to fit the norms of those societies in which it is practised. The concept of social work as a set of interlinked processes in practice is, as Shakespeare's Hamlet would say, 'a custom, more honour'd in the breach than the observance'. That is to say social work practice rarely follows such steps rigidly, and this is how it should be. Social work necessarily concerns developing and working at relationships with people in uncertain and often precarious situations and settings. However, we will consider an overview of the four processes we have identified here as a way of introducing some of the core ways in which we practise social work.

Assessment: social work process 1

Assessment represents the keystone that strengthens social work practice, the stone that locks together all surrounding pieces in an arch (McDonald, 2006; Parker, 2015). However, unlike an archway in which the keystone is fitted last, assessment is one of the first elements of the social work process that social workers undertake before engaging with those people they are working with in any action. Having said this, assessment is not a single point process. Whilst, as a social worker, you may be asked to complete a proforma assessment (part of the procedure of your agency, or part of the requirements of guidance), this relates to only one aspect of assessment and if you were to stop 'assessing' at that point it is unlikely that you would work very effectively (SCIE, 2007). Rather it is an aspect of inclusive and participative critical inquiry into the issues, circumstances and goals of the people you are working with that continues throughout the time you are with them (Parker and Ashencaen Crabtree, 2018; Parker, 2020). Consider the following case study.

Case study 6.1

A social work assessment report on a teenager experiencing depression was required by the team manager. The assessment report detailed home life, likes and dislikes and a social assessment that indicated a range of hobbies and friends. However, in subsequent meetings the teenager indicates that she is feeling bullied at school by teachers and peers. This was not part of the original report but is certainly pertinent to an assessment. It is not necessarily the case that the original assessment report was inadequate but rather that assessment continues as the social work relationship continues.

Social work assessments comprise a range of things. They can refer to one-off reports on particular aspects of a person's life as part of an official process or as part of an 'intervention' protocol. The former may include an assessment for hospital admission or an assessment of a young person in court for offending, whilst the latter may be an assessment of drug-taking behaviour, or the behavioural assessment of a toddler whose tantrums appear more often than expected. However, whatever form of assessment it employed, it can be part of the working relationship that social workers develop with those people with whom they practise. Some are required by law, policy, agency procedure or particular mode of working, but all require relationship skills and a focus on values that keeps the needs and context of the person central at all times (Folgheraiter, 2007; Ruch et al., 2010).

It is important in social work assessment to keep firmly fixed in mind aspects of the work that concern control and regulation. You will be assessing behaviour, personal and social functioning, and making judgements about adequacy of performance. This does not always sit well with social workers who will want to focus on values that are participative and inclusive that work with, rather than do to, people. It should be remembered that you are not necessarily judging the worth or deservingness of another person (being judgemental) but making an evaluation of expectations and doing so with a view to working alongside that person to achieve goals they want to achieve.

Another central area of social work assessment, risk assessment, needs to be mentioned. It may also raise feelings of discomfort and is something social workers need to grapple with. Risk assessment has developed as an almost ubiquitous practice in social work and other helping professions. There are debates about whether this can be quantified or remains at a qualitative level and it is beyond the scope of this chapter to discuss the arguments. Suffice to say that different models reflect the different theoretical or 'tribal' allegiances of practitioners and organisations.

Risk assessment relates to identifying, making clear and working to mitigate risks and dangers in the life choices and situations of those you work with (Crisp et al., 2005; SCIE, 2007). As such, it also reflects the imperative that organisations have to deflect public and political blame from them when things go wrong; this in turn is something that you as a social worker may feel pressured to do, reflecting organisational 'back-covering' at a personal level. Again, this illustrates the need for a critically reflective approach to your practice that questions why you are doing what you are doing and the consequences of your actions. Considering whether the motivations for your risk assessment are predominantly motivated by the needs of the person or group you are working with, a response to agency demands, or driven by your allegiance to a particular mode of working can be assisted by referring to Figure 6.1. The following case study shows some of the difficulties inherent in risk assessment.

Case study 6.2

Zanisah worked in a multidisciplinary team working with older people with dementia. She had been asked to undertake a risk assessment in respect of Tom, an 89-year-old former teacher who had spent his early retirement taking walking holidays around the world with friends. The team had been working with Tom and his family for two years as

(Continued)

(Continued)

his dementia progressed. His family were now extremely worried by his walking behaviour. He was a fit man and liked still to go out walking. However, he frequently walked miles from his home, becoming lost and disorientated and having to be brought home by the police. Zanisah believed passionately in people's rights to determine the course of their own lives, but also the right to be protected. She knew the local authority she worked for had become increasingly risk averse since the publication of scathing reports of lack of intervention in the case of a woman who died in a fire in her own home a few years before. She was aware that her nursing and occupational therapy colleagues in the team and Tom's family were requesting that he be found a safe place in residential care. Zanisah needed to conduct a fair, unbiased assessment that she could defend in the light of this knowledge.

There are no easy answers to a situation like Tom's, but it highlights many of the complex decisions that are made and which need to be taken candidly and reflectively.

Planning: social work process 2

Assessments provide the basis on which plans for work, services and change can be made. When we consider planning as part of the process we may perhaps see where participative or relational social work can come to the fore (Folgheraiter, 2007; Ruch et al., 2010). Planning concerns developing and negotiating what needs to be done to meet agreed goals or outcomes. However, it is not as clear as it first seems, as the goals and means of achieving them could be set or heavily influenced, either by yourself as a social worker, or people may feel pressured or even intimidated to follow your suggestions. The people you work with may also be required to follow them to avoid unpleasant consequences, for instance a child being removed from a parent's care if they don't engage with the schools and health services in respect of the child. So, planning requires you to act with the people you are working with as co-workers on identified issues and this requires openness and transparency throughout.

There are different levels and forms of planning in social work. At the top level, too often removed from people who may use the services, is strategic planning which concerns decisions about using the available resources to meet the range of prospective needs in a certain area and relating to a certain issue. For instance, this may relate to a plan to employ a certain number of social workers in a busy child safeguarding team based on numbers of referrals over a certain period. It is unlikely that you will be directly responsible for such planning for some time in your career. You are likely to be involved in making plans on behalf of your agency in respect of people's care. This may involve care planning on behalf of children or adults, permanency planning for children removed from their birth families, or discharge planning for people when they are ready to be released from hospital.

Many methods of planning in social work are related to decision-making, which is often driven by agency process or legislative requirement and may not always fully include those people you are working with (Leeson, 2007). As a social worker it is important to the working relationship, the work you do and the goals you agree together to act as inclusively as you can. Planning can, as we noted above, represent the site of social work that cements a participatory process. Read the following case study which provides some indications of how this might work. Imagine you are the social worker.

Case study 6.3

Jennie is a 33-year-old single woman with learning difficulties who is moving into independent accommodation from her parents' home. She is very positive about this but both she and her family have felt let down by social services in the past and are reluctant to trust you.

Jennie responds well to visual cues and active ways of making decisions and you suggest developing a SMART plan together. SMART is an acronym for decisions, plans and goals being:

- **S**pecific
- **M**easureable
- **A**chievable
- **R**ealistic, and
- **T**imely

On a large piece of paper you begin to draw together a plan for when she is going to move into her independent flat. Jennie can read and write a little and is encouraged to take the lead. Once the acronym is explained she finds the process fun as it makes a word that she likes. As well as focusing on the plan, she decides to decorate the paper and says she will hang it on her bedroom wall at her parents home and take it to the new flat to check that you have done what you say you will do. You ask if you can take a photograph with your phone and acknowledge that she owns the plan.

Having the plan allows both you and Jennie to reflect on what has been achieved, on ensuring that you are honest and clear about what is possible and what is not. As a physical entity it is something that can, with Jennie's permission, be shared with her parents and used to check everyone's responsibilities and roles in meeting the plan.

Plans such as these are useful in delineating the actions and tasks to be taken to achieve goals. This is usually referred to as a process of intervention and it is to this that we now turn.

Intervention: social work process 3

Intervention is one of those many contested words that we face in social work. To intervene suggests either having the right to become involved in another person's life or the power to do so or, indeed, both. As such, it requires close consideration to ensure that we are considering social work intervention in ways that tally with social work's underlying values (see Chapter 2). Intervention is usually associated with theories and methods and there are numerous works to consult in this regard (see, for example, Payne, 2020; Teater, 2020).

Referring back to Figure 6.2 we can see that intervention may be directed by statute, policy or procedure and so be politically driven. This means that power relations in the work must be taken into account. However, intervention may also represent a 'tribal' allegiance to a particular school of thought. These may be individualistic such as psycho-analytic, behavioural or person-centred social work practice amongst others, or they may represent working across collectivities and groups, for example, family therapy, group work (see Chapter 12) or community development (see Chapter 29) (Parker, 2017). You will come into contact with a range of theories and methods and ways of applying these in practice during your qualifying degree.

Contemporary social work in the UK is increasingly concerned with management, brokering and negotiation when practised in statutory settings (Parker, 2019a). However, it is important to have an awareness of the different types and methods employed to assist people in developing new and more constructive ways of being and to alter situations and behaviours that are counterproductive. Also, in specialist teams and in third sector settings you may be called upon to intervene using specialist skills yourself.

Intervention also carries with it the perspective of expert. This may not sit comfortably with many and is, indeed, challenged by the concept of those people using services as being experts on their own situation. So, it is important that you question what you are doing, why, how and what the consequences might be.

Activity 6.2

Reflect on some of the reasons why you think you might be intervening in people's lives. What is it that you are seeking to do?

On completing this, you may have suggested that you are trying to achieve change. However, are you by this seeking to 'fix' something that is 'wrong' in a person's life (which may suggests a pathological reason for intervening), or are you seeking to enable the person to learn, develop and apply the skills to achieve a goal they themselves have chosen (a more empowering approach)? You may reflect on being instructed to intervene by your agency or by your practice educator as part of your learning. However, this may not result in positive outcomes as it is not led by the person themselves.

It is crucial that you involve the person or group that is the focus of the intervention as this will tell you whether it is the right way of proceeding as well as increasing 'buy-in' from that person or group.

The approach you take to intervention will be determined by a range of interacting perspectives including your own personal and professional value base, your theoretical preferences, your agency's specific brief and outlook and the structural and legislative context in which you are working. As well as the model proposed in Figure 6.2, you may wish to consult the paradigmatic model developed by Howe (2008) from Burrell and Morgan's (1985) sociological taxonomy of organisations. This model separates the types of theories and methods employed into those that are about 'mending something broken' or regulating society (see also Davies, 1994), or raising people's consciousness and seeking radical change. These two dimensions are split across objectivist positions that look at the wider context in which social work is practised and the subjectivist positions that focus on the people involved. Models such as these help us to understand what we might be doing and what some of the consequences of our actions might be for the people with whom we practice.

Review/evaluation: social work process 4

Since the introduction of modernising approaches in social and health care targets, monitoring and accountability have been promoted. This can inform the review and evaluation process of your role as a social worker. It can also be used to constrain your actions and to monitor your work. It is important to be aware of why you are undertaking an evaluation and to ensure it is completed ethically and to the advantage of the people you work with first and foremost.

Research summary

Blom and Morén (2010) develop a critical realist perspective as a means of analysing and reviewing the social work process. Critical realism is a means of moving beyond experiencing the world (empirical reality) to developing a causal analysis of why things happen in the actual world that we may not experience, and identifying the mechanisms that operate to cause things to happen. Their study of social workers' evaluations of practice indicated that Pawson and Tilley's (1997) realist evaluation theory that contexts and mechanisms produce outcomes was insufficient and, therefore, Blom and Morén proposed the CAIMeR model. CAIMeR stands for:

- **Contexts**
- **Actors**
- **Interventions**
- **Mechanisms**
- **Results**

This model allows a dynamic interplay between each section to be developed from which social workers and their services users can develop causal analyses to understand how change occurred and what might have led to it.

There are some forms of review and evaluation that you can and should undertake with those people using your services. These relate to their impressions of what you have done together and can help not only inform your agency, provide feedback or be used for monitoring purposes but can help you to develop practice wisdom in applying your professional skills to the best effect with people in the future. These are formal methods of evaluation and can be driven by organisational demands or by the needs of theoretical models. For instance, the dates and times of a formal assessment may be needed to ensure the agency is complying with statutory guidance, or completing behavioural observation forms may help you to demonstrate the effects of an intervention programme with the parents of a child with behavioural difficulties.

There are also individualised modes of evaluation that can be used developmentally. For instance, good evaluation and review practices can help cement change and positively reinforce a person's self-efficacy. They can help you determine how best to work and develop, identify areas of training and development need for you as a social worker, and contribute to your agency review and development. This part of the social work process can be marginalised or be overtaken by funding or regulatory body needs but done right it represents an important part of the social workers' repertoire as helping professionals whose first line of responsibility is to their service users and secondly to their employing agency. An evaluation of this kind is not solely mechanical, quantitative and cognitive; it is affective as well. Social work itself is a demanding and emotionally charged profession. Reviewing how we feel we have practised and allowing our service users to express their emotional perspectives adds an important roundedness to our work. A practice developmental evaluation should always be affective (concerned with feelings) as well as cognitive (concerned with thoughts).

Conclusion

Openness and transparency are prerequisites for good social work practice throughout the process. Since social work treads that fine line between state regulator of personal, family and social lives and empowering and liberating people from oppressive circumstances, it is fundamental to developing trust and rapport that you are open with people about the possible consequences of actions, behaviours and positions adopted and about your own role within this system. You may be, at times, required to act authoritatively and in ways that people do not like. This does not mean that you hide your role, the reasons you are practising in the way you do or what possible outcomes may ensue from working or not working together. Rather, throughout the social work process you need to be open and honest, stemming from a critically reflective stance that questions everything that you do at all points in the process, focusing on the positives as well as the things you might change, develop or do better in the future.

Key points summary

- Social work is an interwoven set of processes that do not always act in linear ways; they are circuitous and interact continuously.
- Social work processes may be separated out simply into four, or more, processes but it must be remembered that such a separation is artificial and practice is more complex and nuanced. In this chapter we have identified the main processes as assessment, planning, intervention and review.
- All social work processes are political and politicised. Critically reflexive social work is central to recognising the political underpinnings and 'discourses' that influence practice and inform how social work may be viewed by service users, other helping professions and the general public.

Suggested further reading

Parker, J. (2017) *Social Work Practice: Assessment, Planning, Intervention and Review* (5th ed). London: Sage.

Payne, M. (2020) *How to Use Social Work Theory in Practice: An Essential Guide.* Bristol: Policy Press.

Teater, B. (2020) *An Introduction to Applying Social Work Theories and Methods* (3rd ed). London: Open University Press.

Part Two

Social work skills

7

Anti-oppressive practice skills

Prospera Tedam

Chapter objectives

By the end of the chapter you should be able to:

- recognise the different forms of oppression;
- understand and apply the MANDELA and SHARE models in social work practice;
- recognise your own privilege and the impact this might have on your practice and decision making.

Introduction

The purpose of this chapter is to provide social workers with some practice tools which can be used to work non-oppressively with their colleagues and service users. The chapter will examine the concept of oppression and the different forms of oppression which exist in contemporary society. The chapter will draw on the MANDELA model (Tedam, 2012) and the SHARE model (Maclean et al., 2018) as two contemporary frameworks which, if used effectively, can assist social workers to disrupt oppression and oppressive practice. There will be a discussion of key cognitive, emotional and professional skills needed by social workers in their daily practice with colleagues and service users to ensure practice that is fair, non-oppressive and useful.

What is oppression?

There are many ways to define oppression but quite simply put, it is a cruel, harsh and exploitative approach by others who usually (but not always) wield more power than us. To feel oppressed means to feel unfairly held down either by systems, structures or people. Oppression can be gradual, progressive, subtle or obvious, all with lasting negative consequences on people who these oppressions are directed towards. Oppression is as old as humanity (Thompson, 2016) in that the world over, inequality has existed from the start of human existence.

Oppression is defined by Barker (2003) as:

> *the social act of placing severe restrictions on an individual, group, or institution. Typically, a government or political organization that is in power places these restrictions formally or covertly on oppressed groups so that they may be exploited and less able to compete with other social groups. The oppressed individual or group is devalued, exploited, and deprived of privileges by the individual or group who has more power.*

(pp306–307)

Two key ideas emerge from Barker's definition of oppression, with the first being around the issue of restrictions on individuals, groups or institutions. In the area of neglect in the United Kingdom for example, it has been found that families from lower socio-economic backgrounds are more likely to come to the attention of authorities and social workers than more affluent families (Bernard and Greenwood, 2019). Such practice can be considered oppressive on the part of social workers towards less affluent families and communities in the UK. Reminding ourselves that social workers are part of organisations and institutions leads to the conclusion that this form of oppression, if allowed to go unchecked, will ultimately continue to devalue and exploit families from low socio-economic backgrounds resulting from institutional oppression.

The second idea from Barker's definition is the reference to oppression as a 'social act'. This suggests that oppression is initiated and sustained by people through social interaction resulting from the actions and reactions of people. It would be useful, therefore, if in trying to undermine and disrupt oppression social workers recognise the value of reacting to oppression by enforcing strategies to enable this to occur. One such approach is anti-oppressive practice, which is a key principle in social work practice and is here to stay as a legitimate strategy to deal with issues around discrimination, oppression and unjust treatment.

Anti-oppressive practice is used to obstruct the impact of discrimination, inequality and disadvantage between and among people. It should be acknowledged that social workers are routinely 'disadvantaged by association' resulting from the people they work with (Parker 2007) in that service users are often assigned to categories of deserving and undeserving, rich and poor, good or bad. This is similar to Colton et al. (1997, p249) who found that 'social workers might come to consider themselves stigmatized through a series of job-related experiences'.

Anti-oppressive practice must take into account the role of power relations, recognising the power dynamics at play, as this is central to understanding oppression and how it is sustained and used to maintain oppression's systems and processes. Social workers have the power to deny or allocate resources to people who use services, yet it is common to find that many children and families who are in need are often left without support or intervention due to protocols and guidance that make people ineligible for assistance. This is articulated powerfully by Dominelli (2002, p36) who states that:

> anti-oppressive practice addresses the whole person and enables a practitioner to relate to his or her client's social context in a way that takes account of the 'allocative and authoritative resources' that both the practitioner and the client bring to the relationship.

In order to operationalise what Dominelli (2002) suggests, it is crucial that social workers remain aware of their own positionality and privilege, which influence decision making and the delivery of services in social work.

Activity 7.1

Who am I?

Think about who you are. What is your name, where are you from, what is your heritage, how old are you, what is your motivation for studying social work?

Next, consider the socio-political context of social work practice. Where do you work? Who holds the budget? What are the organisational or strategic funding priorities? Who are your service users?

This activity requires you to be critically self-aware of your role and position in relation to your own power and professional autonomy. This is an important anti-oppressive strategy which lends itself to engaging holistically with the person and their circumstance.

What can social workers do to minimise oppression?

Oppression is a divisive strategy and can impinge on individual and group behaviour and opportunities to develop their full potential. It is therefore useful to outline the role of social workers in minimising oppression, beginning with the global definition of social work.

The global definition of social work is a useful foundation from which non-oppression can be discussed. Social work has at its heart the principles of social justice, social cohesion, empowerment, liberation of people and respect for diversities. In 2014, the International Federation for Social Work amended the global definition which now reads:

> Social work is a practice-based profession and an academic discipline that promotes social change and development, social cohesion, and the empowerment and liberation of people. Principles of social justice, human rights, collective responsibility and respect for diversities are central to social work. Underpinned by theories of social work, social sciences, humanities and indigenous knowledge, social work engages people and structures to address life challenges and enhance wellbeing.

> (IFSW, 2014)

The definition makes no secret of the profession's commitment to minimising oppression through utilising social justice principles. However, unsurprisingly, as social workers we have to continuously remind ourselves about these principles and challenge our own and colleagues' practice on a daily basis.

The MANDELA model and anti-oppressive social work practice

I have argued elsewhere of the need for models and frameworks which can assist social workers not only in practising in an anti-oppressive way but which can also enable them to evaluate their own practice using a tried and tested template of ideas and cues. The MANDELA model (Tedam, 2012) was developed to promote anti-oppressive practice between supervisors and supervisees and can be used when working with users of social care services. The model is an acronym, which stands for: Make Time, Acknowledge Needs, Difference, Education experiences, Life Experiences and Age.

Making time to develop rapport and get to know service users is the first requirement when using this model. It could be argued that whenever we rush interviews, interventions and discussions with service users we are not providing them the opportunity to fully articulate their circumstances, nor take in what is on offer by social work agencies. Time constraints exacerbated by large caseloads sometimes make it difficult for social workers to give service users the time required; however, research has found that if we do not invest the time with service users, they are more likely to have to return to our services. Not making time for service users is in itself oppressive, especially when we spend the time we do have instructing and telling them what our service can provide without enabling them to have much input into these discussions.

Writing about children and families social work in relation to the practice of home visiting, Ferguson (2017, p1021) concluded that:

> the more that social workers are given time to do quality work, opportunities to talk, reflect on feelings and to think critically about their lived experiences, the less risk there will be that children will become unheld and invisible.

This lack of time for social work interventions provides yet another angle from which oppressive practice might emerge in practice.

Social workers should acknowledge the needs of service users in a manner that does not further stigmatise or oppress them. Colton and colleagues (1997) argued that service users felt stigmatised by society for needing and having a social worker and often felt judged by social workers who did not always acknowledge or respond to their needs. An anti-oppressive approach would be one in which service users feel enabled to discuss their needs without fear of being stigmatised, ridiculed or discriminated against. For example, when working with a service user who is struggling financially, social workers should carefully consider the value in asking them to attend the office or agency regularly for meetings. It is important that the financial needs are taken into account when such a decision is made and that non-attendance and lateness should not always be interpreted as a lack of engagement on the part of the service user. An experienced practitioner should be able to work with the service user and negotiate the least oppressive strategy in ensuring ongoing interactions.

Depending on the situation, the discussion about ethnic, racial, gender or other difference may not necessarily be useful; however, it is important that social workers acknowledge the power differentials inherent in their relationship with service users. Every person has multiple identities and so social workers need to be acutely aware of the possibility of oppression of service users linked to one or more of their multiple areas of difference. Consideration of differences cannot be undertaken in the absence of acknowledging similarities. The similarity could be in the area of wanting the same outcome; for example, the social worker and the service user might agree that parents need to work on their parenting skills to improve their interaction with their child.

Social workers need to be aware of the language they use when they are working with service users. Language must be accessible, clear and respectful and should leave no room for interpretation. A service user may choose the language which they feel most confident using, and it is imperative that social workers attempt to source interpreting services wherever possible, as leaving the service user without a way of communicating with their social worker is oppressive and discriminatory. Understanding the educational experiences of service users is important for ensuring that we offer them the appropriate language, reading or writing support required to work effectively with them. Simply handing a form to a service user to complete is not considered good practice as we must first ask about a service user's ability in completing the required documents. In seeking this information, social workers must avoid equating English language proficiency with level of education, as such a perception is in itself oppressive and discriminatory. Linguistic capital is important and a service user with multiple language proficiency skills needs to be acknowledged, not ridiculed, as this can exacerbate disadvantage. Similarly, where English is the main or first language, care must be taken not to classify or rank accents as upper, middle or lower class. In the same vein, people with hearing or sight difficulties face oppression when social workers do not plan adequately to meet their needs. Understanding the Deaf population as a linguistic minority will go a long way towards working in an inclusive, non-oppressive way.

In the area of lived experiences, service users are the owners of their narratives and their experiences and it is again important that social workers not try not to take this away from them. Indeed, service users may have experienced discrimination, exclusion or oppression in previous interventions or in their lives and may be hesitant to engage with social care services. It requires a skilful social worker to work with such a service user so they develop trust which can then result in meaningful professional relationships supported by a rebalancing of power in relation to who 'owns' the story or narrative. In sharing their lived experiences, service users can resist oppression by contributing to their own empowerment, thus challenging dominant narratives about particular groups.

Finally, the 'A' in the MANDELA model stands for 'age' as a marker of difference and deserving of discussion linked to anti-oppressive social work practice. Age discrimination is ever present in social work practice and as Duffy (2016) notes it is important for social workers 'not be co-opted into using ageist language, discourse and communication styles when working with older people in social care services and health care settings' (p2069). Age related oppression is also present in social work discussions about specific types of intervention (teenage pregnancy, gang related violence, youth justice) for example. Research by Broadhurst et al. (2015) found that younger mothers are most at risk of experiencing the recurrent removal of children from their care and reappearing in the family justice system.

Activity 7.2

Applying the MANDELA model

Think about the ways in which the elements of the MANDELA model might assist you in working non-oppressively with a service user. For example, what are their needs and how much time can and should you require to support them? Use Case Study 7.1 to guide your thinking.

Case study 7.1

Jadwiga, a 36-year-old mother of two five-year-old children, moved to the UK ten years ago. Her partner works away in Dubai and she and the children only see him for two weeks every three months. They have regular visits to her mother who lives in Krakow and Jadwiga has a group of strong friends who she sees at work, as a florist, and outside. Recently, the children have experienced taunts about their Polish heritage and absent father. Jadwiga has been very upset by this and has said she feels the children might be in danger in Britain.

Think how you might use the MANDELA model with this family, and, as you read further, consider the use of SHARE and the skills you might need.

What skills do social workers need?

Social workers do a difficult and emotionally draining job with many becoming burnt out through stress and ill-health during their careers. In this chapter I am proposing skills which are necessary for social workers to be able to demonstrate non-oppressive practice. These are skills in critical reflection, critical thinking, reflexivity, interpersonal skills, respect and emotional intelligence.

Critical reflection

Critical reflection, according to Field et al. (2016), entails being able to practice drawing upon a robust evidence base with the ability to develop new knowledge, approaches and strategies in response to the social care context which is fluid and ever changing. This ever-changing context requires a social worker who is able to understand the nature of these changes and the implications on their practice. For example, a practitioner working in the area of mental health will need to understand the ways in which the changing landscape in relation to funding and resourcing can result in oppressive and unfair social work practices towards service users.

Critical thinking

Critical thinking is an integral part of social work practice and involves the ability to think on one's feet, not only in a logical manner, but also in a way that examines weaknesses and strengths, and evaluates research and practice on a regular and ongoing basis. A critical thinker will be able to identify the need to continually evaluate available evidence in relation to service users they may be working with. Graham and Schiele (2010) argue the importance of social workers understanding and valuing the 'equality-of-oppressions paradigm' which challenges social workers to be mindful of promoting a view that one form of oppression is given more prominence than another. Consequently, I would argue strongly here that social workers need to ensure that, increasingly, their work is grounded in an approach that gives due regard to all forms of oppression and that utilises relevant research about the ways in which specific groups become multiply oppressed due to the intersectional nature of being.

Reflexivity

Reflexivity refers to the ways in which social workers appraise knowledge for understanding of experiences of service users. It involves social workers remaining aware of the ways in which their own social locations (race, gender, age, class, ethnicity, socio-economic status, sexual orientation) influence their understanding of the problems facing services users and the way solutions may be constructed. It is important because it enables social workers to scrutinise their assumptions about issues such as 'mental illness', for example.

Interpersonal skills

Interpersonal skills are basically one's ability to get alongside others through the way they communicate and interact with others. Interpersonal skills are an important skill set required of social workers. While some people are perhaps natural communicators and can interact with others with ease, for others this may not come as easily; consequently the skills need to be developed. There are a range of interpersonal skills which are essential for social workers and which can either exacerbate oppression or support anti-oppressive practice. These interpersonal skills, according to Trevithick (2000) include: verbal and non-verbal communicating, listening, emotional intelligence, being able to empathise, assertiveness, empowering and enabling, offering encouragement and validation, to mention a few.

Respect

A study by Gibbard (1990) found that the way in which service users were shown respect was often more important to them than what the social worker did to assist them with their problems. In that regard, respect could be said to be a sort of catalyst supporting change and progress in service user–social worker relationships. Respect is a thoughtful approach to someone or something and is one of the key values of social work. Being respectful in social work entails being polite in verbal and non-verbal communication. It is rare that social workers will be rude to service users, not least because they are likely to complain about such behaviour; however, disrespect may come in the form of subtle microaggressions such as not returning a service user's call, not allowing service users the opportunity to speak, interrupting, or using jargon which the service user may not understand. In terms of non-verbal communication, social workers should be aware of how, through their actions, facial expressions and other mannerisms, service users might feel disrespected.

A study into how social workers demonstrate respect to elderly clients by Sung and Dunkle (2009) found that older people preferred what they called 'linguistic respect' (p3) which was how social workers referred to them and the language used. It is also important to have some insight into cultural etiquette wherever possible, in order to demonstrate sensitivity towards people who may use social care services.

Emotional intelligence

According to Goleman (1996, cited in Morrison, 2007), emotional intelligence concerns:

> *being able to motivate oneself and persist in the face of frustrations; to control impulse and delay gratification; to regulate one's moods and keep distress from swamping the ability to think; to empathize and to hope.*

The SHARE model and anti-oppressive social work practice

The SHARE model (Maclean et al., 2018) was developed to highlight the importance of reflexivity, self-awareness and stakeholder voices in social work education and practice. It can be used to effectively navigate the complexities of oppression whilst promoting anti-oppressive practice in social work. The acronym SHARE stands for: Seeing, Hearing, Action, Reading and Evaluation, and will be examined in the section that follows.

Seeing

In the course of their careers, social workers will witness discrimination and oppression towards their service users from family members, employers or other professionals. It could also be the case that social workers may be part of the structures that perpetuate oppression towards service users through their policies in relation to eligibility for services or during the actual intervention. Social work intervenes at the points where people interact with their environments, and we need to be aware that these environments are not always visible to everyone. Ferguson (2017) has argued that in child protection processes and interventions for example, children are often rendered 'invisible' because, although social workers and other professions were often in the presence of abused children, they rarely got close enough to discover the abuse. In order to work anti-oppressively with any family, social workers must see the service user for who they are. They cannot expect to ignore the environment or key stakeholders and successfully intervene with that family. This *seeing*, therefore, aids practice which is grounded in respectful dialogue, clear goals and objectives as well as supporting relationship-based practice.

Hearing

What do we do when we overhear oppressive language in the form of direct communication with a service user or as 'banter' between and among colleagues? The 'hear' in the SHARE models enables us to reflect on the power of language and consider the ways language can contribute towards oppressing others. Social workers listen and speak to and on behalf of service users on a daily basis and their training has exposed them to working in ways that promote anti-oppression. That said, as educators and researchers, we acknowledge that there are times when social workers may hear oppressive language or see oppressive behaviour and do nothing about it. This is an area which requires further development on social work programmes which can be reinforced during practice learning and post-qualification.

For both the seeing and hearing components, the SHARE model encourages social workers to draw upon all the senses including touching, feeling, smelling and tasting – acknowledging and respecting the diversity of human disability.

Action

What could a social worker do when they recognise oppression, either towards themselves, a service user or a colleague? Failing to act when we witness oppression can send the message that we are condoning oppressive and discriminatory actions and behaviour of others; however, we need to be mindful of how difficult it can be to openly challenge oppressive practice. Challenging oppressive practice can be made more difficult in the presence of power differentials. In terms of direct practice, social workers can also design anti-oppressive programmes and interventions or signpost service users to specific services which are more likely to meet the needs of particular service users.

Reading

It is important for social workers to have up-to-date knowledge about the manifestations of oppression in their daily practice, and so reading becomes an important strategy to enhance knowledge in this area. It is also recognised that social workers read (and write) reports which concern service users and it is vital that the language we use does not perpetuate discrimination or oppression. Being respectful in our writing about service users and their families means practitioners need to remain current with the development of language which may have been used previously but which is currently challenged as inappropriate or oppressive. MacLaughlin (2012), writing about anti-oppressive research, encourages social workers to not only question issues around whose voice is being sought and heard, but also to recognise and challenge oppressive research practices. For example, Young (1990, p53) encourages social workers to read about and understand marginalisation as a form of oppression that isolates the disadvantaged people 'from useful participation in social life and thus [leaves them] potentially subjected to severe materials deprivation and even extermination'. Such research is relevant and will aid anti-oppressive social work practice. What we read as social workers will greatly influence the knowledge we hold about specific groups, interventions and practices. As you are reading this chapter, ask yourself what your current learning resources are in the area of anti-oppressive social work practice and consider what impact they have had on you.

Evaluation

This is the final component of the SHARE model and it is concerned with the ways in which social workers make sense of their practice by revisiting standards, values, principles and evidence which strengthens their daily practice. The idea of evaluation in social work is important because of the fluid nature of human experience. How can anti-oppressive practice be promoted and sustained by what social workers see, hear, read and do? How might social workers utilise the skills discussed in this chapter to champion anti-oppressive practice in contemporary practice?

The SHARE model is not a linear model; it is flexible enough for social workers to move between the components as required and its use in a linear way in this chapter is merely for the purposes of illustration.

Conclusion

Oppression is a multifaceted complex concept; consequently it requires a diversity of strategies to assist in understanding and disrupting its many forms. In this chapter, I have drawn upon the MANDELA and SHARE models to unpick practical ways in which social workers can enhance anti-oppressive practice in their daily interventions with service users. I have purposely selected models which have wide and flexible application beyond the social work profession and beyond the United Kingdom. Thompson (1997) argued over two decades ago that social work intervention either adds to oppression, condones oppression or can attempt to disrupt oppression, and it is concerning that the

Bernard and Greenwood (2019) study into social work engagement with affluent families found the existence of oppressive and discriminatory processes and practices arising from classism and socio-economic status of particular families. More than anything else, the findings from this study tell us that social workers need to keep anti-oppressive practice on the agenda at all times and that social work researchers and educators must continue to develop effective evidence-informed models, methods and resources to support anti-oppressive social work practice.

Key points summary

- Anti-oppressive practice creates an environment where people feel safe, respected and listened to.
- Social workers must develop and use skills which are empowering, supportive, fair, transparent, honest and non-oppressive in order to maximise the possibility of positive outcomes for service users.
- It requires more than good intentions to minimise and disrupt oppression and oppressive practice.

Suggested further reading

Tedam, P. (2012) The MANDELA model of practice learning: an old present in new wrapping? *Journal of Practice Teaching and Learning*. 11(2): 60–76.

Maclean, S. Finch, J. and Tedam, P. (2018) *SHARE: A New Model for Social Work*. Litchfield: Kirwin Maclean.

8

Writing skills for social workers

Lucy Rai

> **Chapter objectives**
>
> By the end of this chapter you should be able to:
>
> - identify the importance of and challenges in social work writing;
> - explain the importance of understanding the context and requirements of writing in academic and professional contexts;
> - identify strategies for writing effectively at university and in practice.

Introduction

Writing undertaken by social workers is variously referred to as paperwork, recording or report writing, and there is an implication that it is at worst a distraction from the 'real work' or at best a necessary requirement to meet the statutory obligations of the job.

This chapter explores some of the challenges involved in both professional and academic social work writing and ways in which learning can be transferred from university to practice writing. The focus here is both on the writing that social workers do in practice and academic writing undertaken during professional training. Academic writing is considered as an important opportunity for student social workers to learn the practice of professional writing. Through a consideration of the essential elements of writing, the chapter offers some strategies for students, educators and practitioners to make writing more effective by approaching it as an integral part of professional practice, rather than a discrete 'skill'.

Research summary

The quality of social workers' writing has been identified as a concern in official reports and investigations repeatedly over the past decade (Lillis et al., 2020), and there have been many writing skills books published to advise students and practitioners on how to write (Musson, 2011; Seymour and Seymour, 2011; Healy and Mulholland, 2007; Weisman and Zornado, 2013; Dyke, 2016; Watt, 2013). Admission assessments in literacy postgraduate social work training notwithstanding (Hamilton, 2018), concerns are still expressed about the quality of social work writing (Lillis et al., 2020). The issue is more complex than individual writers' literacy skills. An academic literacies perspective provides an ideologically based approach to supporting writers which tries to understand writing difficulties within the complex social contexts in which the writing takes place. This approach argues that a 'skills deficit' model of writing support locates responsibility for writing difficulties only on the writer, whereas the problem is broader and more complex. As such, Lea and Stierer (2000) argue that there are rules of writing, often subtle and implicit, which are specific to disciplines. Recent research into professional social work writing (Lillis et al., 2020) suggests that social workers commonly spend more than 50 per cent of their time writing. It is not surprising, therefore, that as writing takes up a larger and larger proportion of social workers' time, frustration has bubbled up.

Assessed academic writing on social work programmes measures:

- whether knowledge and understanding has been demonstrated, mapped against course learning outcomes;
- academic skills gained, for example the ability to seek and perform a synthesis of relevant information, to formulate a well-argued and evidenced critical analysis and to apply theory to practice contexts.

The ability to undertake professional writing that will form a significant part of the qualified social worker's role is rarely an explicit assessment outcome. It can also be unclear where professional writing is formally taught, either on social work programmes or subsequently in the early years of post-qualifying practice. Some social work programmes will set writing tasks that simulate practice texts as part of the academic assessment, such as writing a court report or assessments, but students primarily learn how to write professional texts informally through their practice placements, and both during training and in early professional practice the source of support for writing varies greatly (Rai and Lillis, 2013).

Why is writing challenging?

Writing can generate many anxieties and for some this may hark back to difficult experiences in school learning to write, as illustrated by 'Bernie' and 'Mark' in the following case studies.

Case study 8.1 (Bernie)

I was born in Jamaica where I spoke Patois, I still use it with many of my friends and with family, depends who I am talking with though, with some people I might use London English but the odd word of Patois. In school I had to learn to speak differently and I remember it being hard to write when I first came to the UK. Lots of us Black kids missed out because teachers assumed we were not academic, but I wanted to read and learn. It was hard though because it wasn't just that I would use different words and have an accent, the grammar is different too, like the word order, so I had to work hard to learn to write in Standard English. I still feel more 'me' speaking in Patios or with bits of Patios, but I would never use it at work or at uni. That makes it hard to do the reflective writing as I don't really feel as if I am writing as me, I have to think myself into someone else, the kind of professional me.

Case study 8.2 (Mark)

I found a school report tucked away in a drawer. It said, 'Mark is an able child until he puts pen to paper.' Even 40 years later that comment stung and brought back the hurt and humiliation I felt at school. I had lots of ideas, I enjoyed learning and I was always a very active participant in class. I actually also enjoyed writing, but my spelling was always poor and so my marks for written work were never good. Looking back now I see things differently. I gained a degree, so I don't think I lack intellectual ability. The real impact on me was that for much of my adult life I have felt an imposter in the academic world and as a social worker I found numerous strategies to avoid writing in public unless it was mediated through a computer. I do now also enjoy writing professionally, but only because I am less worried about getting caught out and judged for my poor spelling.

Writing is frequently associated with formal testing or official paperwork which are judged by others as measures of our ability or competence. Meanwhile, the place that writing plays in our lives is constantly changing as are the ways in which we express ourselves through the written word. For example, writing is increasingly undertaken in digital environments which can provide some assistance, such as spell-checking software, but also open up diverse sets of rules and expectations about how to write depending on the context. Such rules and expectations for specific writing tasks predate digital environments, but the amount of writing that now takes place in informal contexts such as social media reminds us of the fluidity of writing as part of a range of communicative tools.

Activity 8.1

Stop for a moment and think about four examples of your own written communication over the past week. Make sure that each one was written using a different tool or digital platform (so for example text, WhatsApp, Twitter, paper note, email or blog post). For each example note down:

1. Who were you communicating with? Was it one person or a group?
2. What was the purpose of the communication?
3. Did you include anything other than just words (such as images, emojis or sound)?
4. Would you describe the language you used as formal or informal? Did you use any colloquialisms or words that some of your friends or colleagues wouldn't necessarily understand?

Written communication, as with other forms, can be directed at one person or a group and we commonly moderate how we write, or talk, depending on who we intend to be 'listening'. Sometimes we are writing to specific people who are known to us (for example a group of friends on a WhatsApp group) but in more formal communication the specific identities of the readers are unknown, such as when writing online or for publication when you will have less control over who reads your words. Much of the written communication we use in our social lives is informal and can use a wide variety of language and abbreviations which we may not use in more formal contexts. Texts and messages increasingly also include emojis and images through which the digital channels we use enable us to express ourselves in new and more dynamic ways.

With any single communication there will be multiple decisions that you make, many of them unconscious, about the words and images that you use based on who you are communicating with and what the purpose of the communication is. This is no different from face-to-face communication where we also have many variables in how we might choose to communicate, including not only the words we use but also our tone of voice, body language, gestures and expressions. Written communication, therefore, is not something that is learnt as a one-off skill, something to be ticked off as having been acquired. It is a complex interpersonal practice that involves the writer drawing on a wide variety of skills and making many decisions, often unconsciously, about how to convey meaning most effectively.

Learning to write effectively in university

Activity 8.2

When you think about learning to write effectively, what skills and knowledge come to mind? What are the written skills that you would expect student social workers to be competent in before they begin their training?

Writing support in higher education is commonly offered through centralised learning support centres and frequently taught as a technical skill which is made up from a combination of elements including spelling, punctuation, grammar, 'lexicon' and 'syntax'. Lexicon refers to the vocabulary used and syntax refers to the structure of words within a sentence. All of these elements make up the structure of written language; the building blocks that enable the writer to construct a written text. While these elements are important and can help with the clarity of a text, competence in technical skills alone does not necessarily enable the writer to convey their meaning effectively. To illustrate the difference between effective communication and correct language use, read the following quotation:

> Transformative change within social work from an anthropogenic worldview to an ecologically centred worldview is crucial for addressing impacts of the global environment crisis (Gray and Coates, 2015). This conceptualisation represents a significant shift in consciousness about the place of humans in the natural world and challenges social work's conventional ontological base.

> (Boetto, 2017, p48)

This short extract from a journal article is technically correct and makes effective use of all of the elements of written language referred to above. In its own context it also conveys meaning very well, but how easy did you find it to understand? Do you think that friends who are not academics or social workers would understand it? What about a ten-year-old child or one of your service users? If you found this difficult to understand, or thought that other people may struggle with it, does this mean that it is 'badly written'? This example illustrates the importance of thinking about written texts within their context, what the purpose is and who is the audience who it was written for (Rai, 2011). The correctness of language alone does not mean that the writing necessarily conveys meaning effectively for other purposes, contexts or audiences. The important point here is that writing is primarily a form of communication and as such we need to vary it depending on the purpose, context and audience.

One very important element of context is the discipline that is being written for. Practice-based disciplines, including social work, are particularly challenging as they constitute multiple disciplines; for example, sociology, law, psychology and social policy, all with their own diverse writing conventions. Conventions refers to a range of rules and expectations, which may or may not be explicitly explained to students, on which writing is judged. These can include expectations of quotes and referencing, vocabulary, layout and use of the first person (discussed below). Practice-based disciplines have also developed conventions of writing around specific texts, such as reflective writing and practice case studies in social work. While the influence of such nested disciplines' use of written forms like reflective writing may be common across social work programmes, the specific expectations of how students should write within them differs from institution to institution and even tutor to tutor. This presents a challenge to writers that goes beyond the individual writer's accomplishment in using generic, structural writing skills.

Components of academic writing

Activity 8.3

If you were planning an essay, what are the tasks that you would need to do as part of your preparation? What advice have you been given about what makes a 'good essay' and what do you think you should be doing before writing your first draft?

Writing is the product of a range of processes that underpin and inform what we write. The kinds of processes involved will vary depending on the purpose of the writing; this applies to both academic and professional writing. The undergraduate essay provides a useful illustration of the range of processes or tasks involved in writing. An essay is a particular kind of academic writing commonly used to assess the writers' ability to understand a particular body of knowledge and construct an argument in response to the essay question. While it would be misleading to suggest that the essay is a 'clearly defined genre' (Lillis, 2001, p20) it is commonly used as an assessment tool across higher education.

The processes that you think of will have been influenced by the guidance that you have been given in the range of educational settings you have experienced. You may be able to think of contradictory advice that you have been given as you move between school and higher education settings. There are likely to be some common tasks and these might include:

- careful reading of the question;
- searching for relevant literature;
- reading and taking notes;
- synthesising ideas, information and arguments from reading;
- critical thinking and analysis of ideas and arguments;
- drafting a plan;
- identifying potentially useful quotes and evidence to draw on.

There is no definitive list of tasks or processes, but these give us some insight into the purpose of the academic essay as a tool of assessment. The term 'essay' is used very loosely, and the specific requirements vary from programme to programme and even from module to module within a programme. There are some general principles, however, which are commonly applied to essays.

- **Description** – there is a place for some description in essays but the expectation is that this reduces at higher levels of study as the degree of critical analysis increases. There is some variation; for example in more practice-oriented essays, where there might be a requirement to describe a practice incident which is then analysed. Some programmes would not refer to this as an essay but perhaps as a practice study.
- **Argument** – an essay would always be expected to contain argument in some form. Argument here refers to using evidence (from reading) to present a reasoned explanation of the pros and cons of different perspectives and arriving at a clearly justified conclusion.

- **Reflection on practice** – generally essays are based on theoretical learning rather than on practice, but this is not always the case. Some assessment tasks will ask students to apply theory to their own practice or professional development and write an 'essay' based on both reflections and reasoned argument. Assignments which have 'reflection' and 'practice' as a key focus are more commonly referred to as reflective essays, reflective assignments or practice studies.
- **Description of personal experience** – it would be very unusual for *personal* experience to be required in an academic assignment and students should be very cautious about using this unless it is explicitly required in the assignment brief. Where it is used, it would be the basis for reflection to develop practice, and the assignment would be less likely to be labelled as an essay.
- **Case studies** – it is common for case studies to be used in social work assessments, but such assignments may not be labelled as essays. Case studies might be provided by the course as the basis for a practice reflection but sometimes students might be asked to write a case study based on their practice. This form of assignment would more normally be referred to as a 'case study' or 'practice study'.
- **Anecdotes** – an anecdote would be an account that came from a third party and rarely, if ever, has a place in any form of academic assessed text. All evidence provided should be from published sources, from personal experiences of practice or given hypothetical case studies.
- **Critical analysis** – critical analysis is an element of academic writing which many can find challenging. It is closely associated with forming an argument and refers to the process of forming a well-reasoned, critical view based on an exploration of the evidence. Critical analysis is at the heart of most academic writing typified by the essay and is often the measure used for the quality of an assignment. At its highest level it demonstrates the writer's independent and original thinking based on a thorough understanding of relevant evidence.
- **Referencing of quotes and literature used** – referencing can be experienced by many students as a confusing and frustrating set of rules which have little to do with measuring their understanding. Nonetheless, referencing is an essential element of all academic writing and epitomises good academic practice. Referencing sources used is about giving credit to the original author, but it is also the way in which the writer demonstrates the basis for the arguments and critical analysis presented.

This reflection on some of the thinking tasks involved in writing a social work essay introduces some of the other forms of writing that are commonly used as academic assessment tools, such as reflective writing, case studies and practice studies. As a practice-based discipline, social work academic writing commonly requires students to refer to practice (their own or hypothetical case studies) and also to demonstrate that they can reflect on their learning and professional development. The inclusion of reflection on practice can create a tension in the context of academic writing in which the identity of the author is not traditionally visible (Rai, 2011). This can be illustrated by thinking about the use of the first person in academic writing. Academic writing across all disciplines commonly requires students to write using the third person or passive voice rather than the first person. To briefly illustrate, look at the three examples in Table 8.1.

Table 8.1 Passive voice, third and first person

Example	Passive voice	Third person	First person
1	The service user was interviewed on three occasions.	The author interviewed the service user on three occasions.	I interviewed the service user on three occasions.
2	Attachment theory will be evaluated and applied to human development.	The author will evaluate attachment theory and apply it to human development.	I will evaluate attachment theory and apply it to human development.
3	It could be argued that an understanding of psychology is essential for effective social work practice.	The author argues that an understanding of psychology is essential for effective social work practice.	I would argue that an understanding of psychology is essential for effective social work practice.

Activity 8.4

Looking at the examples in Table 8.1, which style would you feel most comfortable using? Is there any specific guidance that you have been given about which you should use? Does this differ for particular kinds of written assessment? Would any of the styles be problematic for writing tasks where the writer reflects on their practice or professional development?

While universities commonly penalise the use of the first person in traditional academic essays, this is not usually the case for reflective or practice-oriented writing. There is, however, no firm or universal rule on this, so it is always important to check the specific requirements set on the course. Reflective writing, however, places the author at the centre of the writing and so the distance created by the use of the third person or passive voice can appear clumsy and unhelpful, as illustrated in example 1 in Table 8.1 above. Reflective writing can be particularly challenging as it frequently requires the writer to reflect on and discuss their personal values, beliefs and experiences, in a way not normally associated with the personal distance that is more typical in academic writing (Rai, 2011).

Academic writing as a preparation for practice writing

Students on placement will write a wide variety of texts such as court reports, assessments and case recording, and this should be taken into account as an element of practice assessed during placements. Rai and Lillis (2013) suggest that social work students are able to transfer learning and skills from academic to practice writing:

Social workers identified a number of ways in which academic writing enabled them to develop their practice writing in discrete and specific ways such as learning to be more selective and concise in preparing essays and reflective assignments had direct parallels when writing case notes or reports.

(Rai and Lillis, 2013, p8)

Transferable learning included being able to adapt to the requirement of a range of text types. Research reported in Lillis et al. (2020) identified 341 differently labelled text types in everyday social work practice. The most frequently occurring text types were case notes, assessment reports, emails and handwritten notebooks, with important variation across each kind of text. Lillis et al. identified four key variables between text types:

- *Voice*: the ways in which the social worker represents herself and others within a text, such as the use of 'I' and the ways in which the service user's voice is represented, possibly using direct quotes.
- *Explicit evaluation*: the degree to which the social worker includes evaluations of, for example, situations, people or events.
- *Addressivity*: who the explicit or implicit intended reader of the text is and how this is reflected in the writing.
- *Style*: this refers to many features including the layout, punctuation and level of formality reflected by the language used.

(Adapted from Lillis et al., 2020)

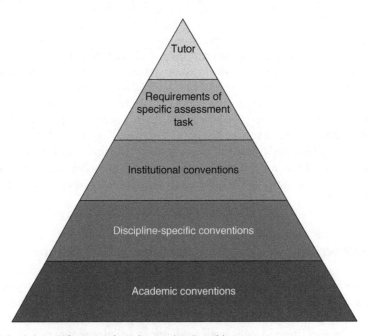

Figure 8.1　Layers of conventions in academic writing

Adapted from Rai (2014) *Effective Writing for Social Work*, Bristol: Policy Press, p.13. Republished with permission of the Licensor through PLS Clear.

There are some commonalities here with the differences between academic texts discussed above. Just as with professional writing, student writers need to use an appropriate voice for the specific assignment task. This will include decisions about whether to use the first person 'I', to draw on experience and how evidence from literature is used, for example through quotes and references. As discussed above, expectations of the degree of critical analysis generally increase in line with the level of study, but it is a feature of all types of academic writing. The focus of the critical analysis may be different in essays and reflective or practice-based writing, but both require the writer to use evidence to support well-reasoned arguments. Addressivity is an interesting issue in academic writing. The explicit intended reader is the tutor or lecturer who will assess the assignment, but in reality writers need to consider complex layers of often implicit expectations, which underpin the assessment of their writing. Rai (2014) suggest that there are layers of conventions in both academic and professional writing (see Figure 8.1). These conventions influence many aspects of writing, including the style used, and influence whether an assignment, or piece of practice writing, is considered to be successful or not.

In this figure the influence of the tutor as a reader is underpinned by the layers of conventions, or implicit rules, embedded at each level. First, there will be requirements of the specific writing task such as an essay, practice study or portfolio. Second, there will be institutional conventions (so the university-wide regulations or guidance on how to write), then the discipline-specific conventions (commonly held within social work across institutions), and finally the broad academic conventions that would generally be common across disciplines and universities. For the experienced and confident student writer, many of these layers of conventions would already be established and understood, but for less experienced writers or students transferring into social work from other disciplines, these layers of often implicit rules and expectations can be confusing. These layers of conventions are mirrored in practice, as illustrated in Figure 8.2.

As with academic writing there are several layers at which the writer may need to consider rules, many of which will be assumed or implicit. The audience for professional writing is in many ways even more complex than it is for academic writing. Depending on the text being written, the audience can include the service user, other social workers, and professionals from other agencies or the courts. Some texts are intended for several audiences, and the writer needs to consider how to communicate effectively with each of them.

One team of independent reviewing officers is piloting writing all reports addressed specifically to children, rather than to the other professionals who will read them. This means that the reports refer to the child as 'you' rather than 'the child', and the language is carefully crafted so that it accessible for the child to read and understand. This approach is an important recognition of the importance of making sure that professional texts are genuinely accessible for service users, and that while professionals should be able to understand a report directed at a service user, it may be difficult for some service users to fully understand reports aimed specifically at a professional audience.

Activity 8.5

Consider how you would write a report, for example, so that a child would understand it? How might this be different from how you would write for a court? What might the differences be in how you write?

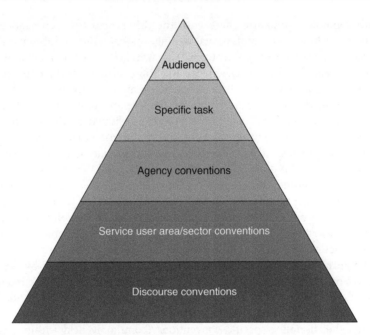

Figure 8.2 Layers of conventions in professional writing

Adapted from Rai (2014) *Effective Writing for Social Work*, Bristol: Policy Press, p.13. Republished with permission of the Licensor through PLS Clear.

As with academic writing, there are specific requirements of each type of professional text and these vary between agencies and services. Some requirements are embedded within the software used with agencies, some are based on local or national guidance, and some arise from the expectations of managers. This variation in requirements presents a real challenge, not only for students but also for social work programmes as it is not possible to 'teach' or practice every text type that a newly qualified social worker might encounter. It is for this reason that students and early career social workers need to learn how to identify the requirements of new text types that they encounter and seek out support from people within their agency. The following plan provides a useful starting point:

1. What is the purpose of the text?
2. Who is the intended reader or readers?
3. Is there anything you should be aware of to make sure the reader can understand the text?
4. Is there any guidance from the agency on what to include and how to write the text?
5. Do you have a line manager, supervisor or senior colleague who can read some of your texts and advise you?

While the purpose of some social work texts is to describe and record, many texts require social workers to use their professional judgement to put forward an argument. This is where experience of writing academic essays can be very useful, as there are many commonalities in terms of selecting evidence and using this critically to construct a persuasive argument. This is not the same as writing your personal opinion, which is considered to be subjective, but rather an objective consideration of the evidence drawing appropriately on professional training. This is particularly important when writing reports and assessments, where it is expected that the social worker draws on professional knowledge and provides clear evidence from their own observations and reports from professional colleagues.

Conclusion

This chapter has highlighted the importance of understanding the wider context of writing in academic and professional contexts. The effectiveness of academic and professional writing relies on more than the structure of writing being grammatically correct. Effective writing requires an understanding of the explicit requirements and implicit expectations, the rules and conventions which underpin all texts but vary from task to task. Most important, however, is an understanding that social work writing is a core aspect of professional practice and many of the competencies of social workers inform effective writing. For example, effective writing should take account of the communication needs of the reader, it should respect rights and confidentiality and it should demonstrate an ability to apply theory to practice.

Key points summary

- Social work writing is a core aspect of professional practice and many of the competencies of social workers inform effective writing.
- Effective writing requires an understanding of the explicit requirements and implicit expectations, the rules and conventions which underpin all texts but vary from task to task.
- The effectiveness of academic and professional writing relies on more than the structure of writing being grammatically correct, for example considering the context in which it is written.

Suggested further reading

Rai, L. (2020) *Writing in Social Work Practice*. London: Sage.

Rai, L. (2014) *Effective Writing for Social Work*. Bristol: Policy Press.

Rai, L. (2011) Reflections on writing in social work education and practice, in Seden, J., Matthews, S., McCormick, M. and Morgan, A. (eds) *Professional Development in Social Work: Complex Issues in Practice*. London: Routledge.

Healy, K. and Mulholland, J. (2019) *Writing Skills for Social Workers* (Social Work in Action Series). London: Sage.

9

Critical thinking and reflective practice

Joanna Rawles

Chapter objectives

By the end of this chapter you should be able to:

- understand what is meant by critical thinking and reflective practice;
- understand why critical reflection is important for social work;
- experience different ways to critically reflect.

Introduction

Social work is not just about doing; it is also about thinking. It is the thinking that makes the doing meaningful. Thinking itself is informed by knowledge but it is also influenced by a whole host of other things that we as human beings experience in our lives, often without realising it. The key to effective thinking for social work is to be able to uncover and understand what these influences are. In other words, to make them explicit rather than leave them as implicit. This is the essence of what critical thinking is and why reflective practice that adopts a critical stance needs to be the bedrock of social work.

You are likely to have noticed the phrase 'critical thinking' and even more so 'reflective practice' or 'critically reflective practice' throughout things you have read or heard in your social work education so far. They appear in textbooks, journal articles and in the professional frameworks upon which your social work education is based. As these phrases are ubiquitous, it is easy to assume we all know exactly what they mean and that incorporating these approaches into our practice must be straightforward.

Many social work students are not sure what 'reflection' or 'critical reflection' actually means in practical terms. Many are uncertain whether they *can* reflect or know how to do so, what they should be reflecting on, when reflection becomes critical reflection, or indeed how they would recognise it when they are doing it. If you are asking these questions of yourself it should not be a source of concern but a recognition that you are actually beginning to engage in the very thing you think is eluding you – reflection. The first lesson to learn about critically reflecting is that it is not always a comfortable place to be because it can, and many would argue that it should, take you out of your comfort zone.

This chapter will cover the *what, why* and *how* of critical thinking and reflective practice; what it is, how it has been defined and understood, and why it is necessary for social work, for your intervention in the lives of people who use services and for your own learning and development and how you might effectively engage in it. I will begin by exploring the notion of critical thinking before moving on to reflection and what we need to do to embed critical thinking into our reflective practice.

Critical thinking

A useful starting point to understand critical thinking is to clarify what it is not. The word 'critical' can be misleading because in general conversation we use it to denote something negative or something we disagree with, as in the following sentences.

- They were always critical of how I dressed.
- The teachers were critical of the government's policy.

A further common use of the word is as something significant, vital or serious such as:

- It is critical that we get these supplies by tomorrow.
- The patient is in a critical condition.

The word 'critical' in critical thinking does not mean any of these things. It derives from the concept of critique which means to analyse and evaluate. Whilst the teachers in the second example above may well have critiqued (analysed and evaluated) the government's policy, they could have concluded that the policy was positive and this would still have been a critique. Critical thinking does not mean disagreeing with or taking an opposite view to something. It means being sceptical and questioning everything that you read, see or hear, then analysing and evaluating it before drawing a conclusion.

The 'critical' in critical thinking refers to the way in which something is thought through, not to the specifics of the actual conclusion that is drawn (Brookfield, 1997).

There are differences in the way the concept of critical thinking has been defined and interpreted depending on ideological traditions (Brookfield, 2009) as well as varying approaches toward how knowledge is constructed (Mathias, 2015), referred to as one's epistemological standpoint. Brookfield's approach to critical thinking comes from a critical theory perspective, and as such provides a good fit for how the concept is usually understood in relation to social work and, I would argue, how it can be of most use to social workers. The focus of critical thinking from a critical theory perspective is on 'uncovering power dynamics and detecting the creation and maintenance of hegemony' (Brookfield, 2009, p296). Cultural hegemony was a theory espoused by the political philosopher Gramsci. It refers to the maintenance of the uneven and unequal power structures in society, not by someone directly wielding power over people, but by these inequalities being sewn into the fabric of our society and becoming part of our culture so that we all consider them to be 'just the way things are' and therefore accept them unquestioningly. It is therefore to Brookfield's (1997) conceptualisation of critical thinking that I turn to in order to explain the relevance of critical thinking to social work.

Brookfield (1997, pp7–9) identified four components that constitute critical thinking. He said that 'identifying and challenging assumptions is central to critical thinking'; 'challenging the importance of context is crucial to critical thinking'; 'critical thinkers try to imagine and explore alternatives' and 'imagining and exploring alternatives leads to reflective scepticism'. Drawing on this conceptualisation, I suggest that we can explore the extent to which we are engaging in critical thinking in social work by scrutinising it in relation to the following questions which in turn should increase the likelihood of us practising reflective scepticism:

1. Am I identifying and challenging *assumptions*?
2. Have I explored the importance of *context*?
3. Have I imagined possible *alternatives*?

In order to understand why these questions are important for social work practice, I will explore further the relevance of assumptions, context and alternatives.

Critical thinking: assumptions, context and alternatives

Activity 9.1

Read the following statements and make a note of whether you agree or disagree with each.

1. Boys who grow up with absent fathers are more likely to struggle with boundary issues and are at risk of joining gangs.
2. It is more of a risk for an older person living with dementia to remain at home alone than to move to a residential home.
3. Immigration is bad for the UK.

You may have been able to respond to each very quickly and decisively or you may have remained unsure. Choose the one you felt most decisive about or that was easiest to answer and ask yourself the following questions.

• Where did you get the information or knowledge from to enable you to answer this question?
• How reliable is this source of knowledge and is it likely to have been influenced by a pre-existing perspective such as a political persuasion?

It is this scrutiny and scepticism that begins to transform a viewpoint from being based on assumption to one informed by critical thinking.

A social work student once asked me, with some frustration, 'Can't I just think or believe something, can't I just have an opinion?' We should acknowledge that social work education often changes the way you think. It should also be acknowledged that whilst this can be a very positive, enriching experience, it can also be difficult. Picking apart why things happen in the way that they do or beginning to question long-held beliefs can feel uncomfortable and set you apart from friends and family if this has not previously been the way you navigate the world. We need, therefore, to explore what the implications and risks are for social work in simply having an opinion which is unsubstantiated, meaning it is founded seemingly on nothing more than you believing it to be so.

Social workers are required to form judgements. You will be required to form your own professional judgement about service user needs, level of risk, how best to meet those needs and risk, the most appropriate way to work with others, be they service users or work colleagues, and many more things besides. You are unlikely to be the ultimate decision maker in many situations, but the crux of your role is that you bring your professional recommendation to bear upon the decision being made in order to achieve the best outcome for people who use services.

So how is this professional judgement formed? You are probably already aware that your judgements should be based on evidence. This might be evidence directly obtained from observation and interaction with service users as well as evidence from research. Your judgement is also informed by other knowledge including theory, law and policy. What we need to be aware of, however, is that neuroscience tells us that we also use our emotions in decision-making (Damasio, 1994) and that we resort to heuristics to interpret information (Taylor, 2016). Heuristics means using mental short-cuts to help our brain sort and sift the huge quantities of information that it continually takes in. Emotions and heuristics are inevitable parts of how we interpret and make decisions as human beings, and should not be seen as inherently negative. The problem is that both heuristics and our emotional reactions are formed and influenced by the biases, stereotypes and assumptions that exist within society which we have grown up with, so unless we force ourselves to critique our own assumptions and reactions we are at risk of merely perpetuating these biases, stereotypes and assumptions and, as social theorists would say, leave the hegemonic power structures unchallenged. In short, decision-making is not a value-neutral activity (Beckett and Maynard, 2005). In other words, the evidence may inform you but you still need to choose how to respond to this evidence, and this choice is influenced by your values, which in turn are influenced by how you have experienced the world, your cultural socialisation. To illustrate, read the following case scenario and consider what might be influencing Laura's conclusion.

Case study 9.1

Laura is a social work student who has recently started her placement in a county council team working with adults. Her practice educator has allocated her a Care Act (2014) assessment to complete with Mrs Sybil Jones. The referral states that Mrs Jones is 87. She has arthritis in her knees and hands, and she has heart disease, which means she struggles to carry out many tasks of daily living independently without tiring and being in pain. She has recently been diagnosed with Alzheimer's disease, which is still at a relatively early stage, but she is already experiencing confusion and memory loss. Mrs Jones lives by herself but her daughter, who is 58, lives ten minutes' drive away. Mrs Jones's son, who lives in a neighbouring town, has suggested that his mother should be considered for a residential home near him where there is a vacancy. During Laura's visit with Mrs Jones she concludes that despite Mrs Jones still having capacity to make the decision she has not been able to get a clear view from her whether she wants to stay living at home or move to a residential home. Laura has identified some risks to Mrs Jones remaining at home, but she thinks these can be managed by her daughter visiting frequently and providing support. Laura is determined to ensure Mrs Jones remains in her own home for as long as possible and is not pressured by her son to move to the residential home.

Few would doubt that Laura has Mrs Jones's wellbeing at the forefront of her intervention and is demonstrating a determination to advocate on her behalf, but despite it seeming like a very positive approach, is Laura's judgement here being influenced by assumptions? She may have developed her assumptions from experiences in relation to her own family, friends or beliefs and may have a strong emotional reaction to the idea of an older person living anywhere other than the family home. By framing it in this way we can see that this viewpoint is not an indefatigable 'truth'; it is a viewpoint that has origins in her own experience of the world. It may be that this is what Mrs Jones would want – it also may be that there is research Laura could draw on that indicates older people generally have a better quality of life when looked after by a family member – but at this point, from what we know, Laura is not drawing on these sources of knowledge but on assumptions derived from her own view of the world. She is using her world rather than Mrs Jones's world as the frame of reference for her decision-making.

In order to broaden our analysis we also need to consider the societal and cultural conventions that may be framing Laura's thinking. There is an assumption built into the case scenario that Mrs Jones's daughter should provide the required support for her mother and indeed that Mrs Jones would want her to do so. The presumption that women should, are able to and are willing to provide care in the family is, again, not an indefatigable 'truth' but is a societal and cultural construct. Without using critical thinking to recognise that this is not a 'truth' but a construct it is easy for this to become an unchallenged assumption. Unless we make a specific attempt to unsettle and disrupt (Fook and Gardner, 2013) these 'taken for granted' assumptions, their influence in framing our professional judgement and decisions remains hidden. Privileging independence leads to a general assumption that living alone at home is bound to be preferable to living in a residential facility with others. There may also be influences from the current socioeconomic situation of contemporary services. Laura may know that it is unlikely her council will fund residential provision in this circumstance and the knowledge of the likely outcome may be fuelling her assumption that in circumstances such as this it is usual that the person does not move to a residential home.

Using the case study of Laura and Mrs Jones we can see why identifying assumptions is a necessary first step in any analysis in order to know what is influencing your judgement. Identifying the source of potential assumptions is a helpful way of identifying what is influencing your thinking in any given situation. This then enables you to be open to 'imagine and explore alternatives' (Brookfield, 1997, p8). This may have enabled Laura to be more active in her listening and more facilitative in her communication with Mrs Jones, assisting her to arrive at her own conclusion rather than Laura's own pre-existing preferable solution unwittingly influencing the interaction. Critical thinking can pave the way for more empathic responses as it opens up the possibility to view a situation from the perspective of the other rather than from one's own assumptions.

So far I have concentrated on identifying assumptions. The other important element of critical thinking is to understand the importance of context. The professional judgement you will need to formulate relates to human situations and these situations are contextually specific and therefore rely on the 'situated judgement of professionals' (Polkinghorne, 2004, p2). Put another way, the issues that people face are not solely, or often not at all, a consequence of their own psychology; they are created, or at the very least impacted by, the circumstances affecting their lives. To fully understand the lives of people you encounter in social work you need to not only be aware of the changing context of their lives but also subject this context to the same critical rigour you would in order to identify assumptions. Social work in the UK has evolved to take an individualist approach. Jones et al. (2008, p19) argue that the history of social work, being rooted in psychoanalysis, has encouraged a reductive approach in which the difficulties faced by people are reduced to 'the individual failings of clients'. Whilst our experience tells us that most social workers do not intentionally attribute difficulties to the 'failings' of the service user themselves, the focus on changing the individual can often be at the expense of critically analysing the context, and this is still apparent in much of social work practice in the UK. Consider the scenario below.

Case study 9.2

Kemi is a social work student on placement in a children's services team. The team receives a referral from a local school. The referral raises concerns about five-year-old Salim. It says he comes to school hungry and tired, his clothes are ill-fitting and very worn, he is often late and can become tearful for no reason. His mother Aisha seems reluctant to engage in conversation with the school staff and they don't think she takes their concerns seriously. The school was also aware that her mother had some mental health problems in the past. A colleague who shares an office with Kemi says, 'There are definite risk factors for neglect there, seems to me that the mother isn't managing. I would be quite concerned.'

Knowledge of law and agency procedure will guide Kemi but will not tell her what is happening in the lives of Salim and Aisha. She needs to formulate her professional judgement.

She has already received two perspectives about this situation, which indicate that Aisha is potentially neglectful of her son. At this point Kemi has a choice: she can either be led by these viewpoints from her more experienced colleagues, or she can subject all she has heard so far to a process of critical thinking by identifying assumptions, being open to alternatives and exploring context.

When visiting Aisha and Salim, Kemi takes an approach explicitly aimed at understanding the context of their lives by encouraging Aisha to talk broadly about what is happening for them, their 'lived experience'. Kemi discovers that Aisha's only source of income is welfare benefits. She no longer uses public transport due to the cost, so she walks everywhere with Salim, which sometimes makes them late for things. She was late for a benefits appointment and now she has been 'sanctioned', so her benefits have been stopped for several weeks. She doesn't know if there is a way of challenging this. She has been to a food bank occasionally but prefers to try to make the food last as long as possible rather than return, as she is worried about who will see her going there as they might think she can't cope and can't look after her son properly.

An exploration of context transforms an understanding of this situation from the individual 'failings' of the mother to the impact of how the economic and political structures are inhibiting the mother from being able to care for her child in the way that she and others would wish.

Critical reflection

So far I have discussed critical thinking without much mention of reflection. This is because I believe a focus on reflection without a prior understanding of critical thinking risks rendering reflection ineffectual. Academics emphasise the importance of distinguishing between 'reflection' or 'reflective practice' and 'critical reflection' (Fook and Askeland, 2006; Fook and Gardner, 2013; Brookfield, 2009). They argue that simply reflecting on what you have done does not challenge any of the premises underpinning what is happening in any given situation, so does not lead to change and can risk perpetuating stereotypes, discrimination and assumptions as was discussed earlier. Thompson and Thompson (2018) advocate the use of the phrase *critically reflective practice* rather than merely drawing a distinction between reflection and critical reflection. They suggest that using reflective practice in social work that is not critically informed is 'poor practice' and could be dangerous due to 'unwittingly reinforcing patterns of discrimination' (Thompson and Thompson, 2018, p21). They also state that including 'practice' in this phrase emphasises the need to ensure critical reflection is considered as 'part and parcel of the practice world and not an activity limited to education programmes one or more steps removed from the day-to-day activities of practice' (Thompson and Thompson, 2018, p21). Despite some differences in conceptualisation, what all these academic writers argue is that critical thinking and reflection should come together to ensure good social work practice and effective learning for social work practice.

So, what do we mean when we say we need to 'reflect'? Building on the discussions so far, the act of reflecting in relation to social work practice can be seen as a *mechanism* to facilitate critical thinking. Some common phrases used to describe what you are doing when you are reflecting are: thinking through; taking a step back; getting under the skin; or taking a helicopter view of the situation. I think the latter provides a useful visual cue, particularly if you are struggling to pin down what you do in order to reflect. Thompson and Thompson (2018, p54) describe this as

the ability to: (i) rise above a situation to get the overview of how the component parts fit together and how they create the overall situation; and (ii) descend back into it to be able to deal with it in an informed way.

Whilst these phrases are useful as a way of beginning to understand the mechanics of reflection, we must guard against placing ourselves outside the reflective gaze. As discussed previously, we naturally have pre-existing views about a situation, either from our own values and cultural socialisation, from societal constructs, or from unwittingly absorbing the perspectives of others. It would therefore be remiss of us to place ourselves too steadfastly as 'objective observer' in the reflective endeavour. We do need to 'get the overview of how the component parts' of a situation 'fit together' (Thompson and Thompson, 2018, p54) in order to proceed in an informed way. At the same time we need to turn the reflective gaze on ourselves and our pre-conceptions, otherwise we will not be effectively scrutinising what is informing our judgement.

There are many definitions of reflection throughout the literature on professional practice, spanning several professions and disciplines. You can find some of these within the suggested further reading at the end of this chapter. I like the following from Jasper (2013, p1):

Reflective practice means taking our experiences as a starting point for learning. By thinking about them in a purposeful way… we come to understand our experiences differently and take action as a result.

Jasper's definition encompasses several important elements of reflective practice. These are learning from experience, being purposeful in our approach to thinking and harnessing both of these in order to take action. I will explore the connection between reflection and learning from experience before discussing ways in which we can engage purposefully in reflection.

Reflective practice: learning from experience

Reflective practice is linked with the concept of experiential learning, and to understand this we need to look at the origins of both and consider why they were transformative for professional practice and professional learning.

The ideas associated with both reflective practice and learning from experience were first discussed by educationalists. For centuries, in 'Western' tradition, learning had been perceived as a linear process in which 'knowledge' existed in books and in the minds of great thinkers, and students learned this knowledge then used it to inform what action they took. Schön (1987) called this a 'technical-rational' approach to learning. There was little appreciation that learning could happen in the reverse, in other words that you could learn from the experience itself and that this could inform and create new 'knowledge' that in turn could be used to inform experience and create a cycle of learning. It is important to note that reflection is not a substitute for formal knowledge or evidence

(Knott and Scragg, 2013; Thompson and Thompson, 2018). Formal knowledge and evidence should be incorporated into reflection along with experience in order to use all possible sources as a means of understanding a situation.

Learning from experience is such a commonplace idea to us now it is hard to perceive this as revolutionary or at all controversial. Educationalists Donald Schön and David Kolb were both instrumental in establishing the idea that you can and indeed should learn from practice in order to first understand the situation you are encountering and second learn from this understanding so that your practice can be improved and your expertise developed. What is important, however, is that you *learn* from experience, not merely that you *have* the experience, and this is where the idea of actively reflecting on that experience becomes relevant. Thompson and Thompson (2018, p57) sum this up in the following way:

> *Experience creates the potential for learning but, in itself, it teaches us nothing directly, it is what we do with experience that is the best teacher.*

John Dewey, an American philosopher and educational reformer writing in the early to mid-twentieth century, is often credited as being one of the earliest proponents of the value of learning from experiencing and interactive learning as well as the need to think reflectively on that experience. Sections of his work provide a forerunner for the way in which we understand critical thinking as a component of reflection. Dewey (1910) proposed the need to take an active role in reflection, illustrating that it is something we need to work at. This is very much about active rather than passive learning and practice. As the definition by Jasper (2013) states, reflection needs to be purposeful.

Helping you to reflect

There are many mechanisms and frameworks that have been developed to help students and practitioners to reflect. Before exploring some of these it is worth re-visiting the ideas of Donald Schön, as his conceptualisation of how professionals reflect has been influential. He put forward the dual notion of 'reflection-on-action' and 'reflection-in-action' (Schön, 1983). The former identifies the way in which you purposefully think through an experience after it has occurred in order to learn from it, whilst the latter refers to the thinking through whilst the experience is happening. Contemporary writers in social work have suggested that there needs to be a further dimension to this and that is reflection *for* action (Thompson and Thompson, 2018; Mantell and Scragg, 2018) in order that we draw attention to the thinking that needs to occur in anticipation of an experience. This has links with the concept of preparatory empathy (Shulman, 1984; Cournoyer, 2011) anticipating the possible feelings and perspectives of service users in order to inform your preparation for intervention.

Most mechanisms that exist to aid reflection are more readily orientated to reflecting on action after the event. It may be that reflecting to sufficient depth during the event makes reflecting in action seem too challenging. I would argue that the aim should be to practise a process of reflection on action in order that this becomes habit-forming and second nature, so that you can mentally draw on a distilled version of this reflective process at the point at which events are occurring. We need to be able to think through our interactions whilst we are in the middle of them in order to guide our actions in an informed and planned way, as well as subjecting them to greater scrutiny and depth of thought after the event.

During the course of your social work education you will need to write reflectively and you will also need to discuss your reflections, but you may have preferences that work for you so it is worth trying out a few different ways of doing this. One important thing to bear in mind is that whichever mechanism you find easiest may be useful to get you started, but remember the aim of critical reflection is to move you beyond your comfort zone, so you should look to challenge yourself to answer questions you may not ordinarily pose (see Mantell and Scragg, 2018; Higgins, 2018; Scragg, 2018). Writing a reflective diary or log can be useful as this enables a free flow of ideas and encourages a regular habit-forming activity. There are many frameworks that are rooted in the idea of experiential learning. Their aim is to facilitate you to think through an experience by writing down or talking through a sequence of steps that start by you describing the event or interaction, commenting on your feelings and emotional reaction, analysing the situation then considering how you would take action as a result of these. Popular and established versions of this are Kolb (1984), Gibbs (1988) and Johns (2017).

'Abstract conceptualisation' in Kolb's model is the stage at which you begin to hypothesise about why things happened in the way that they did and what does this mean. It is the stage at which you analyse. I advise learners that it is at this stage that they should incorporate more formal knowledge such as evidence, and theories can inform them to help analyse the situation. Such frameworks, however, often do not explicitly mention the incorporation of knowledge and this can be a limitation.

Activity 9.2

Think of an occurrence or interaction, preferably in a work or placement context, or it could be in your personal life if you don't have this experience to draw on. It does not have to be anything remarkable – it could be something you do or did often and it doesn't need to be anything negative or that went wrong (we can learn a lot from things that went well). Complete the following activities:

- Write an entry for a reflective journal about this experience. Write without stopping for ten to 15 minutes, or longer if you wish. Try to avoid just describing what happened, try to delve deeper into your thinking with regard to this situation.
- Now use the same example and write (or talk through with a colleague) a response to each stage of a reflective cycle framework such as Kolb or Gibbs.

When you have finished, consider (a) which felt easier and (b) which enabled you to think at a greater depth and helped you uncover new thinking about the situation

---

This may help you to work out what aids to reflection might work best for you, but remember that this may vary in any given situation and at what stage you are of your learning. It is worth experimenting with different models.

Adding a critical thinking dimension to reflective frameworks

The frameworks and mechanisms to help you reflect discussed in the section above can help to make your thinking explicit, but they do not by default encourage the critical thinking discussed earlier. It is possible to use these mechanisms to reflect without identifying assumptions, considering context and imagining alternatives; these methods of reflection have the potential to do this but also they could easily be completed without using much critical thinking in the way it has been discussed above. Read what you have written for the activity to see to what extent you have incorporated critical thinking in your reflections. I would suggest that, whatever reflective framework you use, posing the critical reflection questions about assumptions, context and imagining alternatives should be inserted at strategic points as a checking mechanism to ensure you are adopting critical thinking.

Conclusion

This chapter has introduced you to the idea of critical thinking and explained why it is important in social work to be reflectively sceptical in order to minimise the extent to which your professional judgement is influenced by the biases, assumptions and inequitable power relations that exist within society. In order to do this you need to identify and challenge assumptions, consider context and imagine alternatives. We then considered reflective practice and mechanisms to assist you to reflect. Finally, we considered how to combine the two in order that you can develop into a critically reflective practitioner.

Key points summary

- Critical reflection involves deep, analytic thinking and sceptical questioning.
- It can be a disturbing and difficult process that demands effort and time.
- Everyone approaches critical reflection in different ways and you should experiment to find the ways that suit you best.

Suggested further reading

Brookfield, S. (2009) The concept of critical reflection: promises and contradictions. *European Journal of Social Work*, 12(3): 293–304.

Ferguson, H. (2018) How social workers reflect in action and when and why they don't: the possibilities and limits to reflective practice in social work. *Social Work Education: The International Journal*, 37(4): 412–427.

Mantell, A. and Scragg, T. (2018) *Reflective Practice in Social Work*. London: Sage/Learning Matters.

Thompson, S. and Thompson, N. (2018) *The Critically Reflective Practitioner*. London: Palgrave Macmillan.

10

Communication and interpersonal skills

Juliet Koprowska

Chapter objectives

By the end of this chapter you should be able to:

- explain how context at many system levels influences communication;
- identify differences between everyday informal communication and professional communication;
- describe asymmetry in professional talk.

Introduction

Most human activity relies on good communication, and social work is no exception. Human beings are social animals who live interdependently, so from birth onwards we pay a great deal of attention to other members of our species. We develop a sophisticated repertoire of words, gestures and facial expressions and have a pretty good idea of how other people are feeling. Social workers employ everyday skills that many people possess without specialist training: we ask and answer questions, listen to what people say, share ideas, dispense advice, make recommendations, explain our views and decisions, show our feelings of warmth, amusement, sadness and shock.

Just as social work draws upon the resources of everyday communication, it often takes place in apparently informal environments – the homes of service users – and explores everyday subjects such as relationships and the management of day-to-day living. Like health visiting (Raymond, 2010), social work communication shifts between everyday talk and a distinct work focus, and the chapter explores this terrain. Social work communication is shaped by many layers of contextual expectations. The chapter details some of the core skills social workers use, and considers the asymmetry of professional relationships, where social workers ask about service users' lives but rarely reciprocate with stories from their own. These factors transform professional talk from the everyday informal conversation that supplies its building blocks.

An important question concerns whether the quality of social work communication matters – does it make a difference? It certainly makes a difference to people who use services (see Penhale and Young, 2015), and the chapter also draws on research that studies social work in action (Ferguson, 2011, 2016; Forrester et al., 2019).

The overarching concepts used here are Agazarian and Gantt's (2005) definitions of *context, goal* and *role*, and Drew and Heritage's (1992) distinction between *informal* and *institutional* talk.

Building working relationships

Social workers use communication to forge working relationships with service users, carers and colleagues. We cannot *do* social work without making a relationship, and we cannot make a relationship without communicating.

Figure 10.1   Building the foundations for purposeful social work

Koprowska, 2019.

The purpose of building a relationship is to work with people to improve their lives. The quality of the relationship depends on many factors, including frequency of contact, where we meet, and our remit. Social workers are often under time pressure with daily tasks and reporting deadlines. Sacrificing relational skills to 'get the job done' may be tempting, but Ferguson (2016) shows that without skilful communication, including creative use of play with children, people do not open up to social workers, and vital information may be missed. Meanwhile, Forrester et al. (2019) found that relationship-building and the use of *good authority* (Ferguson, 2011) led to better outcomes in social work with children and families.

The context for communication

We know intuitively that context affects communication. We communicate and behave differently at home, as a visitor, at college, at work or on holiday. Most of us readily learn new norms as we mature. Citing anthropologist Ruth Benedict, Agazarian (2004) argues that the environment (context) influences our behaviour more than our individual traits. The social environment endorses some behaviours and prohibits others. Agazarian and Gantt (2005) further state that every context has a *goal* or goals, and people take up particular *roles* in relation to the context and the goal. We occupy multiple roles in our lives, and as we shift context, we shift role. We have a pool of interactional resources and draw on only some of these in each role. Humour that is appropriate with friends may not be with parents, colleagues or service users.

Social work takes place through purposeful, goal-oriented conversations, and the immediate conversational dynamics are influenced by multiple and overlapping contexts. Lishman (2009, p5) highlights the *tension between accountability to the agency and accountability to users of services*, and here I take her idea a step further (see Activity 10.1).

Activity 10.1

Here are some contextual factors that influence social workers' communication with service users and carers.

* The International Federation of Social Workers.
* The legal system: statute, government guidance and policy, the courts.
* Social work regulators. The four in the UK are: Social Work England; the Scottish Social Services Council; Social Care Wales; and the Northern Ireland Social Care Council.
* Employers in the public, independent and third sectors.
* Specialist services within organisations.
* Service and team managers.
* Social work education programmes in different universities.
* Social work research.
* The media representation of social work.

Choose two or three to investigate further. What can you deduce about the goals of social work and the social work role? Is there alignment or do you see tensions between them? How might they influence your direct work and communication with service users?

This exercise illustrates the complexity that social workers manage. During contact with service users we are never truly alone, as we have in mind the law, policy, codes of conduct and the expectations of our seniors. We may worry that a judge, the local newspaper or a social media posting will cast doubt on the quality of our work, and these anxieties may impair our effectiveness. Supervisors and practice educators are crucial sources of support to manage these complexities.

When we take on new social work responsibilities, it takes time to understand the goals and our role. Although the influence of context is powerful, we bring our prior experience and preconceptions with us, so our role behaviour may not align with the contextual goals until we know them. Consider the following case example.

Case study 10.1

A social work student on first placement visits an older woman living alone who has had a fall. The student's goal is to complete the assessment form her practice educator has given her. Without preamble, she starts on page one. The woman does not answer her questions, avoids eye contact, and says, 'Ask my daughter.' The student abandons the interview. After talking with her practice educator, she makes a second attempt. This time she puts the form aside, initiates a conversation about home and family, and develops the discussion so that much of the information she needs for the assessment emerges.

The student experiences natural anxiety when taking on a new role, and has preconceptions about professional behaviour. She is formal, stilted, preoccupied with the assessment form and frustrated that the service user is 'uncooperative'. In Munro's words (2010a, p14), she is concerned with 'doing things right' rather than 'doing the right thing'. The practice educator encourages her to be interested and friendly, without losing sight of the goal.

Institutional talk

Social work 'talk' is a form of *institutional talk*, that is, talk that prevails in the workplace (Drew and Heritage, 1992). The concept of institutional talk has its roots in conversation analysis. See the following research summary.

Research summary

Conversation analysis (CA) is a sociological approach to the study of interaction which provides insight into *naturally occurring* talk, i.e. not scripted or simulated (Drew and

---

Heritage, 1992). *Turn-taking* is central to communication, and CA shows how people take turns in given situations. In some, people choose when to speak; in others, a teacher, a judge, a game show host controls the flow of talk. In CA, the word *context* is used to refer to the unfolding sequence of interactions. The question, 'What would you like to drink?' provides a context where 'Coffee' is a much more likely answer than 'Vegetable oil' or 'Nail polish'. Talk performs social actions: the offer of a drink is an act of hospitality, and acceptance or refusal are not just factual. They signal cultural norms, or show acceptance or rejection of the person making the offer. According to Drew and Heritage (p19),

> the basic forms of mundane talk constitute a kind of benchmark against which other more formal or 'institutional' types of interaction are recognized and experienced.

CA studies show that talk is characteristic of particular environments, e.g. the courts, or medical consultations. For research in social work see Hall et al. (2010) and Hall et al. (2014).

Countries and regions have different languages and dialects, and so do work environments. *Jargon* refers to the specialised words and abbreviations that insiders use. In addition, institutional talk refers to styles and patterns of interaction that differ from informal talk. People new in social work who talk with no difficulty in everyday conversations may suddenly be at a loss for words. They neither know what to say nor how to say it, as they have not yet acquired a repertoire of professional knowledge and institutional talk.

Getting started

In first meetings with service users or carers, follow this guide.

1. Introduce yourself! Use your first *and* last names, unless you are talking to a small child. Write your name down or repeat it. It is common to forget names immediately and people are embarrassed by asking, so make it easy.
2. Tell them what to call you: 'My name's Joseph Mangwende, you can call me Joe.'
3. Smile. Be friendly – but not over-friendly. Bring interest into your voice tone. Make eye contact.
4. Ask the person what you should call them. Despite the prevalence of informality, only use someone's first name with permission. Cultural norms mean that older people or people from other parts of the world may prefer their title of Mrs, Ms, Mr, etc, and may want to address you in the same way.
5. Children and young people usually prefer to use their first name. Find out if they use a different name or nickname.
6. If you have arranged the meeting, explain its purpose, and say how much time you have. If the other person has initiated contact, ask the reason.
7. Use simple everyday language. Avoid or explain professional jargon and abbreviations.

Time management: an interpersonal skill

It is polite to be punctual, neither early nor late. Let people know if you are delayed. Stating the amount of time available for the meeting helps you and service users manage the discussion. Research into GP appointments (Heritage et al., 2007) found that asking *early* in a meeting if there are other issues the person wants to discuss helps time management. Eliciting this information early means you can agree a rank order for topics. Remember, service users have other obligations too. Except in emergency situations, do not make them late! Keeping an eye on the time is polite behaviour, not something you need to do by stealth. Say something: 'We've got about 10 minutes left so let's see where we are. Have we covered everything important?' Even if you have little time, you can create the illusion of time by your pacing. Obvious rushing flusters people.

Written material

When making notes or completing forms, explain what you are writing and why. Offer to show the service user and explain who will see it. If giving leaflets or written information, consider reading key points aloud in case they cannot read very well (but do not draw attention to this).

Phatic communication

Social workers commonly use pleasantries, called *phatic* communication, at the beginning and end of contacts, something the student in the case study did not realise. As you get to know a person, you learn the topics that suit. Phatic communication bridges the space between the informal home environment and the more formal, goal-directed talk of the working environment. The *talk itself* transforms the service user's home into the workspace. To support the goals of the work, take up your authority to reduce distractions, for example, by asking for the TV to be switched off.

Difficult topics

Some meetings are occasioned by a difficult topic. A neighbour has reported child neglect, or a GP has referred a vulnerable adult. It is awkward to bring up failures or shortcomings (Koprowska, 2017) so we may fear upsetting someone or attracting hostility. We take up our role using good authority and get to the point quickly:

> I've come to see you because of worries about you and your children after your neighbours called the police last night. Your partner's under arrest for assaulting you, and I'm here to see what we can do to help.

This is an example of a difference between *mundane* and *formal* talk (Heritage and Drew, 1992). Striking the balance between politeness and directness is a skill. With difficult topics, conveying interest, openness and empathy help build the relationship.

Asking questions

A key social work activity is asking questions that relate to the goals of the work. It becomes second nature to social workers to ask questions, but service users do not automatically know why we are asking. An early UK study found that people who wanted financial help from social workers were mystified by questions about their upbringing (Mayer and Timms, 1970). The social workers conceptualised early experience as influencing adult financial competence, but the service users did not. A *preamble* explaining why we ask can be simple: 'I'm going to ask you lots of questions today, to understand your situation better.'

Many writers discuss *closed* and *open* questions, *clarifying* and *probing* questions, *leading* questions and *multiple* questions (e.g. Kadushin and Kadushin, 2013; Koprowska, 2014; Lishman, 2009; and Trevithick, 2012). I describe these and thers here.

Examples of *closed* questions:

- Have you always lived here? (Yes/No)
- When did you and your partner meet? (Two years ago/In 2018)
- Who collects you from school when mummy isn't well? (Robin does/No one)

These require yes/no answers, or brief factual answers. In reality, people often expand on initial responses.

Examples of *open questions*:

- What's it like living here?
- How do you and your partner get on?
- What do you do at home when mummy isn't well?

These invite more expansive answers. The service user has more choice about what to say.

Probing questions follow up on what has been said and deepen the discussion, while *clarifying* questions do exactly that: make something clear that was vague.

Leading questions imply the answer.

- You're all right for food, aren't you? (Yes)
- You haven't got enough food for the weekend, have you? (No)

Note the form of the question *projects* a yes or no response.

Double or *multiple* questions create confusion (Kadushin and Kadushin, 2013). According to Sacks (1987), first answers relate to second questions, and second answers to first questions.

Q: How did you get home last night? What time did you get in?

A: I got in about 11. I caught the last bus from town.

I have seen social work students in role play ask a double question, receive no answer to the more important *first* question and, satisfied with the answer to the *second* question, move on without noticing. Ask one at a time.

We also use expressions that are not formed as questions but elicit new information:

- Tell me about your time in the army.
- Tell me what happened yesterday afternoon.

Declarative questions are formulated as a statement and the rising inflection at the end signifies the question.

- You moved here two years ago?

Delicate questions

Sociocultural norms limit the subjects that are permissible for discussion early in acquaintance. Social workers sometimes have to set these norms aside, and ask about personal issues on first meeting. While service users are entitled not to answer, this could have implications related to risk, especially if it indicates deceit.

Case study 10.2

Mrs Chitambo

Mrs Chitambo is a 75-year-old who may be eligible for home care.

Well, Mrs Chitambo, some people pay the whole cost of home care, and some only have to pay a proportion. It partly depends on a person's financial situation, so I'm going to ask you some questions about money before I can work out how much you would pay. Is that all right with you?

Rob

Rob is 16 and in foster care. He has started his first sexual relationship with another young man. He has been telling his social worker how happy he is about the relationship.

Rob, I know this sounds a bit personal but are you guys using condoms? I'm asking because it could be really important for your health.

Marie

Marie has two daughters aged eight and 10. Her new partner Greg has convictions for sexual assault against pre-adolescent girls.

I know Greg comes over as a supportive person to you, but I'm wondering what you think about your relationship with him now you know about his sexual offences.

In these scenarios, the social worker introduces the awkward topic with an explanatory or empathic preamble. Mrs Chitambo might prefer to pay the full cost or refuse the service rather than share her private finances. Rob might blush and avoid an answer, but the social worker has given him information he can use later. Marie might protest that Greg has explained he was wrongly convicted, and this would contribute to a risk assessment.

Reflecting back and paraphrasing: active listening and empathy in action

Reflecting back someone's words is unusual in everyday Western conversations. 'So this morning you got up late, had a shower, ate some breakfast and went to the shops.' Yet in social work, counselling and therapy, reflecting back and paraphrasing are vital to demonstrate understanding. They convey understanding without recourse to self-disclosure and are more convincing than platitudes such as 'I know how you feel, I completely understand'. They entail attuning emotionally as well as listening carefully to the words. Sometimes novices are not listening but planning their next turn; it takes practice to listen and reflect. These are among the *relationship-building* skills that Forrester et al. (2019) identify as improving outcomes. (To hear a wonderful parody, find Venning and Ramsden, 2016.) Reflecting back and paraphrasing are useful when *summarising* key points and *agreeing next steps*, which social workers often do towards the end of interviews.

Non-verbal behaviour, facial expression and emotion

Human beings are good at scanning for emotional cues and clues and do this from infancy; being able to assess the mood of our carer is an important survival skill. Social workers attend to non-verbal communication, and while some of us attune more easily than others, everyone can improve by observing people closely. Gestures, movement, facial expression and complexion give valuable information about the emotional state of the other person, as does *paralanguage,* the non-verbal elements of speech such as speed, pitch, volume, intonation and breathiness. These provide clues to their reactions to what we say and do – they are a form of feedback.

Our own non-verbal presence has an impact, and in my experience most social work students do not need to modify their behaviour much. Be friendly and do what you can to appear relaxed even when you are anxious. Avoid crossing your arms tightly across your chest, slouching, towering over people or invading their space. Use the information that comes from your own bodily responses: are you anxious, tense, tearful? Do you feel nausea or disgust (Ferguson, 2011)? You may be reacting to something in the context. You could be picking up the service user's worry, or responding to intimidation, dirt or unpleasant smells.

Asymmetry

Conversation analysts identify *asymmetry* as a common characteristic of professional interaction (Drew and Heritage, 1992). We have seen this already with questions, since social workers often ask questions, placing service users in the role of *answerer*. Asymmetry signals power differentials, and who has control of the discussion (Freed and Erhlich, 2010).

Second stories

A social norm is to tell a *second story* from our own experience when with friends or relatives, conveying understanding and empathy. Here are two women talking about their teenage sons.

I'm worried about Leo, he's not doing any revision and I think he's going to mess up his exams.

You know, Faisal was just the same. He only came to his senses after he failed a couple.

An alternative strategy is to offer someone else's story. 'My friend/mother/Rhianna went through something like that and …' Professionals rarely offer personal second stories (Drew and Heritage, 1992). Sometimes the anonymised experience of other service users becomes a resource: 'I worked with someone else who self-harmed, and …' (Lovell, 2017). This effectively conveys understanding without offering information about ourselves that could be distracting or render us vulnerable.

Advice-giving

Professionals give advice, another form of asymmetry. The timing of advice-giving affects how it is received. A study of health visiting (Heritage and Sefi, 1992) suggests that advice delivered as soon as a service user names a problem is often rejected, sometimes obliquely, with silence or an 'Mm.' Advice given after the person has explained their own understanding and efforts to solve the problem is better tailored and therefore more likely to be heard, indicated by a more definite response such as 'Oh right!' This finding is relevant to social work, though no similar studies exist.

Case study 10.3

Jenny is in her 50s and has a long history of drug and alcohol use. She attends a group at a substance misuse service. Members must be sober during group sessions, and the social work student who co-runs the group can smell beer on Jenny's breath when she comes in. After greeting her, the student says,

SWS: *Jenny, I'm thinking about the group, and how everyone's got to be sober during group sessions. And I think you've had a drink today – am I right?*

Jenny: *I know I shouldn't have, I just felt so awful that I picked up a can before coming in here. I only had one.*

SWS: So how come you felt so awful?

Jenny: I don't know, I didn't sleep well, and I wanted to come to the group but I was dreading it as well.

SWS: So part of you wanted to come, and part of you was dreading it. What were you dreading?

Jenny: I don't want to get anyone into trouble. [Starts crying]

SWS: Sounds like something's happened that's really bothering you.

Jenny: It has, it has. I'm going to have to tell you because I don't want it happening again.

SWS: Okay, I'm listening. Take your time.

Jenny: Well after last week's group, Pete, in the group, kind of followed me on my way home. He wanted to go for a drink but I didn't. I've been trying so hard not to drink.

SWS: Okay, so Pete followed you and wanted to go for a drink, and you didn't. And what happened then?

Jenny: Well first he was acting nice, but when I wouldn't go in the pub he started calling me names, and pushing me around, and tried to drag me by the arm. It was awful.

SWS: So what happened then?

Jenny: I was really lucky. A friend of mine, Nick, came out of the pub, and saw me, and saw Pete was pulling me and told him to leave me alone, and Pete gave him a mouthful but he let go of me and I went home with Nick. He's a good guy, Nick. But I'm scared of seeing Pete again.

SWS: And that's why you had a drink today?

Jenny: Yeah.

SWS: And you want to carry on with the group, even though you can't attend today?

Jenny: Yeah I do. It's been helping me.

SWS: Okay, right. I'm really glad you came in and told me all this, and you can come to the group next week of course. So you're saying that Pete followed you, tried to get you to go for a drink, and wouldn't take no for an answer. He called you names and pulled you around, and it just so happened a friend of yours was able to step in. You still want to come to the group and this event has got in the way. Have I got everything?

Jenny: Yeah, that's about it.

SWS: Okay, so here's what I'm going to do. I'm going to talk to one of the managers so we can decide next steps. We'll need to talk with Pete and see what he's got to say. Is that okay with you?

Jenny: I don't want to get him in trouble but I don't want it happening again.

SWS: Okay. Do you want to stick around and have a cup of tea before you go? I can ask Mary if she'll sit with you for a bit. I've got to go into the group soon, so I want to speak to the manager now.

Jenny: Yes, thank you, I'd like that.

Activity 10.2

Read through the dialogue between the student and Jenny, in your head or with someone else, taking one part each. Identify questions, reflections, and other conversational features. Listen to the music of the talk and pay attention to the images that your mind produces in relation to it. Now take a moment to imagine Jenny's posture, her gestures, her eye contact with the student, the timbre and steadiness of her voice, the speed, pitch and volume of her speech. Does this change during their talk?

The social work student asks questions, listens, reflects back and paraphrases. She offers empathy through questions reflecting Jenny's feelings ('So how come you felt so awful?'), acknowledging the unspoken ('Sounds like something's happened that's really bothering you'), and with a symbolic gesture ('Do you want to stick around and have a cup of tea before you go?'). She summarises key points and uses good authority to explain what she will do next. Her behaviour indicates the goal-directed nature of the discussion. She refrains from telling her own second story: 'I've got a friend like that, always trying to get me smoking again.' She explores Jenny's understanding and wishes, without giving advice, and does not condemn Pete (who may have a different version of events). She manages and contains her own feelings.

Conclusion

The key objectives of the chapter have been met by considering the influence of context on communication and exploring some of the similarities and differences between informal and institutional talk. The chapter has shown that social workers draw upon the resources of everyday communication and are thus often well-equipped to communicate with service users. However, context and asymmetry shape the work goals of social work interaction, so the chapter has identified role behaviours that characterise professional talk, such as asking goal-directed questions, reflecting back and paraphrasing, and refraining from telling personal second stories or giving premature advice. It has discussed how to address difficult and delicate topics that are often avoided between comparative strangers. It has highlighted the importance of being friendly, open-minded, and active in explaining what we do and using our authority effectively. When embarking on a social work career, or taking up a new social work position, we need to learn about the norms, goals and roles of the new context, and accept that sometimes we make mistakes as we find our way.

Key points summary

- Communication operates at informal and professional levels and social workers learn to be aware of these different levels in their practice.
- Understanding common and contextual norms in communication is central to working with people as a social worker.
- Communication is not an exact science and developing one's own 'naturalness' is important.

Suggested further reading

Ferguson, H. (2016) Making home visits: Creativity and the embodied practices of home visiting in social work and child protection. *Qualitative Social Work*, 17(1): 65–80.

Koprowska, J. (2020) *Communication and Interpersonal Skills in Social Work* (5th ed). London: Sage/Learning Matters.

Lishman, J. (2009) *Communication in Social Work* (2nd ed). Basingstoke: Palgrave Macmillan.

Trevithick, P. (2012) *Social Work Skills and Knowledge: A Practice Handbook* (3rd ed). Maidenhead: Open University Press.

11

Courtroom skills for social workers

Allan Norman

Chapter objectives

By the end of this chapter you should be able to:

- appreciate why social workers need courtroom skills, and understand the environment within which those skills are deployed;
- identify the core social work skill as giving compelling evidence as a witness;
- anticipate likely questions with reference to the strengths and weaknesses of a case and what has, or has not, been covered in written evidence; and
- answer questions in a way that is compelling and authoritative.

Introduction

It is much more likely now than in the past that a social worker will at some point be called upon to give evidence in court. The case study below illustrates a number of the reasons we may end up in court. It is significant in particular that as human rights pro-fessionals we have a growing awareness that many social work interventions are interferences with rights that need some kind of judicial oversight.

'Judicial oversight' implies that we are not fully in control of a number of social work processes. Asking for a court order is not a simple administrative step. The court is independent, it has its own rules, and the legal professionals have their own ethical code. Seeking a court order may feel like the heavy end of social work, particularly to a service user, but to the social worker, it may feel very much like relinquishing control to an alien profession in an unfamiliar arena. This chapter therefore seeks to explain the courtroom – its actors, its structures and processes – to make it less alien.

What emerges is that, almost invariably, the social worker has the same specific and narrow role: to provide the evidence of the social worker's interventions and conclusions, and in giving evidence, to assist the court to decide what the right outcome should be.

Activity 11.1

Often in the courtroom, a service user with whom we have been working, and with whom we may continue to work, sees us giving evidence with which they disagree. How will the service user be feeling? Is there anything we can do as professionals to address this? We will be considering these questions throughout the chapter.

Having identified the core courtroom skill for a social worker as giving good witness evidence, and after exploring the various roles and processes, consideration will be given in turn to types of evidence, what makes evidence compelling, the stages of giving evidence, and how to anticipate lines of questioning.

Understanding the courtroom

Why do social workers need to go to court?

Consider the following case study. This is a real case. The title at the top is known as the case citation, which uniquely identifies the case, so you could look it up.

Case study 11.1

Y (Autism – Care Proceedings – Deprivation of Liberty), Re [2018] EWHC B63 (23 April 2018)

Y is a teenager with autism, without speech, and with severe behavioural difficulties. Y is one of three children. Neither of the other two has disabilities, and no concerns have ever been raised about the parenting of the other two children.

(Continued)

(Continued)

Y's parents asked the local authority for help to manage Y's increasingly difficult behaviour, and have had an intensive package of support, of between 20 and 30 hours per week. When difficulties continued and Y's parents continued to press for additional support, the local authority became increasingly concerned that they were not taking advice or managing behaviour in accordance with the local authority's recommendations. Court proceedings were started, but eventually it was agreed that the local authority would accommodate Y in a residential unit, under Section 20 of the Children Act.

However, Y's parents became increasingly concerned that the unit was not appropriately looking after Y. Their concerns in particular included that the unit made excessive use of physical restraint; that the unit had made him clean up his own mess when he soiled himself; and generally that he was unhappy, and was losing weight. It emerged that he was not receiving an education, and that the unit did not have the skills to communicate with him. Y's parents eventually withdrew consent to the placement under Section 20 of the Children Act. They wanted Y returned to their own care.

The local authority issued care proceedings. The local authority asserted that Y was beyond parental control.

So, why did this case end up in court? First, observe that trying to work with the family voluntarily had failed because consent had been withdrawn. Often, if we cannot work with consent, it is a court order that gives us the authority to do what is necessary. Court orders are effectively tools in the social worker's toolkit.

Of course, it is not always the case that the local authority is bringing a case. Sometimes it will be defending a case that is brought against it. Although the local authority brought this particular case, it is easy to see that the parents had a number of criticisms – that on proper examination turned out to be well founded criticisms – and if the local authority had not brought proceedings, the parents might have brought proceedings themselves, with the local authority being the defendant. One type of court case in particular, called judicial review, can be used by individuals to challenge the fairness of the procedures of public bodies, and this includes cases brought by service users against the decisions made by social workers.

It is not just if consent is withheld or withdrawn, but also if a person is unable to consent, that it might be necessary to bring a case to court. In this case, the court pointed out that since Y was approaching adulthood, an application to the Court of Protection might be needed – this is a court that deals with issues under the Mental Capacity Act, and social workers are increasingly in the courtroom because the service user cannot consent, rather than because they will not. Moreover, Y was deprived of his liberty, which engages human rights. That, in particular, often means that social workers need a court order.

Social workers and service users are not always on opposite sides. We might be supporting an outcome that some of those we are working with want; or, if we are putting something in front of the court simply because the court must review our decisions, we might be supporting an outcome that everyone wants.

Nor is the local authority necessarily one of the parties to a case. Sometimes, a social worker might be brought in as an expert in a dispute – for example between parents in private law proceedings – where the local authority is not a party. Social workers might also intervene on behalf of their service users in other kinds of cases. For example, social workers acting as corporate parents of looked-after children have been more proactive in acting in the children's best interest in immigration matters, and this might also bring the social worker into a court or tribunal setting.

We have seen, therefore, that a social worker might need courtroom skills:

- bringing a case, or defending a case;
- because there is an actual dispute that a court needs to resolve, or because even where there is not a dispute the court needs to have oversight of what is happening; and
- where the social worker's decision is actually what the court is looking at, but also where the social worker is trying to help the service user in some other kind of dispute.

The court system

In England and Wales, the Ministry of Justice runs a Courts and Tribunals Service. Tribunals are bit like courts, but normally more informal, and set up to make decisions in specialist areas. However, there are also specialist courts, and the social worker may encounter in particular the Family Court, which makes many decisions in respect of children and families, and the Court of Protection, which makes decisions for those who lack the mental capacity to make decisions for themselves. Most of the time these courts are more formal, but some hearings are around a table in a manner more akin to a typical tribunal hearing.

First instance and appeal courts

The term 'first instance' is used for a court where a case starts off. After a decision has been made, there can be an appeal to a higher court, or a higher level of judge. Typically, and certainly the higher up the appeal structure a case goes, appeals are about points of law, rather than a rehearing of the facts. The practical consequence for social workers is that we are not likely to be appearing in the appeal courts, but only in the lower courts that make findings of fact. That reflects our role as a witness giving evidence, which happens in the lower fact-finding courts.

Civil and criminal courts

A further distinction that can be made is between criminal courts that deal with those accused of crime, and all the other courts, which are civil courts. The Family Court and the Court of Protection are both civil courts. Rules of procedure in the civil courts are generally more flexible than in the criminal courts, and, in particular, there is greater leeway about what kinds of evidence are admissible. Given our role as a witness giving evidence, those differences are important.

The courtroom

The exact layout of a courtroom will depend on many factors, including when and for what purpose it was built, but for more formal court hearings of a kind social workers may attend, some points about the layout offer useful markers about court hearings.

The judge is usually raised, and facing most of the other actors, able to see everything going on in court. This is the front.

The rows facing the judge will have advocates (see below) at the front; any members of the public, observers and those not involved at the back; and other lawyers, parties and witnesses in between. The social worker will sit behind their own advocate.

From one side to the other, the advocates will sit in the order they expect to be presenting their cases, which also provides you with an indication of the order in which cross-examination (see below) takes place.

The witness giving evidence sits sideways to both the advocates and the judge. This is important, allowing the witness to clearly see both, and both to clearly see the witness.

Reflections on the role

The social worker's role, in almost any courtroom situation, is that of a witness giving evidence. Consideration of three other roles in the courtroom allows some insights into what the social worker giving evidence should *not* be doing.

The judge

The judge is the decision maker. In many other situations, the social worker is the professional making decisions. Here, the social worker is trying to persuade, and the judge is the person to persuade. You may want to make a good impression on your employer, your service user, or the advocate who is asking you questions – but none of them are the decision maker. You should look at the judge when you answer questions, even though it is unnatural to be asked a question by one person and to direct your answer to someone else. There are many other reasons for this advice – it helps to stop you being distracted or even controlled by the reactions of the advocates, for example, and to better focus your evidence – but the need to engage the decision maker, and take cues from the decision maker, is one of the more important.

The advocates

An advocate is someone who speaks on behalf of another person. Social workers and lawyers both use the term, but in slightly different ways. In the courtroom context, the advocates are the lawyers – either solicitors or barristers – who are representing the parties to the case. You may understandably think that advocating for service users is part of the social work role. That might even be your formal role, for example as an Independent Mental Capacity Advocate. However, as a witness you are not acting as an advocate. It is not your place to make any kind of legal argument. You might refer to legal principles within your evidence, but you don't get to argue about what the law means.

The parties

The parties are the people or organisations that are bringing or defending the case. There will need to be at least two parties but can be many more. For example, in a care case or in a Court of Protection case a number of different relatives might be separately 'joined' as a party. Each party might have their own advocate, but the advocate is not a party themselves. Each party might have their own witnesses, but (although a party can go into the witness box to give evidence) witnesses are not necessarily parties themselves, and social workers almost certainly are not.

Sometimes a social worker is giving evidence as the employee of a local authority. Sometimes, we have more specialist role that gives us a greater degree of independence in exercising professional judgement – for example, as a Best Interests Assessor in relation to an adult, or a Children's Guardian in relation to a child. Sometimes, a social worker is asked to provide an independent social work assessment, and give evidence on that. Whatever the exact role, and even where a social worker is employed by the party bringing the case, as a professional the court expects the social worker to demonstrate a level of detachment, and of reflective thinking, that is not expected of 'lay witnesses', members of the public giving evidence for a party.

Giving good evidence

The nature of evidence

Evidence may be considered as anything that a party puts forward in support of their claim. That definition is broad, and it means that something is still evidence even if it is (a) untrue; (b) deliberately manufactured; (c) not credible; (d) not relevant; or (e) not admissible. That is why such an important part of the role of the court is to test the evidence. That in turn should help the social worker to appreciate there is nothing personal in the forensic process of testing the evidence. Indeed, a thorough testing process gives legitimacy to the result. There is a benefit to society as a whole in being able to have confidence that people accused of crimes will not be found guilty without a fearless testing of the evidence against them. Social work decisions, too, have grave repercussions – individuals can be deprived of their liberty, families can be split up, sometimes forever.

Testimony

Evidence can take many forms, including objects or recordings, but the most common are documentary evidence and testimony – the oral evidence you give in the witness box. It is testimony evidence that is at the heart of courtroom skills, and it is also highly valued as a form of evidence. Statements may be poorly drafted, may be ambiguous, may lack context, may lack relevance, or may have been drafted deliberately in such a way as to minimise or disguise facts that might be unhelpful to the case being advanced. A social worker whose statement stands up to being tested through the courtroom process, which is designed to test for such things, has given the best and most helpful evidence to the court.

Opinion evidence

There is a technical rule of court that only an expert witness can offer an opinion. When the social worker is in the witness box, however, that technical rule will feel completely illusory. First, it has already been observed that whether or not the social worker is technically an expert witness, they are a professional rather than a lay witness, and will be treated accordingly. Second, it is the social worker's judgement and analysis that is frequently at the very heart of the dispute the court has to resolve, and therefore that is going to be tested. Third, while a criminal trial will be necessarily focused upon the question of whether something happened in the past, most social work cases have a strong future-looking focus. That means that there is a greater element of speculation and uncertainty, not least because what happens in the future may be contingent; it also means that opinion necessarily plays a more significant role.

Hearsay evidence

This is another term with the technical meaning. Although it is generally understood to mean second- or third-hand evidence, it is more accurately when you give evidence of what someone else has said or recorded on the basis that what was said or recorded is true. The civil courts in which social workers appear do allow hearsay evidence and you will give hearsay evidence. It is still really important to be clear to the court when you are doing so, and to be conscious of the possibility that it is not true. In particular, if you want to rely on the truth of someone else's words or records and another party is disputing their truth, you may not be the best witness, and someone who can give direct evidence may be needed instead.

Scientific evidence

Social workers have a troubled relationship with scientific evidence. Often, we hope that science can provide certainty when we are uncertain. We might hope that hair-strand testing can accurately detect drug use; that medicine can confidently assert that a baby was deliberately shaken, or that an injury was deliberately inflicted, or that sexual abuse has taken place. That list, however, is a list of forms of scientific evidence that have all been questioned. It is not that there is no scientific basis, but that in each case there have been flaws in the scientific process, which means that rarely is certainty possible. Sometimes there is a real risk of false positives, leading to an accusation of abuse or harm when there was none. It is important that a social worker giving evidence understands the scientific conclusions, but also that they are not unduly reliant on them. The social worker should be confident to say what they have or have not observed, whether they did or did not have concerns, irrespective of whether the scientific evidence points in a particular direction. If we give evidence as though the weight of the science pointing in a particular direction were infallible, and discount our own observations, then the court loses an important part of the picture that would help it to make the right decision.

Research summary

The Inns of Court College of Advocacy

This is a body providing specialist support to barristers in particular. It has produced guidance to help barristers in the process of testing evidence. One of these documents deals generally with expert evidence, and the other, jointly written with the Royal Statistical Society, deals with specific statistical evidence specifically. They are:

- 'Guidance on the preparation, admission and examination of expert evidence' at https://www.icca.ac.uk/wp-content/uploads/2019/06/Expert-Guidance-final-copy-with-cover-2019.pdf; and
- 'Statistics and probability for advocates: Understanding the use of statistical evidence in courts and tribunals' at https://www.icca.ac.uk/wp-content/uploads/2019/06/RSS-Guide-to-Statistics-and-Probability-for-Advocates.pdf

Although these are not written for social workers, they are written for those who will be cross-examining social workers in court. The guide to statistical evidence in particular is designed to explain it to non-statisticians. Social workers, and in particular any social workers who may rely upon research evidence in their reports, might find these guides helpful in developing an insight into how legal advocates may approach testing their expertise and the authority of the research they rely on.

On the epistemology of evidence

If this chapter appears to treat the court process as benign, its conclusions as legitimate, and the evidence given by the social worker as objectively neutral, then it may be helpful to reflect upon the epistemology of evidence.

Epistemology is a study of how knowledge is constructed and understood, something rarely reflected upon outside of the context of academia. One of the crucial distinctions within epistemological thinking is between those who proceed upon the basis that there are objectively discernible facts, and those for whom knowledge is primarily constructed.

The ways in which we can discover and know whether or not a crime has been committed are likely to be very different to the ways in which we can discover and know whether or not an adult is at risk of abuse or neglect, or what their best interests are, or whether a child is suffering or likely to suffer significant harm. Roets et al. (2017) introduce a distinction between truth-telling and story-telling. Wilkins (2017) uses this distinction to reflect upon the process of giving evidence. If you consider you are primarily a truth-teller, you are likely to focus upon the 'knowable' history, and

(Continued)

(Continued)

minimise your professional role in interpreting it. However, we might consider that what constitutes abuse or neglect, significant harm or best interests, is in reality socially constructed. On this view, the 'knowable' history does not lead inevitably to a particular finding or conclusion, because your evidence and the court's judgement are constructing what abuse or neglect, significant harm or best interests actually are. Roets et al. locate this as story-telling rather than truth-telling.

Reflecting upon whether a social worker is or should be a truth-teller or a story-teller is an epistemological question; it is also one that may cause any individual social worker to be more or less troubled about exactly what they are doing when they step into the witness box in any particular case.

Being compelling

It goes without saying that the courtroom skill of giving evidence is enhanced if a social worker is compelling. Three characteristics of compelling evidence are discussed here – the social worker should be able to be reflective, caring and authoritative.

Being reflective

It is sometimes believed that, given the adversarial nature of a courtroom, and given that a social worker is seeking a particular outcome, this is best achieved by focusing all one's attention on the evidence that supports that particular outcome. In terms of being a compelling witness, however, that is a serious mistake. Being balanced in evidence is a critical skill. Indeed, there are both good legal and social work reasons for acknowledging the weaknesses, as well as the strengths, of your case. A conclusion that appears to have been reached without considering the contrary arguments is of limited assistance to the court. Really one-sided evidence can even mean the social worker may be accused of lying because a service user simply cannot see themselves in the evidence. Balance can be demonstrated by acknowledging counterarguments. This may involve setting out advantages and disadvantages that do not seem compelling. There may be an acknowledgement that 'I can see the force of your point, however …' There is an important role in making appropriate concessions when challenged in cross-examination. Balance means, on the one hand, that it is normally possible to find something good to say about any service user. As Dyke (2016, p93) puts it, 'families rarely have a life with nothing but dysfunction and the most dangerous households can have happy and enjoyable times'. On the other hand, good evidence-giving does not allow for simply accepting every concession you are asked to make in cross-examination. Social workers must be alive to the moments to answer with a 'but' or 'however', and even more alive to those concessions that would effectively undermine their case.

Being caring

It is possible that the search for balance and objectivity can result in seeming detached from the lives of the service users with whom you work. But being caring is not incompatible with balance. Being able to demonstrate warmth and concern, being able to demonstrate that you are vested in the service users' interests, will make your evidence all the more compelling.

Being authoritative

In the courtroom context, there are two likely ways of being able to create an aura of authority. One of these relates to the depth of your knowledge of the individual, and the other to your experience as a practitioner. Sadly, the service user at the centre of a case is frequently absent from the courtroom, with the practical effect that decisions are made about them without them. If you know the case well, know the service user and the family well, and are able to convey the depths of your knowledge, alongside the frequency of your contact and the range of circumstances in which you've worked with them, that is going to create compelling evidence. If you have significant experience, and in particular in-depth experience of a particular kind of situation, you need to convey this. It is not uncommon to find disagreement between social workers, one of whom has an in-depth knowledge of the situation, and the other of whom has significantly more experience of the area of practice. Whatever your strength is, you will be relying on that to lend credibility to your evidence, and should expect to be tested on it.

Anticipating questions

In order to prepare for the process of giving evidence, it is helpful for you to read your own statement, but also the main statements of the other parties, and as you read to reflect both upon what has been said and what has not been said, upon what strengthens and what weakens your case. This exercise can help you in particular so that you are not taken unawares in cross-examination. It can be expressed as follows:

Table 11.1   Preparing to give evidence

	Strengthens case	Weakens case
Said	What has been said by a witness – you or other witnesses – that strengthens your case is likely to be the main message that you are trying to convey. Cross-examination is likely to be focused on undermining it.	In your own statement, what you have said that weakens your case is likely to have been said in the interests of fairness and balance. The same is true of other witnesses, though sometimes cases are undermined unintentionally. Cross-examination is likely to be focused on bolstering such points.
Unsaid	If you have left unsaid something that strengthens your case, it can be difficult to introduce it. You may not be given the opportunity, or you may be challenged if you try. It is best to address this by good drafting, or good examination-in-chief, although new evidence that genuinely emerges from cross-examination is, of course, admissible.	It can be tempting to leave unsaid what weakens your case. However, noticing what has not been said, both in your own statement and in those of other parties, is often important in predicting the direction cross-examination will take.

> **Activity 11.2**
>
> Draw up a sheet with four boxes and headings as shown above. Consider a case with which you are involved, where there is disagreement. See if you can identify in particular the weaknesses and gaps in your evidence, and the evidence that would support the other perspective. Reflect on how far you ought to acknowledge those points, if the matter came to court and you were being cross-examined on them.

The process and the stages

In the witness box, there are three distinct stages to giving evidence and having your evidence tested. Cross-examination, sometimes used incorrectly to refer to the whole process, is actually the middle of the three stages.

- **Examination-in-chief** is the process of being taken through your own evidence. Since you have normally put a written statement into evidence, this can often be brief. However, it is an opportunity for your own advocate to ask open-ended questions by way of scene-setting, or dealing with developments. The difficulty with open-ended questions is that your advocate cannot give you any help about the reason for their question or the answer that was looked for.
- **Cross-examination** refers to the questions asked on behalf of each of the other parties to the case. It is cross-examination that normally induces most anxiety. These are the questions that probe and test, that may seek to undermine your case, or your credibility, or your judgement. These can be leading questions – you are likely to know exactly what answer the advocate is hoping for, even if you don't understand why, and you still have to try to give a fair and professional answer. This is the point where you need to be alive to whether to make concessions, and whether to qualify those concessions by restating your case.
- **Re-examination** concludes the process. Your own advocate is able to pick up any points that have been misunderstood, or emphasised incorrectly. They may try to regain control of the narrative. Particularly after lengthy and hostile cross-examination, it can be easy to forget at this stage that your own advocate is there to try to help you and your case. Remember these are open-ended questions where you are invited to expand upon, reinforce or summarise your case.

Conclusion

We have seen that while social workers may assist in bringing or defending a case, or sometimes participates as an independent witness, nonetheless the social work role is almost invariably that of a witness, and therefore the core courtroom skill is to perform that role well.

The chapter then introduced features of the courtroom where familiarisation and understanding might help you to be more at ease: the court system, the significance of the courtroom layout, and the roles of those in it were explored.

To prepare you for giving evidence, types of evidence were considered, with guidance on what makes evidence compelling, and consideration of the different stages and types of questions being asked. An activity encouraged preparation for giving evidence – and anticipating likely areas of questioning – by working through the strengths and weaknesses of the parties' positions, including with reference to what has, and what has not, been said.

Key points summary

- A social worker in a courtroom will give evidence. This may include evidence of *fact* and of the *analysis* that has led to the social worker's *conclusions*.
- Questions asked as examination-in-chief and re-examination are an opportunity to *set out* the evidence. Those asked on behalf of other parties in cross-examination are *probing and testing* that evidence.
- Good evidence will be compelling when it is delivered in a way that is reflective, caring and authoritative.
- You will need to become familiar with when to be concise and when to elaborate, when to make concessions and when to restate your evidence.

Suggested further reading

Davis, L. (2015) *See You in Court: A Social Worker's Guide to Presenting Evidence in Care Proceedings* (2nd ed). London: Jessica Kingsley Publishers.
Page, C. and Johnstone, L. (2019) *Supporting Good Court Craft*. Dartington: Research in Practice.

For insights from service users into their experiences and perceptions of the court processes:

Neary, M. (2011) *Get Steven Home*. Morrisville: Lulu Press.
Tickle, L. (2016) 'I saw his fluffy little head going out the door': one woman's fight to keep her baby. *The Guardian*. Available at: **www.theguardian.com/lifeandstyle/2016/feb/20/children-taken-into-care-mother-fighting-to-get-baby-back-louise-tickle**

Websites with **practice-based resources:**

CC Inform has a 'Court skills knowledge and practice hub' with a landing page for all its resources on report writing and courtroom skills here: **www.ccinform.co.uk/knowledge-hubs/court-work-skills-knowledge-and-practice-hub**
Research in Practice (**www.rip.org.uk**) and Research in Practice for Adults (**www.ripfa.org.uk**) are website resources including videos, practice guides and other tools, focusing respectively on children and families and adult practice. Both include guidance on courtroom skills, and there is a subdomain funded by the Department for Education, specifically dedicated to 'Court Orders and Pre-Proceedings' (**https://coppguidance.rip.org.uk**).

12

Groupwork skills

Timothy B. Kelly and Toby Berman-Rossi

Chapter objectives

By the end of this chapter you should be able to:

- define what is meant by 'skill';
- articulate a range of groupwork skills;
- understand the difference between skill and being skilful;
- describe the importance of skills across the phases of groupwork practice.

Introduction

This chapter begins with a brief definition of skill and the difference between skill and skilful. At the end of the chapter there is an exercise where you can explore this difference more fully. The chapter then provides an overview of stages of group development and phases of groupwork practice. The idea that different tasks and skills are required at different stages/phases is introduced. We then move to a description of many different groupwork skills so that your skill vocabulary increases. The chapter ends with an exercise whereby you will practise skill labelling, reflecting on effectiveness, and trying out new skills.

Understanding the difference between skill and skilful

The word skill often is used to mean some task or activity that a person learns through practice. It can also refer to a proficiency or competence. Examples include dribbling in football or basketball, keeping thread tension when cross-stitching, or drawing blood from an artery. Doel and Kelly (2014) place a professional slant on the meaning of groupwork skill by saying that a skill is knowledge in action (Phillips, 1957). In this sense, a skill becomes more than muscle memory, and instead has an intellectual component, whereby professional knowledge is used to do something. Professional knowledge is applied to a situation in a helping relationship and the worker *does* (verbally or non-verbally) something – hence, knowledge in action or purposive action with the intention of influencing group process or individual behaviour.

Many groupwork skills are skills that social workers might employ when working with individuals, families or in other social work contexts (Gitterman and Germain, 2008; Gitterman and Shulman, 2005; Shulman, 2015). The other chapters in Part II of this book provide a range of such skills. But as Schwartz (1971[1994]) points out, groupwork skills are used in a small-group situation where there are many helping relationships (the worker and all the group members). No longer is there a 1:1 relationship, but a multiplicity of relationships all within the same space. As such, those familiar individual skills must be adapted to be used skilfully in groupwork practice (Doel and Kelly, 2014).

At this point it is useful to differentiate between skill and being skilful. A skill is the verbal or non-verbal action that a worker does. Being skilful is an evaluation of the effective use of a particular skill. The same skill can be used skilfully or unskilfully, and assessing the difference can be complex. Take for example the skill of 'asking for information', used in the following case study of an early group for men who have perpetrated domestic violence.

Case study 12.1

Member: *So I kind of hurt her a bit.*

Worker: *How did you hurt her? (asking for information)*

Member: *I hit her a bit.*

Worker: *You hit her? Where? (asking for information)*

Member: *On her arm and face.*

Worker: *Did you use your fist or hand? (asking for information)*

Member: *Nah, my fist.*

(Continued)

(Continued)

Worker:	*A fist to the face? (asking for information)*
Member:	*Yeah, her nose, like blood everywhere.*
Worker:	*What happened next? (asking for information)*
Member:	*I knew I shouldn't have done it. I freaked. I screamed it was her fault and pushed her down and she hit her head. I ran before the police came, being on probation and all. I freaked. That was so stupid.*
Other members:	*Sit silently nodding their heads in agreement.*

In the case study above the worker uses a simple skill of asking for information using what, when, how questions. The worker knows that men who commit gender-based violence minimise their actions and their consequences. The skill of asking for information shows willingness on the part of the worker to talk about the 'nitty gritty' of violence. Asking for details also prevents minimisation. So the worker has intention in their action; they are putting knowledge into action. Importantly, in groups, the rest of the members witness this interchange and also learn that the worker is interested in their lives and it is safe to discuss the specifics of their actions. One could evaluate the skilfulness of these questioning skills based on the outcome. The group member did confront his actions in a small way.

However, basing one's evaluation of skilfulness only on outcome can be problematic. Asking the same questions to another member or the same member on another day could result in very different results, as shown in the next case study.

Case study 12.2

Member:	*So I kind of hurt her a bit.*
Worker:	*How did you hurt her? (asking for information)*
Member:	*I pushed her a little and hit her a bit.*
Worker:	*You hit her? Where? (asking for information)*
Member:	*It was nothing, just a little push and tap to get her out of my space.*
Worker:	*What do you mean a tap? (asking for information)*
Member:	*You know like a tap. (makes a waving motion with hand)*
Worker:	*Did you hit her with the back of your hand? (asking for information)*
Member:	*Man it was just a tap. She made a big deal out of nothing. Ask someone else. I'm done talking.*

At the same time, sometimes workers can use a skill and get a great outcome, even though the use of skill was not skilful. Imagine the same situations as above but though the same skill is used (asking for information), the next case study looks and feels different.

> **Case study 12.3**
>
> *Member:* So I kind of hurt her a bit.
>
> *Worker:* How long have you been together? (asking for information)
>
> *Member:* About five years.
>
> *Worker:* Do you have any children with her? (asking for information)
>
> *Member:* Yeah, a daughter, she's three.
>
> *Worker:* Any other children? (asking for information)
>
> *Member:* Another girl by my wife's first husband. She's five. I'm so glad they were with their gran. When I punched her face, it was her nose, like blood everywhere. I knew I shouldn't have done it. I freaked. I screamed it was her fault and pushed her down and she hit her head. I ran before the police came, being on probation and all. That was so stupid. Thank God the girls didn't see that this time.

Here the worker uses a skill, in an unskilful and disconnected way. Yet it appears as if the member did not minimise his actions, and as such, a claim could be made that there was a good outcome. However, this would not be a skilful use of 'asking for information'.

Rather than define skilful based on outcome, we define skilful in terms of the level of connection between what the group member or group as a whole says or does, and what the worker says or does. In other words, skilfulness relates to how close the worker gets to the member's or members' primary message. Take for instance the questioning in examples 1 and 3 above. The skill 'asking for information' was very connected with the member in example 1, but totally disconnected from the member in example 3.

Tasks across the phases of helping and stages of group development

Before articulating groupwork skills, there are two other important overlapping but distinct groupwork concepts that influence the type and timing of groupwork skills a worker should use. These concepts are phases of work and theories of group development. Phases of work describe the dimensions of time over the course of the helping process and are typically described as preliminary, beginnings, middles and endings. During each phase of the helping process, the worker is required to complete different tasks (Doel and Kelly, 2014; Gitterman and Shulman, 2005; Kelly and Berman-Rossi, 1999; Kelly et al., 2006; Schwartz, 1971/1994; Shulman, 2015).

The preliminary or preparation phase of groupwork practice is often a neglected phase (Kurland, 2005) and it consists of thinking through and planning for everything required prior to a group having its first session. The beginning phase of work is that initial period of meeting with the members as a group and the main tasks of the worker are to help the group make connections around their shared purpose and establish ways of effective working. The third period of time is the middle phase of work and the tasks of the groupworker in this phase are primarily focused on helping the members stay focused on and working on the group purpose. The final phase of work is the ending phase. Here, the main task of the worker is to help the group continue to focus on the remaining work of the group and to begin to transition to life without the group.

Stages of group development refers to how the group as a whole changes and matures over time. One of the main jobs or central tasks for a groupworker is to help the group members work together as a collective. There are tasks and skills that the groupworker can use to help the collective become stronger, more cohesive and focused on the work that brought the members together. There are many different theories of group development that identify varying patterns of group development and contextual factors that influence development (Bennis and Shepard, 1956; Kelly and Berman-Rossi, 1999; Schiller, 1997; Tuckman, 1965; Tuckman and Jensen, 1977).

Bion (1959) and Bennis and Shepard (1956) initially identified two key dynamics that emerge in groups – authority and intimacy. Groups grapple with who has power within the group and with how close they need or want to be to each other. The development of professionally facilitated groups was independently theorised by a group of social workers (Garland et al., 1965) and a psychologist (Tuckman, 1965; Tuckman and Jensen, 1977). These theorists built on the authority and intimacy themes and provided a framework for how professionally facilitated groups developed from the early formation stages through to endings or termination. The stages conceptualised by Garland et al. (1965) are known as pre-affiliation, power and control, intimacy, differentiation, and termination. Tuckman and Jensen (1977) describe forming, storming, norming and performing. Later, groupworkers such as Berman-Rossi (1993) and Gitterman and Germain (2008) articulated the differing skills required at different stages of group development. Kelly et al. (2005) later noted that, as groups develop, even the number of skills required changes.

An articulation of groupwork skills

Linguistic relativity teaches us that our language shapes the way we think. Having the concept of something is required if we want to learn to do that thing. As such, it is useful to be able to conceptualise and articulate a wide vocabulary of groupwork skill. Once we have the concept and vocabulary we can identify the skill in the actions of others and begin to learn to put that concept into action ourselves. In addition, to be skilful we must be able to use the skills with purpose. In essence, we do X so that Y happens.

This listing of groupwork skills is based on our years of teaching groupwork skills in the classroom, agencies and within placements/practice/internships and on the works of numerous authors who have influenced our thoughts about groupwork practice. These authors include Doel (2005; 2014) Gitterman and Shulman (2005), Gitterman and Germain (2008), Northen and Kurland (2001), Mullender et al. (2013), Shulman (2015), and especially Schwartz (1971[1994]).

Many of the groupwork skills are used across individuals, families, groups and communities. This is in keeping with the ideas of Schwartz who was instrumental in developing a generic vision of social work practice (Berman-Rossi, 1994). However, some of the skills are unique to groupwork practice or practice with other collectives.

In order to show the relevance to work with groups, the ending clause in each description of the skills begins with 'so that' and clearly articulates one potential hoped-for group-work outcome when using the skill. The 'so that' clause also demonstrates how a worker can put knowledge into purposive action. Based on our professional knowledge we do X, so that Y happens.

A list of skills and 'so that' clauses

- *Tuning in to group members' feelings* – preparatory empathy so that the worker is able to recognise subtle messages from group members and respond accordingly.
- *Tuning in to workers' feelings* – becoming aware of one's own emotional state so that personal feelings will not cloud work with a group or so that worker's feelings can be used if appropriate.
- *Reviewing previous session (if one occurred)* – reflecting on process and content from previous group session, so that the worker is able to help members transition into the work of the new session and keep momentum.
- *Structuring space* – making changes in the physical environment, so that group culture is supported.
- *Attending* – giving undivided attention to the individual group member and the group as a whole, so that members feel supported, heard and understood.
- *Using humour* – making jokes or funny statements that are kind, gentle, self-deprecating and well timed, so that members are put at ease and/or social bonds are made.
- *Offering a statement of the fit between members' felt need and agency mandate* – stating in user-friendly language how the group purpose is connected to both the agency's reason for existence and the problems in living that brought members to the group, so that the offer of assistance is placed within the agency context.
- *Generalising members' needs* – connecting individual members' needs/problems to others in the group and beyond, so that members realise they are 'all in the same boat'.
- *Partialising members' needs* – breaking big problems down into smaller chunks, so that problems are manageable and not as overwhelming.
- *Providing information* – giving members information relevant to their situations, so that the group as a whole and individual members can make informed decisions.
- *Reaching for feedback* – asking members for their thoughts, feelings or opinions about what is occurring within the group, so that clarity and shared understanding and meaning are established.
- *Summarising* – pulling together group content, themes, and/or process into a coherent statement, so that a new group session can pick up where it left off, or so that members develop a shared understanding before moving forward.
- *Attending to non-verbal communication* – put non-verbal communication into words, so that members feel heard and understood and veiled communication becomes explicit.
- *Inviting members to tell their stories* – using non-threatening but specific questions encourages members to share themselves, so that connections can be made.
- *Putting feelings into words* – sharing the affective portion of the messages that members may be unable to express, so that the worker comes closer to understanding the member's experience and the member can share a greater portion of what is real to them, and so that members experience empathy and learn to connect with their and others' feelings.
- *Clarifying the groupworker's role and purpose* – using jargon-free language to describe the role of the worker in the group and within the agency, so that members have clarity about authority and power and can choose to engage (or not) with informed consent.

- *Exploring differences* – pointing out divergent beliefs, views or thoughts and helping members engage with the differences, so that members learn from each other and identify new ways to think, believe or act.
- *Reaching for information* – asking what, when, how questions so that situations are understood and members see that the worker is interested in the details of their lives.
- *Challenging obstacles to group functioning* – pointing out patterns of interaction that block the work of the group and asking the group to problem-solve about the obstacle, so that group members learn problem-solving skills and focus on the work of the group.
- *Challenging the illusion of work* – pointing out when groups engage in empty meaningless conversations, so that resistance to work can be addressed and the group can return to meaningful work.
- *Focusing* – pulling the conversation or activities back to the topic or issue at hand, so that the group can continue to work and be productive.
- *Addressing the authority theme* – directly address overt and covert plays to or challenges of worker authority, so that members understand critique of the worker is allowed, the air can be cleared and ambivalence towards authority loses its potency as a block to work.
- *Pointing out similarities between members/pointing out common ground* – connecting the stories, experiences or feelings of members to one another, to foster connection, cohesion and mutual understanding.
- *Mediating* – helping sub-groups hear each other's point of view, so that problem-solving through the dialectical process can occur, or so that tenuous/strained connections can be strengthened.
- *Raising taboo subjects* – naming the topics or issues that carry stigma and are difficult for group members to bring up or discuss, so that members learn the group is a safe place to speak about difficult topics of concern.
- *Scanning* – looking around the group to observe all behaviours, so that group dynamics can be observed and group-based interventions can occur if needed.
- *Naming* – articulating unspoken or unrecognised group processes, group norms or group achievements, so that the unacknowledged becomes explicit and learning can take place or changes can be made and mutual aid can flourish.
- *Parking* – stopping or putting a hold on topics that are deflecting immediate concerns or processes, but acknowledging the topics will be picked back up later, so that immediate issues, concerns or processes can be dealt with.
- *Redirecting communication* – shifting the communication patterns so that members are speaking to the person the communication is intended for, so that meaningful dialogue can occur between group members.
- *Reflecting communication* – pointing out patterns of communication in the group, so that the group can change them if getting in the way of the work or continue if supporting the work of the group.
- *Reframing* – putting a different spin on a situation or putting actions into context, so that members can consider different points of view.
- *Sitting with silence* – patiently allowing quiet periods to occur in the group so that members may reflect.
- *Stacking* – when several people are talking or want to talk at the same time, creating an order in which they will speak, so that all members are able to speak and be heard by the group.
- *'Thinking group'* – a cognitive skill whereby the worker consistently thinks of all interactions, activities and processes as being in and part of the group, rather than of individuals, so that interventions help the group as a whole develop.

- *Gatekeeping* – bringing quiet members into the discussion, so that all voices are heard.
- *Noting multiple themes* – helping members see that, though one topic/situation may be the focus of discussion or work, several themes may be underlying discussion, so that differences are clarified and new ways of thinking emerge.
- *Pointing out the connection between the general and the specific* – helping members bring their discussion about generalities down to the level of their individual and collective experiences, so that externalising is minimised and members can work on their issues/problems/concerns.
- *Pointing out the connection between individual difficulties and public issues* – highlighting how group members' problems/issues are a case in point of larger social issues or public policies, so that collective social action becomes a possibility for the group.
- *Pointing out group endings* – highlighting the ending of the group, so that transitional aspects of groupwork can be discussed (e.g. highlighting topics to be carried over to next session or identifying other sources of support if group is coming to an end).
- *Lending a vision* – communicating messages of hope for a better future or belief that things can be different for members, so that members see the possibility for something different until they are able to believe it themselves.
- *Externalising oppressive forces* – pointing out the impact of social injustices on the lives of group members, so that internalised homophobia, sexism, racism, etc. are understood and decreased.
- *Teaching group problem-solving approaches* – explicitly explaining problem-solving steps and supporting members to work through them, so that group effectiveness is enhanced.
- *Reaching inside of silences* – using empathic understanding to state what members might be thinking or feeling in periods of silence, so that unstated communication can be brought out into the open for the group to note or work through.

Increasing our groupwork skill repertoire

Groupwork skills are learned through study, reflecting on practice, supervision, practising and further study of one's own practice. The first step is studying skill and developing a vocabulary. This chapter provides one taxonomy of groupwork skill, and there are many other taxonomies you can choose. However, increasing vocabulary is not sufficient without putting newfound vocabulary to use by applying it to practice. We find that the study of practice in detail (what was actually said and done) helps with the skill building process. Using an example of someone else's practice is a helpful first step. In Activity 12.1 and Case Study 12.4 you will find a group process and steps for analysing the skills used by the groupworker. Using the same process on other groups, especially groups you facilitate, is a good way of increasing your skill repertoire and your effective use of groupwork skill. Practice, reflection on practice and further practice will not create perfect groupwork practice as there is no such thing, but it will create the conditions for effective groupwork practice and the development of expertise. Consider the following activity and case study in the light of your reading.

Activity 12.1

The purpose of this exercise is to identify and analyse the skills that groupworkers perform as they carry out their function within the group situation.

Using the group recording provided in Case Study 12.4 below (or one from your own practice), complete the following analysis.

1. Underscore the things the worker did and said. Where a silence or lack of response was deliberate, use the margin to call attention to this as an act.
2. Number all of the acts, chronologically.
3. Create a table listing all of the acts in the left-hand column. Use the number <u>and</u> the words underlined in the record.
4. Finally, fill out the remaining columns using the categories listed below as column headings.

   a. **Response**: the act.
   b. **To whom**: the person, or persons, to whom the verbal or non-verbal response was directed.
   c. **Stimulus**: whatever the worker did or said was precipitated by some remark, or condition, or act, by a member or several, or perhaps the group as a whole. Indicate that stimulus which is most specific and closest in time to what the worker did.
   d. **Reading member(s) or group**: how did you 'read' this stimulus? What did it mean to you?
   e. **Hoped-for-immediate-response**: what did the worker hope would happen as a result of what was done or said?
   f. **Degree of connection**: what is the extent to which you think the worker connected with the members' primary message?
   g. **Reading myself**: putting yourself in the worker's shoes, state exactly what the worker was thinking or feeling in the moment. Use the 'I' voice.
   h. **Re-do**: if you were to re-do the act, what *exactly* would you do? Say the *exact* words, describe the *exact* behaviour. Don't characterise the act, e.g. 'I would offer support,' rather state the actual words, e.g. I would say: 'I can see that losing your job is very hard for you.'
   i. **Skill label**: name the skill used. If you did not re-do the original act, label the initial action. If you offered a re-do, label the new act.

(Adapted from Schwartz, 1971)

Case study 12.4

Setting: a home and hospital for the aged in the US.

Group members: all males living together on a floor within a long-term care facility. Eighty per cent of the members on the floor were white, non-Hispanic; 10 per cent were white Hispanic; and 10 per cent were African-American. The average age was 86. All members in the following session were white non-Hispanic.

The worker: a 30-year-old German-American first year social work student.

The group itself: the group was an open-ended floor group meeting for the 31 residents living on an all-male floor. The group met weekly for 1½ hours. It was designed to provide an opportunity for residents to work on problems, issues and concerns arising from institutional life and from being older persons. There was a student on the floor the year prior, but there had not been any meetings over the summer following the departure of the student. Floor groups had been in existence for only one year.

The excerpt: this was the group's fifth meeting. Present were: Mr Boxer, Mr Scher, Mr Dodge, Mr Livesey, Mr Katz, Mr Waxman, Mr Fox, Mr Palmer, Mr Schwartz and Mr Gold.

(As explained in Activity 12.1, the sections that have been underlined denote actions on the part of the social worker.)

The meeting began with the residents speaking about the recent election. The group listened and talked a bit. Mr Dodge then introduced a problem he had at breakfast, that his food did not come up very correctly. Other members in the group said we had discussed food in this group before and that nothing gets done about it. Mr Dodge said yes, nothing can be done, nobody can get to the higher ups. We are all helpless. I asked him if he felt that helplessness in other things beside the food in the hospital (1). He replied that he did. The other men joined in and said they felt helpless about everything. Mr Katz joined in and said, yes, we are very helpless; we are just here waiting for the end. Mr Dodge said yes, that's it, you just hit it right on the nose. Mr Scher then said as soon as I came into the hospital I gave up; nothing can be done. I asked him why he had given up (2). He said he was old and waiting to die. Mr Dodge then said that's what happens, some of the men just don't do anything. Others want to make the most of it and others don't. That's why nobody comes to the meetings anymore. I asked others in the group for their reaction (3). Most of them agreed that everybody has given up and very few of them haven't. Mr Gold said if I give up then I will die; I'll have lost everything. Have you seen it at lunch time – when nobody talks to one another? I said I had eaten lunch up there the last week (4). He said you know what it's like; nobody talks to one another; there is no communication here. Mr Dodge said yes, there is just apathy everywhere, and then he pointed to Mr Scher and said, look, he's given up. Mr Schwartz, who was new to the group, said to Mr Dodge that he eats lunch with Mr Scher and though Mr Scher does not say anything he enjoys eating with him. I asked for Mr Scher's reaction (5). He said he was pleased with what Mr Schwartz said. Mr Dodge then turned to Mr Waxman and said Mr Waxman, he is a foolish man – all he does is sing songs and clap his hands. Mr Waxman answered, well, some things just don't click, you know. Anything you say to me goes in one ear and out the other. I asked Mr Waxman if he was angry at Mr Dodge for saying what he said (6).

Conclusion

In this chapter we defined skill as knowledge in action. We also made the case that skilful is defined by the amount of connection between members' primary messages and what the worker says or does. We explored the importance of different types and amounts of skills used across the life of the group. Finally, we articulated a range of skills and identified some of the purposes for which the different skills may be used and we ended the chapter with an exercise that is useful in applying the concepts introduced in the chapter and for increasing skill vocabulary and repertoire.

Key points summary

- A skill is a knowledge based purposive action with the intention of influencing group process or individual behaviour.
- Being skilful is evaluated in terms of the level of connection between what the group member or group as a whole says or does and what the worker says or does.
- A central task of the groupworker is to use their skills to help the group mature over time and stay focused on the group purpose.
- Developing a vocabulary of groupwork skills allows workers to identify the skill in the actions of others and begin to learn to put that concept into action.

Suggested further reading

Berman-Rossi, T. (1993) The tasks and skills of the social worker across stages of group development. *Social Work with Groups*, 16(1–2): 69–81.

Doel, M. and Kelly, T. B. (2014) *A-Z of Groups and Groupwork*. Basingstoke: Palgrave Macmillan.

Middleman, R. and Wood, G. G. (1990) *Skills for Direct Practice in Social Work*. New York: Columbia University Press. (Especially Part III, 'Skills for Working with Groups'.)

Shulman, L. (2015) *The Skills of Helping Individuals, Families, Groups and Communities* (8th ed). Boston, MA: Cengage Learning. (Especially Chapter 5.)

13

Leadership and management skills in social work

Trish Hafford-Letchfield

Chapter objectives

By the end of this chapter you should understand:

- the roles of management and leadership in social work and their significance for providing quality and effective services;
- theories and models of leadership and their relevance for social work;
- your potential for leadership and followership and opportunities for developing your leadership qualities and skills during your social work training.

Introduction

This chapter explores concepts about management and leadership and their application to social work. Effective leadership and management are cited as the key to successfully 'transforming services' (Dougall et al., 2018) in UK government policy, and internationally. We need to continuously review and improve the way we deliver care services, despite very difficult challenging environments over time and in rapidly changing legal, economic, social and technological circumstances. Finding more effective ways of collaborating and responding to contemporary and sometimes intransigent social issues is needed. These unprecedented challenges and uncertainties have led policy makers and those responsible for commissioning, arranging and delivering services to assert that good management and leadership are essential to achieving these transformations (Tafvelin et al., 2014). As a metaphor, leadership is deeply embedded in policy discourse about care provision. This involves constant dynamic exchange of ideas and willingness to learn and experiment with leadership models, styles and skills appropriate to managing the unique settings of care. Further, leadership capabilities should be developed at every level of the workforce as well as in the community (Hafford-Letchfield et al., 2014).

Why study leadership and management in your degree

During your training, your approach to social work will engage with practice which offers choice, flexibility, person-centred and innovative support to enable service users to access services in a seamless and empowering way (DHSC, 2014). Perhaps developing leadership and management skills wasn't something you considered in social work, but being able to navigate through the complex structures, processes and culture of your own organisation, and its relationship with other providers and the communities they serve, will demand you be creative and resourceful at every level as you progress through your career. The framework for developing your practice in different contexts and organisations and your own professional leadership is described in Domains Eight and Nine of the Professional Capabilities Framework (BASW, 2018).

Leadership needs to address the sheer complexity and enormity of the world's problems, especially injustices experienced by the world's most impoverished, oppressed and vulnerable people, which can seem overwhelming and can result in pessimism inertia or compassion fatigue (Hawkins and Knox, 2014). International social work (IFSW, 2012) draws attention to the importance of learning about global patterns of social and economic injustice and to understand the world beyond our own. These are concerned with rapidly developing networks of global communication, deepening interconnected economies, expanding migration patterns, and globalisation of social work extending across national borders.

The idea of the social work leader goes back to 1986, when a social work academic (Brilliant, 1986) identified leadership as a missing ingredient in social work education. She noticed that the roots of leadership naturally emerged from her social work students' passion for direct practice. Brilliant found a resistance to taking up leadership roles because of ideological constraints, a sense of powerlessness and a general lack of status in society. Poor management practice leads to poor outcomes for service users (Laming, 2009). The case study below illustrates how trust and belief in the systems involved were undermined and raised uncomfortable questions about the responsibilities of management for the effectiveness of frontline practice and the wellbeing of those they manage. Leadership is significantly associated with the operation of power and influence and some models are privileged and preferred. This is why we need to examine leadership and management *critically* and consider alternative and subjective viewpoints when we theorise about leadership and its direct application to practice.

Case study 13.1

Sir Robert Francis's (2013) enquiry into the failures at Mid Staffordshire NHS Foundation Trust highlighted the lack of dignity and compassion in care stemming from ageism and the dehumanisation of older people highly dependent on both staff and their managers. The older people's own narratives and those of people directly caring for them were dominated by the priorities of senior management. Francis highlighted that frontline staff need to be supported in seeking out patients' needs and accounts, to actively listen and act on what they hear. This needs to happen at different levels in an organisation. Staff should be encouraged to be emotionally resilient and to create an environment where there is a positive emotional 'tone' for the delivery of care, to enable individuals to feel comfortable about raising issues that concern them and to be able to do this visibly and purposely. All staff, managers, services or organisations must be responsive to the individual nature of people's concerns (Francis, 2013).

Activity 13.1

Speaking up and out in an organisation when there is a dilemma can be very challenging but is an essential leadership skill. Reflect on this case study and identify the structures and processes available in your practice learning setting which facilitate these. Examples might include: providing opportunities for service user/carer feedback, supervision, team meetings and participating in community forums.

This chapter examines these dynamics in the different contexts you will be navigating and interacting with, and gives examples of the underlying theories driving these. We explore the contested concept of 'leadership' in social work, and as leadership is frequently associated with 'management', we discuss their similarities and differences. Secondly, we consider the cultural and environmental context for leadership and discuss theories on organisational culture in which leadership might thrive. Finally, we look at the vital role of service users in leadership practice. Recognising service users' own leadership potential embodies the very essence of social work by reflecting an approach that is participative and informed, rights and value based (Hafford-Letchfield et al., 2014).

In summary, it is important to be mindful of leadership early within your educational journey to maximise the conditions for your own leadership development. Social work leadership is about unlocking potential, eroding inequality and being aware of how the appropriate use of power can transform working relationships and services

(Hafford-Letchfield, 2014). This chapter concludes by encouraging you to reflect on your own leadership practice and to evaluate what you bring to it.

The concept of leadership in social work

Traditional language around leadership commonly refers to leading *and* being led, providing direction and guidance, and is associated with hierarchical structures (Bass, 1990). Leadership can also be about survival in competitive and progressive situations where single or small groups of specially gifted or positioned individuals lead through their moral, intellectual, interpersonal, material and political resources (Northouse, 2011). Typically, leadership styles in these situations might be described as 'transformational', 'charismatic' or 'situational' (Bass, 1990). People in leadership roles should be empowered by having sufficient room to manoeuvre or the authority to lead, alongside sufficient resources, time and support requiring effort or commitment from those being led which benefits everyone. Some of the leadership typologies emerging from the literature are summarised in Table 13.1.

Table 13.1   Leadership typologies

Approach	Description
Transactional	Transactional leaders build on trait, behaviourist and contingency theories and pay attention to all the necessary and critical management functions, such as clarifying the roles and tasks and allocating work through the exchange of rewards and sanctions. They adhere to organisational policies, values and vision, are strong on planning, resource management and meeting schedules, but do not cope well with major change or managing the change process.
Charismatic	Charismatic leaders create the impetus for change and have a motivating effect upon others. They create a grand idealised vision and unify people towards that vision by fostering conditions of high trust.
Transformational	Transformational leaders inspire change and innovation (the opposite of transactional leaders) because they deal mainly with abstract and intangible concepts like vision and change. Key attributes are: showing concern for others, approachability, integrity, charisma, intellectual ability and an ability to communicate, set direction and manage change.

Hafford-Letchfield et al. (2009, p32)

Traditionally, the knowledge base in social work has derived from a range of social science subjects, applied eclectically to practice, which is also true of its leadership. Social theory informs our understanding of social problems, social policy enables us to define the role and policy purpose of social work, and management and leadership provide an understanding of how the organisation, management and leadership of practice occur (Lawler and Bilson, 2010).

Many types of leadership activities in care settings are shaped by bureau-professional paradigms which stem from neoliberal policy and reform. Known as 'new public management' (Heffernan, 2006), the principles of marketisation, competition and as a result, much outsourcing of care services, have imported business models and goal-oriented performance in social work. This is a globalised phenomenon with emphasis on constructing and evaluating measures to specify what social work actually does (Hafford-Letchfield, 2009). In recent decades, several crisis points, following service failures, resulted in wider public engagement and debate on the very nature and role of social work in the context of these powerful external influences (Munro, 2011; Narey, 2014; Croisby-Appleby, 2014). Professional autonomy, such as the right to speak out, has been a casualty of the managerial revolution that has sought – on the basis of no real evidence – to portray social work as a 'failing profession' in need of reform (Lambley, 2011). These have not necessarily increased the efficiency and effectiveness of social work organisations and the conditions for practice (Munro, 2011), but have led to more defensive practice (Lawlor and Bilson, 2010). Leadership roles therefore need to promote the softer values of human service organisations and systems change (Healy, 2002; Hafford-Letchfield et al., 2014). In response we are re-introducing more person-centred and community-based legislation and policies, such as the Care Act 2014. These attempt to move away from command and control or heroic leadership styles towards fostering learning cultures that influence the promotion of prevention and strengths-based practice (King's Fund, 2011; Munro, 2011). Adopting a dispersed or distributed leadership style should give people within the service and its providers the confidence to challenge poor practice. Distributed or participatory leadership is most akin to a collaborative approach to social work and seeks to share power and work in the most democratic way. Leadership is not associated with a specific position but is an attribute that arises in different individuals throughout the organisation. Distributed leadership focuses on leadership practice rather than roles. These leadership practices occur when those in authoritative and subordinate positions interact with each other (Hafford-Letchfield et al., 2014).

> **Case study 13.2**
>
> A large provider of care homes for older people wanted to make their service accessible to the needs of older Lesbian, Gay, Bisexual and Transgender (LGBT) people. They know that training is important but is a short-term measure. They engaged LGBT members of the community to come in and discuss issues with their managers and staff. The LGBT community advisors visited the care homes and gave feedback on a regular basis over six months. This helped the care home to develop an action plan, some good relationships and a reputation for inclusiveness in the meantime (Willis et al., 2018).

Management in social work

You may have recognised that there are strong links between leadership and management, often embodied in the term 'leader-manager' (Hafford-Letchfield, 2009), which

demands a mix of analytic and personal skills in order to set out a clear vision of the future and defining a strategy to get there. It requires communicating that to others and ensuring that the skills are assembled to achieve it. It also involves handling and balancing the conflicts of interests that will inevitably arise, both within the organisation and outside it where ... a wide variety of stakeholders will have a legitimate interest.

(The King's Fund, 2011, p12)

Given some of the challenges described so far, leaders require considerable management skills to marshal both human and technical resources to achieve the organisation's goals, and ensuring the administration needed is in place. However, there is a danger of over-emphasising technical knowledge, skills and dependency at the expense of the broader structural issues. Much of social work concerns discrimination, oppression and inequality within communities. Making sense of the complexity and conflict inherent in the management task, to enable greater responsiveness, innovation and challenges in delivering improving services, is a management task. Lawler (2005) talks about humanist or existential management, which reflects social work's professional value base and includes strong personal and democratic elements. This may involve shifting the power and status of service users and carers from recipients of professional wisdom and judgements, to one of co-producers and co-providers of care (Needham and Carr, 2009). Supporting staff and stakeholders to engage in these changing relationships needs appropriate engagement and negotiating skills, and of course a leadership style that buffers professionals between politicians and service users.

Appreciative Inquiry theory (AI) – for creative leadership

AI is an approach used in problem solving. It uses stories told within the system we work in to provide a creative and constant source of learning. There is an emphasis on questioning and drawing on the collective imagination and positive principles about how the future might guide the current behaviour of the organisation. The stages of AI are often abbreviated to the four Ds: **discovering**, which enthuses feeling; **dreaming**, which inspires imagination; **designing**, which invokes innovatory concepts; and **delivering**, which commits to making things happen in practice. AI has gained currency in social work because it enhances morale where participants' contribution is valued and focused on improving outcomes towards appreciative leadership (Bostock et al., 2005).

Social workers often 'become' managers without the benefits of formal training, and tend to adopt styles combining their professional expertise and practice know-how with technical knowledge and skills. They also need the capacity to identify and support organisational leadership, to manage change and to develop a healthy culture, a large part of which requires them to motivate employees to perform well in their jobs. Management skills may suit task-related issues, but motivation and organisational innovation require leadership. Some managers have learned to lead successfully based on their practice wisdom and personal experience through a practice-led approach (Sedan and Reynolds, 2003).

Research summary

Developing management skills

Empirical studies of management in social work have demonstrated:

- the importance of having a vision, promoting values of the profession. Motivating and stimulating employees, facilitating change and leadership was more inclusive and altruistic in social work than in different organisations (Hutchinson, 2000);
- that time with the leader and support from co-workers enhanced the effect of transformational leadership, essential to achieving change. Stability also enables social networks and friendships to develop between people and to enhance relational processes. Acting as a role-model involves demonstrating vision, inspiration and motivation for social workers to deal with the turbulence they may face in their day-to-day work (Tafvelin et al., 2014);
- the application of skills involves: auditing and reflecting upon our current level of skills against relevant standards or frameworks for social work; an understanding of 'what works' – what effective practice looks like; accessing frameworks useful in carrying out responsibilities in that area (e.g. models of change management) (Gallop and Hafford-Letchfield, 2014);
- that opportunities to practise skills go together with sufficient self-awareness and space for reflection on our performance with trusted feedback from others (Hafford-Letchfield et al., 2014).

Critiques of leadership and differences from management

This review of leadership and management demonstrates the complexity involved in delivering services and why we need to give attention to how we want leadership to evolve in social work and serve its unique circumstances. It is fair to say that leadership has been extensively used as a rhetorical or discursive device. O'Reilly and Reed (2010) coined the term 'leaderism' (p971), used politically to justify or redefine any tensions emerging from managerialism in the care sector and as the solution for achieving successful performance management and association with 'excellence'. This will only occur when underlying power relationships are identified, challenged and redirected.

Leadership needs followership. A difference between leadership and management is the ability of some people to get others to do things above and beyond rewarded effort, not purely dependent on sanctions, the use of power, authority and coercion. This is attributed to the followers' expression of beliefs and emotions towards certain ideas or influence over them. This influence is the essence of leadership and draws on 'emotional intelligence' (Goleman, 1996) to develop excellence in work performance. Whilst these characteristics can be used negatively, socialised leaders are motivated by a sense of responsibility and knowledge of social structures to provide empathy and response to the emotion of others. Working in social care triggers stress and anxiety, given the difficult and challenging situations faced. Goleman (1996) identified the ability to understand oneself and others, including competence in self-awareness, self-control, empathy, listening, conflict resolution and cooperation, as characteristics of someone who is emotionally intelligent. Emotional intelligence helps us to cooperate and work together within highly emotional interpersonal relationships to achieve better conditions for change. O'Reilly and Reed recognised this passion for a common goal between leaders and those being led or managed as a core function of authentic leadership. Ford and Lawler (2007) similarly stress the conflation of management and leadership in blurring the relational aspects of leadership and how this might develop beyond the confines of management relationships. They highlight the importance of existentialist and social constructionist thinking into the leadership debate. These promote ongoing and relational acts between people to enable more meaningful and constructive ways for leaders and followers to relate and work together and encompass new forms of intellectual and emotional meaning (p415).

Activity 13.2

Based on what you have read so far, think about the evidence of management and leadership in your own practice experience. What positive and negative role models have you noticed?

You may reflect on levels of trust within your team, the clarity of communication and how clear people's roles are on a day-to-day basis.

Finally, what structures are in place for consultation and encouraging people's ideas, and how is conflict managed and supported?

The cultural context for leadership and organisational theories

So far we have signposted how leaders and managers think about the organisational culture, the nature of their services and some of the external and internal factors that influence how leadership is fostered, developed and supported.

Every organisation has four cultures; the one that is written down, the one that most people believe exists; the one that people wished existed and finally, the one that the organisation really needs.

(NHS Chief Executive, cited in DoH, 2005, p1)

Organisational theorists associate strong unified cultures with commercial success in relation to quality and performance. Many aspects of culture are intangible and difficult to see. Cultures may be multidimensional, concerned with traditions, shared beliefs and expectations of organisational life, such as ways in which people interact and perform. These are all powerful determinants of individual and group behaviour. Some negative aspects of culture result in communication failure, leading to mistakes, challenges and serious incidents as seen in our first case study.

Whether culture can be manipulated or engineered to reflect an organisation's value system remains contested. Systems theory is a useful paradigm for thinking about the interdependency of organisations through its alliances and partnerships. Visible features of healthy cultures for social workers may involve peer support and relationships with service users. Put simply, culture is learned, shared and transmitted through a combination of assumptions, values, symbols, languages and behaviours that manifest as the organisation's norms and values (Hafford-Letchfield, 2009). Although there may be several sub-cultures flourishing, the cultural network is the primary informal means of communication. French and Bell (1995) likened this network to an iceberg. What you see above the surface constitutes the formal organisation, structure, spans of control, rules and procedures and job descriptions. Below the surface, however, lies the informal and invisible organisation made up of grapevines, informal leaders, group norms and sentiments, emotional feelings, needs and relationships. Therefore, cultivating leadership styles to shape organisational culture should model sound philosophy, vision and management styles where staff feel valued and rewarded (Hafford-Letchfield, 2014).

Research summary

Sub-cultures in complex organisations

Scott et al. (2003) identified three types of sub-cultures and their organisational functionality.

- **Enhancing cultures**: representing an organisational enclave in which members hold core values more fervent or amplified than the dominant culture, e.g. specialist, expert teams and centres of excellence.
- **Orthogonal cultures**: an enclave that tacitly accepts the dominant culture of the organisation while simultaneously espousing its own professional values, e.g. clinicians within an integrated service who prioritise their own professional knowledge.
- **Counter cultures**: an enclave espousing values that directly challenge the dominant culture, e.g. resistance by specialists or disciplines to broader management diktats or the limitations of professional freedom as a result of overzealous management.

Service users and leadership practice

It is inconceivable to imagine that leadership can evolve without the active participation of service users. The challenge is to use a variety of organisational and strategic frameworks to embed user and carer participation, both formally and informally, into the fabric of practice. Wright et al. (2006, p8) define participation as service users' involvement in decisions about their own lives, as well as collective involvement in matters which affect them. This requires a culture of listening which enables users to influence both decisions about the services they receive as individuals on a day-to-day basis, and how services are developed and delivered for all. Participation is not an isolated activity, but a process by which users are empowered and supported to influence change within an organisation and by directly leading in policy and service development. It is not judged on any hierarchy and should offer different levels of participation for different groups of users and at different stages of policy and service development.

Research case study

A national study looked at mental health service users' experiences of targeted violence and hostility and how these were aligned with adult safeguarding practice. The team was led by service users who co-designed the study with academics and practitioners. They were trained to conduct research interviews with service users, to analyse the data and make recommendations. People interviewed reported that they found it much easier to speak with people with direct experience of mental health, leading to a much richer and deeper understanding of the issues (Carr et al., 2019).

Conclusion

This chapter explored concepts of management and leadership and encouraged you to think about how these are relevant to all people working in social work and social care and engage them in developing their effectiveness at a personal, team/organisational level and in the wider system through their local communities and beyond. Taking up a leadership role should enable you to constantly reflect on your core motivations, values and ethics for social work and how these impact on your approach to the role and the quality of the work that you do. Leadership and management are not tied to hierarchical roles, but, as demonstrated in the theories and examples given, are clearly embedded in everything we do. Despite these findings, we do not yet have a systematic and purposeful evaluation of leadership models and their applicability to social work research and practice (Colby Peters, 2018). Analysis of leadership theory involves making links between social work theory and practice to establish a strong foundation for a leadership model and definition that advances the mission, values and goals of social work practice and research.

In developing your own potential for leadership and followership qualities and skills during your training as a social worker, you can start by observing and paying attention to those in management and leadership roles in your placements. Through your learning and practice, you can make an active contribution to developing, implementing and evaluating the conditions and tools required and support those leading services through the behaviours required. Hopefully this chapter has provided food for thought about the different roles that leadership plays, how you might maximise your effectiveness in your practice, and, most importantly, take those subject to the systems and impact of care services with you, in the most participatory way.

Key points summary

- Leadership and followership are interrelated; their roles and processes can be embedded in everything we do in social work and are not tied to any particular role or position.
- The best way of leading is to be aware of our values and ethics and how these inform the ways in which we relate to people and how they relate to us. Being thoughtful, aware and attentive can help us embed the principles of leadership as we learn to develop our practice.

- We should take a critical approach when we talk about leadership in social work. Leadership and management can be used as rhetorical devices to steer us away from being transparent and authentic in our day-to-day practice, particularly in challenging and difficult social and economic environments. Good leaders will encourage reflection, open dialogue and enable realistic and difficult conversations to be had as well as the motivational ones.
- Start thinking about leadership early in your social work career and use yourself as an example to develop leadership potential.

Suggested further reading

Faulkner, A., Johnson, N., Kam, M. and Wonnacott, J. (2013) *Effective Supervision in a Variety of Settings: SCIE Guide 50*. London: Social Care Institute for Excellence.

Hafford-Letchfield, T., Lambley, S., Spolander, G. and Cocker, C. (2014) *Inclusive Leadership in Social Work and Social Care: Making a Difference*. Bristol: Policy Press.

Hughes, M. and Wearing, M. (2017) *Organisations and Management in Social Work* (3rd ed). London: Sage.

14

Using research in social work

Brian J. Taylor

Chapter objectives

This chapter aims to:

- clarify why social workers need research-based knowledge to inform practice;
- introduce key concepts in shaping a practice-evidence question;
- give an initial understanding of what is involved in identifying relevant research;
- explain the relevance of survey, qualitative and (quasi-)experimental research; and
- introduce key ideas in appraising research quality and synthesising research findings.

Introduction

Once upon a time if social workers were challenged, they might have answered: 'At least we are doing no harm, even if we do no good!' Or we might have argued that: 'It is just not possible to have sound evidence that social work actually works!' In this age of greater service user awareness, such arguments hold little weight. Vulnerable people have the right not to be the 'victims' of untested interventions, however well-intentioned. Society expects that social workers (often funded by tax-payers) will use the best knowledge available. Knowledge helps us to provide the best service for those in need, and helps in using public and charitable resources most effectively. As well as this moral imperative, there is now a legal dimension in the UK. Professionals claiming that a practice is accepted as proper in defending a claim for negligence now require a knowledge-based rationale for their view (Bolitho v City and Hackney Health Authority [1998]; see Taylor, 2017).

Professionals need skills in identifying, evaluating and using research. A review of social work in England (Croisdale-Appleby, 2014) emphasised the need for social workers to be 'social scientists' as an integral part of their role (Taylor, 2017). In this vein, this chapter introduces the knowledge and skills required to identify, understand and use research to inform practice. This chapter relates to the requirements of the Professional Capabilities Framework for Social Work in England (BASW, 2018). For Scotland, Wales, Northern Ireland and other countries, the relevant National Occupational Standards for social work are a useful point of reference.

This chapter considers in turn:

* shaping a practice question;
* identifying relevant research;
* understanding survey research;
* understanding qualitative research;
* understanding (quasi-)experimental research;
* understanding the principles of appraising research quality; and
* understanding research synthesis.

Each of these topics is explained in greater depth in the book *Understanding and Using Research in Social Work* (Taylor et al., 2015).

Research knowledge for practice

There are various types of knowledge that we need as social workers, including about: needs; experiences of problems and of receiving services; and the effectiveness of psycho-social interventions. Using research to inform practice is a continuing professional development task throughout a social work career:

> *Placing the client's benefits first, evidence-based practitioners adopt a process of life-long learning that involves continually specific questions of direct practical importance to clients, searching objectively and efficiently for the current best evidence relative to each question, and taking appropriate action guided by evidence.*

> (Gibbs, 2003, p6)

Research summary

In 1973 Joel Fischer published a paper questioning whether there was any evidence of the effectiveness of social casework. He was Professor of Social Work at the University of Hawai'i, USA, having previously worked as a caseworker and clinical social worker. The paper sparked a debate and critical reflection across the newly developing profession. Thereafter, Joel Fischer published extensively on the interface between science (i.e. knowledge) and social work, exploring ways of strengthening the evidence base for the profession. The reader interested in the evolution of ideas, principles and skills for evidence-based practice is referred to his monumental work (Fischer, 2009) which brings together four decades of his work, including his seminal 1973 paper.

Shaping a practice question

The starting point is to shape a question relating to practice that might be answered by research. This will become an iterative process involving reflecting on your practice situation in the light of the evidence that you find when searching (see next section).

Case study 14.1

A social work training officer had a role that included leadership for training on adult safeguarding, and managers had expressed interest in the possibility of training staff in family work in adult safeguarding. Preliminary scoping of databases indicated that the broad conceptualisation of 'adult safeguarding' (which includes mental health, disability and elder care social work in the UK) did not exist in most countries, so it was necessary to *narrow* this concept to 'elder abuse' (on which there were many publications) for a manageable review. Conversely the topic of family group conferencing produced little literature, so this was *broadened* to working with families generally. The final search concepts (omitting synonyms and truncations, etc.) were (Kirk, 2019):

[family work] AND [elder abuse OR adult safegarding] AND [older people]

In essence, you create a series of concepts, each of which is an essential element for your topic. When searching a computerised database for publications, you join these concepts with 'AND'. Synonyms for the same concept (for the purposes of this search) are joined by 'OR' within the brackets for that concept, as illustrated.

Activity 14.1

Search concepts

- Identify an aspect of social work where knowledge might improve practice.
- Define each concept for a piece of research to be relevant.
- Use this search to find relevant articles on SCOPUS database, using the structure: [Concept One] AND [Concept Two] AND [Concept Three].

Identifying relevant research

Primary reports of research are usually published as articles in journals. In order to find relevant articles, there are databases which compile the abstracts (summaries) of articles and classify them with 'index terms'.

Some databases useful in social work

- *SCOPUS*: currently the largest database, covering all subjects.
- *Medline*: a large database focusing on medicine, and including child welfare, mental health, addictions and care of older people.
- *PsycInfo*: a large database focusing on psychology; useful for psycho-social constructs such as *self-esteem, resilience, stress*, etc.
- *CINAHL*: focusing on nursing and allied health topics.
- *Social Science Citation Index*.
- *Applied Social Sciences Index & Abstracts (ASSIA)*.
- *Social Services Abstracts*.
- *Social Care Online*: provided by the UK Social Care Institute for Excellence.
- *Social Work Abstracts*.

(For further information about databases see Taylor, 2015, pp47–48.)

There are now various studies on effective database searching for social work (Stevenson et al., 2016), as well as on how World Wide Web search engines compare with bibliographic databases (Bates et al., 2017). Searches for relevant literature normally cover publications across the world as we can often learn from practice elsewhere, although the legal and cultural context should be considered (Palinkas and Soydan, 2012).

Articles in journals include theory papers, policy papers, ideological papers, book reviews and editorials as well as research papers, which are our focus. Amongst the research papers, there may be many research designs. We focus here on three basic research designs and the corresponding research questions for which they are suited:

- surveys;
- qualitative studies; and
- (quasi-)experimental studies.

Understanding the purpose of different designs is fundamental to appraising research quality, and we discuss these three design types in turn.

Understanding survey research: prevalence and correlation

Surveys typically use questionnaires sent out by post, or increasingly by email or administered online. A survey design may also use data gathered from case files or a client database. There are two main purposes of surveys:

- to measure prevalence, i.e. how commonly something occurs within a population or group; and
- to measure correlation, i.e. whether the occurrence of one factor correlates with some other factor occurring.

For more detail see Campbell et al. (2016).

Research summary

Survey measuring prevalence

An online survey was conducted with health and social care professionals working in community dementia services regarding risk communication (Taylor et al., 2018). Of 270 staff, there were 70 complete and 55 partial responses (about 20 per cent were social workers).

- 86 per cent reported using numeric information in practice.
- Participants' numeric estimates of verbal terms for likelihood (such as 'very common', 'common', 'uncommon', 'rare', 'very rare') were widely variable.
- The risks most commonly encountered were (in rank order): falls, depression, poor personal hygiene, medicines mismanagement, leaving home unsupervised, financial mismanagement, malnutrition, swallowing difficulties, abuse from others, risks to others, home accidents and refusing equipment.
- Respondents generally over-estimated the likelihood of serious harmful events by approximately ten-fold (having a missing person's report filed with the police; having a fall resulting in hospitalisation) and by approximately double (being involved in a car accident; causing a home fire), with wide variation between respondents.

Research summary

Survey demonstrating correlation

A survey of suicidal ideation and behaviour amongst young people (age 16 to 21 years) leaving state care by a Senior Social Work Practitioner used data from 164 case files in 16+ teams in the authority (Hamilton et al., 2015). Data were extracted by the social workers using a standard data collection tool.

- 27 per cent of the young people engaged in self-harm or suicidal behaviour.
- There was a strong correlation between the number of self-harm incidents and the number of suicide attempts.
- Risk factors correlating with self-harm and suicidal behaviour were: male; unemployed; alcohol and drug misuse; adverse childhood experiences; higher number of placement moves; and older age when entering care.

Understanding qualitative research: perspectives and constructs

There are two main purposes of qualitative studies:

- to understand the perspectives of people (e.g. service users, family members, providers of services) about a situation that they have experienced (e.g. needs, receipt of services, providing services); and
- to create a conceptualisation, model or understanding of how a psycho-social situation (such as a family, a care environment or the relationship between social worker and client) operates.

For more detail see Campbell et al. (2016).

Research summary

Qualitative research of perspectives

This qualitative study of older people's understandings of elder abuse used data from eight focus groups involving 58 people aged over 65 years across the island of Ireland. Increasing lack of respect within society was experienced as abusive. The vulnerability of older people to abuse was perceived as relating to the need for help and support, where standing up for themselves might have repercussions for the person's health or safety. Emotional abusiveness was viewed as underpinning all forms of abuse, and as influencing

(Continued)

(Continued)

its experienced severity. Respondents' views as to whether an action was abusive required an understanding of intent; some actions that professionals might view as abusive were regarded as acceptable if they were in the older person's best interests. Preventing abuse requires a wide-ranging approach including re-building respect for older people within society. Procedures to prevent elder abuse need to take into account the emotional impact of family relationships and intent, not just a description of behaviours that have occurred (Taylor et al., 2014; https://www.tandfonline.com/doi/full/10.1080/08946566.2013.795881).

Research summary

Qualitative research to create a model

Risk management systems in health and social care need to take into account the conceptual frameworks of professionals. This grounded theory study used data from 19 focus groups and nine semi-structured interviews (99 staff in total) to explore perspectives on risk in the long-term care of older people. Focus group participants and interviewees comprised social workers, care managers, consultant geriatricians, general medical practitioners, community nurses, occupational therapists, home care managers and hospital discharge support staff. Social work and health care professionals conceptualised risk and its management according to six paradigms that appeared to be in a state of reciprocal tension: (1) *identifying and meeting needs*, (2) *minimising situational hazards*, (3) *protecting this individual and others*, (4) *balancing benefits and harms*, (5) *accounting for resources and priorities* and (6) *wariness of lurking conflicts*. Each conceptualisation of risk had its sphere of relevance, and inconsistencies at the boundaries of this. Professionals used the conceptualisation that was most appropriate for the situation, changing to another conceptualisation when more useful. The translation into practice of risk management strategies needs to address the complex practice issues facing health and social care professionals (Taylor, 2006).

Understanding (quasi-)experimental research: effectiveness

In order to measure the effectiveness of a planned intervention, such as a social work helping process, some form of experimental or quasi-experimental study is most appropriate. (The term 'quasi-experimental' means 'like an experiment', and these are sometimes used as the requirements for a research design to be termed 'experimental' are strict.) At a basic level, we could measure the effectiveness of an intervention by measuring some relevant dimension before and after the intervention. This is known as 'pre-post testing'.

Research summary

Pre-post testing to measure effectiveness

A social work team leader was asked to measure outcomes in an aspect of day-care services so as to demonstrate whether or not there was measurable benefit to clients. The focus was participants' own perception of mental well-being after participating in a *Positive Living Programme*. Two self-report scales were used in a before-and-after study to measure change from admission until the end of the programme at 16 weeks. Across the six day centres, 51 day centre members completed measures at the start and 37 completed measures at the end. A paired-sample t-test was conducted to compare the score of each individual at the start with the score of that individual at the end. This gives a more accurate measure than comparing the average score of the group of participants at the start and at the end. There was a statistically significant decrease (improvement) in *Perceived-Stress Scale* scores from the start (*Mean* = 24.59, *SD* = 6.38) to the end of the *Programme* (*Mean* = 18.89, *SD* = 5.35), t (36) = 5.35, p <.001, (two-tailed). 'SD' refers to Standard Deviation, and means that about 68 per cent of the responses were within this 'distance' from the mean score. So at the start of the study, 68 per cent of respondents had scores between about 18 and 31. As this is a standardised scale, it is also possible to compare scores with studies on other populations. So, for example, a Harris Poll of 2,387 members of the general public in the USA gave a mean score for men of 12.1 (SD 5.9), and for women 13.7 (SD 6.6) (Cohen, 1994). The mean score for this group was approximately double the level of perceived stress of the general population on this scale. The mean decrease in the scores was 5.7. So for this group undertaking the day-care programme, the mean improvement brought them about half-way back towards the population average, so that on average they were about 50 per cent above the population mean, rather than double it. This is a large improvement for a psycho-social intervention. The eta-squared statistic (widely used to understand the effect size of health and social care interventions) was 0.44, regarded as a large effect size. The measures were effective and useful in demonstrating client outcomes in the *Positive Living Programme*. This project demonstrated the potential and value of using validated scales to measure client outcomes in a low-intensity day-care programme, encouraging the use of validated scales to measure outcomes for other social care settings (Gillespie, 2014).

However, simply measuring before and after an intervention leaves the possibility that the participants in the study may have improved even without the intervention. There may have been other factors (for example a change of family circumstance or government policy) that influenced the change. Experimental studies are where some people with the problem are assigned to receive the intervention of interest and the others do not. The change (if any) between the two groups is then compared. For more detail on the design of experimental and quasi-experimental studies (often called 'randomised controlled trials') see Taylor (2012).

Appraising research quality

Understanding the basic research design and the type of question for which it is most appropriate (as above) is the most important step in appraising research quality. There are numerous systems for quality appraisal of research. Some are for use with only one type of research design. Others have more general questions that can be applied as appropriate to a wide range of research designs, as in the example below. More detail on appraising research quality is in Taylor et al. (2015).

Research summary

Key points in quality appraisal of research

1. Is the rationale for the study adequately described?
2. Is the study design appropriate?
3. Is the sampling strategy clearly defined and justified?
4. Are ethical issues adequately addressed?
5. Is the method for data collection appropriate?
6. Are the methods used for analysing data appropriate?
7. Are the research findings adequately presented?
8. Are the research findings credible?
9. Are the discussion and conclusions justified and appropriate?
10. To what extent are the findings of the study transferable to other settings?

(Taylor et al., 2015, Appendices: QAT Quality Appraisal Tools)

Synthesising research

There are three distinct approaches to synthesising research on a topic:

- statistical meta-analysis of experimental studies to calculate mean effect size;
- meta-synthesis of qualitative studies using principles of qualitative research; and
- narrative synthesis of studies of various designs, focusing on key themes.

For the practical purposes of social work, narrative synthesis is achievable and useful, particularly when built on a rigorous search process to identify relevant studies, thereby creating a *systematic narrative review*.

Activity 14.2

Systematic narrative reviews

Look at the full text of a systematic narrative review such as one of those listed below. What can we learn from seeing studies 'side by side' and synthesised? In what ways do systematic narrative reviews contribute to our knowledge base?

- Protective factors for children in out-of-home home care: Zabern and Bouteyre (2018)
- Social media and mental health of young people: Best et al. (2014)
- Intimate partner violence: perpetrator perspectives on change: McGinn et al. (2020)
- Resilience and burnout in child protection social workers: McFadden et al. (2015)
- Physical disability and carer resilience: Glover et al. (2018)
- Older people and loneliness: Hagan et al. (2014)
- Older people's conceptualisation of abuse: Killick et al. (2015)
- Professional decision making on elder abuse: Killick and Taylor (2009)
- Risk communication in dementia care: Stevenson et al. (2018)
- Social worker involvement in advance care planning: Wang et al. (2018)
- Bereavement needs assessment in palliative care: Agnew et al. (2010)

Cochrane and Campbell Collaboration systematic reviews

The Cochrane Collaboration (**www.cochrane.org**) is an international, non-profit, independent organisation dedicated to making up-to-date, accurate information about the *effectiveness of health and social care* readily available through systematic reviews of rigorous studies. It was founded in 1993 and involves 11,000 members and 35,000 supporters from 130 countries.

The Campbell Collaboration (**www.campbellcollaboration.org**) is similar, founded in 1999, and focuses on informing people of the effects of interventions in crime and justice, education, international development and social welfare. The methods are parallel to those of the Cochrane Collaboration.

There are over 100 reviews in the Cochrane Library of interventions relevant to social work. Some require post-qualifying training (for example in cognitive behavioural therapy or systemic family therapy). Some might be commissioned by social workers; for example in residential or day-care you might employ a sessional worker for art therapy, exercise, music therapy, massage, dance or drama therapy.

Activity 14.3

Cochrane and Campbell Collaboration systematic reviews

Look at a systematic review in the Library of the Cochrane or Campbell Collaborations, such as one listed below, or search for a topic of particular interest. What can we learn from seeing studies 'side by side' rather than individually? What types of possible bias are documented by the reviewers? How do systematic reviews of effectiveness contribute to our knowledge base?

- Home-based child development interventions: Miller et al. (2011)
- Group-based parenting training: Barlow et al. (2014)
- Interventions for self-harm in children and adolescents: Hawton et al. (2013)

(Continued)

(Continued)

- Cognitive behavioural interventions for children who have been sexually abused: Macdonald et al. (2014)
- Counselling for mental health and psycho-social problems in primary care: Bower et al. (2011)
- Collaborative care for depression and anxiety problems: Archer et al. (2012)
- Cognitive behavioural therapy versus other psycho-social treatments for schizophrenia: Jones et al. (2012)
- Family interventions for schizophrenia: Pharoah et al. (2010)
- Parent training support for intellectually disabled parents: Coren et al. (2010)
- Behavioural and cognitive behavioural interventions for outwardly directed aggressive behaviour in people with intellectual disabilities: Ali et al. (2015)
- Cognitive stimulation to improve cognitive functioning in people with dementia: Woods et al. (2012)

Service users can be involved usefully in the synthesis of research, and are involved in the Cochrane and Campbell Collaborations. Their insights may highlight the importance of certain findings for 'real life' and for the improvement of services (Hayes et al., 2012; Stevenson and Taylor, 2019).

Knowledge translation into practice

A key challenge for the social work profession is to develop a research-minded culture. Professional bodies and employers (Health and Social Care Board, 2015) have a role and responsibility in this, as well as individuals having a responsibility to use the best available knowledge to inform practice.

Activity 14.4

Knowledge translation into practice

How effective are the mechanisms for getting knowledge into practice in your organisation, such as:

- continuing professional development (training) opportunities;
- knowledge transfer systems (such as knowledge hub or emails);
- informal learning possibilities; and
- general research-mindedness of the working culture?

Conclusions

With the World Wide Web, there are now many opportunities to access information, including research. This vast amount of information makes it more important than ever that professionals are able to identify relevant materials; discern quality; and synthesise studies to form a coherent message to inform practice. This requires individual commitment, but also commitment by employers and professional bodies.

Key points summary

- The social work profession needs research-based knowledge to inform practice.
- Using research to inform practice involves shaping a practice-evidence question; identifying relevant research; appraising research quality; and synthesising findings.
- Employers, professional bodies and individual social workers have responsibilities to ensure that practice is based on the best knowledge available.

Suggested further reading

Campbell, A., Taylor, B. J. and McGlade, A. (2016) *Research Design in Social Work: Qualitative and Quantitative Methods*. London: Sage. This readable book explains in detail how to carry out research using qualitative and survey designs.

The Social Care Institute for Excellence (SCIE) (**https://www.scie.org.uk**) improves the lives of people by co-producing, sharing and supporting the use of the best available knowledge and evidence about what works in practice in England, Wales and Northern Ireland.

Taylor, B. J. (2017) *Decision Making, Assessment and Risk in Social Work* (3rd ed). London: Sage. This readable book includes a chapter on using knowledge to inform professional judgement and a chapter on legal perspectives on reasonable decisions.

Taylor, B. J., Killick, C. and McGlade, A. (2015) *Understanding and Using Research in Social Work*. London: Sage. This readable book teaches in detail the 'how to' of the key points in this chapter, including: shaping a practice question; identifying relevant research; appraising research quality; and synthesising study findings.

15

Looking after yourself as a social worker

Jo Finch

Chapter objectives

The aims of this chapter are:

- to examine how social workers can effectively look after their health and wellbeing, given the demands and challenges of practice;
- to explore what stress and burnout are and the damaging and adverse impact they can have on us, our practice, and service users;
- to highlight the importance of assertiveness in prioritising our own health and wellbeing and developing a work-life balance.

Introduction

Social work is a very stressful occupation, not least because of the daily exposure to human suffering and distress, working in organisations that are subject to intense political surveillance and inspection regimes, and the constant state of change. Social work is also a much maligned and misunderstood profession, often seen as failing in terms of either removing children from their parents inappropriately, as in Cleveland and the Orkney Isles, or else failing to spot obvious signs of abuse and neglect, resulting in children's deaths at the hands of their parents or carers (see Chapter 17). This chapter reviews research on what can exacerbate stress for social workers alongside an examination of compassion fatigue, secondary vicarious trauma and resilience. To begin, however, we explore why we need to look after ourselves as social workers.

Why is looking after ourselves important?

The question may seem obvious, but it is an important one to ask, as well as something we should remind ourselves of on a daily basis. The first answer is that we cannot do our jobs effectively, that is, contain and manage the daily stresses and challenges of practice, if our wellbeing is compromised; wellbeing in this sense meaning both physical and mental wellbeing. In other words, we cannot look after others if we cannot look after ourselves first. An obvious analogy is an airline safety demonstration, whereby passengers are advised to put on their own oxygen masks first, before helping others (Grant et al., 2014; Maclean et al., 2018). Looking after ourselves, in its widest sense, will ensure our practice is reflective, thoughtful and decision making accurate and safe. It will ensure our relationships with users of social work services are the best they can be, and that we maintain our capacity to listen to and effectively contain other people's emotional distress (Cooper, 2018). We should, of course, have due regard for ourselves, whatever occupation we are in, and it is far from selfish that we focus on our own health and wellbeing. It is important to acknowledge at the outset that there is not currently the evidence to suggest that social work is more stressful than any other caring profession (Lloyd et al., 2002) but all caring professions will inevitably contain stressful elements, in terms of the close proximity to other people's emotional and physical suffering and distress (Cooper and Lousada, 2005). Indeed, the social worker's role in any speciality should be the promotion of the wellbeing of others, and as such we must also promote our own wellbeing and that of our colleagues. Stevenson (2014), writing in the context of promoting wellbeing in early years settings, argues that practitioners much recognise how essential their own wellbeing is, if they are to be able to form bonds with children (or young people and adults) that are personal as well as professional. Clearly, service users will be impacted by high staff sickness levels, as well as staff whose conduct is impacted adversely by suffering from stress. The chapter now goes on to explore how significant an issue workplace stress is, both in general terms and within social work in the UK.

The extent of the problem

The CIPD (2018), in their annual report of health and wellbeing at work, noted that in the public sector, mental ill health, followed by stress, is the main reason for long-term sickness absence, with mental ill health the reason cited for the most short-term sickness absenteeism. The same report also noted an increase in stress related absences across a number of professions. Similarly, the Health and Safety Executive (HSE), on their website, report that 11 million days are lost at work due to stress and, indeed, employers have a legal duty to protect workers from stress. Research commissioned by the British Association of Social Workers (BASW) in 2018 found that working conditions of social workers overall are poor (compared with other comparative professions) and are 'adding to high levels of stress, presentism, job dissatisfaction and intentions to leave both the current job and the social work profession as a whole' (Ravallier and Boichat, 2018, p5). Nonetheless, it is not all doom and gloom, as the research on stress and wellbeing more generally focuses on what can help, which will be discussed later on in this chapter. The discussion for now, however, considers what stress and burnout are.

What are stress and burnout?

Stress is a normal part of everyday life; indeed it can be essential for getting up in the morning and for completing everyday tasks, or indeed helps us to finish a last minute task. Stress describes the physiological process of hormone release when a person experiences a shock or a threat, i.e. the fight or flight response, originally identified by Selye (1955). Selye (1975) later identifies different types of stress: eustress – which is related to situations when stress enhances functioning; stress which is a reaction; and a stressor which is something that causes distress, i.e. when stress continues unresolved and can lead to negative outcomes. Stress, therefore, is more than a physiological reaction; indeed, Maslach et al. (1996) described stress as the emotional as well as physiological reactions to stressors. Stress is defined by the HSE (2007) as the 'adverse reaction a person has to excessive pressure or other types of demand on them' and the Mental Health Foundation defines stress as 'the degree to which you feel overwhelmed or unable to cope as a result of pressures that are unmanageable' (2018).

The term burnout is used to describe the process whereby the worker becomes cynical and disengaged. In other words, they may fail to respond professionally to other people's distress and concerns. Maslach and Leiter (1997) describe this very evocatively. They argue that burnout has occurred in a worker when they experience

> the dislocation between what people are and what they have to do, it represents an erosion in values, dignity, spirit and will – an erosion of the human soul. It is a malady that spreads gradually and continuously over time, putting people into a downward spiral from which it is hard to recover ...

> (1997, p17)

Croucher (2010) argues further that a burned out worker may display detached behaviours, is likely to be exhausted, with motivation and drive severely impaired, and may feel an overwhelming sense of helplessness and hopelessness.

Activity 15.1

Stress and impact

Consider the following questions before reading the next section.

1. Have you worked with someone who you felt was suffering from stress?
2. What behaviours did they exhibit?
3. What was the impact of your colleague's stress on you and others around them?
4. What was the impact on service users?

The impact of stress

Long-term exposure to acute stress can have significant implications for the health and wellbeing of individuals and cause a range of short-term physical health issues, such as stomach aches, headaches, and skin complaints, as well as longer term health issues. Indeed, medical research has found that long-term exposure to stress is a contributory factor in the development of metabolic syndrome, which is a risk factor for the development of type two diabetes (Chandola et al., 2006), cardiovascular disease (Rosengren et al., 2004) and stroke, angina, coronary heart disease and hypertension (McEwen, 2008). There are also the poor health outcomes associated with maladaptive stress related behaviours, i.e. excessive consumption of alcohol, smoking or risk-taking activity.

Stress can therefore impact on us in three distinct ways: physiological, emotional and behavioural. It is worth noting that stress impacts on us in different ways at different times. Some common physiological reactions to stress can include: aches and pains, headaches, muscle tension, exhaustion, sleep disturbances, indigestion, hair loss, disturbance of normal bodily functions, and exacerbation of skin problems, such as eczema or psoriasis to name but a few (Maclean, 2011).

In terms of the emotional impact of chronic stress, feelings we might normally manage easily become overwhelming. Therefore normal everyday feelings, for example, frustration, being miserable, feeling tense, angry, anxious and under pressure may become exacerbated, all of which in turn can impact on our wellbeing both physically and emotionally. It can become a difficult vicious cycle to break out of and, in turn, may lead us to engage in certain behaviours to manage the physical and emotional effects. It is easy therefore to use particular coping strategies, which may work in the short term, but add to the cycle of adverse physiological and emotional impacts. For example, feeling overwhelmed with work tasks may hinder sleep, which makes us tired and exhausted during the day, which may make us increase caffeine intake, which may then, in turn, impact on quality of sleep. Similarly, we may respond to stress by over- or under-eating, which may impact on stomach complaints, which may then impact on future food choices.

Whilst we may not have control over our workloads, or other organisational pressures, it is important to stress that what we do have a choice about is how we appropriately respond to these pressures. The first step, therefore, in managing stress is to ensure our behavioural responses to the issue at hand are positive rather than negative. So, avoiding the more obvious negative response, such as increasing alcohol consumption, additional caffeine intake and indeed excessive consumption of chocolate!

Activity 15.2

Stress

Identify the physical and emotional symptoms you experience when under stress and consider the positive and negative behaviours you engage in as a result.

Vicarious trauma and secondary traumatic stress

The term vicarious trauma or secondary traumatic stress refers to the stress caused by being in close contact with other people experiencing trauma. Figley (1995) defines it as:

> *the natural, consequent behaviours and emotions resulting from knowledge about a traumatising event experienced by a significant other. It is the stress resulting from helping or wanting to help a traumatised suffering person.*

(1995, p10)

Chrestman (1999) argues that symptoms of secondary traumatic stress (STS) can mirror those of people suffering from post-traumatic stress disorder (PTSD) and could include intrusion, avoidance and arousal behaviours and reactions (Figley, 1995). Intrusion refers to re-experiencing the traumatic event, through dreams, flashbacks or intrusive thoughts (Bride, 2007). Avoidance concerns avoiding any stimuli or situation that may provoke memories of the traumatic event. This may include avoidance of particular people or space, or avoidance of thinking about the traumatic event, resulting in some instances in memory loss of the event (Townsend, 2018). Arousal symptoms can include anxiety, irritability, anger, hypervigilance and difficulties falling or staying asleep (Newell and MacNeil, 2011). Bride (2007), in an American study of 282 social workers, found that almost 98 per cent of the people they worked with had experienced trauma and their interventions focused on supporting service users with trauma. Bride (2007) found that the majority of social workers in the sample experienced low levels of STS symptoms, whereas a small number were showing severe symptoms of STS. Bride (2007) concludes from the findings that, independent of any other trauma that social workers may directly experience, the rate of PTSD in social workers due to indirect exposure to trauma is twice that of the general population. The chapter now goes on to explore compassion fatigue.

Compassion fatigue

The term compassion fatigue is often used interchangeably with the terms burnout, vicarious trauma and STS as discussed previously. Indeed, the interchangeability of terms in use in the literature is noted by Kapoulitsas and Corcoran (2015). Whilst there may be subtle nuances between the differing terms used, the term compassion fatigue may be a more appropriate, and perhaps less pathologising and medicalising term to use in social work contexts. Essentially, therefore, compassion fatigue refers to the response associated with the exposure to other people's stress and trauma; it can affect an individual's emotional wellbeing, and importantly can be accumulative, i.e. the adverse impacts can build up slowly and over time. Therefore practitioners must be vigilant and self-aware, as will be explored later on in this chapter.

> ### Case study 15.1
>
> Juliet has been a social worker for 15 years. She has worked in child safeguarding and now works in the Looked After Children team. You have noticed her cynical approach to the work, to change in policies and procedures and an increasing tendency to make negative comments about the children and young people she is working with. In the context of your reading so far, consider what might be happening and why.

What factors contribute to stress and burnout in social work?

There can be a range of external factors that contribute to social workers' stress and burnout as well as a person's individual capacities, or resilience, to manage the demands of social work. It is important to consider both environmental and individual issues. As discussed earlier, being in close proximity to other people's trauma or stress may be a contributory factor to social workers experiencing stress, and indeed secondary trauma.

> ### Research summary
>
> A study by Gibson et al. (1989), focusing on occupational stress in a sample of 176 Northern Ireland social workers (which also included managers), found that whilst social work staff felt positive about their roles and social work in general, many reported that they felt a significant amount of work-based stress. Stressors included: too little time to undertake work, with associated feelings of not being able to meet their own expectations, pressures of external deadlines, a lack of agency in influencing decisions particularly around resourcing, and lacking a sense of personal accomplishment. The study utilised two standardised schedules, the General Health Questionnaire (Goldberg, 1978) and Maslach Burnout Inventory (Maslach and Jackson, 1981). The study found that one third of social workers reported psychiatric morbidity, which includes somatic symptoms, anxiety and insomnia, social dysfunction and severe depression. The study found this was higher than teachers and nurses (who were also included in the study), and the general population of Northern Ireland. In terms of the burnout inventory, less than the norm were experiencing burnout. It was disappointing to note that, in this study, supervision was reported as not being effective in ameliorating workplace stress. Given the study took place in 1989, the impact of the Northern Ireland Troubles might have also played a potential part in the findings.

More general research on workplace stress found that stress increases when workers have high demands coupled with low control in their working lives (Langer, 1983). A systematic review of stress by Coyle et al. (2005) amongst mental health social workers found that contributory factors to workers feeling stressed included role conflict, role ambiguity and fulfilling statutory responsibilities. Stress increased when workers felt a lack of achievement, high workload and not feeling valued as an employee. The HSE management standards identified six areas that can impact on employees experiencing stress (Health and Safety Executive, date unknown, [a]).These include:

- **Demands**. This refers to workload, work patterns and the general environment.
- **Control**. The extent to which employees feel they have control (or agency) over their work.
- **Support**. This includes encouragement, sponsorship and resources provided by the organisation, as well as from the line manager and colleagues.
- **Relationships**. This includes promoting positive relationships within organisations and working to avoid conflict, as well as managing behaviour from employees that might be considered unacceptable.
- **Role**. This concerns the extent to which people understand their roles in an organisation and how the organisation ensures employees do not have conflicting roles.
- **Change**. This concerns the way that organisational change is managed and communicated within the organisation.

As can be seen, public sector organisations, by their very nature, will inevitably be in constant flux and change, not least due to austerity, and, because of austerity (not least the closing of support services) demands on services have inevitably risen and so workloads will be demanding. Further, the role of the social worker has always been a challenging one, not least the perennial role conflict between care and control.

What factors mitigate against stress and burnout in social work?

As stated at the outset of this chapter, this is not intended to put anyone off becoming a social worker. It is a stressful job, but research from across professions and disciplines evidences a range of organisational and individual practices that help support practitioners to effectively manage the day-to-day stresses and challenges of the job. There are two competing theories or approaches about managing and dealing with stress (Lazarus and Folkman, 1984). The first one is known as vigilant coping, in other words active coping or finding solutions to address or remove the initial cause of the stress, and emotion focused coping. Emotion focused coping involves approaches which try to find ways of more successfully or positively managing emotional distress (Carver et al., 1989). In terms of the first approach, one strategy concerns support in the workplace (as identified in the HSE six management standards discussed earlier). The Health and Safety Executive (date unknown [b]) has produced a useful guide in the appendix of a report (pp62–64) about positive management responses to the six areas that can cause stress in employees. It also details negative management responses that can exacerbate stress. This is useful in itself, i.e. perhaps one can assess the responses of those in authority around them (including practice educators) as well as use it as a reflective guide to consider one's own response to service users and colleagues.

Activity 15.3 (with one worked example)

Having knowledge of what can potentially cause stress in workplaces is useful and the following asks you to reflect on these areas. Consider the worked example and add your own thoughts to the other fields.

Table 15.1 Stress in the workplace

Potential work place stressor	Currently on my social work programme, placement, or as an NQSW or SWer on a scale of 1–10 1 = negative 10 = very positive	What can I do to manage this? Positive strategies and coping skills?
Demands – this refers to workload, work patterns and the general environment.	*It is very busy, as I am managing my placement and my university work. Currently at number 2. I feel quite overwhelmed at times.*	*I am organised and I have prioritised completing my mid-way portfolio. I have a week off and will focus on my course work. I know this is time limited.*
Control – the extent to which employees feel they have control (or agency) over their work.		
Support – this includes encouragement, sponsorship and resources provided by the organisation, as well as from the line manager and colleagues.		
Relationships – this includes promoting positive relationships within organisations and working to avoid conflict, as well as managing behaviour from employees that might be considered unacceptable.		
Role – this concerns the extent to which people understand their roles in an organisation and how the organisation ensures employees do not have conflicting roles.		
Change – this concerns the way that organisational change is managed and communicated within the organisation.		

Collins (2008) identifies a number of what he termed 'positive focused coping strategies' (2008, p1177) which can be usefully employed. These include planning, suppression of competing activities, restraint and seeking out social support. Colleagues may also be a primary source of support for social workers (Gibson, 1998; Smith and Nursten, 1998; Thompson et al., 1996; Um and Harrison, 1998). Linked to support within the work place is the protective impact of supervision (Lloyd et al., 2002; Collins, 2015). Lloyd et al. (2002) noted further that high workload was manageable if support levels were high. Indeed, research by Wilkins et al. (2018) argued that there was evidence to support the claim that good supervision can help individual social workers to improve their self-efficacy, confidence, resilience, retention and stress levels. A concern, however, has been raised about the purpose of supervision increasingly concerning management oversight and surveillance, rather than providing a supportive and educative function (Beddoe, 2010). Morrison (2007) identified that help seeking activities were also useful in combatting stress.

Wagaman et al. (2015) explored the extent to which social work practitioners' levels of burnout and STS would be mitigated by practitioners' skills in developing and practising empathy. The study argued that if practitioners can learn and develop their empathic skills and practise them consistently, then it will protect, to some degree, the practitioner, and will promote 'compassion satisfaction' rather than compassion fatigue. Compassion satisfaction is 'the positive feelings about people's abilities to help' (Stamm, 2010, p8).

Resilience is a concept that is often used in social work, both in terms of service users we may work with and ourselves. You will have heard the word used on your social work training course and, indeed, being resilient to the stresses and strains of social work is positive. As Grant and Kinman (2012) argue, resilience can be defined as the ability to manage and overcome stressful situations, or indeed negative life events, and 'find personal meaning in them' (2012, p605). Grant et al. (2015) therefore advise that techniques to improve self-awareness, reflective ability and developing emotional literacy were significant in helping social works develop resilience. A word of warning, however, in that the focus on individual resilience can be criticised because it locates the problem within the individual, rather than taking the structural issues into account. The next section of the chapter, therefore, focuses on employers' responsibilities.

Promoting wellbeing: employers and employees

The HSE is a governmental regulatory body which aims to reduce workplace accidents, workplace deaths, and injuries at work. They also include workplace stress as a potential workplace hazard. The HSE ensures all employers conform to various legislation and policies to ensure worker safety. Employers have a duty to promote the wellbeing of employees. The Management of Health and Safety at Work Regulations (1999) requires employers to identify what could cause stress at work and enact measures to combat stress. Health and safety at work, therefore, encompasses more than just physical risks but also risks that may cause psychological harm. As such it is worth locating your employer's (or if you are a social work student, your placement agency's) policy relating to workplace stress. Of note in these policies is that it remains your responsibility to inform your manager (or practice educator) that you are suffering from stress.

Many large organisations have in service occupational health advisors, or indeed can refer you to externally contracted occupational health advisors. Often you can make a self-referral and your manager or human resources departments do not have to be informed, but often if you require 'reasonable adjustments' in your workload and working conditions then a manager's referral is required. The important point to note is whilst organisations have duties of care to employees, employees must also raise issues that impact on their health and wellbeing. It is also important to be aware of your own organisation's policy around managing workplace stress. Of course, when you are a student social worker on placement, those employers will not view you as an employee, and so if you are impacted by stress then you must discuss this with your practice educators and university tutor. Universities also have duties of care towards their students. There has been a lot of media interest recently in how universities support students with issues around wellbeing and supporting students with mental ill health. What is clear, as a would-be professional, is that you need to be open and honest about any health or personal issues that may impact on your ability to meet the course requirements.

Self-care in action

There are lots of resources available to support you to develop and practise self-care, although a few examples are provided here. Maclean (2011) advises keeping a stress diary to check how many of the usual stress symptoms a social worker might experience in their day-to-day work. Devising a self-care action plan may also be a useful strategy, or indeed using, either individually or collectively, the self-care cards produced by Collier and Boucher (2019). There are 50 cards to choose from, including useful self-care strategies such as:

- take ten minutes to plan tomorrow's lunch;
- take a walk;
- allow yourself five minutes to day dream.

A really lovely but simple idea by Maclean (2011) is that of creating a 'Stress Aid Kit' (2011, pp122–123) – this could be individually, or a team could devise their own Stress Aid Kit. Maclean (2011) asks us to consider what we would have in such a kit. For example, some music, treats, positive photographs or images.

Key points summary

- There are a number of international studies that focus on stress, burnout, compassion fatigue, vicarious trauma and STS experienced by social workers.
- Social work can be considered a stressful occupation, like many other caring professions in direct contact with distressed and vulnerable people.
- The importance of being alert to stress symptoms is clear, as well as engaging in positive coping strategies rather than negative coping behaviours which will only cause further physical harm and tend to exacerbate stress.

(Continued)

(Continued)

- Whilst employers have legal responsibilities, it is important we also take responsibility for managing our health and wellbeing. In other words, a proactive response in managing our wellbeing is necessary in social work. Devising a self-care plan, therefore, and engaging in positive self-care activities, rather than behaviours that can cause harm in the long term, is an absolute must.

Suggested further reading

Maclean, S. (2011) *The Social Work Pocket Guide to Stress and Burnout*. Litchfield: Kirwin Maclean Associates.

Grise-Owens, E., Miller, J. J. and Eaves, M. (eds) (2016) *The A-to-Z Self Care Handbook for Social Workers and Other Helping Professionals*. Harrisburg: The New Social Worker Press.

Collier, K. and Boucher, S. (2019) *50 Acts of Professional Self Care for Social Workers*. Litchfield: Kirwin Maclean Associates and Self Care Psychology.

Grant, L. and Kinman, G. (eds) (2014) *Developing Resilience for Social Work Practice*. London: Palgrave Macmillan.

Useful resources

The HSE have produced a useful stress checklist covering the six key areas that can contribute to work place stress: **http://www.hse.gov.uk/stress/standards/pdfs/indicatortool.pdf**

The HSE have produced a talking toolkit with managers in mind, but this is nonetheless a useful resource for thinking about how our own stress may impact adversely on those we work with: **https://www.hse.gov.uk/stress/assets/docs/stress-talking-toolkit.pdf**

16

Creative skills for social workers

Jonathan Parker

Chapter objectives

By the end of this chapter you should be able to:

- describe different creative ways of working as a social worker;
- identify how these might be used sensitively to build rapport, trust and a positive working relationship;
- reflect on the most appropriate use of creative techniques – what may work well, where and under what circumstances and what may not;
- develop a plan for increasing your knowledge and skill in working creatively.

Introduction

At times it may seem that such a serious profession as social work, dealing as it does with people at their most vulnerable, exploited and distressed, cannot be trivialised by resorting to creativity and artistic ways of practising. However, this would be to mistake part of what makes us human; we are playful, responsive and creative (Winnicott, 1971; Parker, 2019b). So, thinking deeply about how we are to work best with our fellow human beings requires us to be adaptable, agile and creative in using what resources we can to build a positive working relationship and to stand alongside people whilst we work together on the problems of living.

As we have seen earlier in Chapters 1 and 6, UK social work, in the main, has developed a focus on safeguarding and statutory work. However, its roots also include community and youth work, groupwork (Chapter 12) and more therapeutic approaches that are more akin to continental social pedagogy where creative ways of working are championed.

Before we enter discussion of using creative approaches, we should define what we mean by creative social work, creativity and creative approaches, and creative skills for social workers. All of these terms interlink to some extent. However, creative social work differs to a degree to creative approaches as the latter concerns specific ways of working that might include creativity, arts and performance, whereas the former relates to ways that might engage social workers in their role and tasks and might enhance their experience as much as that of those with whom they work. In this chapter we will focus most of all on the creativity that social workers bring to their role and explore creative techniques. However, we will assume that being creative creates a positive space for social workers to engage with their profession and to enhance their professionalism by exploring novel and innovative ways of working (McFarlane, 2017). We are going to consider the use and development of life storybooks across the life course; with children and young people to ensure they have memories when moving into new families, and with people with dementia as a means of encouraging reminiscence.

We will consider poetry, drawing and cartooning, and photography and film. We will consider the use of theatre with young people, groups and communities who are marginalised from or feel disadvantaged within society.

Activity 16.1

Before we start considering some creative techniques that can benefit your work as a social worker, take some time to reflect on your own creativity. List all the creative things you do, whether that is writing letters or stories, playing a musical instrument, taking photographs, even decorating! Think about how some of these talents can be used creatively to form working relationships with people. If you were to use any of them, what would you need to keep in mind? Think about the need for sensitivity, respect and not patronising the people you work with. You may need to develop a 'toolbox' of resources that you keep with you as a social worker; you can also use your laptop or tablet.

Life story work: creative biographies

When I was training as a social worker there was a balance between working 'therapeutically' with individuals, working with family systems and groups, and working with wider communities to seek change in the structures that were recognised as contributing to the problems experienced by people. Today, social work is practised in a more regulated and controlled environment where the wishes of employers, driven by budgets and targets and the whim of populist reactions to social work when things go wrong, hold more sway than those of people using social work services (Lavalette, 2019). This has changed what you are taught, and to an extent what you can do as a social worker. However, it is important to remember that it is the human-to-human relationship that is most wanted and found most satisfying in working with people, and this is often assisted by creative approaches that recognise the individuality of those people.

When working with looked after young people I was introduced to using life story work and developing life story books as a way of both working together with those young people, finding our more about them and thus informing my assessments and developing positive working relationships in which the person began to make sense of their life, movements and situation. At first I used the British Association for Fostering and Adoption (BAAF) guidance by Ryan and Walker, which is still available today in a revised edition (Ryan and Walker, 2016). This book provides useful methods for forming relationships with children, developing communication and gathering and constructing information about children's lives in meaningful ways.

When I first worked with children and young people I would use flip chart paper, marker pens, coloured card and magazines, alongside a physical scrapbook that would form the life story book itself. These materials are still useful and, indeed, can act as a safe 'third object' between you and the person you are working with that allows them to explore painful aspects of their lives whilst gradually building trust with you. However, as Ryan and Walker (2016) explore in their new edition, a range of digital techniques can also be used (see also Hammond and Cooper, 2013). So, today, developing and creating videos, photo collages, soundtracks and computer drawings can all be used to help young people explore their lives, build a sense of self and enhance self-esteem.

Later, when qualified, I adapted the life story book method for use with older people with dementia, building on reminiscence groups and the biographical assessment tool reported by Johnson (1976); see also Gearing and Dant (1990). Reminiscence work can use themes or biographies depending on whether you are working with an individual, a family or a wider group of people. One useful way of encouraging memories is to use an array of prompts. These can include smells associated with the past – soaps, perfumes, lavender bags, herbs and flowers; music from different times; films and photographs; sporting events, and so forth. The use of reminiscence can be formal, aimed towards producing a set of memories, or informal and spontaneous. You will need to take your lead from the person you are working with to determine how to proceed.

If you are completing a more structured storybook with an older person, perhaps someone living with dementia, knowledge of their life history and experiences can be important. This is where a biographical assessment can help, and the genogram, ecomap and life flow chart tools set out in Parker (2017) can assist that work by engaging practically in the tasks, recapturing playfulness which, in turn, can raise self-esteem and a sense of accomplishment.

These models continue to be useful, although they have adapted considerably from the coloured pens, flip charts, letters, physical scrapbook and polaroid pictures that I originally used, to include digital media. However, the relational aspects remain. The physical effort of working together, searching for information and images and making sense of it together allows working relationships to form and memories to be elicited.

Activity 16.2

Think of your own life to date. If you were compiling a biographical account or storybook of your life, what would you include, where might you find out information, and how might some of the findings make you feel about yourself, your life and significant people within it?

Comment

Everyone will have different things to include and different reasons why, but most people will turn to family members, friends, schools, work and clubs or organisations that have been important in some way. It is important to think reflectively how this may make you feel, because if you are working with people to help them understand their lives there are likely to be instances of upset and powerful emotion, and you need to be able to deal with this.

The use of theatre and drama

It may seem strange to consider theatre or drama as something you might use in social work. However, before dismissing it as too playful, abstract and removed from the seriousness of contemporary social work, read the following section.

Family sculpting

Much of child safeguarding and childcare social work is conducted with families. Indeed, this is the context in which most children and young people live and in which we hope they will be able to live. In this area of work there are many pressures and many administrative demands to complete. However, often the mundane, quotidian demands of practice can be addressed in creative ways, using approaches that are at once playful yet focused and engaging. Imagine you are asked to undertake an assessment of the ways in which parents and children interact in a family that has been referred to you because of alleged child neglect. You have time pressures to work to and a report to construct on the ways in which the children and parents interact based on the Assessment Framework (Department of Health, 2000). How are you going to complete this? Of course, you may ask other professionals and people involved with the family for their perceptions. However, you might ask questions of the family, and that will certainly provide you with some information, but it may not help too much in developing a rapport or working relationship with members of the family. You might observe passively but again, whilst giving you some information, it may be construed as too artificial to get to the 'real' dynamics between family members in the timescales allowed. Taking a perspective from family therapy may pay more dividends. Virginia Satir, a psychiatric social worker in the US, developed an approach to working with families called 'conjoint family therapy' that involved all members of the family (Satir, 1964). From this she developed a technique termed 'family sculpting' which is used in many different family settings (Zastrow, 2009). This involved members of the family putting other members in different physical positions – higher, lower, crouching, slightly hidden – as a way of showing how each member perceived the others. Of course, this method has been criticised for seeing family relations in a systemic way in which the actions of one family member influences the action of the others and that this tends to excuse abusive behaviour. However, we are suggesting that this kind of sculpting process is very useful in non-physically or sexually abusive family situations. The following case study gives some clues as to how this might be used.

Case study 16.1

Andreas presented as a sensitive boy of 12 who was said by his parents to be timid, often alone in his bedroom and, if told he had done something minor wrong like not putting his school shirts to be washed, would often burst into tears. His parents were worried that he was not growing into a 'strong' young man. After discussing the situation, and experiences of bullying at school and when out with his peers, and his feelings that his parents expected too much of him, the social worker, Janine, asked the family if they could all work together on expectations and feelings. They agreed and Janine introduced the idea of family sculpting to them.

After some encouragement to express his feelings, Andreas placed himself on a kitchen chair with his parents below him looking up. He said he felt that he was not living up to their expectations and felt very small. This shocked his parents who, when asked to sculpt the family as Andreas stood on the chairs themselves and asked Andreas to look up to them, saying they are so proud of him and want him to fulfil his dreams. The family had never expressed these things to each other, and it allowed them to consider different ways of talking and expressing concerns. Andreas himself gained a new perspective on the way he was looked at by his parents, which began to give him a greater sense of self-worth.

Theatre of the oppressed

Taking the dramatic method a step further, we can draw on the work of Augusto Boal, a pioneer of political theatre who developed the 'theatre of the oppressed'. He considered theatre, dance and poetry to be originally freeing but rigid forms detracted from this. He called, therefore, for people in distress to change their role from spectators to *spect-actors* taking an active role in 'trespassing' on the stage and forming alternatives. In this he was claiming that all drama is a political act and that acting in this way can act as a challenge to structural oppression in community development projects. This is a legitimate forum for social workers to be involved and Boal's ideas can be employed at a range of levels.

It might be difficult for people to encourage in a full theatre of the oppressed. There are a range of different activities that can be used in building confidence and esteem, consciousness raising, encouraging peer support, expressing solidarity, experience and experiences.

Case study 16.2

Arkdale was a small community that had, over the last few years, lost their post office, had reduced public transport services and were now faced with the threat of closure of their community centre which hosted a local dramatic society, scout group, badminton society and Women's Institute, along with other community meetings. They were an ageing community and somewhat conservative in their views, but were appalled at the reduction in services they were experiencing. The community development officer, a social worker, developed with members of the community a play that considered the various positions of people and groups in the community and officials responsible for the current situation. The community play acted as a place to 'dream' a future on their preferred terms, which gave them confidence to voice their opposition to the changes and to seek ways of expressing their outrage to the local council.

Poetic inquiry as a social work method

In 2019, I was asked to speak about poetic approaches at an innovative conference on the use of performative and creative arts in higher education. This concerned using innovative methods in teaching, learning and assessment. However, the same techniques are equally applicable to social work practice and can help in collecting information, forming a positive working relationship, expressing wishes, needs and goals and allowing citizens involved in the work with you to comment on the work.

Poetic inquiry is well tested as a research tool. Poetic inquiry creates a space for unheard and marginalised voices to be heard by exposing positions between the 'researched' and 'researchers' (Görlich, 2016; Lambert, 2016; Schoone, 2017). It can construct communicative spaces across a range of diversities (Weems et al., 2009). Poetry can be used to mould reflections on research and teaching (Leavy, 2010). It has been employed in school education, such as Prendergast et al.'s (2009) research into developing *haiku* to explore high school music education, or producing new knowledge through 'educational poetics' (Gitlin, 2008). However, it need not focus on the aesthetic quality and skill of those creating the poetry. Poetic inquiry is used in health care and therapeutic settings. Day and Yallop (2009) explore the technique as a means of connecting insights in nurse education, something Galvin and Todres (2011) also used for presenting their research concerning dementia care. Pillay et al. (2017) indicated that poetic inquiry also deepens self-knowledge and recognises distinctiveness, complexity and plurality of voices – something that is very important in social work practice.

Poetic inquiry uses the writing of poetry to allow people to explore meaning and emotion about the subject in hand. The writers of poems do not need to be highly skilled but simply be able to convey what one thinks is important through poetry. The potential for reflection and meta-learning (learning about the ways and processes through which you learn) is significant. This can be useful not only with people you are working with but also for your own professional development as a social worker.

Owton's (2017) accessible and practical book on poetic inquiry is not written specifically for social workers but offers a range of advice on developing the technique for use as a therapeutic tool in a range of human service professions including social work. There are problems associated with the use of the term 'therapeutic' which need to be outlined briefly. The word refers to healing which may suggest that something is wrong or sick and therefore healing is needed. From this a person may be considered to be the source of their own problems of living, whilst in social work we would seek to avoid such conclusions. However, if we are careful to articulate our meanings in terms of the enhancement and improvement of human experience at an individual and wider social level, and if we acknowledge that people with whom we work are often distressed, hurt and upset, we can see that therapy can be a human-to-human interaction that does not demand the pathologisation of anyone.

Poetic inquiry can also be used to highlight political and structural inequalities and to give voice to seldom heard people as the following research summary shows.

Research summary

The Seldom Heard Voices project worked with young and disabled people to develop performance poetry, raising awareness amongst the public and self-esteem in those taking part. Young people were introduced to creative activities with the goal of exploring their experiences and feelings about risk and safety and their 'connectedness' to their local community. They built on the insights of earlier research suggesting that young people felt that they were not listened to or had little influence in their neighbourhoods, and participatory and arts-based approaches were employed to demonstrate the value of their social and cultural capital. Participation allowed them to develop an effective arena and process in which young people learned new skills to tell their stories (Fenge et al., 2011). The use of performance poetry was used especially with young disabled people to challenge society's perceptions about them and to gain voice (Hodges et al., 2014). This has been extended to using poetic inquiry to explore the experiences of homeless people and to give them a voice to challenge societal assumptions, whilst raising self-esteem and making the unheard heard (Fenge et al., 2018).

Activity 16.3

Haiku is a form of Japanese poetry that focuses on intensity, simplicity and form to convey deeply felt ideas and thoughts. It is only three lines in length with 17 syllables in total; five in the first line, seven in the second and five, again, in the third line.

Using this poetic form, write your own *haiku* to explain why you have chosen to study social work. This is something you can keep and look at throughout your course, reflecting on the reasons and identifying changes or underlying and fundamental motivating factors that have led you into social work.

Cartooning and drawing

Drawing is often a good way of engaging with a child or young person. It can act as both a third object and as a communicative device in the same way as creative work towards a life story book. However, it is something that can be employed with adults and older people as well. Drawing cartoons does not have to be a skilled artistic device; it can rather open opportunities to portray aspects of one's life in pictorial and comic form through which people can begin to make sense of their world and experiences and to construct plans to change and develop. Indeed, you can use stick figures to make a cartoon or even simple shapes.

Again, it is a good device to use as a student social worker to reflect on aspects of the role, your values and developing professional self. The research summary provides an example here.

Research summary

Dean (2015) asked his class to experiment using drawing to examine their perceptions of homelessness. The research highlighted that students reproduced stereotypical images reflected in the media and particular local scenes. There were many common themes and common misconceptions of homelessness. Dean analysed the approach as something that allows critical debate to develop on the basis of what was produced. His conclusions were that drawing could form part of a critical pedagogy that encourages debate and deconstruction.

Whilst Dean's (2015) research was not focused on social work we can see potential in drawing to:

1. gather information concerning beliefs and perceptions;
2. create a focus for discussion and debate;
3. generate individual and community perspectives that can identify needs for change and development.

Case study 16.3

Jaz was Nazrin's social worker. The plan for Nazrin was to work towards his adoption. His prior family experience, before being looked after from the age of four (he is now nearly seven years old), was physically and emotionally abusive. Whilst he was recognised to be a well-adjusted and bright young boy, he expressed some ambivalence about the plan for his adoption.

Jaz wanted to work with his feelings and ambivalence and to ensure that the plans were right for him before working towards a matched placement. One of the ways she did this was to draw with Nazrin and she asked if he would mind drawing his future family. When he did so he drew pictures of him crying, being shut in his room and an angry father figure alongside pictures of enjoyment, happiness and lovely sunny days out. Nazrin was able to explain these to her as feelings that he might enter a similar family situation to his birth family, and he was frightened of this but also wanted to be in a loving family. This allowed Jaz to work with him towards understanding that his safety and future were her main priority.

Of course, art therapy is recognised as a specialist psychotherapeutic means of working with distress and emotional upset and you are not training to be an art therapist. However, using these creative approaches offers another medium to use to create professional working relationships in a range of settings.

Conclusion

In this chapter we have extolled the virtues of working creatively in social work. This is important because social work, in whichever field or country that it is practised, is human focused and human beings are changeable, playful and creative and, therefore, demand an approach that is responsive to the human condition. We have explored a number of different creative ways of doing social work but have left out a wide range of artistic and creative approaches. Indeed, as a social worker you are in a unique position to use your own creativity to best help the people you are privileged to work with.

Activity 16.4

Think of the ways we have introduced biographies and storybooks, theatre and drama, poetry and drawing. Write down the various ways you might use them to improve your own practice, and to work with others. Then consider what other creative ways of working you might wish to develop and use. You should develop a plan to experiment with creative ways during your practice education, remembering it must be done sensitively and in a spirit of participation and never imposition. Think back to the first activity and amend your list if you wish and add to your developing 'toolbox'.

Key points summary

- There are many different creative ways of working as a social worker that can be adapted for working with children and young people, adults, and in reflecting on your own role. These might include life story work, drama, poetry and drawing which we have reviewed in this chapter, but could also comprise music creation and appreciation, collage and painting, and creative writing, amongst others.
- These creative techniques help to develop trust, explore painful aspects of one's life, and give voice and meaning to one's experiences.
- Creative techniques can raise awareness, self-esteem and feelings of self-worth amongst those people with whom we work.
- You can use creative techniques to reflect on your own learning and development as a beginning social worker.

Suggested further reading

Boal, A. (1979) *Theatre of the Oppressed*. London: Pluto Press.
Owton, H. (2017) *Doing Poetic Inquiry*. Basingstoke: Palgrave Macmillan.

Part Three

Social work interventions in practice

17

Social work and safeguarding children

Nancy Kelly

Chapter objectives

By the end of this chapter you should be able to:

- understand the legislative framework and practice guidance in relation to safeguarding children;
- understand the process and role of a social worker in safeguarding children in a statutory context;
- understand the concepts of significant harm, risk and threshold criteria;
- understand the role of the social worker in the assessment of children and families;
- apply your knowledge through a series of activities and case examples.

Introduction

Social work and social work practice are constantly evolving. Change is the result of a complex interplay between political, legislative and social factors; changes in knowledge based on learning from professional practice, and research and evaluation. Discourses surrounding statutory working with children and families reflect such change, with language moving through 'battered baby syndrome', non-accidental injury and child protection to the current term, safeguarding children. These changing discourses reflect the move from identifying and developing interventions with children who have been the subject of abuse to a more universal position of recognising that all children have a right to live in circumstances where their safety and wellbeing can be nurtured so that they might realise their full potential throughout the life course.

The Care Crisis Review (2018) highlighted the increasing numbers of care applications and numbers of accommodated children in England and Wales since 2013. These applications are where concerns of a local authority are such that they require a court to impose a plan and decision on where children should live in order that their welfare is best supported. The comprehensive review advocates the ideal that we are all responsible for helping families understand and deal with concerns around children's welfare and that, wherever possible, we should be developing systems that help children remain within their own networks of family and friends. The Chair of the review also proposes

moving away from an over reliance on the language of assessment and intervention and more towards understanding and helping. It's about being less adversarial, risk averse and harsh and much more collaborative and kind.

However, when the welfare of children is potentially compromised to the extent that compulsory intervention by the state is required (rather than early help which is considered in another chapter in this book), then central to all practice is the concept of risk; what are the factors that constitute risk/s to children, how do we assess those risks comprehensively and effectively, how do we develop interventions to mitigate those risks and how do we monitor whether our interventions have been effective?

This chapter explores these questions and provides you with guidance and examples of practice in relation to safeguarding children. If we are to impose what some see as 'draconian' measures to intervene in family life to varying degrees, then we have a responsibility to evidence that our decisions are sound and proportionate to the needs of children and families.

Activity 17.1

- When you first considered becoming a social worker, which group/s of people did you think was/were the primary focus of social work?
- Who were social workers working most to help?
- Where did you form this impression from?
- What did you think social workers did on a day-to-day basis in their work?

Whilst social work is much more than safeguarding children, it is likely that the first activity will have led you to thinking about (to name a few) cases of serious injury or deaths of children, historical investigations and public inquiries into child sexual abuse, investigations into abuse of children in residential care, and investigations into child sexual exploitation. Some high profile examples of these include: The Independent Inquiry into Child Sexual Abuse in the UK (IICSA) or Westminster Inquiry (ongoing), The Scottish Child Abuse Inquiry (ongoing), The Independent Inquiry into Child Sexual Exploitation in Rotherham 1997–2013 (Jay, 2014), The Victoria Climbié Inquiry Report (Laming, 2003), and The Protection of Children in England: A Progress Report (Laming, 2009) following the death of Peter Connelly (Baby P).

The legal framework for safeguarding children

The history of child care law dates back to the late sixteenth century Poor Laws, and can be charted through the development of organisations and policies designed to promote the welfare of children. As society changed there was a move from the welfare of vulnerable children being primarily undertaken by charitable and philanthropic organisations to becoming the responsibility of the welfare state. The emergence of social services departments saw the development of social work as a profession, such that agencies duty bound to seek the best developments for children deprived of a normal home life were staffed by personnel professionally trained in psychosocial sciences and aware of human development, relationships and needs. Between 1889, which saw The Prevention of Cruelty to and Protection of Children Act, and 1989, there were several Acts where local authorities were given the duty of investigating instances of abuse or risks to children. In these Acts measures were set out such that the state could intervene in order to provide families with advice, guidance and support, or in the most serious cases of risk to children local authorities could apply to the courts in order to remove children from their birth families.

In all of this legislation a balance had to be achieved between protecting the welfare of children whilst at the same time protecting the rights of children and their families to live together without interference from the state. In the 1980s there were several child abuse inquiries that raised questions about this balance. The Inquiry Reports into the deaths of Jasmine Beckford (1985), Tyra Henry (1985) and Kimberly Carlile (1987) were critical of local authority failings to protect these children, who were already known to social services. In other words local authorities should have intervened in different ways to prevent their deaths. Yet in the Cleveland Report (1988), the local authority was criticised for removing children from their families too quickly following alleged instances of sexual abuse. In other words, they should not have intervened to remove children.

It was in this context that the Children Act 1989 was developed and, despite several revisions to this Act, culminating most recently in the Children and Social Work Act 2017, it remains the case that the fundamental principles of the Children Act 1989 determine contemporary social work with children and their families (Holt, 2019; Eekelaar and Maclean, 2013).

The Children Act 1989

The Children Act 1989 was based on a guiding principle that children are best looked after by their family, with both parents playing a full part in the upbringing of their children. Subsumed under this are two further principles: the 'welfare principle' and the 'principle of non-intervention'. The welfare principle concerns the fact that the welfare of children should always be the prime consideration when making decisions about intervening into family life. Section 17 (1) of the Act states:

It shall be the duty of every local authority to:

- *Safeguard and promote the welfare of children within their area who are in need*
- *So far as is consistent with that duty to promote the level of upbringing of children by their families by providing a range of services appropriate to those children's needs.*

The principle of non-intervention is concerned with the fact that where a court becomes involved in decision making with respect to a child, it has to be satisfied that intervention is better than no intervention.

The mechanisms by which the Act were to be put into place included the duty of local authorities to promote the upbringing of children within their families, including the need for partnership working, such that children and families be included in decision making and planning about their needs and their future. Importantly, the Act also introduced the concept of 'significant harm'. This concept is a single standard for compulsory measures of care where a local authority must provide evidence to a court that a child has suffered or is likely to suffer significant harm should a decision be made to provide a care or supervision order that might include removal of a child from the family on a temporary or permanent basis.

Section 31 (2) of the Act states:

A court may only make a care order or supervision order if it is satisfied:

- *That the child concerned is suffering, or is likely to suffer, significant harm, and*
- *That the harm, or likelihood of harm is attributable to:*

    The care given to the child, or likely to be given to him if the order were not made, not being what it would be reasonable to expect a parent to give to him; or

    The child's being beyond parental control

In Section 31 (9) of the Act, harm is to mean ill treatment, impairment of health or development and where health or development should be compared with that which could be reasonably expected of a similar child.

With a care order, the responsibility for a child will be taken from the parents and given to the local authority or another appropriate adult. The child is likely to be accommodated separately from the parents or source of risk to the child, although contact may be granted. A care order will last until the child reaches 18, or it is discharged because the situation changes such that a court deems it is no longer necessary or a child becomes adopted during that time. With a supervision order, parents retain responsibility for looking after a child, but the local authority retains the statutory responsibility for making plans for the child and family and monitoring progress. Supervision orders will normally be for 12 months with a possibility to request that the order be maintained for three years.

Essentially what the Act does is require that a local authority not only provide evidence that a child has been the subject of harm, but also, for the first time, that there is a prediction that further harm may occur unless some form of intervention is implemented.

The Children Act 1989, and subsequent versions, are put into operation by practice guidance in 'Working Together' documents. The number of revisions to the original Working Together (1991) document currently stands at six, with the latest document, Working Together to Safeguard Children: Statutory Guidance on Inter-agency Working to Safeguard Children and Promote the Welfare of Children, coming into effect in 2018 (HM Government, July 2018). The changes reflect different emphases on assessment frameworks, differences in identified agencies responsible for safeguarding children, and different definitions of abuse. Working Together (2018, pp103–104) now incorporates definitions of abuse in general with reference to technological facilitated abuse: physical abuse, emotional abuse, sexual abuse, child sexual exploitation and neglect.

The document outlines who is responsible for safeguarding children, an assessment framework by which agencies should assess the needs of children and families, guidance on developing a clear analytical focus with the needs and views of children at the centre, and guidance on the monitoring and evaluation of decisions and interventions with families. Working Together to Safeguard Children (2018) continues to make it clear that there are multiple agencies responsible for the safeguarding of children, and that it is the duty of these agencies to ensure that coordinated arrangements are in place locally in order to achieve their duties. Safeguarding partners are defined in the document as: the local authority, a clinical commissioning group for an area and the chief officer of police for an area (2018, p73). In addition, documentation with regard to education states that education establishments should have Designated Safeguarding Officers (DfE 2015, updated September 2019) and safeguarding partners should ensure that arrangements are in place to allow education providers to be involved fully in any safeguarding duties. Thus social workers are required to work within their local authority but also to engage in multiagency working when making assessments or planning for children and their families.

Working Together to Safeguard Children (2018, p24) outlines the purpose of assessment as:

- to gather important information about a child and family;
- to analyse their needs and/or the nature and level of any risk and harm being suffered by the child;
- to decide whether the child is in need (Section 17 Children Act 1989) or is suffering or likely to suffer significant harm (Section 47 Children Act 1989);
- to provide support to address those needs to improve the child's outcomes and welfare and where necessary to make them safe.

Local authorities are given the responsibility of developing and publishing local protocols for dealing with cases once a child has been referred to children's social care.

Activity 17.2

Use the internet to explore local protocols for safeguarding children. (These may be found under Local Safeguarding Children Board sites for different local authorities.)

- How detailed are they?
- Do they make clear the criteria for the assessment of children and their families?

What actions do social workers undertake when a child is referred to children's social care services?

The following flow charts in the Working Together to Safeguard Children (2018) document outline the process of actions to be taken when children are referred to a local authority children's social care services.

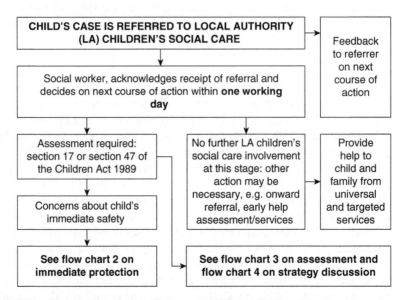

Figure 17.1   Working Together to Safeguard Children (2018, p33)

As this chart demonstrates, a social worker has one working day to make an initial decision following a referral of a child to a local authority. That decision might be that there is no necessity for further statutory involvement, in which case referrals might be made to other early help services; or that further assessment under Section 17 of the Children Act 1989 (Children in Need) or Section 47 of the Children Act 1989 (the imposition of duty to investigate with respect to concerns around significant harm) is necessary.

The assessment framework in the guidance involves three components (see Figure 17.2), so in the initial stages of information gathering and decision making the following should be considered, importantly with the child's welfare and views at the centre of deliberations: the child's developmental needs, parenting capacity and family and environmental factors.

Whilst the flow chart is prescriptive and the elements of assessment stipulated, it remains the case that a social worker must still gather and, importantly, analyse information to determine the level of risks to children. Following that, appropriate levels of support or intervention needed for the child and the family must be identified, plans drawn up and shared with multiagency partners and records kept. Within Working Together to Safeguard Children (2018) there is acknowledgement that risk can never be

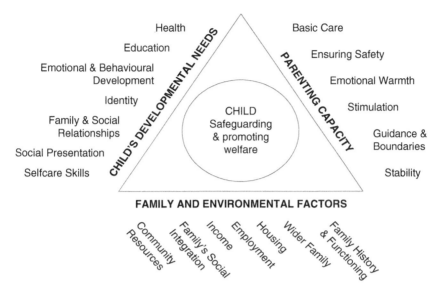

Health   Basic Care

Education   Ensuring Safety

Emotional & Behavioural Development   Emotional Warmth

Identity   Stimulation

Family & Social Relationships   Guidance & Boundaries

Social Presentation

Selfcare Skills   Stability

PARENTING CAPACITY

CHILD'S DEVELOPMENTAL NEEDS

CHILD Safeguarding & promoting welfare

FAMILY AND ENVIRONMENTAL FACTORS

Community Resources — Family's Social Integration — Income — Employment — Housing — Wider Family — Family History & Functioning

Figure 17.2 Assessment Framework, Working Together to Safeguard Children (2018, p. 28)

fully eliminated, but that social workers, their managers, supervisors and other professionals should make informed decisions, being appropriately challenged at all stages. Where there may be more than one child from the same family of concern to a local authority, social work assessments must consider the needs of individual children and not conflate them with those of their siblings.

If at this stage there are risks of immediate significant harm to a child it is the duty of the local authority, the police or the NSPCC to act immediately to secure the child's safety. This would normally involve removal of the child from the situation presenting significant risk. Where immediacy is not as urgent the local authority should convene a strategy meeting with multiagency representatives and make an application to the courts for an Emergency Protection Order, preferably having sought legal advice. These EPOs will normally last for eight days (Section 45, 1) and allow the opportunity for Section 47 investigations where social workers can meet with the child.

Following the outcome of the process in Figure 17.1, the flowchart (Figure 17.3) outlines the next stage of the assessment and action process for social workers.

In this process a social worker must carry out a multiagency assessment with the child at the centre and either create a Children in Need plan identifying any support and intervention necessary, or initiate Section 47 investigations. A social worker should meet with the child and family members and make an assessment of the situation informed by them. An assessment of the child in need will consider what works well in a family, what support may be needed and who can provide that, what the child/family agree to and what expected outcomes are. Services that may be provided range from financial assistance, day care facilities for children under five, advice and counselling, and respite care (Child Law Advice, 2019).

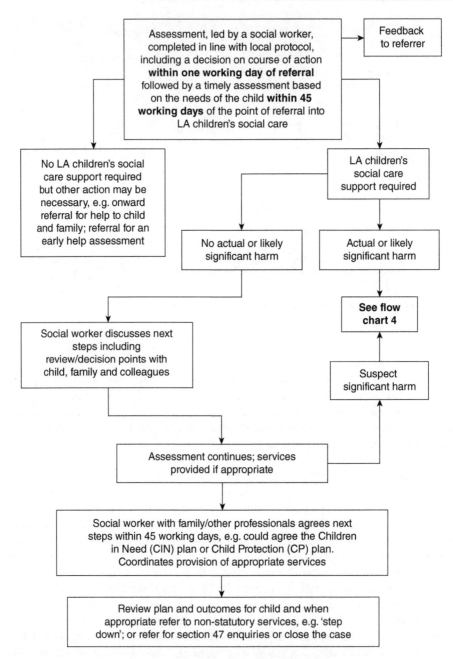

Figure 17.3   Working Together to Safeguard Children (2018, p38)

If a Section 47 investigation is required, the flowchart in Figure 17.4 indicates the process a social worker should follow after a strategy discussion.

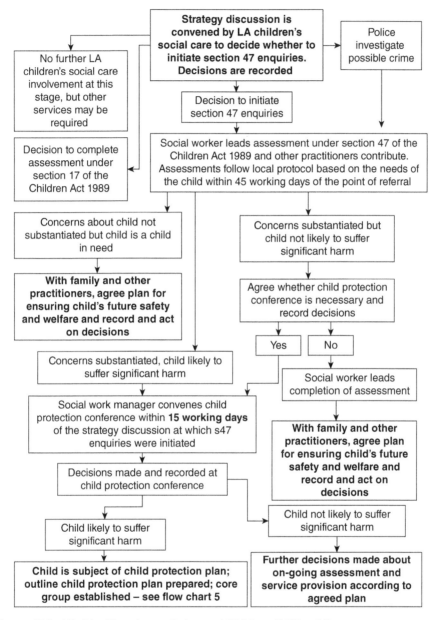

Figure 17.4 Working Together to Safeguard Children (2018, p41)

Social workers should lead the assessments in this process, and where concerns of significant harm are upheld they should convene an initial child protection conference. This multiagency conference is tasked with making decisions about a child's future safety, health and development and to make child protection plans.

These plans should be formulated with clear actions and timescales and be explicit in recording how and what needs to change in the child's life so that the health and wellbeing of the child are ensured. The conference also has a responsibility for supporting the wider family if it is in the best interests of the child. The initial child protection conference should deliberate according to the evidence as to the need for legal action, and a core group should be established to clarify plans, actions and required outcomes should plans to support the family at home be taken forward. Following the conference, a designated lead social worker is tasked with follow up actions, including continued assessment of the child and family, drawing on other professionals and agencies where necessary, ensuring plans are detailed and circulated to other safeguarding partners, coordinating reviews and progress reports on the plans at timely intervals and leading on core group activity. Child protection plans may be discontinued if a local authority deems that the child is no longer continuing or likely to suffer significant harm, or where the decision making process is stepped up to involve applications for care or supervision orders through the courts.

The welfare checklist: assessment and threshold criteria

The Children Act 1989 in s1 (3) specifies seven criteria that must be considered by a court when making decisions about children. These criteria, the 'welfare checklist' are:

1. the ascertainable wishes and feelings of the child concerned;
2. the child's physical, emotional and educational needs;
3. the likely effect on the child if circumstances changed as a result of the court's decision;
4. the child's age, sex, background and any other characteristics which will be relevant to the court's decision;
5. any harm the child has suffered or maybe at risk of suffering;
6. capability of the child's parents (or any other person the courts find relevant) to meet the child's needs;
7. the powers available to the court in the given proceedings.

As seen earlier, the assessment framework in Working Together to Safeguard Children (2018) is reflected in this welfare checklist, so assessments and evidence should be tailored by social workers around these factors. Once evidence is gathered and an analysis put before the court then 'threshold criteria' need to be met for a decision to be made to make a care or supervision order. As such, social workers must establish a threshold statement in which the facts of the case can be put forward and decisions about significant harm and the no order principle considered. In 2013 the President of the Family Division, Sir James Munby, stated that threshold statements should be concise and the court needs to

> know what the nature of the local authority case is; what the essential factual basis of the case is; what the evidence is upon which the local authority relies to establish its case; what the local authority is asking the court, and why.

There is concern that social workers and local authorities are not always clear in their threshold statements, but the basis for such a statement is at the heart of assessments with children and families. An example of a clear threshold statement by a local authority might be:

The child (five-year-old girl) has suffered significant neglect evidenced by:

- *Parent failing to take child for medical treatment deemed necessary.*
- *Child had several teeth removed due to serious dental decay.*
- *Home conditions are insanitary and present a danger to the child.*
- *Sporadic school attendance, when attending presents with inadequate clothing with a strong smell of urine.*
- *Parents do not appreciate the severity of the situation and seem unable to meet the needs of the child within timescales and given extensive support thus far.*

Activity 17.3

Consider the pros and cons of using the welfare checklist in all cases, not just those where a care or supervision order is being sought.
  Using the template above, write some evidence for threshold statements in relation to significant emotional harm, neglect, and physical harm.

If threshold criteria are met, and the parents are willing to accept that they need help and support in order to meet the child's welfare needs, then a supervision order may be granted to allow time for the family to demonstrate positive change and positive outcomes for the child. If, on the other hand, the parents dispute the evidence of significant harm or show an unwillingness to change then a care order may be considered more appropriate. In some instances, Interim Care Orders may be granted to allow for further assessment or fact finding.

Care planning and partnership working

In any case where the local authority deem that children are in need or where care or supervision orders are sought, the robust assessments of social workers should inform plans where goals can be set, interventions and support planned and implemented, and effectiveness monitored. Outcome based planning is now central in social work (Heslop and Meredith, 2019) and crucial to this is the skill of a social worker in negotiating realistic plans with all stakeholders in a case, including children and their families, and other safeguarding agencies. There have been many criticisms of social workers no longer having the time or skill to engage in partnership working or relationship based practice with families; rather risks are reduced by gathering more information with a lack of analysis. In addition, more procedural and bureaucratic approaches to decision making have become the norm (Parton, 2008; Broadhurst et al., 2010a, 2010b; Munro, 2010b, 2011; Gupta et al., 2016; Featherstone et al., 2017). However, as Howe suggests,

If you really render social work to its basics then there isn't much left other than the relationship between worker and client, practitioner and service user.

(2015, pvii, in Megele, 2015)

Holt and Kelly (2018) outline issues in relation to partnership working, but importantly identify areas of practice where relationship working with children and families has been extremely positive. See, for example, Lewis-Brooke and Bradley (2011) who report on the development of Family Intervention Projects where key workers were pivotal in building trusting relationships with families with multiple difficulties; and projects such as Family Drug and Alcohol Courts (FDAC) that demonstrate how effective working with parents can be (Harwin et al., 2014). Holt and Kelly (2019) also outline case studies where local authorities supported relational working with families and reduced the numbers of children in child protection plans or in care proceedings. The DfE Children's Social Innovation Programme supported these initiatives and as reported (Holt and Kelly, 2019) the first were Hertfordshire Family Safeguarding (Forrester et al., 2017), Leeds Family Valued (Mason et al., 2017), North East Lincolnshire: Creating Strong Communities (Rodger et al., 2017) and No Wrong Door – an example of good practice with adolescents (Lushey et al., 2017) (across North Yorkshire). Each demonstrated multidisciplinary working and clear commitment to strengths-based approaches to working with families, moving away from what had arguably become default deficit approaches.

By now you should be able to consider the issues in the following case study.

Case study 17.1

Ruth is a 25-year-old mother of two children, Bobby, aged five and Aiden, aged six months. The father of Bobby is not resident in the UK, the father of Aiden is currently living with Ruth and the two children and has been for 12 months; he is unemployed and known to have issues with drug and alcohol misuse. Ruth has support networks with her mother and grandmother who have in the past looked after the elder child for short periods of time. Ruth has a history of mental health issues and has in the past been in contact with the local authority to ask that her older child be taken into care as she is concerned that he deserves better in life than she can provide for. There is evidence that she changes her mind around this when she feels supported by her own mother. There is evidence that Ruth has been involved in domestic incidents where the police were called out and which Bobby was witness to. Ruth does not engage consistently with the social worker or other agencies and Bobby is regularly absent from school.

Activity 17.4

Assess the needs of the children and family based on the welfare checklist.

- Is this a case of child/children in need, or is there a need for child protection plans?
- What factors would need to be considered if supervision or care orders were sought?
- What evidence would need to be provided to support a threshold statement?

Key points summary

- When social workers are engaged in safeguarding children, they are bound by the Children Act 1989, and its current revision, the Children and Social Work Act 2017.
- Current practice guidance, Working Together to Safeguard Children: Statutory Guidance on Inter-agency Working to Safeguard Children and Promote the Welfare of Children (2018), outlines the processes that social workers should go through to inform decision making.
- Social workers must assess risk to children using the welfare checklist and the concept of significant harm.
- Social workers must make plans, implement them and monitor them in order to achieve objectives and outcomes that place the welfare of children at the heart.
- Best practice is achieved through partnership/relationship based working with children and their families.
- Social work with children and families is complex, requiring skills of professional judgement and decision making (with assessment and planning at the core), and skills to negotiate and build trust with children and families and to engage in effective multiagency working.

Suggested further reading

Davies, L. and Duckett, N. (2008) *Proactive Child Protection and Social Work.* London: Sage/ Learning Matters.

Featherstone, B., Morris, K. and White, S. (2014) *Re-Imagining Child Protection: Towards Humane Social Work with Families.* Bristol: Policy Press.

Heslop, P. and Meredith, C. (2019) *Social Work: From Assessment to Intervention.* London: Sage.

Holt, K. (2019) *Child Protection* (2nd ed). London: Macmillan International.

18

Social work with children and young people in need

Melanie Watts and Nick Frost

Chapter objectives

The aims of this chapter are:

- to present the legal and regulatory context of work with children in need;
- to analyse theoretical perspectives on family support;
- to explain the social work knowledge, skills and values in working with children in need;
- to critically explore research approaches and findings.

Introduction

This chapter explores social work with children in need: we identify these practices using the umbrella term 'family support'. Family support, in varying forms, has a legal mandate across the devolved nations that make up the United Kingdom. The legal mandate means that family support is central to social work practice, although people sometimes mistake 'statutory work' as applying only to safeguarding and work with looked after children and young people. We argue that family support is an important and often under-valued aspect of social work. Family support is strongly consistent with the values of social work, as it emphasises partnership work, empowerment, strengths-based and relationship-based practice. Social workers can work with families to challenge the impact of poverty and inequality (Featherstone et al., 2014). One of the authors of this chapter has argued elsewhere that family support can be embedded in the following principles:

1. Family support offers inclusive and engaging practices based on the idea of offering support to families and children who feel they require it. Family support is therefore strongly suggestive of partnership, engagement and consent.
2. Such support can be offered early in the life of the child or early in the emergence of the identified challenge facing the family. It is important that family support services can be relevant to all children and young people, and not only to younger children.
3. Family support is a proactive process which engages with the parent(s) and/or young person in a process of change. Implicit in the term 'family support' is the suggestion of bringing about change within the family network.
4. Family support attempts to prevent the emergence, or worsening, of family challenges.
5. Family support is necessarily based in a theory of change. Any family support intervention should aim to result in some desirable change, and it draws on a belief that change is achievable.
6. Family support draws on a diverse 'tool kit' of skills and approaches. It attempts to develop and encourage local, informal support networks.
7. Family support aims to generate wider social change and benefits. Such results may lead to a saving in public expenditure, a decrease in social problems, an improvement in the quality of family life or a reduction in measurable outcomes, such as the number of children coming into care.
8. Family support works with children and young people in partnership and encourages and develops their resilience (Frost et al., 2015, p151).

This chapter commences by exploring the legal mandate for family support; it then analyses some useful theories and perspectives on such work. We then explore elements of the skill set required to practice in this field. We move on to outline some approaches to research and some relevant data, which can help inform practice.

Children in need: prevalence and the legal context

Across the devolved nations of England, Scotland, Wales and Northern Ireland the legal frameworks for defining 'children in need' share some elements and are contained in the following legislation: for England, the Children Act 1989, the Children (Scotland) Act 1995, the Social Services and Wellbeing (Wales) Act 2014 and the Children (Northern Ireland) Order 1995. In England, the Children Act 1989 was designed to create a threshold for assessing and offering services to children and families who have a designated need around their health, development or education which is not otherwise being met by universal services. The law sets out a legal 'general duty' (a must comply) rule, for local authorities to safeguard and promote the welfare of children and families who are in need, or who have additional needs, including those related to disability. The concept of embedding the 'in need' powers within the Act was in recognition of the growing body of research which overwhelmingly concluded that children had better developmental outcomes when they were supported to be brought up by their families, and that difficulties in childhood or in parenting, including family breakdown, are best alleviated when early support is given to reduce such challenges (Jordan, 2012). Thus, the way services are designed should reflect this concept of ensuring that there is a range of community family support services in recognition that 'early help' can prevent the escalation of family difficulties. To reinforce our earlier point it is important to note this legislative basis for family support and for working with children in need: it therefore is statutory work, a term that is often, wrongly, reserved to describe safeguarding practice and work with looked after children.

Family support can be utilised to address a range of challenges during childhood; for example, being a young carer, coping with parent and child conflict, addressing parental mental ill health and adult use of substances. Westwood cautions that, in reality, statutory services are subject to gate-keeping through the use of thresholds and that those families with the greatest need are 'in practice those who are receiving support services but are not subject to other statutory interventions' (2014, p5).

The devolved nations of Scotland, Wales and Northern Ireland address support to families similarly. In Wales, the Social Services and Wellbeing Act 2014 uses the language of 'prevention' with an emphasis on assessing needs holistically. This seems to be less directive than the English, Northern Ireland and Scottish counterparts and it could be argued that this provides practitioners with wide parameters in their judgement about what interventions, if any, should be considered. Whilst these primary Acts contain the specific duties for 'in need', the devolved nations also adhere to wider overarching legal frameworks about the design of services to children and families. The responsibilities for nation states to provide social care interventions that are ethical and proportionate responses to human needs are enshrined in international treaties, such as the European Convention of Human Rights 1950 – enacted in English law though the Human Rights Act 1998 – and the United Nations Convention on the Rights of the Child 1989. These legal principles emphasise transparency and non-discrimination in the exercise of state powers in the endeavour to promote the upbringing of children and the provision of their education in safe and supported environments that facilitate families' opportunities to meet these needs (Jordan, 2012). Partly as a result of the United Nations (UN) Convention, family support exists in different forms across the globe (see UNICEF, 2015).

In England data is gathered through an annual 'in need' census, conducted by the Department of Education (DfE), the purpose of which is to plan and monitor trends within families and communities to assist with service design and delivery. This data provides some useful information as to who is a child in need and what the need is.

Research summary

The data reveals a correlation between poverty, social inequality and becoming 'in need', as 30 per cent of children subject to Child in Need Plans (CINP) lived in deprived areas:

Bywaters et al. (2016) conclude that there is a ten times higher rate of social care interventions for children in deprived areas compared to more well-off areas. The reason that children and young people came to the attention of social care professionals relates to domestic abuse in 49.9 per cent of cases, and child/parental mental ill health in 39.7 per cent of cases. Gender data reveals that male children and young people (54 per cent) are more likely to be in need. The largest age group subject to CINP was ten to 15 years of age (31.2 per cent) with under-fives making up 23.1 per cent. The majority of these children and families come to the attention of social workers via police referrals (27.5 per cent), followed by schools (17.7 per cent) and health service referrals (14.4 per cent) (Department of Education online). Data on indices of deprivation in Wales also show similar patterns in relation to the characteristics of children and young people in receipt of interventions (Elliott and Scourfield, 2017).

The type of services a local authority can provide may include a range of services which at the higher end includes specialist interventions, such as support to parents whose children are disabled, and providing respite care breaks to families on the brink of breaking down. Lower level services could be 'assistance in kind', such as small amounts of funding or referrals to community groups and welfare agencies where families facing short-term financial hardship can sometimes gain support to meet immediate needs for food and basic needs. In England the statutory guidance is provided by 'Working Together to Safeguard Children' (WTSC) (2018), which acts as the legal directive to all professionals and partner agencies that hold safeguarding duties on the expectations required of them. This 2018 version emphasises the importance of getting 'early help' right to prevent needs escalating and becoming child protection issues.

For the first time WTSC (2018) sets out what Firmin et al. (2016) term 'contextual safeguarding', which is an approach to safeguarding which sees the child in relation to the context of their social environment. This includes understanding the needs and risks for children and young people in informal community spaces and formal situations (school settings/social clubs) where they spend their time: these spaces are called 'extra-familial contexts' (WTSC, 2018, p15). Importantly there is, at least in England, a statutory recognition that for 'early help' services to be effective, a coordinated and multi-agency response is necessary and stakeholders are reminded that under Section 10, Children Act 2004, they have a responsibility to promote inter-agency cooperation to improve the welfare of all children. Perhaps this attempt to refocus on 'early help' presents an opportunity for social care agencies and other key stakeholders to revise their approach towards keeping families and communities safe enough for children to both grow up and thrive in (Shannon, 2019).

Working with children in need: theoretical perspectives

All high quality social work practice should be underpinned by theoretical frameworks and research findings: these will now be explored in turn in relation to family support. The range of theoretical perspectives about working with children in need available to practitioners is diverse and, arguably, overwhelming. Initially, it is necessary to explore some concepts and definitions. Work with children in need can be conceptualised as preventive work, family support, early intervention or the deployment preferred in 'Working Together to Safeguard Children' (2018), which is 'early help'. There are both nuanced and profound differences between these terms and this terminology has an impact on actual practice, depending on which of these is utilised (for an extended discussion see Frost et al., 2015). Here we prefer family support, which we argue is most consistent with social work values of partnership and working with families, but we also use the term 'early help', which is currently enshrined in English official guidance.

Relevant theories which can inform family support include attachment theory, resilience, ecological theory, restorative practice, social capital theory and social support theory. As well as theories there are ways of understanding social problems and service delivery which we can identify as 'explanatory frameworks'. For example, social structural approaches argue that social challenges (such as children in need) are caused by factors beyond the control of individuals, such as poverty, inequality and discrimination. These social structural explanations contrast with more individualised ones, perhaps drawing on psychology, which would focus more on ability to cope and interpersonal relationships.

Here we argue for a pragmatic approach in recognition of the wide range of problems faced by children in need. Children in need are likely to live in poverty and therefore we need social structural explanations of why social workers most often work with families experiencing poverty (Bywaters, 2013; Featherstone et al., 2014). However, the particular manifestation of their unique situation may include domestic violence, substance abuse, neglectful parenting and parental mental ill health, which may be amenable to more therapeutic and personalised approaches (Allen, 2011). The social worker, therefore, needs to utilise their professional expertise to draw on the theories and explanatory frameworks which are most helpful in the given, concrete situation.

Foremost amongst the explanatory frameworks utilised in this field is that which originated in the work of Pauline Hardiker (Hardiker et al., 1991), which includes the following levels:

Primary prevention – which involves universal, non-stigmatising support for families. Child benefit (before it became means-tested), playgrounds and health visiting provide examples of this intervention: they are universally accessed and do not involve any stigma for those who use such services. Such intervention provides a bedrock of a welfare state, but tends not to involve social workers.

Secondary prevention – moves nearer to direct social care involvement. The secondary level targets parents who experience the lower level of challenges, which may involve isolation, lack of parenting skills or depression. Such situations may respond well to home visiting from a third sector organisation, such as Home Start, or joining local support or drop-in groups. Local authorities have services named 'early help' or similar which work with such families: many suitable services will also be based in community centres, schools or children's centres.

Tertiary prevention – overlaps more with social work and may be provided under Section 17 of the Children Act 1989 in England. Provision is aimed at parents who face severe challenges in their parenting – including issues such as the 'toxic trio' of mental ill health, domestic violence and substance abuse. Provision can be based in local authority, or in the voluntary and community sector. Tertiary provision will sometimes involve evidence-based, manualised programmes – such as those that are promoted by the Early Intervention Foundation.

We provide an example here of how theory and differing practice approaches can be utilised.

> **Case study 18.1**
>
> Claire is a single parent with three children under eight years of age, living in social housing in a large northern city. Claire states that she is lonely and feeling depressed, and feels she is not enjoying being with the children. How can the social worker understand this situation and work appropriately with the family?

We would argue that social structural theories are helpful in understanding Claire's situation. She is living in social housing, which during recent decades has been under-invested in, and carries with it an unfortunate degree of stigma. She may be a victim of government policy which uses work as an incentive – a clear legacy of Poor Law thinking. She may live in the area of the city in which children are more likely to be subject to social care interventions (see Bywaters, 2013). These are all social structural issues that the social worker is relatively powerless when facing. However, there are actions that the social worker can take – by facilitating access for Claire to advice centres in relation to her income and housing situation, they may be able to take action through pressure groups such as professional associations and trade unions. Claire could be supported in working with universal services, such as play groups or day care. On a secondary level they could work with Claire on her parenting, and she may also benefit from working with a parenting class and/or a drop-in group. If her depression is troubling her she may decide to have help from a GP or by accessing CBT (Cognitive Behavioural Therapy).

Here we can see the social worker can use a 'toolbox' – a range of theories, approaches and techniques that are appropriate to each case in order to support families that are facing challenges.

Social work with children in need

All families depend, to some degree, on universal support provided by professionals such as midwives and health visitors and services provided by playgroups and day care centres: this is what Hardiker identifies as primary prevention. Once these services have been accessed and if the needs increase it can necessitate a referral to social care services, triggering an assessment under the parameters of children in need. The child and family can experience a range of social care interventions, including home visiting (Howard and Brooks-Gunn, 2009), direct work and coordinated working with a range of agencies, all aimed at achieving change around the issue of the health, development and welfare of the child. This work could be around reducing any harmful effects of parental behaviours on the child's daily life, improving the home environment, improving health, education or wellbeing.

Frost et al. suggest that the essence of help at this stage is good quality support to families through 'partnership work that encourages and develops their resilience' (2015, p56). As we have seen effective, theoretically informed family support work draws on traditions of a strengths-based approach, which considers how life stressors, such as a crisis in a family, can disturb the status quo and cause disruption to relationships and/or coping mechanisms. Healy writes that the purpose of social work intervention in these situations is to support the family 'to improve the fit between the individual and their social environment' (2014, p115). This is often undertaken by exploring the family networks and identifying their strengths and capacity to improve upon these. There are several social work 'tools' that aid the practitioner to facilitate change and improved coping strategies such as life stress maps, genograms and eco-maps. These are used in one-to-one, direct work sessions, with children and adults. To look at patterns of behaviour and transitional life events can provide powerful conversations about what needs to change and what the future might be (Teater, 2014). In this respect the practitioner facilitates the power of the personal network to adapt, survive and recover from personal distress and challenges that we all experience in life.

A well-researched process that can be utilised to mobilise support effectively is provided by Family Group Conferences (FGCs) (see Frost et al., 2013a, b). Whilst an FGC can be utilised across a number of practice areas (such as child protection or in domestic violence situations) we focus here on their role in family support. FGCs share most of the features of family support – a strengths-based approach, facilitating participation and operating through the mobilisation of community-based support mechanisms. The origins of FGCs are in New Zealand, in an attempt to recognise and build on the extensive reach of community support in the indigenous Maori communities. In the FGC model there are four key stages:

- The **preparation stage** is before the FGC as such when an independent coordinator contacts members of the family network, including neighbours and other significant people. The timing and venue of the FGC will be negotiated at this stage.
- At the **information stage** the relevant professionals provide information, including the strengths of the family network and the concerns that professionals may have.
- The third stage is the **private time** for the family network, to discuss the information that has been provided and to come up with a plan to address the concerns raised by the professionals.
- At the fourth phase the family **share their plan** with the professionals who accept the plan if they feel it has a chance of addressing the concerns that have been raised at the 'information stage'. The FGC may be re-convened and reviewed at a time agreed at the original meeting.

It is apparent that FGCs are a valuable part of the family support skill set. The process evidence in relation to FGCs is very positive – by process we mean the way that practice is undertaken. Many studies report that people taking part in FGCs feel valued, listened to and able to participate (see Frost et al., 2013a, b).

Outcomes studies are more mixed. Exploring Family Group Decision Making (FGDMs) in the United States context, one study found that children subject to the process were less likely to enter the care system and more likely to be placed in the family network. A Swedish study found a minimal impact in child protection cases. One of the authors of this chapter concluded a small-scale study of FGCs in England as follows:

- The FGCs require expert preparation and facilitation if they are to work well, a process which the coordinator has carried out to an excellent standard.
- The system seems to be operating effectively overall in encouraging family participation.
- Most conferences were able to draw up an action plan with clear, achievable and agreed aims. After three months, 61 out of 84 agreed action points were actually delivered.
- Participation levels at the FGCs have been high. Usually all parties have been able to make active contributions during the meeting.
- Older children have been able to contribute, including one instance where a ten-year-old led the feedback following private time.
- It is noteworthy that, in almost all cases, very articulate and helpful aunts and uncles (siblings of parents) have emerged as key carers, able to provide concrete assistance to struggling parents. Grandparents have also played a key role.
- Review meetings have been held to review the plans and check implementation and progress (Frost and Elmer, 2008).

Case study 18.2

Jenna and Ricky are parents from an Afro-Caribbean background, who have two children aged under five. They are both keen to work but cannot find appropriate employment and are therefore dependent on social benefits. The health visitor has referred Jenna and Ricky to the local family support team – she is concerned about them being isolated, their lack of parenting skills and the potential impact on the children. They have a wide family network in the area but relationships are often stressful.

Reflect on how the team could work with the parents and the children. Which theories could be useful? How should their ethnic background be taken into account?

Family support and research

Family support research studies utilise a wide range of research methods: these include qualitative, quantitative and mixed-method studies. Qualitative studies, case studies and project evaluations are dominant in the literature: there are some randomised controlled trials (RCTs) (see Bellfield et al., 2006) but these are rare in the United Kingdom, as are large-scale quantitative studies. Some researchers have adopted a 'futures methodology' to address researching the future-prevention challenge mentioned above (see the LARC studies 1–6, Easton et al., 2011). It is argued in this chapter that these debates about research methods have a direct impact on policy, funding and practice.

As we have stated, social workers have a duty to utilise research findings. There is, however, a challenge in researching family support, as research projects are attempting to research what has been prevented: this is a complex research challenge, and helps to understand why the debates already briefly outlined matter. Godar argues that research in this field can play a fundamental role in service development involving the exploration of:

- prevalence: how many children and families have a particular characteristic, or experience (e.g. number of children living with domestic violence);
- trends: is the number of children with a particular need changing over time? Are the types of needs that children experience changing?

- relationships: is there a relationship between different characteristics and needs (e.g. the correlation between parental substance misuse and domestic violence)? Where a robust statistical analysis is carried out and shows a relationship between two factors, this is called correlation;
- risk: does the presence of a particular need, or combination of needs, increase the probability of a later negative outcome (e.g. the increased risk that the children of young parents will not reach developmental milestones by the age of five) (Godar, 2013, p42)?

In this chapter we argue that family support is a human process based in the relationship between the professional and the family (see Frost et al., 2015, Chapter 8). Many studies, particularly those in the United States, focus on 'outcomes' (the measurable results of family support), which is an approach that has become embedded in the United Kingdom, through the Allen Report (2011) and organisations such as the Early Intervention Foundation. The emphasis on RCTs and outcomes has undermined a focus on the 'process' of family support, which explores the means by which professionals undertake their practice. What is required from research is a holistic approach that takes into account the wider social context and places due emphasis on both the 'outcomes' and the 'process' of family support, if we are to fully understand the complexities of family support:

> In any evaluation of family support, a balance must be struck between the demands of technically achievable, objective measures and the need to adequately represent and address the fundamental purpose of policy and practice.

> (Pinkerton and Katz, 2003, p16)

By emphasising process in this way, we also in turn place an emphasis on qualitative studies, which often provide valuable insights into how people actually experience their lives and service delivery. Qualitative studies enable us to reflect on the narrative of service users – for them to explain in their own words how they experience family support services. Such studies can adopt a range of techniques: unstructured, semi-structured and structured interviews. Sometimes surveys and also observational methods are helpful. These approaches do not necessarily have to concern themselves with the rigorous measurement of outcomes or cost-benefits in the way that quantitative studies do.

Qualitative studies often provide a direct voice for the service user. These studies are also ethically consistent with family support values, which is important, as Weiss states:

> The service delivery values and principles behind family support are challenging evaluators in many countries to experiment with different evaluation approaches and measures.

> (Weiss, 2003, pxvi)

Co-production of research projects is useful in this context. Co-production allows service users a voice in designing, delivering and disseminating research findings. As is consistent with family support values, qualitative methods allow researchers to present the feelings, experiences and perspectives of the service user and to accept these as valid narratives, without the support of statistical methods or a stance of objectivity and statistical validity. This is not an excuse for weak research methodology or design. Canavan et al.

make the case for reflective practice, informed by research, in relation to family support: 'Doing family support requires a mixture of description and questioning informed by action. It is a mixture which provides the basis for reflective practice' (2006, p17).

Conclusion

This chapter has explored social work with children in need, using the explanatory term family support. We have argued that this practice, whilst often overshadowed by safeguarding practice, is core to social work values and skills. Family support is informed by a number of theories, a range of explanatory frameworks and mobilises a wide range of skills and approaches. Family support is central to social work practice and can challenge the impact of poverty and inequality of the most disadvantaged families.

Key points summary

This chapter has:

- presented and analysed the legal and regulatory context of work with children in need;
- explored theoretical perspectives on family support;
- explained the social work knowledge, skills and values required in working with children in need;
- critically explored research approaches and findings.

Suggested further reading

Shannon, M. (2019) *Family Support for Social Care Practitioners*. London: Red Globe Press. A well-written and wide-ranging exploration of family support aimed at social care practitioners, including an exploration of adult services.

Frost, N., Abbott, S. and Race, T. (2015) *Family Support: Prevention, Early Intervention and Early Help*. Cambridge: Polity. This book explores theory, research findings and practice in relation to family support practice with children and their families.

Canavan, J., Pinkerton, J. and Dolan, P. (2016) *Understanding Family Support: Policy, Practice and Theory*. London: Jessica Kingsley Publishers. Written by a team that has influenced policy and practice across the Republic of and Northern Ireland, this book has particular emphasis on the relation between reflective practice and family support.

19

Working with unaccompanied refugee minors

Deborah Hadwin, Helen Guizani and Gurnam Singh

Chapter objectives

The aims of this chapter are:

- to explore the many challenges facing unaccompanied refugee minors (URMs);
- to develop practice interventions rooted in social work values;
- to understand how the dominant government rhetoric may impact on their lives;
- to consider practice issues, including:

  - initial engagement with a URM, specifically in relation to safeguarding and best interest decisions;
  - the care planning process, including preparation and supporting transitions to adulthood;
  - providing support for young people who have precarious futures owing to not having secured permanent settled immigration status in the UK.

Introduction

By the end of 2017, the number of forcibly displaced people around the world was estimated to be 68.5 million, 25.4 million of whom are refugees (UNHCR Global Trends, 2017). The displacement is due to persecution, conflict, violence or human rights violations and an estimated half of those are children (Hill, 2018). In 2017, the number of URMs claiming asylum alone is estimated to be 45,500, with Italy seeing the largest proportion of those applications at 9,900 (UNHCR, Global Trends, 2017). The number of URMs who made asylum applications within the UK in 2016 was 3,290 and in 2017, 2,399. Eritrea, Sudan and Vietnam were the top three countries of origin, with 71 per cent of applicants aged 16–17 years old, and 20 per cent aged 14–15. Of the applicants, 89 per cent were male (Refugee Council, 2018).

It has long been recognised that URMs experience a triple jeopardy, in that they are likely to have experienced trauma and possibly discrimination in their country of origin, on route to the UK and once in the UK (Melzak, 2005). In addition, URMs also face challenges due to uncertainty regarding their future (Chase, 2017; Chase and Sigona, 2017; Chase, 2010; Meloni and Chase, 2017; Robinson and Williams, 2015; Sirriyeh and Ní Raghallaigh, 2018).

Contemporary attitudes toward asylum seeking young people do not take place in a socio-political vacuum, and it is therefore necessary to understand negative attitudes to asylum as not simply an expression of callousness or xenophobia. Rather, they are part of a 'common sense' discourse of competitive individualism, where people who require state support are often described as 'wanting something for nothing'. People seeking asylum viewed through this lens are presented as a drain on British society and rarely as people with whom we should identify or sympathise, let alone to whom we owe an obligation (Hadwin et al., 2019).

The image of URMs presented by parts of the media can have a significant impact on the environment that young people have to navigate. The Levenson Report into press standards published in 2012, recognised that reporting in relation to ethnic minorities, immigrants and asylum seekers was 'discriminatory, sensational or unbalanced … and … is a feature of journalistic practice in parts of the press, rather than an aberration' (Leveson, 2012).

A recent example of this is a headline that stated with total conviction that a person who had arrived claiming to be a 15-year-old URM, and who was attending a school in Ipswich, was actually a 30-year-old man (Parker, 2018). As discussed later in the chapter, there is no entirely accurate way to assess age; therefore, this raises the question of how the journalist could have known that this person was 30 years old? Whilst social workers do need to be mindful that some people may present as older, which could give cause for further assessment, approximately three-quarters of URMs do not have their age disputed. However, headlines of this nature add to what Dorling (2013) suggests is a 'culture of disbelief' that these young people, who are already in a very precarious situation, need to traverse.

Although there is a popular perception driven by media moral panics that young asylum seekers intend to come to the UK at the outset of their journeys, the research evidence suggests otherwise. In 2010, the Refugee Council commissioned research which suggested that people who sought asylum in the UK had little 'choice' over their destination country. Based on first hand testimonies, the research highlighted that *the choices that asylum seekers make are rarely the outcome of a rational decision making process in which individuals have full knowledge of all the alternatives and weigh them in some conscious process designed to maximise returns.*

(Crawley, 2010)

The choices are also often shaped by the circumstances they find themselves in and with issues relating to their identity, such as age, gender and ethnicity. A third of participants that had indicated that they had been drawn to the UK due to historic ties from the colonial period, language, the presence of family and the perception that it was a safe place. However, for the largest group in the research, the decision had been made by agents and facilitators. None had detailed knowledge about the asylum system, welfare support or work (Crawley, 2010). More recently, the MedMig research on the Mediterranean migrant crisis of 2015 suggested that journeys were protracted, often dependent on a series of factors including access to education, employment, being safe and the availability of resources, not least financial, to be able to continue to find safety in another country. When people do have a destination country in mind, it is often to be united with family members already settled in that country (Crawley et al., 2016).

Activity 19.1

Given all the conflicting information coupled with the intense political interference, working with URMs presents a unique set of challenges for professionals. Think what some of these might be, write them down and keep your notes handy as you read this chapter.

Terminology

With regard to terminology, there are many different phrases used to describe children and young people under the age of 18 who arrived in a country without a parent or guardian and have sought asylum as a child in their own right. By definition, according to the United Nations Convention on Refugees, an asylum seeker is a person who has made an application for protection, but this raises the question: whose application is being processed? A person who is a refugee is someone whose asylum claim has been upheld by the government (Refugee Council, 2017). Most recently, to address the anomaly some academics advocate the term 'unaccompanied refugee minors' (Derluyn, 2018; Sirriyeh and Ní Raghallaigh, 2018). They argue that, whether or not the young person has had an asylum claim upheld, on the premise that a person does not need to be defined as a refugee by a government body, they are de facto refugees. Other definitions include 'unaccompanied migrant children' (Department for Education, 2017), 'separated children' (Matthews, 2014) and still, often within local authorities 'unaccompanied asylum seeking children'. However, this can be seen as problematic because it locates the child in relation to their immigration status first and as a minor, second. And so, when you begin working with young people, it is imperative that you understand who you are working with, as a child can be separated or unaccompanied, but may not have made a claim for asylum. Therefore, in determining this, it would be prudent to seek legal advice for the young person, so that any decision is made with the young person being independently represented. In this chapter, we are specifically concerned with young people under the age of 18 who have made an application for asylum in their own right.

Social work values

As social work practitioners, values and ethics unpinning social work practice should encourage social workers to critically reflect on their approach (HCPC, 2016; IFSW, 2014; The Policy, Ethics and Human Rights Committee, 2014). Activity 19.1 is designed to get you to think about your starting point, and what has shaped your understanding of URMs, at the outset.

Activity 19.2

Your starting point

Undertake this activity and share your thoughts with a colleague or supervisor.

1. Look up five newspaper or other mainstream media coverage of refugees and asylum seekers in the UK. What perception does that give you about these people?
2. Now look up the Refugee Council's publication 'The truth about asylum': **https://www.refugeecouncil.org.uk/policy_research/the_truth_about_asylum/the_facts_about_asylum**. In the light of this information, has your view about refugees and asylum seekers changed? If so, how and why?
3. How might this information influence your social work practice with this group of young people?

The tension in implementing the statutory elements of social work is well documented (Banks, 2012; Beckett, 2017; Horner, 2012; Pullen-Sansfaon, 2012) and sometimes referred to as 'care vs control' in that the protection and welfare of the individual is central, but also the responsibility to the wider community. Thompson (2015) suggests that being 'caught in the middle' of this dual responsibility can cause conflict and tension, though these functions don't necessarily need to be seen as incompatible opposites, as in some instances it might be necessary to exert a degree of control in order to care. Nonetheless, how the social worker recognises and responds to the statutory power invested in their role can have a fundamental impact on how the recipient of the intervention views and responds to the social worker. Power can be used either constructively to, for example, enable people to take control of their lives, or destructively in reinforcing existing disadvantage and inequalities (Thompson, 2015). And so, whilst they seek to support and advocate on behalf of people who may have been rendered powerless by institutional practices, practitioners should not forget that they are identified with the very same institutions (Horner, 2012). We suggest that this area of social work practice is one where ethical dilemmas loom large, and therefore establishing a critical reflective approach is essential in unpicking the basis of professional decision making.

New arrivals

Most URMs that enter the UK are facilitated to do so by agents who have usually been paid a fee for this exchange. This is because there are very few safe, legal routes to enter the UK, and most URMs do not meet the criteria for these schemes. Entry to the UK is usually by lorry and on occasion by plane, though more recently the UK has seen an increase in people attempting to enter the UK by crossing the English Channel on boats, prompting the UK home secretary to declare it as a 'major incident' (BBC, 2018). Trafficking is where there is a threat and ongoing coercion and control once the young person reaches the UK, whereas with facilitation, this might not be the case. Trafficking is defined within Article 4 of the European Convention Against Trafficking in Human Beings as follows:

> Any child who is recruited, transported, transferred, harboured or received for the purposes of exploitation is considered to be a trafficking victim, whether or not they have been forced or deceived.

> (Department for Education, 2017)

Most URMs will not fall into this category, and therefore there will not necessarily be the need for an immediate S47 (Child Protection) enquiry in every case. However, for those that do, the importance of early detection is crucial, and immediate safeguards need to be put in place, otherwise there is an increased risk that the young person may have disappeared within the first 24–48 hours. As an attempt to ensure that local authorities are fully accountable for all URMs who come to their attention, they now need to record a URM as 'looked after' under S20 of Children Act 1989 immediately when they come to the attention of the local authority, 'rather than only when they have been accommodated for 24 hours ... if a UASC goes missing in those first 24 hours they should always be recorded as missing from care' (Department for Education, 2018). This should, in time, ensure that local authorities have stringent procedures in place for identifying which young people might have been trafficked. The procedures need to be well known, and consistently implemented across authorities.

Apart from providing for a young person's basic needs, ensuring they have eaten and drunk, and there are no emergency health needs, the immediate assessment of whether a person has been trafficked has to be the first decision a social worker and/or immigration officer makes. Where there is a concern that someone claiming to be a child looks older, and there are also indicators of potential trafficking, the need to address the safeguarding issues around trafficking should be prioritised before undertaking further assessment in relation to age (Department for Education, 2017). Where it is determined that they are an adult, they could be signposted to specialist trafficking provision for adults.

If they are assessed to be a child, then the law is clear: they need to be immediately safeguarded. Practitioners need to look out for signs that the young person may have been trafficked. Sometimes, at the point of referral, immigration officers might state that they think this could be the case. Young people may arrive on false passports, they may arrive with adults who might not be a relative, or they may be from countries already known for high levels of trafficking, such as Vietnam, China and Albania. The London Safeguarding Trafficking Toolkit provides a framework for the identification of trafficked children and a risk assessment matrix for children who may have been trafficked (London Safeguarding Children's Board, 2011).

Where there are concerns, safety planning is imperative. Guidance about steps for social workers on how to safeguard a young person who has been trafficked is available (Harrow, 2011). Where there is a concern that a young person is the victim of trafficking, a strategy discussion should take place (Working Together, 2018). Social workers are first responders, in that they are a public body, as identified in the Modern Slavery Act 2015, and have a duty to notify the National Referral Mechanism of any potential victim of modern slavery or human trafficking they encounter. Failure to do so could result in challenge by way of a judicial review (Coram, 2017). S48 of Modern Slavery Act 2015 also states that URMs should have access to an Independent Child Trafficking Advocate, usually provided by agencies outside of local authorities. The statutory guidance by the Department for Education into the Care of Migrant Children and Child Victims of Modern Day Slavery provides further guidance as to what approach should be taken and what the assessment should include (Department for Education, 2017).

National Transfer Scheme

URMs can become the responsibility of a local authority by being found within a specific locality, though whether they remain in that area or are transferred to another local authority can be considered. From 1 July 2016, S69 of the Immigration Act 2016 allows local authorities to transfer URMs between authorities under the National Transfer Scheme. This was as an attempt to ensure that no local authority had a disproportionate percentage of URMs, compared to other local authorities who might have very few or none. If the total number of URMs in a local authority reaches 0.07 per cent of the total child population, then that local authority can request a transfer to another local authority, usually managed by regional strategic partnerships (Association of Directors of Children's Services, 2018).

The scheme has not been without difficulty, not least because it is voluntary, meaning some local authorities have never signed up and some who did originally have pulled out because they argued they were not getting properly renumerated for supporting URMs (Lepper, 2017). A local authority is supposed to assess whether or not it is in a young person's best interests to be transferred, and transfers should ideally be completed within 72 hours of the person becoming known to a local authority; however, the evidence suggests that this target was only reached once (Bolt, 2018). The updated guidance is not as clear about the timescales; however, it does state that a request for transfer can only be made after a young person's asylum claim has been registered. A decision about whether a transfer will take place should occur within two days (ADCS, 2018). In addition to delays, many transfers are now taking longer than three months. There is a lack of information sharing by the Home Office and inadequate consideration of best interests was problematic (Bolt, 2018; Refugee Children's Consortium, 2017). An independent review in relation to the S55 duty identified that there was very little consideration given to the child's best interests (Matthews, 2018). Any delay is likely to impact the process of settlement (Kohli, 2007) and potentially could disrupt the claim for asylum itself.

Case study 19.1

Ibrahim is 15 years old and originates from Iraq. He describes himself as Kurdish and his first language is Sorani. He is a practising Muslim and identifies that his religion and culture are very important to him.

As a local authority eligible to use the National Transfer Scheme, you are asked to complete a Best Interests Assessment to determine whether it would be in Ibrahim's best interests to transfer to another local authority.

If you were undertaking the assessment, what would be your key considerations?

Care planning

For all URMs, care planning is essential from the outset and as a looked after child, care planning applies to this group as it would to any child in the care of the local authority (Department for Education, 2015). Much can be done to support an unaccompanied young person to settle, whether this is in foster care or other accommodation provision and the role of foster carers can be of immense significance in this (Sirriyeh and Ní Raghallaigh, 2018; Wade et al., 2012). There is considerable evidence that living arrangements with high support correlate with decreased post traumatic symptoms while supporting the young person to feel safe, secure, less isolated and more attached (Hek et al., 2012; Hodes et al., 2008; Wade et al., 2012). A recent study by O'Higgins et al. (2018) identified that mental health varied dependent upon accommodation type, with those in foster care faring better than those in other types of accommodation provision. Young people living with other young people who shared the same ethnic background also had better mental health, and educational outcomes appeared to be better for those young people looked after in foster care.

The relationship between wellbeing and isolation is a well-established fact in social work. In relation to URMs, Rutter (2006) identified that for many URMs the 'relationship web' including friends, family, food, language, community of worship and education is lost. Rebuilding these relationships is what Kohli (2006b) describes as the act of 'regenerating' the ordinary rhythm of life. Social, familial, peer and community supports are significant resilience factors for the adaptation of war-affected children (Beirens, 2007).

As a social worker, it is important to enable young people to establish some control and exercise agency over some circumstances and decisions where they can. Some young people can present as silent and circumspect and only provide very limited accounts of who they are. Kohli (2006a; 2007) refers to these as 'thin stories' and fuller accounts as 'thick stories', which tend to be shared as the young person becomes settled and feels safe

(Passarlay and Ghouri, 2015). This is an area that could present a challenge to a worker's values, if they consider that a young person is being dishonest and therefore potentially making it difficult to trust them and build a relationship. Understanding why young people may only provide limited information or give what appears to be a scripted account in the first instance, could go some way to alleviate this. Social workers need to be sensitive to this and allow the young person's story to emerge gradually, since pushing them to talk may have the opposite effect.

The emotional wellbeing of a URM is therefore crucial in aiding their recovery and enabling them to settle in their new arrangements. Early research identified the importance of the young person's identity including the need to belong, and to preserve the young person's religious and cultural identity. Failure to do so can increase marginalisation, social exclusion and insularity (Owusu-Bempah, 2014; Small, 2000). This chimes with the need for a young person to have a sense of continuity and structure. Chase (2013) also discussed a young person's resilience and wellbeing. She identified that rather than being solely about protection from harm, having a sense of certainty and a trajectory where they could envisage a positive future was a significant factor in a young person's ability to cope, though she warns that this will become more difficult as a young person approaches adulthood (Chase, 2010; 2013).

Returning to the case study of Ibrahim, although assessing what is in Ibrahim's best interest should take place within the first few days, the assessment should consider similar areas to those required when determining Ibrahim's care plan. A social worker would need to consider how long Ibrahim has been in the care of the local authority, including whether he is making relationships and beginning to settle. As Ibrahim is a practising Muslim, other considerations when identifying a placement should be: his religious and cultural needs; in not assuming all mosques are the same, proximity to suitable places of worship, shops selling halal foods; services within the community to support him to rebuild his relationship with other people within the Kurdish community; his wishes and feelings, which, if deemed necessary, should be obtained with the support of an independent advocate.

Care planning with URMs also needs to identify appropriate care and support, trace families and determine the child's best interests in finding a durable solution. This is defined as a sustainable solution that ensures that unaccompanied children are able to develop into adulthood in an environment which will meet their needs and fulfil their rights as defined by the Convention on the Rights of the Child (O'Donnell and Kanics, 2016).

Factors supporting the role of educational attainment and social connectedness have also been explored including building networks with supportive adults and friends, and links with home culture and religion (Farmbrough, 2014). However, access to education may prove difficult, as schools may be hesitant to provide places if there is an outstanding age-related issue, but also due to the availability of school places and administrative delays. Research by the Refugee Support Network identified that not one region in the UK met its 20-day target of finding education places for all URMs within the region. It recommended that even where it is likely that young people may be transferred to another local authority, they should access education in the initial local authority, albeit some interim provision, especially if the transfer is likely to take weeks or even months (Refugee Support Network, 2018). Where URMs do have access to education, 85.3 per cent in mainstream schools, the evidence suggests they perform better than other children in care or 'children in need', and URMs who entered care younger, and lived in foster or kinship care, with fewer behaviour problems, placed in mainstream school or with fewer school changes, had higher exam scores (O'Higgins, 2018).

Case study 19.2

Fatima is 16 years old and originates from Aleppo in Syria, and belongs to a minority ethnic group. Since 2011, Syria has been engaged in a civil war which has resulted in Fatima's family being displaced, losing their home and community.

Fatima has witnessed the killing of her father and other family members, and has been exposed to significant and extreme physical and emotional violence. With the assistance of an uncle, Fatima managed to flee Syria and travel to the UK. She has witnessed abuse, death and violence on her journey to the UK.

Fatima reports that she is Muslim and her first language is Arabic. She has very limited English skills. Fatima's family remain in Syria, which she reports is causing her additional stress and anxiety. Due to her family being displaced, Fatima does not have any contact details for her family and is unable to make contact with them.

From your reading:

1.   What would you need to consider when finding a suitable placement for Fatima?
2.   When completing Fatima's care plan, what do you need to consider?

Age assessment

A further complicating factor when working with URMs is the question with regard to age. There is a significant amount of research, guidance and caselaw dedicated to this issue (Association of Directors of Children's Services, 2015; Cemlyn and Nye, 2012; Crawley and Rowlands, 2007; Department for Education, 2017; Dorling, 2013; Sauer et al., 2016) including how to complete age assessments and the considerations, dilemmas and issues faced in trying to determine something that at best will only be a likelihood, as there has not been any 100 per cent accurate way to determine a person's age. Returning to the example given earlier in the chapter, unless an age assessment had been completed, and documented evidence obtained which could be authenticated, no one would know the age of the allegedly adult male at the school in Ipswich. From the outset, the Home Office can decide that someone claiming to be a minor is an adult as stated in their age assessment guidance, 'if their physical appearance and demeanour very strongly suggests that they are significantly over 18' (Home Office, 2018, p10). In this case, the Home Office had not exercised this discretion; instead, it was the local authority who would need to undertake an age assessment.

The Merton Judgement (*R (B) v Merton London Borough Council* [2003] EWHC 1689) was the original piece of caselaw which laid the parameters for undertaking age assessment. These included that the assessment should be carried out by two experienced and trained social workers, the need to ensure fairness, the need to give reasons for the decision, the benefit of the doubt should be given, and the child had the right to be accompanied by an appropriate adult.

Although practice has developed, the issue of age assessment has remained controversial and it is likely to be the case that most URMs arrive undocumented from many countries where a systematic register of birth does not exist. Dorling (2013, p6) warns that a 'culture of disbelief' had developed over the past decade whereby

the default position taken by immigration officials and social care professionals is that the young person either does not know their age or is lying.

The intent of the 'Good Practice Guidance' was to support practitioners to understand the issues which URMs face, amongst which include trafficking, additional needs and vulnerabilities such as impact of trauma on memory, and how to ensure that assessments are caselaw compliant (Association of Directors of Children's Services, 2015). However, the British Association of Social Workers published a position statement on age assessment at the same time as the ADCS Guidance (BASW, 2015) highlighting the difficulties in undertaking these assessments and the practice and ethical issues raised.

Case study 19.3

As a duty social worker, you receive a telephone call from the local police, advising you that a 14-year-old male from Afghanistan has walked into the police station and said that he has come to the UK to claim asylum. Police inform you that he looks more like he is aged 18–19 years old, as he 'has a lot of facial hair and could grow a beard'. Police have interviewed him using a telephone interpreter, and he states that he does not know his date of birth, but knows that he is 14 years old, as his mother told him shortly before leaving Afghanistan.

What further action do you need to take?

This example is not untypical of a referral a social worker might receive. As discussed above, they should be placed in local authority care, and as someone claiming to be 14 years old, that should be a foster placement pending completion of a Merton Compliant age assessment. The age assessment would usually take place within the first month of the person being in local authority care. Although there are risks associated with potentially placing adults in children's settings, age in itself is not a risk factor. A person's motivation to offend is the risk factor, so a young person under the age of 18 may present more of a risk than an adult, which is why it is important for foster carers to follow safe caring policies for whomever is placed with them.

Social workers need to question their own starting point, including whether they have been influenced by the 'culture of disbelief' around asylum seekers and age. Accordingly, they need to be mindful of the impact trauma may have on their ability to recount a consistent account of reasons for coming to the UK, and need to give the benefit of the doubt and allow the young person to answer any inconsistencies in their account.

Transitions to adulthood

A URM, like any other child in the care of the local authority, should have a Pathway Plan from the age of 16 determining options for their transition to adulthood and beyond. The Children Act 1989 and the Children (Leaving Care) Act 2000 do not mention immigration considerations; however, associated guidance, which has come later, does. The Children and Social Work Act 2017 introduced the duty to local authorities to extend the provision of Personal Advisor support to care leavers until the age of 25. Within the statutory guidance, the exclusion of some former URMs is explained (Department for Education, 2018). Schedule 3 of the Nationality, Immigration and Asylum Act 2002 makes a former URM, who is Appeal Rights Exhausted (ARE) an 'ineligible person' and therefore excluded from accessing leaving care services. Any person who made a claim for asylum at a port of entry, such as Dover, or an airport, is exempt from Schedule 3, therefore social workers need to check these details. Where a young person becomes Appeal Rights Exhausted, the Home Office provides funding to a local authority for three months after the young person becoming ARE and local authorities are only able to provide leaving care support following a Human Rights Assessment, determining that removing support would constitute a breach of the young person's human rights. A URM excluded on this basis is now even more disadvantaged, given that the government now recognises that young people who have been in the care of the local authority need further support to transition to adulthood.

There is a growing body of research considering what happens to former URMs as they reach independence (see for example Meloni et al., 2017; Sirriyeh and Ní Raghallaigh, 2018). They often live in a protracted state of limbo and are unable to envisage a future for themselves. What has become apparent through the research messages is that there is a disparity of service across the country. Some local authorities support all former URMs until the point of removal, whilst others discharge their leaving care duties as soon as they are able to. Pathway planning with URMs should include planning for each eventuality, referred to as triple planning, considering options if refugee status is granted, planning for a period of uncertainty whilst still in the UK and plans for a return to country of origin (Department for Education, 2015).

Leaving care and making the transition to adulthood represents a juncture whereby immigration policy overrides child welfare interests and this will impact on URMs' rights, entitlements, experience of leaving care and ability to plan for the future (Wade et al., 2012). Devenney (2016) found that young people with unsettled status found planning for the future almost impossible, and whilst triple planning requires planning for all possible immigration outcomes at 18, young people with unsettled status could not even consider one. The Immigration Act 2016 suggested that the provision to former URMs as they become 18 was going to be even further restricted, by moving to a provision similar to Direct Provision seen in the Republic of Ireland (Ní Raghallaigh and Thornton, 2017). This, however, has never been implemented and there is no information as to when or whether it will ever be (Coram Children's Legal Centre, 2017).

Conclusions

This chapter has offered an overview of the challenges that confront social workers in working with URMs as well as the young people themselves. Specifically, it has considered how the negative discourse that has been perpetuated through tabloid media reporting and moral panics surrounding URMs can impact on values and attitudes which in turn can determine service provision. The key procedural issues in the care planning process form important factors to consider when a young person arrives as a URM through to when they reach adulthood.

Social work at the best of times can be a very challenging profession, but with URMs, given the hostile climate and the multitude of complex issues that are involved, inevitably, we have only managed to scratch the surface. For example, issues relating to questions of sexuality, belief, trust, trauma, mental health, and particularly where the young person may have been escaping from conflict situations, questions of security and radicalisation are all important. However, whilst remaining critically aware of the complexity of circumstances surrounding a URM, of utmost importance is that the social workers must ground their practice in social work values of social justice and human rights. Though in such cases multi-agency partnership working will be important, social workers must also maintain a critical distance between themselves and the roles of other agencies, especially those concerned with immigration and security.

Key points summary

- The issues of migration and asylum seeking are deeply politicised. Policies guiding local authority practices are value driven, a response to political pressure and public 'moral panics' about asylum, often driven by bias and inaccurate reporting by parts of the media. It is therefore essential that you are aware of your own views and values, and critically question what has shaped them.
- In addition to checking immediate physical and health needs, you need to assess the young person's safety, especially in respect of being trafficked or subject to other aspects of modern day slavery.
- Age is an issue that is at the heart of a person's identity where, unfortunately, a 'culture of disbelief' exists with young people often being assumed to be older than they are presenting (Dorling, 2013). There is also evidence to suggest that many children end up in adult detention (BBC, 2019). However, unless physical appearance suggests someone is over 25, then they must become a looked after child and be age assessed fairly (ADCS, 2015).
- Social workers need to pay careful attention to the best interests of the young person, in determining whether a young person is moved between local authorities as per the National Transfer Scheme.
- Social workers and other professionals need to be aware of why some young people may provide limited accounts of their background, as opposed to concluding they are being purposely subversive.
- Preparing an unaccompanied young person for adulthood is highly complex, and can have a profound impact on their emotional wellbeing. Social workers and personal advisors need to build their knowledge in terms of options and resources available to young people, in order to support them during this period.

Suggested further reading

Clayton S., Gupta A. and Willis K. (2019) *Unaccompanied Young Migrants*. Bristol: Policy Press.
Dorling, K. (2013) *Happy Birthday? Disputing the Age of Children in the Immigration System*. London: Coram Children's Legal Centre.
Kohli, R. K. S. (2007) *Social Work with Unaccompanied Asylum-Seeking Children*. Basingstoke: Palgrave Macmillan.
For research on leaving care, read the six research briefs published at: **https://becoming adult.net**

20

Social work and youth justice

Sean Creaney and Roger Smith

Chapter objectives

By the end of this chapter you should be able to:

* appreciate the complexity of contemporary youth justice practice;
* examine how children's participation in systems and processes can be recognised and promoted as a legitimate and desirable objective of intervention;
* utilise creative interventions to address the complex needs of children in conflict with the law and the youth justice system.

Introduction

The contemporary place of social work within the youth justice arena is very different to the position it occupied in the past. Although in one sense its position is more secure, in that there is a statutory expectation for Youth Offending Services to include at least one social work practitioner, this function itself has undergone very significant changes. At the same time, other developments, including the effects of a prolonged period of austerity and the greater emphasis on inter-agency responsibilities in this area of practice, have combined to reduce the role and influence of qualified social work practitioners in work with young offenders. In what follows, we will try to provide a sense of what this new practice terrain feels like, as well as mapping out the scope of social work intervention, alongside the positive opportunities for enabling progressive practice which still remain for those who wish to pursue this line of work in their professional careers.

Young people in the youth justice system

Children in conflict with the law tend to have poor life chances and have experienced some adverse childhoods. Acknowledging such traumatic experiences and the impact on brain development, for instance, can result in professionals viewing children as having diminished or limited capacities and essentially unable (unless supported) to influence decision making processes (Hollingsworth, 2019). Nevertheless, it can be argued that this group requires a needs-based welfare approach (taking account of age-related capacities, viewing them as a treasured resource, vulnerable and in need of protection), as opposed to an overly punishment focused intervention (Hollingsworth, 2019). Notwithstanding proportionality and due process associated with the justice model, there has been concern that young people have been overly 'responsibilised' for engaging in problematic behaviours, with their disadvantage status or limited life chances not properly understood.

Despite the importance of being child-focused and providing pastoral support, this vulnerable and marginalised group continue to experience unfair treatment. For example, in 2016 it was discovered that children in prison were being unlawfully restrained (Medway Improvement Board, 2016) and in 2017 David Lammy concluded that racially discriminated practices with people who offend were widespread (Lammy, 2017). Indeed, black, Asian and minority ethnic (BAME) individuals have been persistently overrepresented throughout all stages of the youth justice system. Rights and social justice thus become important considerations for those engaged in practice with young offenders; and the nature of their behaviour should not be allowed to override the entitlements to fair and just treatment which should apply to *all* children and young people irrespective of their circumstances, characteristics or character. Before reading the following sections, consider what 'participation' means to young people and practitioners. What are the benefits, challenges and limitations of giving children a voice in youth justice?

Young people and crime: beliefs and evidence

Crime is a socially constructed concept, which means that assumptions we make about who criminals are and their characteristics are not fixed and permanent, but depend on social norms and how these are enacted (Case, 2018). Definitions of what constitutes criminal activity vary, as do public and political understandings of 'normality' and 'abnormality' (Armstrong, 2004, p270). Conventional assumptions about the problems associated with youth are linked to understandings of child and adolescent development. This is a life stage which is often seen as particularly turbulent, and fraught with challenges. Neuroscience now tells us that the 'adolescent brain' has distinctive features which inhibit the capacity to exercise self-control, or to consider the consequences of behaviour. Psychologists associate the teenage years with developmental changes, starting with puberty, which are inherently problematic and destabilising. Sociological perspectives have focused on factors such as family conflict and peer influence as well as poverty and disadvantage to account for young people's involvement in what is identified as 'anti-social behaviour'.

These 'expert' analyses are mirrored in media portrayals and popular beliefs about the threat to public order posed by young people in the absence of effective mechanisms of social control. The dominant perception is that youth crime is an endemic problem which is continually worsening (Case, 2018). Despite what might be described as (recurrent) 'respectable fears' (Pearson, 1983), statistical evidence suggests there have been persistent falls in recorded offences by children and young people since 2007 (Bateman, 2017). Contrary to popular belief, young people – notably between the ages of 16–24 – are statistically more likely to be victims than perpetrators of crime (France et al., 2012).

Explaining youth crime

Often, perhaps in accordance with neo-liberal thinking, young people in conflict with the law are depicted as a source of threat who must accept individual responsibility for their actions. The concepts of 'individualisation', 'responsibilisation' and 'self-realisation' have been emphasised, resulting in the 'social situations, social contexts and social structures [being] relegated to the margins' (France et al., 2012, p6). The principal focus has been on uncovering the 'causes' of youth crime. In this context, developmental criminology has flourished, and in the process heavily influenced government policy in the field of criminal justice, and informed Risk Factor Analysis (RFA), an approach that has its roots in public health analysis. RFA is concerned with scientifically identifying populations of risky individuals who have a propensity to offend in the future (Case and Haines, 2009). These so-called risk factors are predominantly related to psychological aspects of an individual's life, notably their propensity to 'malfunction', neglecting structural aspects for instance, which, as alluded to above, are often viewed as non-significant in terms of their impact on offending (France et al., 2012, p7).

Other criticisms have been levelled at RFA. For example, the authors of a longitudinal study conducted on children residing in Hawaii discovered that, despite being labelled 'high risk' and identified (based on their 'riskiness') as requiring specialist mental health or educative support, a third of participants did not fulfil negative expectations, and 'developed instead into competent, confident, and caring young adults' (Werner, 1989, p73). It is relevant to note here that risk-taking and experimentation are not unusual; it is often part of the adolescent phase and thus common behaviour among young people.

Despite such contrary findings, much work has gone into developing assessment and predictive tools to identify those young people at risk of becoming persistent offenders, notably the Asset tool, which came into operation with the implementation of the Crime and Disorder Act 1998 (Baker, 2005).

The youth justice 'system'

Youth justice in England and Wales has been described as a system that comprises conflict, contradiction and ambiguity (Muncie and Hughes, 2002, p1). Notwithstanding this, the Crime and Disorder Act 1998 underpinned 'the new youth justice' and signalled a shift towards criminalising young people through risk-focused prevention and early intervention (Case and Haines, 2009), even putting in place pre-emptive mechanisms to deal with behaviour which fell short of being criminal but was still defined as 'anti-social'.

An example of the government's drive to 'responsibilise' children was the abolition of *doli incapax* (the presumption of innocence) for ten to 14-year-olds.

Activity 20.1

Read the article: 'The James Bulger case should not set the age of criminal responsibility':
https://theconversation.com/the-james-bulger-case-should-not-set-the-age-of-criminal-responsibility-91342
   In groups, reflect upon how you feel about levels of youth crime in the UK. Discuss whether increasing the age of criminal responsibility would be beneficial to children and society.

The 1998 Crime and Disorder Act created the Youth Justice Board (YJB) and Youth Offending Teams (YOTs). The YJB's role was to oversee the youth justice system and monitor outcomes. It also, somewhat oddly, took on operational responsibility for arranging and commissioning secure placements for young people sentenced to custody. YOTs were established as multi-agency organisations made up of representation from (notably, but not limited to) education, social care, health, police and probation. YOTs were given the remit of working with children in a bid to prevent offending/reoffending – the principal objective of intervention as specified by the 1998 Crime and Disorder Act (Section 37).

This emphasis on preventing offending behaviour was influenced by evidence of the factors associated with youth offending (Farrington, et al., 2006) which was used to support the argument that 'risk assessment instruments could be developed, and risk-focused prevention could be implemented' (Farrington et al., 2006, pi). This approach was described as deficit-based and criticised for an insufficient emphasis on positive aspects of children's and young people's lives (Haines and Case, 2015).

It has been argued that multi-agency Youth Offending Services draw young people into contact with an overwhelming number of adult professionals each with differing agendas, creating, at times, confusion and conflicting messages for young people and their families (Byrne and Brooks, 2015). Despite the support provided by Youth Offending

Teams being potentially beneficial for the child and their family, not least by providing opportunities to have their often complex individual needs addressed by specialist service professionals, the

> challenge is finding the right balance between making available interventions that draw on a range of skills from a number of specialisms and disciplines while at the same time avoiding the involvement of an unnecessary large number of people in face to face work with a young person.

(Ibbetson, 2013, p22)

Principles for intervention

Importantly, in accordance with the emphasis on the promotion of participatory rights, one could argue that children should be provided with opportunities to play a part in determining the response to the problems associated with their behaviour. Rather than focusing on risk/deficits, any work proposed should be built on developing strengths and enhancing resilience (Gilligan, 2006, p41). Creating such a space may be difficult given time constraints, and bureaucratic aspects/procedural requirements severely restricting the ability of the practitioner to be sufficiently responsive or to address the needs of the child/youth requirements.

Individual factors which may encourage offending, such as hedonistic gain or low self-control, have dominated criminological agendas. The system has been geared towards confronting young people with the consequences of their actions, for them to atone and change their behaviour as a result (Muncie, 2006).

Developmental criminologists appear to have marginalised structural aspects or ecological processes, dismissing the significance of their influence on offending. Promisingly, however, critical criminologists have emphasised ecology and the impact such processes have on young people's involvement with crime. However, critics questioned to what extent this acknowledgement of ecology results in a comprehensive analysis that combines micro and macro factors, and relationships inherent in social life (France et al., 2012, p8). It is relevant to note that children's attitudes and behaviours are not determined by the 'external world', but rather 'negotiated [and shaped] through [an interplay of] relationships and social interaction' (France, 2015, p78). Cultural criminology has attempted to provide insight into how children and young people in conflict with the law are impacted upon or affected by social and political processes (France et al., 2012). As Hayward (2008, p119) notes, cultural criminology is related to the construction of rules – those that are respected and those that are broken.

Moreover, children tend not to be perceived as social agents who are able to influence processes. They are perceived instead as people who lack the ability to provide a perspective on crime and offending trajectories (France et al., 2012). However, France and his colleagues (2012) are keen to centralise the authentic voice of children and young people who were often depicted as a 'problem'. According to the authors, they ensured their analysis was 'grounded' in children's, often neglected, perspectives and explanations (France, 2015, p79).

Having read this section, consider the following reflective question: how can practitioners motivate children, who may appear reluctant to engage and participate in the process that they view, initially at least, as a punishment that they wanted 'over and done with'?

Risk practices

Despite pathways into and out of offending being complex and difficult to measure with any degree of accuracy, the youth justice system in England and Wales has continued to be risk oriented and this has remained the case for more than 20 years. Actuarialism in criminal justice first relates to the statistical calculation of risk and probability of (further) offending/harm. Second, it is concerned with 'the application of managerial techniques to control the threat to the community thus identified' (Smith, 2008, p128).

On the other hand, research has identified both the practical limitations of such approaches (Smith, 2014a), and the 'unintended consequences' in the form of labelling and its criminalising effects, which can result in further system involvement as opposed to preventing it (McAra and McVie, 2007; 2010).

Alternative approaches: diverting young people and the consequences

This evidence has encouraged and validated the development of diversionary schemes, designed to keep young people out of the system and signpost them to more appropriate forms of support to address welfare needs and criminogenic factors. Essentially, there appears to have been a return to an earlier model of youth justice, which emphasised minimal diversion, decriminalisation and decarceration. Whether this shift in stance is related to evidence/research or is rather convenient for politicians in terms of economic expediency can be debated.

Despite this, a key cause for concern has been *stubbornly* high reoffending rates (Puffett, 2017). As alluded to above, the vast majority of offending by young people is now dealt with by keeping them out of the formal system. This was underpinned by the introduction of Legal Aid, Sentencing and Punishment of Offenders Act (2012), which reintroduced and extended the practice of cautioning young offenders, and promoting disposals which do not impose counter-productive punishments, or label them.

However, this has meant that the proportion of children with complex needs on court orders has increased. Those under supervision tend to live chaotic lives, experience speech and language communication difficulties, for example, and require intense support. Although this could at least partly explain the increase in reoffending rates, one could question the efficacy of interventions used (Hampson, 2017, p2) and indeed the lack of voice of the child within the process, notably the absence of any opportunity to participate and shape the content of intervention plans; to take responsibility, in fact (Case, 2018).

Desistance-led intervention

Put simply, desistance is the ceasing or termination of crime by those who previously engaged in criminal activity (HMIP, 2016). It is an approach that emphasises the positive aspects of children's lives. Although desistance-focused approaches have been promoted in the adult criminal justice system, this model has been applied sparsely to the field of youth justice. However, the Youth Justice Board appears to have embraced the shift towards desistance-based approaches. As Hampson (2017, p2) notes, this was 'crystallised in the launching of AssetPlus [in 2014], an assessment system purporting to support desistance approaches'. AssetPlus is desistance informed and seeks to balance a persisting concern with managing risk with an emerging emphasis on promoting wellbeing and desistance. Critics, though, have expressed concern that it continues to conceptualise young people as 'objects of risk' (Briggs, 2013; Whyte, 2009) and provides justification for (pre-emptive) intervention in the lives of children to reduce the probability of (further) offending. It can also be viewed as 'a tool of blame' (Turnbull and Spence, 2011, p940) as professionals continue to be preoccupied with threat or potential danger, and a mistrust of young people. As Turnbull and Spence (2011, p941) assert:

> Lack of trust and the fear of what young people might become are manifested in risk management, surveillance and control interventions, with professional services focusing on controlling risks to the individual, wider society, or the organisation itself.

Practitioners are thus faced with the challenge of balancing concern for the young person's wellbeing and future prospects with a mandate to maintain a clear sense of the level of risk associated with the young person's past behaviour and current indicators of concern. Surveillance and control are thus inherent expectations of practitioners, although experimentation and risk-taking behaviours are particularly prevalent during the phases of childhood and adolescence. This preoccupation at times appears at odds with promoting desistance and allowing them just to 'grow out of crime'.

Children's participation: a model for effective practice

All children and young people have the right to a voice, and to be listened to regarding decisions that affect them (UNCRC Article 12). Children should not be subject to processes that alienate them, they should be empowered, and approaches should seek to ensure their active participation (Creaney and Smith, 2014). Approaches to working with young people who offend that foster empathy, trust and children's participation (their voice and ability to influence systems or processes) can help to promote positive outcomes, including self-esteem and self-worth, and lead to reductions in (re)offending. Participatory practices can enhance children's 'trust in the system and their willingness to comply with the law in the future' (Janes, 2018, cited in Hollingsworth, 2019). However, promoting the voices of children and young people in conflict with the law has not been a central feature of youth justice policy to date. Children in conflict with the law have tended to be 'done to' and coerced as opposed to supported to participate effectively (Haines and Case, 2015).

It has been argued that children and young people can be 'experts by experience', capable of providing unique insights and sharing knowledge and experience of being an 'offender' and using criminal justice services (Creaney, 2018; Hylton, 2014; Peer Power, 2018). Children's participation has been promoted, for instance, through the publication of the Youth Justice Board's participation strategy (YJB, 2016), problematising the dominant view that 'professionals know best'. It was acknowledged that children can be active agents, capable of possessing credible expertise. It promoted or reinforced the need to elicit the child's viewpoint on matters that affect them and detailed the beneficial effects of their active participation and meaningful involvement in the planning, design, delivery and evaluation of youth justice services (YJB, 2016). However, inevitably there will be children and young people who treat the experience as an inconvenience that they want 'over and done with'. Young people may be intent on 'playing the [youth justice] game' (Wilson and Rees, 2006) and this may result in passive engagement. Hart and Thompson (2009, p24) found that young people

> described their experiences in very passive terms – something that happens to them, or is done to them, rather than something they can actively engage with, and help shape and design.

There are different levels of participation, with the suitability of each level influenced by a child's age and stages of their development. Although its definition has been disputed, participation generally refers to taking part in an activity or a process. On the one hand it relates to children being listened to, and on the other their active involvement in processes, premised on the idea that they 'have reason to believe that their [participation] will make a difference' (Sinclair, 2004, pp110–111). The former involves children being consulted (opportunities to express their views) but the latter relates to children directly influencing decision making processes (Hill et al., 2004, p83).

There has been criticism that attention has been overly directed at their participation in the delivery of services as opposed to their influence over strategic development and addressing needs rather than empowering them to express their wishes on matters that directly concern them. Other issues relate to feedback mechanisms, consultation or questionnaire overload, participation being top-down and professionals being biased in terms of the types of children and young people they recruit, excluding vulnerable and disadvantaged children from adopting key decision making positions, thus being unable to capture a 'diversity of voices' (Thomas, 2007, p202; also see Badham, 2004 and Tisdall and Davis, 2004). Hart and Thompson (2009, p19) quote from Hogeveen's (2006) study on restorative practices, and refer to the factors that influence a non-participative culture:

> discourses that question the appropriateness of children's political involvement, people who doubt youth's ability to participate, and uncertainties about the form participation should take.

Young people should be given opportunities to have their say and be empowered throughout all stages of the youth justice system to provide 'insights … into the services that are likely to be most effective' (Hart and Thompson, 2009, p8). It is relevant to note that children and young people can 'quickly become disinterested or disengaged from interventions, if they do not feel valued or listened to' (YJB, 2008, p8). A further issue relates to risk scores. As Hart and Thompson (2009, p13) note,

> individual young people may be further disempowered if their own perceptions do not accord with the scores assigned to them by the YOT assessor.

There have been calls for practitioners to work more in partnership with young people, embed a participatory culture within decision making and hold children's interests, rights, viewpoints and needs as central (Case and Yates, 2016, p59). However, although provision should reflect young people's interests and their individual needs, there are specific challenges to overcome for this ambition to be realised. Despite the guiding principles of the children's rights agenda (UNICEF, 1989), and other national or international policies and pieces of legislation that encourage children's participation in decision making, Smith (2014b, p298) points out several barriers to progressing children's participation in the youth justice system:

> inhospitable statutory requirements and an unwelcoming 'culture'; lack of time and resources to engage young people; conflicting organisational expectations; lack of knowledge or understanding within staff teams; and a general absence of a strategic commitment to participatory principles ... [and] prevailing emphasis on [adult-centric] actuarial, risk-based and managerial frameworks for intervention.

The dominant perception is that, because they have done wrong, young people are not deserving of a voice (Hart and Thompson, 2009). As Smith (2014b, p300) notes,

> gaining legitimacy for an approach which appears to be granting special privileges to young people whose rights are properly forfeited in the eyes of many by the very fact of their proven involvement in [crime]

is a substantial challenge that continues to be difficult to resolve.

Although not specific to the youth justice context, Matthews (2003) referred to practitioners' ability and willingness to share decision making with young people. More specifically, there may be 'adult reservations about handing over control and cynicism on the part of young people', and this can lead to a 'culture of non-participation' (Matthews, 2003, p264–265, cited in Thomas, 2007, p202). Furthermore, it has also been argued that there is 'tension between children having the responsibility for decision making and enjoying their childhood' (Percy-Smith, 2005, cited in Thomas, 2007, p202).

As alluded to, the underlying discourse of punishment in youth justice can result in the young person's perspective being seen as irrelevant. Although young people have the right to influence the design and/or delivery of services, promoting the voices of young people who offend has not tended to be a core feature of policy or practice. As Wood and Kemshall (2008, p150) note, 'the loyalties of a [youth justice worker] may be more likely to be vested in victims as opposed to offenders'.

Activity 20.2

Consider how much of a say you think victims should have in deciding how young offenders are dealt with.

- How would you approach your practice to ensure that this did not lead to unequal or unfair outcomes for the young person?
- Can you draw up a list of principles to inform your approach to models for delivering participatory justice?

The issue of striking a balance between the voices of victims and offenders is perhaps most relevant in relation to public or community protection work, notably with those who commit violent or sexual offences. Here, restrictive measures may be imposed on offenders, and they can be excluded from the decision making process, unable to contribute their views (Wood and Kemshall, 2008). However, if professionals provide suitable justification or reasoning to the offender on how the decision was reached, it can prevent them feeling aggrieved or resentful and increase compliance with conditions or the restrictions imposed (Wood and Kemshall, 2008, p151). Arguably, being transparent with young people in terms of decision making is conducive to rehabilitation. If young people are 'active partners' and empowered to influence the shaping of their care, supervision and the services they are receiving, they can provide insight into what does and *does not* work for them (Nacro, 2008, p6).

Relationship-based practice

Although research consistently demonstrates the central role of relational practices (Stephenson et al., 2007), there is often limited attention directed at how to establish and sustain 'effective' young person-worker relationships (Batchelor and McNeill, 2005). Nevertheless, if children have developed caring and trusting relationships with their supervising officers, this can help to increase their self-esteem and self-worth, and can even be transformative and help the young person to cope with distress and feelings of hopelessness (Mason and Prior, 2008).

Positive and constructive relationships are more likely to form when professionals avoid adopting a confrontational stance. Demonstrating belief and being optimistic that young people can change offers most promise in terms of achieving positive outcomes. In the context of counselling and psychotherapy, Westwell (2015, p67) refers to the necessity of practitioners demonstrating 'a heartfelt commitment of goodwill … towards the emotional suffering of [children and young people]'. According to Westwell (2015, p67), this requires 'active, careful, accurate, sensitive and consistent empathic communication' with a view to empowering those in receipt of assistance to 'voice their own emotions and needs', despite the context in which there will undoubtedly be concerns about the young person's behaviour, its impact and implications. Greenberg and Elliot (1997, p184; cited in Westwell, 2015) assert:

if a [child or young person] can fully express a feared, dreaded, unacceptable aspect of experience, such as intense despair or shame, and have it fully received by a [youth justice practitioner] who is sensing the feeling in full intensity and is clearly valuing the [child or young person] with no reservations, this can be a powerful experience that promotes change.

Crucially, service user choice, autonomy and instilling trust and hope are valued in such collaborative relationships. Children and young people construct their own understandings of their lives (France et al., 2012), making sense of their actions and experiences, and how they feel the world treats them (Goldson and Yates, 2008, p116). Recognising this can facilitate positive outcomes, including restorative solutions to the offence, the building of resilience, and desistance from (further) crime or contact with the criminal justice system.

Conclusion: concerns and remedies

An ongoing issue relates to the problems or issues young people experience or circumstances they find themselves in coming to be framed as the fault of the individual. There appears to be limited acknowledgement of the socio-economic context and its impact on aspirations and behaviours. Indeed, it 'converts social and communal risks into individual ones' (Briggs, 2013, p19).

Youth Offending Teams have been subjected to budgetary restrictions, and professionals have been constrained by the circumstances under which they currently practise. As Briggs (2013, p26) notes, practitioners have experienced 'immense pressure in respect of finite resources and time'. In a context of such financially unstable systems, there have been organisational restructures. There has also been a further revamp of national standards and a host of policy and practice changes including a welcome move away from criminalisation and towards non-stigmatising forms of support following the publication of the Taylor Report, which itself drew widely on existing examples of good practice. Decriminalisation, decarceration and diversion have re-emerged as prominent philosophies influencing the development of systems and processes. This has led Smith and Gray (2018, p1) to endorse the emergence of:

a number of 'models' of youth justice practice operating in parallel ... there does not appear at present to be the kind of 'orthodoxy' in place which has sometimes prevailed in this field.

This trend towards local design and creative professionalism is perhaps significant. Additionally, children's direct involvement in the design and delivery of youth justice services not only helps to potentially address their unique needs, it can also contribute to crime reduction (Hart and Thompson, 2009). There may be resistance from professionals and the perception that it is demanding or additional work. What is more, professionals may feel that an emphasis on hearing the voice of the child is in direct conflict with their own oppressive experiences of hierarchical structures, whereby their perspectives are neglected, and they feel 'done to' rather than consulted with.

Key points summary

- Young people who offend should be recognised as young people first.
- Social work interventions should balance assessments of 'risk' with a concern to promote young people's needs, rights and aspirations.
- Participatory approaches to the delivery of youth justice should ensure that children and young people's voices are heard and acted upon, whilst drawing on the insights and expertise of professionals to promote future wellbeing.

Suggested further reading

Case, S. P., Johnson, P., Manlow, D., Smith, R. S. and Williams, K. H. (2017) *Criminology*. Oxford: Oxford University Press.

Fox, D. and Arnull, E. (2013) *Social Work in the Youth Justice System: A Multidisciplinary Perspective*. Maidenhead: McGraw Hill Education/Open University Press.

Muncie, J. (2015) *Youth and Crime* (4th ed). London: Sage.

Smith, R. (2014) *Youth Justice: Ideas, Policy, Practice* (3rd ed). Abingdon: Routledge.

21

Social work and mental health (children, young people and adults)

Toby Brandon, Carole Southall and Steve O'Driscoll

Chapter objectives

By the end of this chapter you should be able to:

* critically discuss the different perspectives of mental health;
* appreciate and justify the importance of 'experts by experience' in mental health social work;
* understand how the law is applied to mental health;
* weigh up how the intersection of different social factors affects the development of mental health distress.

Introduction

In this chapter we will explore mental health in terms of social work with a focus on the views of people who use mental health services, the law and broader social theory. We will use a case study, questions and activities to support the development of your thinking and potential social work practice. The provision of mental health services in both health and social care has often been referred to as a 'Cinderella service' (Mind, 2012), owing to chronic under resourcing and the increase in need of people with mental health concerns being overlooked. The harsh reality in 2016 being reported by the Mental Health Foundation's Fundamental Facts about Mental Health:

- Nearly half (43.4 per cent) of adults think that they have had a diagnosable mental health condition at some point in their life (35.2 per cent of men and 51.2 per cent of women).
- In 2014, 19.7 per cent of people in the UK aged 16 and older showed symptoms of anxiety or depression.

The term mental 'health' or 'illness' or 'distress' are highly contested due to disagreement about causation. This in turn leads to different perspectives on how people should be supported and what their 'recovery' should look like. Below is a case study to help you to begin to consider the role of social workers in mental health.

Case study 21.1

Martin (aged 28) describes a stable childhood with a good relationship with his mother. His father he found very controlling, critical and impossible to please. Martin feels anything he did achieve was undermined by his father's negative attitude. At school Martin had reasonable success with his GCSEs but left sixth form before completing his A levels. His parents became concerned about changes in his behaviour. He disengaged from his friends, isolated himself in his room, lacked motivation and his personal care deteriorated. This went on for some time until eventually his parents called the GP who made a referral to a psychiatrist. Initially Martin refused to see the psychiatrist, but eventually he did attend an appointment, but declined to allow either of his parents to go in with him. The psychiatrist identified some paranoid thoughts and disordered thinking; medication for psychosis was prescribed. The medication did suppress some of Martin's symptoms but it did not eradicate them completely. It also has side effects, which Martin finds difficult to cope with. A Community Psychiatric Nurse (CPN) is allocated to monitor Martin taking his medication. He has never worked and is struggling to find a way to take his life forward.

Different perspectives on mental health

The predominant model of mental health in Western societies is the disease or medical model which developed in the mid-nineteenth century, replacing earlier moral and/or religious explanations (Coppock and Dunn, 2010). Led by psychiatry, the medical model identifies mental distress as an illness with physical causes. Poor physical health, substance misuse, or brain injury caused in numerous ways may all be possible contributing factors.

In response to these physical causes, a range of treatments have been developed, the prime being medication, though electro-convulsive therapy (ECT) has been administered, while psycho-surgery is also used (but rarely). To consolidate and legitimise the medical approach, manuals using medical terminology were developed to identify objective symptoms for specific disorders. The most widely used is the Diagnostic and Statistical Manual of Mental Disorders (DSM) published by the American Psychiatric Association (2000). The World Health Organization has also published a similar manual, the International Classification of Diseases and Related Problems (1992). The validity of these diagnostic manuals has been called into question by critics of the medical approach (Pilgrim, 2014). The reasons for these questions are, first, that identifying symptoms is based upon subjective interpretation of human emotions, behaviour and experience rather than observable biological characteristics and, second, that the research evidence base for biological causation, symptom identification and diagnosis is weak at best. Both these factors reduce rather than support the scientific legitimacy of the medical framework (Pilgrim, 2014). In addition, the DSM has been revised numerous times with conditions being added or, in the case of homosexuality, removed. In addition, mental health is viewed differently in some societies, supporting the criticism that psychiatric diagnosis is culturally defined and the perception of mental 'illness' as an objective biological fact is not sustainable. These concerns formed the basis of critiques of psychiatry by members of the anti-psychiatry movement in the 1960s such as R. D. Laing (1965) and other commentators such as Thomas Szasz (1972) who argued that mental illness was a misrepresentation of people's reactions to 'problems with living' (Glasby and Tew, 2015), though Tew (2011) does suggest the exception to this would be the work around dementia.

Despite these criticisms, the medical model has maintained its dominant position. More recently, however, increasing recognition has been given to other alternative models that have developed alongside it. These include psychological models with a focus on cognitive, emotional and behavioural process that can be addressed through a variety of therapeutic interventions. Perhaps more pertinent still for social work has been the development of social models of explanation. Pilgrim (2014) identifies different theoretical threads that come within the social model in Table 21.1 below.

Table 21.1   Social models of mental health

Social Causation	The focus here is on models that emphasise the role of external social forces on mental health.
Critical Theory	Integrates psychological and structural factors to explore issues such as family socialisation, ego development, mass media and culture.
Social Constructivism	For the mental health field the most relevant elements here are the consideration of how social forces determine what is identified as a social problem and the work of Foucault (1965; 1981) (French Post Structuralism).
Social Realism	Acknowledges the reality of 'madness and misery' but the words to use them are themselves socially constructed.
Social Reaction or Labelling Theory	This is the process whereby certain behaviours are labelled as deviant (primary deviance). A range of social and psychological factors then influence if a person receives a diagnosis and the individual is seen to take on the deviant role (secondary deviance). Deviance tending to trigger punitive responses.

Drawn from Pilgrim (2014)

The social causation model focuses on external forces such as unemployment, discrimination, inequality and powerlessness as triggers for poor mental health. Tew et al. (2012) found evidence to suggest connectedness and social inclusion were central to long term recovery. Social workers need to have an understanding of all these models of explanation to give them a holistic understanding of the person's situation. Criticisms of the medical model have proved difficult to ignore, and in practice a number of combined models of intervention have developed. These include the psychosocial, biopsychosocial and recovery models. Tew (2011), whilst acknowledging a role for the medical model, suggests a more balanced emphasis is needed between approaches with a greater focus on social, political, cultural and economic influences; and reclaiming from medical science the meaning a person's experience has for them. Mental health recovery is also a contested term as it is often unclear who defines, measures and assigns it. A person's perception of their recovery may not correspond to that of the professionals working with them. The Scottish Recovery Network (2012) defines recovery as:

being able to live a meaningful and satisfying life, as defined by each person, in the presence or absence of symptoms. It is about having control over and input into one's own life. Each individual's recovery, like his or her experience of mental health problems or illness, is a unique and deeply personal process. It is important to be clear that there is no right or wrong way to recover.

One of the key challenges social workers in the mental health field face is to raise the profile of social and psychological concerns as it is these areas that will be core to effective social work intervention with individuals providing a balance to the more medically orientated approaches of other professionals.

Case study 21.2

A service user perspective:

My first thoughts on reading this case study (Martin) are that this is a mirror of my life and how I was when I was a teenager. I think the social workers should look into getting Martin into supported accommodation with the view to him going onto living independently as 28 in my view is not a healthy age for a person to still be living at home especially with a father who gives his son no positive encouragement and with Martin socially excluding himself in his bedroom. If there is a Recovery College in the area maybe the social worker could support Martin to access this and it would help build Martin's self-esteem and meet people with lived experience with a view to getting him a Peer Support Worker. This would give Martin structure and something to get up for in the morning, also with Martin's permission working with the father to alter his perceptions and give his son some praise might be positive move for both of them. All decisions regarding Martin should be made with co-production at the root of everything. Also, possibly working with Martin to develop a Wellness Recovery Action Plan (WRAP 2019) which he could use in his day-to-day life. Whilst the social worker is working with Martin they should give him encouragement in a meaningful way to boost his self-esteem.

Legal context for mental health practice

The historical policy for supporting people with mental health concerns was originally characterised by the great confinement of those deemed 'useless eaters' in the 1800s (Scull, 1979) followed by a dramatic shift to deinstitutionalisation with the closure of the large psychiatric hospitals from the 1970s onwards with a view to integrating people back into their communities. This was coupled with the rise in patients' rights movements advocating for people experiencing poor mental health care, or even 'surviving services'. As such, the legal framework for supporting people with mental health concerns in the community is the same as that for everyone else. The Care Act (2014) was intended to provide a framework to ensure health and social care agencies communicate with each other to ensure they provide services to promote mental health recovery and personal wellbeing. Following assessment, a person, if eligible, will be allocated a personal budget with which they can purchase support. A challenge for social workers is that the 'provision of care services' model operationalised under the Care Act by local authorities does have significant limitations in its application to people with mental health concerns. It can only be easily applied to situations that are stable and predictable and when needs can be quickly and readily identified. Glasby and Tew (2015) point out that for people experiencing fluctuating and unpredictable mental health conditions the one-off assessment and provision of a care plan model is woefully inadequate. Alongside the Care Act (2014), the Mental Capacity Act (2005) may also apply to the person's situation, as may the Deprivation of Liberty Safeguards (2009), though the latter are to be replaced in the near future (see Chapter 4 for a more detailed examination of this legislation).

Direct payments to individuals have formed part of a shift in social care towards the individualisation of services, which are intended as highly flexible means to facilitate people arranging their own care. They were introduced by the Community Care (Direct Payments) Act (1996) which came into force in April 1997. A direct payment is a cash payment that can make up part of or a person's entire personal budget. In mental health direct payments have not had a significant take up (Davey et al., 2007). The suggested reasons for this (Disability Rights UK) include a lack of awareness about direct payments and a risk aversion from professionals to promote them.

Activity 21.1

With reference to the case study, make a list of all the aspects of Martin's life (social, psychological, professional and family) that you rate important enough to protect with the help of social work and a personal budget.

On occasion people with mental health concerns may need a hospital admission. This can be achieved informally as with other hospital admissions. However, a small but significant number of people may refuse admission to hospital, when the professionals working with them feel it is essential an admission goes ahead. In these circumstances, if certain thresholds are met, the person can be admitted against their wishes under the Mental Health Act (1983, amended 2007). To achieve this, application is made usually by an Approved Mental Health Professional (AMHP) supported by two medical recommendations. Social workers make up the majority of AMHPs, though other professionals such as mental health nurses, occupational therapists (OTs) and psychologists can also train to become AMHPs. The thresholds for compulsory admission, particularly for Section 2 of the Act, which is for assessment of the individual's mental health, has a focus on the nature and degree of any mental distress present and the health or safety of the person or the protection of others. Given its coercive nature, it is not surprising that the development of mental health law has been characterised by the tensions that exist between individual empowerment, self-determination and treatment for the individual and protection of the public. It is this tension that dominated the debates leading up to the reform of the Mental Health Act in 2007. Service user and professional groups formed a 'Mental Health Alliance' and argued for reform that promoted a more rights based, less coercive approach with a focus on individual autonomy and reciprocity. This was compared to what they argued was a political agenda to assuage 'moral panic' about public safety, fuelled by negative media coverage of a small number of tragic cases. The application of the Mental Health Act (2007) must be underpinned by the Human Rights Act (1998), in particular article 5 and the Equality Act (2010).

There has been a raft of other policies relating to mental health over the last 30 years, variously focusing on risk management, crises response, introduction of community based services, and organisation of services and co-ordination of multi-disciplinary services. Despite this, the nature and availability of mental health services has remained an issue, with pressure on budgets resulting in higher thresholds for access and eligibility. The most recent policy of note, No Health Without Mental Health (2011), set out a number of objectives. These are that everyone should have good mental health and people experiencing mental health concerns should not be subject to any harm. More people should recover, have good physical health, and have a positive experience of support. In addition, fewer people should be subject to discrimination and stigma. Glasby and Tew (2015) suggest that, while laudable in its aims, measuring the outcomes of this policy is difficult to achieve due to a reliance on existing data sets without commissioning any new ones around recovery rates. In addition, no strategy was produced on how these targets would be achieved. Perhaps in response to this lack of clarity, in 2014 further policy, 'Making Mental Health Services More Effective and Accessible' suggested mental health concerns be given the same status as physical health issues. This harks back to the Cinderella service status mentioned earlier. The priorities for Public Health England in this include increasing accessibility, particularly to psychological services, providing funding for campaigns to challenge stigma and discrimination, and reducing mental health concerns. However, there is no reference to the crises in inpatient bed availability, and it does little to highlight explicitly the social, economic and cultural factors that may constrain progress toward achieving its outcomes.

The role of social work

As a social worker, the initial intervention with a person is likely to be completing an assessment of their situation and needs. This should be undertaken using core social work values and good practice principles of effective engagement, working in partnership with the person, listening to and developing an understanding of their experience and how they perceive their needs. As work progresses and a support plan is being considered, the roles of protecting the person's rights and representing their interests become paramount. Please see the core elements of both assessment and intervention outlines below.

- Take a person centred approach, exploring the person's understanding of their situation, their wishes and desired outcomes
- Does the person wish to co-produce their assessment and support package
- A full picture of the person's needs should be established and how they impact on the person's day-to-day life
- What is the person aiming for in their life and what are the barriers
- Consider strengths, levels of resilience and coping mechanisms, emotional and psychological wellbeing
- Risk and protective factors
- Previous history, diagnosis, treatment and response to it
- Holistic assessment of family and social relationships, sources of support or lack of them
- The stability of housing and finances
- Social capital employment, education, social contacts and engagement
- Communicate effectively with the person
- Financial assessment (after social needs assessment is completed)
- Social capital

Figure 21.1 Core elements for social work assessment in mental health

- Supporting the person's choice for support rather than coercive options
- Helping the person identify community services and activities that may support their recovery
- Use therapeutic techniques to provide positive encouragement, modify thoughts and behaviour and manage traumatic elements of their experience
- Act as a link between services
- Assessment and support for carers
- Education for the person, carers and other parties relevant to the person's situation
- Advocating for the person
- Challenging discrimination and attempt to address the impact of stigma
- Identifying the need for independent advocacy
- Managing risks/having a crises plan. This includes socio-economic risks

(Adapted from Golightly and Goemans 2017)

Figure 21.2 Core elements of social work intervention

As mentioned before, the legal entitlement to an assessment and support comes from the Care Act (2014). Numerous elements, however, can impact on the social worker's ability to intervene effectively. This may come from a lack of knowledge about mental health or not having the skills needed to intervene. For example, few social workers in mental health continue to receive training in therapeutic approaches, but limited funding (exacerbated by austerity measures), a lack of viable community resources, exhausted carers and discrimination, stigma and overly paternalistic attitudes by family and professionals can all impact on what can be achieved. Some of these issues, such as attitudes, discrimination and to some extent funding can be challenged, but others, such as balancing the needs of a carer, may require a sophisticated negotiation and compromise by the social worker and others.

Children and young people

Over the last 20 years a plethora of government policies and initiatives have targeted the mental health of children and young people. In its 2011 document 'No Health without Mental Health: A Cross Government Mental Health Outcomes Strategy for People of all Ages' the Department of Health states that one in ten children aged between five and 16 years has a mental health problem, and many continue to have problems into adulthood, half of those experiencing mental health symptoms by the age of 14 and three quarters by their mid-20s. In addition 10–13 per cent of 15- to 16-year-olds have self-harmed, and certain groups such as children who are in foster care (Minnis et al., 2006) and care leavers more generally have a greater risk of experiencing mental health and other emotional and psychological difficulties (DOH, 2011; Butterworth et al., 2017). Prevalence data is conflicting and confusing, making it difficult to get an accurate picture; the mental health charity Young Minds (2018) suggests one in ten children and one in five young adults have a diagnosable mental health disorder with anxiety, depression, self-harm and suicide being significant issues. They also suggest half of all mental health problems manifest by the age of 14, with 75 per cent by age 24. The Nuffield Trust (2018) suggest a six-fold increase in children and young people experiencing mental health conditions over the last two years, whereas The Government Statistical Service Survey by Sadler et al. (2018) suggests only a slight increase in prevalence of mental health issues in the five to 15 age group from 9 per cent in 1999, 10.1 per cent in 2004 to 11.2 per cent in 2017. The increase is seemingly accounted for by a rise in emotional disorders.

Equally, there is also a range of research that explores the characteristics of children and young people from high risk groups that do not develop mental health concerns (Rutter, 1999; Vostanis, 2007). It is important for social workers to understand those protective factors that enhance resilience and prevent difficulties developing rather than being purely reactive to problems once they have occurred (Walker, 2011). The types of mental health issue will vary across the age range. For younger children, indicators may be problems sleeping, communication, behavioural and relationship problems, response to trauma, hyperactivity and school refusal. For older adolescents other problems such as eating disorder, self-harm, suicide, depression, anxiety or psychosis may become evident (Golightly and Goemans, 2017; Burton, 2014). The identification and presentation of some difficulties may also be complicated by comorbid substance and/or alcohol use. Neuro developments may also occur across the age range; these may include Attention Deficit Hyperactivity Disorder (ADHD), autism and learning disability.

A key challenge for social work is to understand what is going on. Some of these issues may fall within the realm of 'normal' behaviour and responses. It is, however, important to identify what has shifted it beyond that, indicating mental distress. Interventions are generally in the form of supporting the family as a whole, which can raise the problem of balancing the needs of the child or young person with parental demands and expectations. Policy emphasis is on early intervention (DOH, 2015) with the support of schools, local authority children's services and Child and Adolescent Mental Health Services (CAMHS). CAMHS were established following the Together We Stand Health Advisory Service Report (1995). Four tiers of service were introduced to provide a framework for the commissioning, organisation and delivery of mental health services for children and young people (see Table 21.2).

Table 21.2 CAMHS Tiers (National Archives, 2010)

Tier 1
This level is provided by non-specialist services such as GPs, school nurses, teachers and social workers, youth and residential workers recognising that it is usually parents and professionals in universal services that initially identify something is wrong.
Tier 2
Service is provided by uni-professional groups connected through networks. While providing some direct intervention they may also act in a consultative capacity for workers at level one and screen for access to levels three and four. Professionals may include child psychologists/psychiatrists, nurses, family therapists, educational psychologists.
Tier 3
A specialist service for more severe and complex disorders. Typically a multidisciplinary community based team of child and adolescent psychiatrists, psychologists, nurses, occupational therapists, family therapists, social workers, art and music therapists.
Tier 4
Access to tertiary service such as day centre and hospital inpatient services and outpatient services for those with severe mental illness or those at risk from self-harm or suicide. The professionals involved are the same as those in tier 3.

McDougall and Cotgrove (2014) argue the evidence base for Tier 4 CAMHS is weak and provision of service remains hospital admission, with intensive outpatient and home based treatment services being poorly developed (Lamb, 2009). Effectiveness of intervention depends on early intervention, knowledge of the individual and the multiple factors affecting them and levels of engagement by the child or young person (Kurtz, 2009). SCIE (2017) also suggests good communication, quality relationships, staff training and recognising the child and young person as the expert in their experience are important factors for successful intervention. A significant range of interventions with children and young people are therapeutic in nature. To intervene appropriately, knowledge of mental health is required alongside the necessary therapeutic and communication skills needed to engage the individual. The demise of the therapeutic elements of the social role and replacement with more bureaucratic and administrative models is well documented (Payne, 1997; Adams et al., 2002; White, 2013; Trevithick, 2014); the increasing emphasis on purchasing family and therapeutic support has led to a reduction in the skills base of social work in this area (Walker, 2011). Local authority social workers face the challenge of trying to manage risky, complex situations while waiting for specialist services and trying to balance this with the child protection elements of their workload on which a priority is placed.

Despite these limitations, social workers at all levels can intervene in a number of ways. Psycho-educational methods can help the child and their family understand the nature of their condition and how to promote their own mental health. Taking a holistic and systemic approach to situations will enhance understanding of the person within a relational and environmental context exploring family dynamics and identifying factors impacting upon them on a day-to-day basis. In addition, facilitating self-expression and developing coping strategies are all ways of supporting individuals and their families. Always remember to see the real person and not just the diagnosis and symptoms. Access to specialist services has been problematic for a number of years (DOH, 2004; Walker, 2011), an issue echoed in more recent media coverage.

A child or young person under the age of 18 who needed support would be subject to Section 17 of the Children Act (1989) as a child in need drawing on the outcomes of Every Child Matters (2003, revised 2018). Under the Act the definition of a child in need has several elements, one being that the child is disabled. This includes a child or young person with mental disorder. The Mental Health Act (1983) can also apply to children, but the least restrictive option should, as with adults, be considered first and facilities in which they are accommodated should be age appropriate.

Activity 21.2

Consider the following questions and answer as best you can in the light of your reading. How can the 'social' in social work support people with mental health distress? What pressures in society can have a negative impact on people's mental health? What socio-demographic factors increase the likelihood of mental health distress?

Conclusion

In returning to Martin's case study the presented theory, policy and practice has intended to help you appreciate that mental distress is a particularly complex and challenging area for social workers to effectively engage with. Confident diagnosing is often patchy and even defining 'madness' problematic (Macneil, 2010). Similarly, the increased diagnosis of children with mental health distress is a wider concern for our society, in both our appropriateness to do so and how we should respond to it. Social work offers a skill set outside of the medical model that does not rely on people's pathologies, looking instead to possible social causes and solutions. For instance, Martin may see recovery in terms of his personal growth and development.

Future work in mental health appears to be focusing on the significance of early child-hood trauma (Treisman, 2017) and developing new more sophisticated ways of defining the needs of people. The importance of considering intersectionality when understanding people's situations is also key. The role of poverty, ethnicity and other factors cannot be considered in isolation as they combine to produce serious impacts on people's mental wellbeing.

The stigma of mental ill health cannot be underestimated. Social workers need to resolve the tensions between acting as an advocate for a mental health service user whilst at the same time upholding any legal obligations around protection and the potential need to intervene in their lives. Social work is at the forefront of a paradigm shift towards a greater social understanding of mental health where we can all work more positively with people in co-productive ways.

Key points summary

- Social work is both uniquely and powerfully placed to work in creative ways to support people experiencing mental health distress.
- The application of the law in mental health is complex and needs careful consideration in the light of people's rights and liberty.
- Mental health is influenced by an intersection of many social factors, which need to be examined in detail when considering any intervention.

Suggested further reading

Beresford, P. (2000) What have madness and psychiatric system survivors got to do with disability and disability studies? *Disability & Society*, 15(1): 167–172.

Matthews, S., O'Hare, P. and Hemmington, J. (2014) *Approved Mental Health Practice*. London: Palgrave Macmillan.

Rubio-Valera, M., Aznar-Lou, I., Vives-Collet, M., Fernandez, A., Gil-Girbau, M. and Serrano-Blanco, A. (2018) Reducing the mental health–related stigma of social work students: a cluster RCT. *Research on Social Work Practice*, 28(2): 164–172.

Russo, J. and Sweeney, A. (2016) *Searching for a Rose Garden: Challenging Psychiatry, Fostering Mad Studies*. London: PCCS Books.

22

Social work and disability (children, young people and adults)

Sally Lee

Chapter objectives

By the end of this chapter you should be able to:

- understand the terms impairment and disability;
- understand the responsibilities of social work practice with disabled children, young people and adults;
- consider theories of disability and the implications for social work practice;
- understand some of the challenges disabled people experience in contemporary society;
- consider some contemporary challenges for social work with disabled people.

Introduction

This chapter will consider social work practice with disabled people throughout the life course. Whilst many disabled people have little or no contact with social care services, social workers often work with disabled children, young people and adults who require care and support to achieve their personal outcomes. It is therefore important that social work professionals have knowledge about issues related to the experience of living with impairment and disability and practise in anti-oppressive and anti-discriminatory ways.

Disability is *everybody's* business

Being human is an embodied experience; humans have a physical form which is shaped by a combination of biological factors and interaction with the physical world. The body is subject to multiple influences resulting in diversity of shape, size, colour and form. We are all born unique with physical and sensory differences, and the human life course is marked by changes to our bodies. Trauma, injury, disease and poor nutrition are only a few of the unpredictable, even random, factors which can impact on the body. Other factors, such as poverty and the associated health inequalities related to disability, are more available to analysis and intervention and consequently, prevention. The body is key to human identity because we experience our lives through embodied senses and physical differences contribute to different experiences of the world. For example, a heavy door can be an inconvenience to a non-disabled person, but to an individual with mobility impairment such a door can be a barrier to opportunities and implies their inclusion is devalued. Disability is, therefore, a complex phenomenon, reflecting the interaction between a person's body, identity and social environment.

Activity 22.1

Think about a journey you make regularly. Imagine you have a sensory or physical impairment which impacts on your mobility. Would your journey be the same? Think about how long it might take and the preparations you might need to make.

Significant numbers of people identify themselves as disabled: there are currently 13.9 million disabled individuals in the United Kingdom (Office of National Statistics (ONS) and the Department of Work and Pensions (DWP), 2018) and one billion globally (World Health Organization (WHO), 2011). These figures are unlikely to represent the true number of disabled people but do demonstrate that disability and impairment are universally relevant as a current or potential experience. Social workers need to be able to work with disabled people across the life course and within all forms of social work; for example, someone requiring social work support with a mental health issue may also have a physical disability.

Traditional models of disability

Disability is a protected characteristic identified by the Equality Act 2010 (s6) meaning that it is illegal to discriminate (treat unfairly) on the grounds of that characteristic. The Act states that a person has a disability if they have:

a physical or mental impairment which has a long term and substantial adverse effect on their ability to carry out normal day to day activities.

This definition includes physical, sensory and mental impairments or severe disfigurement and includes individuals born with impairments and those who become disabled at any stage in life. This definition of disability is used within social care legislation, including the Children and Families Act 2014 in relation to social work with disabled children and the Care Act 2014 in relation to work with disabled adults. It locates disability with the individual, not their social or physical environment.

However, disability is a contested term and it is important that social workers acknowledge the debates and political associations reflected in the language commonly used in relation to disability. Language is a powerful, value-laden tool (Healy, 2014) and can be used to challenge or reinforce oppressive ideas. How disability is defined is key to the lived experience of disabled individuals and the social status accorded to disabled people (Simcock and Castle, 2016). Wendell (1996) points out that the definition of disability depends on cultural expectations of what a 'normal' life looks like, including what activities are essential to survival and what aspects of personhood are valued by a specific culture. The concept of normalcy has led to the pathologising of atypical bodies, leading to their being viewed as though the impairment is a symptom of disease rather than embodied diversity (Simcock and Castle, 2016).

Disabled people are not a homogenous group and the diversity of experience and impact of impairment should be acknowledged. However, the power of collective voices and action, exemplified by the long and effective history of campaigning, rights focused activities and academic challenge by disabled people has resulted in extensive change to the law, public services and the environment in terms of accessibility and social inclusion of disabled people. Organisations including the Union of the Physically Impaired Against Segregation (UPIAS) in the 1970s and the campaigns for anti-discrimination legislation and direct payments for personal assistance in the 1990s have brought about significant improvement in the lives of disabled people (Oliver et al., 2012). The disability movement has resulted in rethinking disability, moving away from responses based on charity to those based on rights, partly in response to the historical treatment of disabled people, who were frequently dehumanised, segregated, neglected and isolated (Swain et al., 2014). Hahn (1984) sees legislative change as a transition from thinking about disability and impairment in medical terms to considering disabled people as a minority group at risk of social exclusion, discrimination and oppression, which emphasises the political dimensions of disability. Understanding the definition and use of the terms disability and impairment is crucial to social work practice because how they are used will determine how disabled people are approached and inform the nature of subsequent relationships, impacting on the individual's experience of the service and the values demonstrated by professionals (Morris, 2001).

The social model of disability

A key part of the work emerging from the disability movement has been the develop-ment of the social model of disability (Oliver, 1990) which is an alternative way of understanding disability from the dominant medicalised discourse which frames disability as a wholly individual, negative or tragic experience to be avoided, treated or 'cured'. The social model considers how illness, impairment and medical treatment relate to social status with health inequalities reflecting experiences of poverty and social exclusion. Swain et al. (2003) also note how medical science selects valuable characteristics and devalues atypical bodies.

The social model instead locates the cause of disability in the disabling social, economic and environment which is designed by and for non-disabled people (Oliver, 1990). The model emphasises how society can be organised in ways which directly aid or hinder inclusion with social policy choices impacting on the experience of impairment and creating disability, thereby making disability a political matter.

The social model became the unifying idea for a 'collective disability consciousness' (Oliver, 2013, p1024) and is a key influence on social work with disabled people. The model distinguishes between disability and impairment, with the former caused by social processes leading to exclusion and discrimination. The model promotes the agency, strengths, expertise and equal right to self-determination of disabled people (Oliver et al., 2012), emphasising the diversity of human beings leading to the concept of 'normal' being both unhelpful and misleading.

But the social model is not a static concept; it is subject to debate and development, reflecting how disablism is not just a matter of how the organisation of society exerts an impact on people, but also how the individual personally experiences their environment and social world (Swain et al., 2003). Other models of disability have also developed in response to dominant medicalised discourse, including the Affirmative Model which emerged from the disability arts movement of the 1980s and has successfully reclaimed language such as 'cripple' (Mairs, 1986) through its development of 'crip culture' (Kuppers, 2006). This model of disability challenges the oppressive assumption that dis-ability is a wholly negative experience, with disabled people wanting to conform to normative ideas about bodies (Morris, 2001). The Affirmative Model is concerned with positive social identities of disability and the benefits to life experience impairment offers (French and Swain, 2000).

Activity 22.2

Think about experiences you have had or witnessed where a disability of some kind has resulted in someone finding difficulty in managing their daily lives or needing more support to undertake everyday tasks.
Was the difficulty caused by the impairment or the environment?

Traditional social work with disabled people

Social work has often been experienced by disabled people as a disabling barrier in their lives (Simcock and Castle, 2016), and part of the welfare response to disability which has viewed disability as a problem to 'manage' (Oliver et al., 2012).

Research summary

Swain et al. (2003) discuss how forms of 'care' can be characterised as activities 'feeding off' disabled people with an industry created around disability with professional jobs based on existing power structures rather than any expert knowledge or skills. This has led to the creation of new categories of people being deemed in need of assistance, with jobs then created to meet these needs and reinforcing negative notions of dependency: it is 'like a market seeking new growth potential' (Swain et al., 2003, p142).

Empowering social work practice works with disabled people to enable informed decision making, including choice and control over care and support. Empowerment challenges risk averse practice which is reluctant to cede responsibility or power. However, often it is agencies which think in terms of risk, rather than the people subject to risk management policies, who instead want greater control over their routine, access to rights, order and sensitive care (Furedi, 2011). Physically disabled people are often defined as 'at risk' because of their impairment, denying their agency and rights (de Than, 2015; Quarmby, 2011). Empowering social work practice needs to challenge such oppressive views of disabled people.

Activity 22.3

Write down the practitioner skills you think are important for empowering practice; refer to the BASW Code of Ethics and SWE Professional Standards.

Social work practice across the life course

Legislation enables social work practice with disabled people throughout the life course. The Children Act 1989 (section 17) defines a child in need as someone aged under 18 who

- needs local authority services to achieve or maintain a reasonable standard of health or development;
- needs local authority services to prevent significant or further harm to health or development;
- is disabled.

The Children and Families Act 2014 builds on the Children Act 1989 and states that councils must inform children and young people and their parents what they need to know about their disability and what support is available. This includes enabling people to actively participate in determining the nature of the support and making sure education, health and social care services work together to develop one overall assessment and plan for meeting their education, health and social care needs (DoE, 2014).

Young disabled people aged 14 to 18 who are moving from children to adult services may be supported by transitions workers, who operate under both the Children and Families Act 2014 and the Care Act 2014, sections 58–66. Young disabled people face the same issues as any young person but may have additional barriers to attaining the markers of adulthood such as 'employment, independent housing and the establishment of one's own family' (Simcock and Castle, 206, p43). A core part of the social work role with young people is supporting the development of social networks, life goals and personal identity.

Case study 22.1

(Written by Bob Ashe, social worker with the Children with Disabilities team in Dorset.)

Jenny is 13 years old and has a severe learning and physical disability. She is considered a 'child in need' within the definition of the Children Act 1989 (Section 17).

Jenny's health diagnosis is complex and affects many areas of her life. Jenny has frequent admissions to both local and specialist hospitals.

The ability for Jenny to communicate her wishes and feelings is complex, requiring the social worker to have knowledge of how Jenny uses communication; for example, what sounds and gestures mean. At times, it is difficult to interpret what she is communicating so it is unclear if Jenny is able to communicate if she is in pain. The social worker observes how Mrs Foster, Jenny's primary carer, communicates with Jenny, as she is a person who knows Jenny well. In addition, the social worker consults the Speech and Language Therapist Assessment.

Children's Services are involved as Jenny is considered to be a child who is disabled under the Children Act 1989 and therefore Children's Services has a duty to assess Jenny's needs (Broach et al., 2010). Child Protection investigations and procedures (Children Act 1989, s47) have also been undertaken due to allegations of fabricated or induced illness (Bools, 2008); concerns were raised by nursing staff that Jenny had been given additional medication by her mother. A plan is agreed to ensure Jenny's safety.

The social worker reads Jenny's file, including the chronology, which provides information about the family history and any previous involvement with Children's Services, health and education services. The chronology details that Jenny's parents are divorced, and communication is difficult between them. Jenny receives home tuition as her health prevents regular school attendance. This is a flexible arrangement and provides education when Jenny is well.

Jenny lives with her mother in a property that has been adapted following occupational therapy assessment. Mrs Foster's own life expectations changed as she became Jenny's main carer. She is offered a Carer's Assessment (Carer's Recognition and Services Act, 1995) in her own right because of her caring role (Broach et al., 2010).

(Continued)

(Continued)

The social worker observes that Jenny she likes her patio doors open so that the wind can blow into her room. She also enjoys the feeling of soft toys in her bed.

Social work visits allowed observation of the relationship between Jenny and her mother.

- How do you make friends?
- What barriers is Jenny experiencing in establishing a social network and what ideas do you have to support Jenny to overcome these?

The Care Act 2014 and social work with disabled people

Social workers working with disabled adults offer care and support assessment to explore the impact of the individual's impairment on their wellbeing. The Care Act identifies nine domains of wellbeing which may be considered during the assessment process. These domains include physical and emotional wellbeing, ranging from personal relationships to physical function and personal safety. Approaches focused on the individual's strengths are promoted, which explore factors that help or enable the individual to meet their needs and achieve their desired outcomes. These factors include:

- personal resources, abilities, skills, knowledge, potential;
- social networks, resources, abilities, skills (SCIE, 2015a).

Case study 22.2

John is referred to adult social care services by his GP, who is concerned that John is showing signs of self-neglect. John agreed to the referral, although he is rather cautious about what might happen.

Polly makes contact and arranges to visit John at home, explaining that the visit will be an opportunity to provide information and discuss any concerns or issues he has. John is reassured that the visit will be informal and focused on his situation.

John was diagnosed with a degenerative neurological condition three years ago. He has recently experienced increased dizziness, disorientation and numbness. He has fallen on several occasions, scalded his hand and lost confidence. This is affecting his work, his mood and his intimate relationships, especially with his partner.

Polly visits John and they discuss his circumstances and explore the barriers he is currently experiencing. This collaborative assessment identifies the impact of his changing condition on his ability to meet his desired outcomes and John is given the opportunity to consider his strengths and how he wants his needs to be met. Areas he requires support with are located in his ability to meet his personal care and nutritional needs, and a support plan is subsequently designed where John is empowered to control how his needs are met. The significant impact on the wellbeing domains resulting from his disability means he meets the eligibility criteria for care and support services.

How might you identify and use John's strengths to assist the assessment and development of his care plan?

What good practice with disabled people looks like

Whilst the particular social work skills employed, activities undertaken, and legislation drawn on will vary according to the individual, their age and the nature of the impairment, there are universal social work skills required when working with disabled people of all ages. These skills relate to anti-discriminatory and anti-oppressive practice and include addressing the processes which lead to discrimination (Thompson, 2015) and oppression (Young, 2005). For example, Thompson (2015) identifies how invisibilisation operates as a process of discrimination. In relation to disabled people invisibilisation is evidenced in the limited representation of disabled people in the media, on mainstream television and in films. Powerful dominant groups are constantly presented in ways associated with positions of power, status, prestige and influence, whilst disabled people are rarely seen in such positions; it is as if they have been rendered invisible. Young's (2005) work examines the processes of oppression, including marginalisation. The marginalisation of disabled people can be evidenced by their historic separation from general society and ongoing access issues.

Ethical, rights based social work with disabled people of all ages needs to be informed by the social model of disability with its focus on the person's agency and active participation (Oliver et al., 2012). Good social work practice with disabled people should communicate genuine care and compassion, respect privacy, promote advocacy and empowerment and demonstrate professionalism by communicating confidence in the role. Social workers need up-to-date knowledge about relevant issues (including barriers to inclusion often experienced by disabled people), and honesty and commitment to exchange relationships where each party's contribution is respected and valued (Simcock and Castle, 2016). These qualities and skills relate to professional standards identified by the registration body, currently the Health and Care Professions Council and the social work Professional Capabilities Framework.

Challenges for social work with disabled people

Despite the success of the disability movement in creating change, disabled people continue to face discrimination and barriers to full social inclusion. The UN Equality and Human Rights Commission report (2017) highlights how progress has slowed or deteriorated in areas such as access, opportunities and service provision, leading to poor life chances for disabled people.

This means social workers and social care organisations need to work with disabled people to address the discrimination and barriers to inclusion faced by disabled people, as well as the underlying causes in order to improve lives and social circumstances. However, the following section highlights some of the challenges faced by social work practitioners working with disabled people.

1. *Personalisation*

Personalisation concerns individualised, person-centred approaches to care and support, working with people, valuing their strengths and enabling self-determination (Brent, 2016). The Care Act 2014 has extended the scope of personalisation within social care and promotes it as a way of enhancing personal wellbeing (Department of Health, 2014). However, introducing personalisation since the financial crisis of 2008 has risked implementation being undertaken in ways which respond to budgets rather than the principles of choice and control (Lymbery, 2013). Personalisation originally referred to a sum of money (direct payment) provided to an individual eligible for care and support in lieu of services and was seen as the mechanism for achieving equality through increased choice and control. Whereas direct payments were originally introduced to disabled people as a form of liberation, Beresford (2013) argues that the more recent interest has an ideological rationale, extending the marketisation and bureaucratisation of care. Spicker (2013) also highlights how using consumerism as a means for driving up quality and efficiency is flawed as numerous scandals and care provider failures have indicated. The challenge for practitioners concerns how the consumer model simplifies social work with adults and fails to acknowledge the multiple social work roles they undertake.

Further barriers to meaningful personalisation are identified by the Social Care Institute for Excellence (SCIE, 2012). First, the persistence of the medical model amongst social care providers, rather than an acknowledgement of services resulting from rights associated with citizenship. Second, SCIE highlights ongoing barriers related to funding cuts, lack of a market in care services, inflexibility about how personal budgets can be used, risk assessments acting as a block and lack of support for people who are isolated (p9). Such critiques are extremely challenging to social work as they indicate how relationships built on consumerism rather than empathy are prioritised (Lymbery, 2013).

2. *Social work in the age of austerity*

Cuts to welfare benefits and care and support services have had a disproportionate and negative impact on disabled people of all ages (Scope, 2014). Disabled people are more likely to live in poverty, and on average life costs £550 more a month for disabled people (Scope, 2014). Disabled people in employment are also disadvantaged as, after housing costs, 28 per cent of working age disabled people are living in poverty in comparison to 18 per cent of working age non-disabled people (Households Below Average Income (HBAI), 2015/16). The impact of austerity measures on the social inclusion of disabled people needs to be core to social work practice with disabled people. This requires social workers to be actively supporting disabled people to access welfare benefits, paid employment as appropriate for the individual, suitable housing, opportunities of social inclusion and other services to maximise material wellbeing.

3. *Negative narratives about disability*

Negative narratives about disability have a corrosive impact, reducing self-confidence and hope (Quarmby, 2011; Briant et al., 2013). Characterisation of disability in the media creates and reinforces negative perceptions. UK media reports commonly associate disability with benefit fraud, adding more public support to government policy to reduce benefits contributing to a 're-evaluation of who is and who is not deserving of benefits' (Briant et al., 2013, p880). In addition, the promotion of ideas suggesting the welfare system creates a negatively conceptualised form of dependency has been part of the justification of substantial cuts to welfare provision. Reducing state intervention will lead to disabled people living lives characterised by isolation and poverty, financially penalised for not conforming (Oliver et al., 2012; Beresford, 2013).

The absence of realistic and positive cultural representations of disability contributes to the 'otherness' of disabled people and increases fear and ignorance about disability (Wendell, 1996; Briant, 2013). There has been an increase in hate crime targeted at disabled people since 2010, which studies have linked to UK government welfare policy (Ballan and Freyer, 2017). Hate crime refers to often violent crime where disabled people are targeted because of a perpetrator's prejudice towards their disability.

Individualistic notions of independence based on an ideal of self-sufficiency are part of the negative perception of impairment and disability. An alternative understanding of independence acknowledges human interdependence and the importance of self-determination and control over life; something which someone with total care needs can experience if support is organised in a person-centred, self-directed way (Swain et al., 2003; Secker et al., 2003).

Conclusion

This chapter has highlighted the importance of social work practitioners having the knowledge and skills to work with disabled people of all ages, which includes working in ways which promote human rights and address the discrimination and oppression disabled people continue to experience. Social workers have a professional obligation to promote social justice, which means proactively challenging injustice and collaborating with others to address the social and cultural processes which marginalise individuals and groups, including disabled people. Social work practice, underpinned by the social model, emphasises disabled people's strengths and expertise, leading to collaborative ways of working to achieve outcomes. This chapter has suggested how such approaches to practice are enabled by the Care Act 2014 and Children and Families Act 2014.

However, current challenges to social work practice have also been highlighted, including the impact of austerity on disabled individuals' lives and social support structures along with discrimination disabled people continue to experience. This means that for social workers to fulfil their professional duties as stated in the code of ethics (BASW, 2012) and professional standards (SWE) they must proactively engage in actions to promote social justice, including the fair distribution of resources which may create tension with competing interests.

Key points summary

- Disability is an embodied experience and relevant to everyone.
- Disability is created by social and environmental structures rather than impairment.
- Concern for human wellbeing is key to social work, so knowledge about factors impacting on wellbeing is essential for effective practice.
- Disabled people can experience discrimination and oppression; therefore practitioners need to be alert to processes leading to discrimination and address these through anti-discriminatory practice.

Suggested further reading

Oliver, M., Sapey, B. and Thomas, P. (2012) *Social Work with Disabled People* (4th ed). Basingstoke: Palgrave Macmillan.

Simcock, P. and Castle, R. (2016) *Social Work and Disability*. Cambridge: Polity Press.

Swain, J., French, S., Barnes, C. and Thomas, C. (2014) *Disabling Barriers: Enabling Environments* (3rd ed). London: Sage.

23

Social work and learning disability/difficulties (children, young people and adults)

Emma Evans and Sally Lee

Chapter objectives

By the end of this chapter you should be able to:

- consider some of the challenges and risks relating to social work practice with people with learning disabilities/difficulties;
- describe some of the law relating to social work and people with learning disabilities/difficulties;
- explore ways of working with individuals and their parents/carers.

Introduction

This chapter will define and identify the differences between learning disability and learning difficulty. Three key themes in working within the field of learning disabilities, across the life course, will also be explored:

- Transitions from childhood to adulthood.
- Older carers.
- Consent to sexual and other relationships.

These themes form a significant proportion of social work in community learning disabilities teams and are the areas that pose the highest level of challenge and risk.

What is a learning disability or learning difficulty?

The Oxford English Dictionary (Oxford University Press, 2019) defines a disability as: 'a physical or mental condition that limits a person's movements, senses or activities', whilst a difficulty is defined as: 'a thing that is hard to accomplish, deal with, or understand'. By pairing the words disability with learning we get the following definitions: 'A reduced intellectual ability and difficulty with everyday activities – for example household tasks, socialising or managing money – which affects someone for their whole life' (Mencap, 2018a). There are similar definitions used in the NHS who add that 'a learning disability happens when a person's brain development is affected, either before they are born, during their birth or in early childhood' (NHS, 2018a). The language and terms used are constantly in flux and the term learning disability is often used interchangeably with intellectual disability; these are simply different ways of describing the same thing.

The British Institute for Learning Disabilities (BILD) states that

in UK education services, the term 'learning difficulty' includes children and young people who have 'specific learning difficulties', for example dyslexia, but who do not have a significant general impairment of intelligence.

(BILD, 2019)

They recognise that these terms are labels given by society and are open to change (Hardy and Tilly, 2012). In this chapter, we use the term learning disability (LD) to describe those who may need support from adult social care.

Statutory social care defines an LD as an IQ of 70 or below and difficulties with social functioning and communication (Valuing People, 2001). Someone with a learning difficulty is likely to have an IQ above 70 and good functional ability.

If an LD was uncertain, psychology services could complete an Intelligence Quotient (IQ) Test based on the Wechsler Intelligence Test. The Weschler Intelligence Test measures abilities in four areas:

- reasoning;
- retention of information;
- processing of information; and
- verbal comprehension.

Each area is scored, and an overall IQ calculated (Weschler Test, 2019).

In addition, an Occupational Therapist would undertake a functional assessment called an Assessment of Motor Process Skills (AMPS) in which a person's activities of daily living (ADL) are observed (Royal College of Occupational Therapists, 2018). If the individual's IQ was below 70, and they had difficulties undertaking ADL, along with sequencing of activities, then they would be identified as having an LD. This screening is designed to determine the service that is best placed to assist them.

Identifying an individual as having an LD effectively labels them, but enables professionals to tailor support and communication and to determine whether mainstream services can be adapted to meet individual needs. However, social workers must not lose sight that the individual is a person first and their LD is one aspect of them and that labels may draw the focus away from their strengths (Howe, 2009).

Number of people with a learning disability

It is estimated that approximately 1.5 million people in the UK have an LD (Public Health England, 2016). The number is estimated because not all individuals with an LD are known to services. Emerson and Baines (2010, cited on BILD) state that although the life expectancy of people with an LD has increased over the last 70 years, individuals are 58 times more likely to die before the age of 50 compared with the general population. Mencap's report, *Death by Indifference* (2007), states that institutional discrimination contributes to this poor outcome, with individuals admitted to hospital considered a low priority, poor understanding of capacity amongst staff, and professionals not having specific training in LD. The Learning Disabilities Mortality Review (2017) was established to review the deaths of individuals with an LD and to use learning to improve services. The programme found that a greater number of individuals die in hospital compared with the general population. Those who are younger and have multiple or profound disabilities are more at risk. Although not explicit in the report, this is likely to be due to existing health needs and communication difficulties. Whilst increased life expectancy is positive, it can bring its own challenges, with individuals facing potential discrimination due their disability and their age. Individuals with an LD may be at higher risk of developing a secondary diagnosis due to genetic factors. For example, people with Down's syndrome are at high risk of developing early onset Alzheimer's, while Prader-Willi syndrome increases the risk of Type 2 diabetes. Health checks and national screening are especially important for people with an LD. Health Action Plans and Hospital Passports provide information for the individual and professionals supporting them (Turner and Bernard, 2014).

Social work and learning disability through the life course

Individuals make many transitions throughout their life course and may require different services; there are, however, similarities when working with people with an LD of all ages. Communication and advocacy are key considerations when working with individuals with an LD. Ascertaining the individual's wishes and ensuring these form part of the assessment alongside care and support planning are essential elements of person-centred work.

Ways of communicating with individuals can be adapted to the level of LD and the information needing to be shared. For example, breaking down tasks into several stages. Signing and pictures can be used alongside verbal communication to aid understanding. Visual aids are useful when explaining complex information, for example, potential medical treatment or accommodation changes.

Advocacy, family and the impact of austerity

Individuals should be encouraged and enabled to participate in discussions about their lives as far as is practicable. This may involve independent advocacy. It is a requirement of the Care Act 2014 (s67) that independent advocacy is available if an individual is unbefriended, or there is conflict amongst carers. It is also the role of the social worker to advocate on the individual's behalf. Advocates should help individuals explore the choices and options available to them and ensure they are involved in all decisions, whilst not expressing personal opinion or the view of others (Mencap, 2018b).

Whilst families can be advocates, there may be conflict between the outcomes both wish to achieve. Balancing differing views can be difficult. Person-centred practice keeps the focus, decision making and agenda firmly on the individual. For example, what is important to and for the individual (Helen Sanderson Associates, 2019a)? When advocating for an individual it is important to acknowledge the views and feelings of the family. Families are a system within which the individual sits. Working with, not against, the individual's family will increase the likelihood of better outcomes and secure their ongoing support (Howe, 2009).

Austerity presents a further challenge, with local authority budgets being cut. These cuts are reflected in the reduction and scrutiny given to support packages for those with an LD. The Care Act 2014 (s2) requires local authorities to identify community services that could meet need, with paid services only considered when all other options have been explored. A balance needs to be struck between essential services that keep individuals safe and promoting independence. Budget restraints can mean that decisions sit uncomfortably with practitioners. Carter (2017) reported in Community Care that social workers feel under pressure to make reductions that are 'unfair and unsafe', that they are not exercising professional judgement and that adult services are at a 'tipping point' with the long-term sustainability of adult social care being questioned (Carter, 2017).

When approaching funding there needs to be a balance between what the individual wants, what will meet their needs and what is cost effective. Any services/budget should focus on achieving outcomes and building skills for the future. A clear support plan with measurable outcomes is essential (Helen Sanderson Associates, 2019b).

Law and legislation

The areas of law and legislation most commonly used when working with individuals are:

- Care Act 2014;
- Children Act 1989 (amendments in 2004)/Children and Families Act 2014;
- Mental Capacity Act 2005.

The Children Act 1989 and Children and Families Act 2014 are used for individuals up to the age of 18. These Acts ensure that the child's welfare is paramount. There is also a duty for the local authority to promote the safeguarding and welfare of a child in their area who is in need. The Children Act 1989 (s17) states that a child is considered to be in need if he/she is disabled. The Children and Families Act 2014 (s22) states that a local authority must be aware of all children in the area who have a disability.

The Care Act 2014 provides for individuals aged 18 years old or over and care and support assessments identify 'eligible needs' based on the conditions and criteria within this (s9). The eligibility criteria states that the individual's care and support needs must arise from a mental or physical impairment and the individual is unable to achieve two or more outcomes which include a range of needs such as maintaining nutrition and managing personal care. If the individual is unable to meet these outcomes and there will be a significant impact upon their wellbeing, they have eligible care and support needs.

Some individuals with an LD meet these conditions and support services are put into place to assist them in achieving their outcomes. Others may not associate themselves with having an LD, require support services or wish to engage with professionals. However, they can be vulnerable to exploitation and abuse. The Care Act 2014 states that local authorities are required to provide information and advice relating to care and support to all adults in its area, extending beyond those who have an immediate need for care and support.

Engaging with individuals who do not want contact with services is a challenge to practitioners and, in these cases, it is important to determine mental capacity to ensure the person is making an informed decision. The Mental Capacity Act (MCA) 2005 (s1) sets out five principles to be followed when assessing capacity:

- Presume that the individual has capacity.
- The individual can make unwise decisions.
- Practicable steps should be taken to involve the individual.
- Any decision should be made in the individual's best interest.
- If a decision is made it should be the least restrictive option.

The MCA states that capacity is decision specific and if the individual has capacity to make the specific decision, and they choose to engage in something that poses a risk, they may be making an unwise decision. When an individual is assessed as lacking capacity it is essential to include everybody involved in their life to discuss decision making and how the level of risk could be reduced and managed.

If the threshold for formal safeguarding procedures is not met under the Care Act 2014 (s42), then a Multi-Agency Risk Management Meeting (MARMM) can be a productive forum in which to discuss and record concerns about individuals. A MARMM is a locally developed protocol. Although it has no statutory basis it is part of the wider safeguarding adults system with the expected outcome of formulating an agreed risk assessment and management plan for the individual (Bournemouth, Poole and Dorset, 2017).

> **Case study 23.1**
>
> Sarah has a mild LD. There are concerns around Sarah's risky relationships, but she has been assessed as having capacity in this area. Sarah will often contact the police saying that she has been assaulted or raped by the men with whom she has had a sexual relationship or encounter. Sarah accesses services at her local sexual health clinic. Whilst Sarah's behaviour cannot be changed, regular MARMM meetings are held with representatives from adult social care, police and the sexual health clinic. The MARMM enables actions to be set and measured, for example, adult social care will contact Sarah every month, Sarah will attend the sexual health clinic for appointments every six weeks, etc. The approach is joined up and any concerns are shared.

Models, theories and approaches

There are many models, theories and approaches used in LD, but we will cover the following in this chapter:

- systemic;
- outcome focused;
- task focused;
- strengths based;
- advocacy services;
- person-centred practice (personalisation).

Models, theories and approaches are interlinked. Person-centred practices (PCP) ensure the individual is at the centre of care and support planning. PCP tools are easy to read, use pictures and ask questions that relate to the individual (Helen Sanderson Associates, 2019a). PCP relates to advocacy whereby the individual is supported to make their views known and to participate in decisions about their life (Mencap, 2018b). When assessing, it is important to utilise PCP and to remember that the individual is part of a wider system and network. A systemic approach acknowledges this, and the impact the environment and family may have upon them. Assessment requires outcomes to be set including identifying what outcomes the individual wants to achieve, how this might occur and their strengths such as a good support network and community links. The individual's system and network can both facilitate and prevent their outcomes from being achieved. If the individual's family is not supportive then advocacy services may be required to ensure that their voice is heard. If the environment does not offer what the individual needs, then this can impact upon the achievability of the outcomes set. Outcomes agreed with the individual need to be measurable, include time scales, what they can do themselves and lead to task focused practice (Howe, 2009).

Social workers never use just one approach, model or theory, but a variety, in order to support the individual to achieve a greater level of independence.

Transition from child to adult

Transition from children's to adult's services can be an adjustment for parents/carers who may know what they want for their son or daughter, but local authorities are unable to provide it. Resources in adult services are generally different to those in children's services, for example respite. Respite options available to individuals, especially those with complex needs, are limited. Drives in some areas to close residential settings mean that future accommodation and staffing needs to be searched for, recruited and planned. This setup works well for some individuals, but it puts pressure on the staff team who may be isolated.

Heslop and Abbott (2008) completed research that suggested any move for an individual with complex needs was likely to be permanent, owing to limited options. For those with less complex needs, having a stepped approach to independence may be successful as more resources are available. It is important to manage parents'/carers' expectations and for children's and adult's teams to work closely to ensure a smooth transition and continuity of care and support.

Although transition typically takes place when an individual is aged 17 or 18, they still attend school. The bigger transition arguably occurs when this provision ends at age 18 or 19. Complex individuals should be referred to community teams at an early age. Some providers cannot work with individuals until they are 18 years old so creative opportunities, such as shadowing existing staff, should be explored to build confidence. This can be frustrating for parents/carers, social workers and education as systems and processes do not always support what is needed (Intellectual Disability and Health, 2019).

Where individuals have complex needs, discussions around health versus social care funding can cause delays. The authority/organisation funding care when the individual becomes 18 years of age should continue to do so on a 'without prejudice' basis until any dispute has been settled. The criteria for Continuing Health Care Funding differs from child to adult; however, the main disputes are regarding cognition, behaviour and psychological/emotional needs. It is argued that these areas do not relate to physical health, but they are part of the assessment for this funding stream (NHS, 2018b).

Activity 23.1

Think of a transition you have made. For example: leaving school, moving to a new house, changing job.
Write down three factors that made this successful. Would you do anything differently if faced with a similar situation now?

Older carers

Gant and Bates (2017) report that the majority of individuals with an LD live with parents. Life expectancy for these individuals has increased, so many of the parents are older carers.

Their research suggests older carers talk of their caring roles as a responsibility, as opposed to the practical tasks they undertake. Many carers have taken on this 'life-long' role to the detriment of other areas of their lives, for example, employment. Older carers often only come to the attention of services in a crisis. Work with carers needs to recognise the reciprocal nature of relationships. As carers become older, their son/daughter can take a more significant role in practical household tasks and provide emotional support and companionship. Within the Care Act 2014 this strong reciprocal network could be a strength and should be considered during assessment. This should not, however, detract from the individual's outcomes. Financial interdependence can be a reason for an individual remaining at home. Finances are often not separated, with an individual's benefits included in the general household income. This can be problematic if the individual wants or needs to move, as this money is relied upon.

Limited resources within local authorities could mean more pressure is put on older carers to manage and 'keep going'. When completing assessments, the caring role should be acknowledged and consideration given to longer term arrangements (Gant and Bates, 2017). The following case study highlights older carer issues.

Case study 23.2

Mrs Smith is an older parent and carer for her son David. Mrs Smith is 90 years old, has a visual impairment and is unable to meet her own needs. David is 70 years old and has a severe LD. He smokes heavily and has Chronic Obstructive Pulmonary Disease (COPD). Mrs Smith also has COPD due to passive smoking. David is incontinent of urine and wears pads both day and night. He is unable to change these himself. David attends a day service five days a week, where he has a cooked meal at lunchtime. David has one overnight respite break every fortnight which enables him to have a shower.

A support provider has been assisting David at home with an evening meal, medication and personal care. Mrs Smith has also benefited from the support. The support provider gave notice due to David's smoking and an alternative has not been found. It is very important to Mrs Smith that she and David remain living together. David's mother is important to him, but he does not express any concerns being apart from her when he attends the day service or respite. Without evening support there are concerns for David in the following areas:

- personal care;
- medication;
- nutrition;
- skin breakdown.

David's smoking also increases the risk of fire within the home.

What ideas do you have to help keep both Mrs Smith and David safe whilst ensuring their wishes are taken into consideration?

You may have suggested:

- a home safety check from the fire service;
- David showering at the day service;
- the day service managing medication during the week.

Sexual capacity/relationships

Support workers interviewed by Abbott and Howarth (2007) recognised that the topic of sexual capacity and relationships among people with LD was largely ignored and usually only discussed in a crisis. One support worker commented that when two men were found having sex in a shed it was taken down. This managed the perceived crisis but didn't address the relationship.

Relationships should be more widely discussed, especially as the Department of Health (cited in Abbott and Howarth, 2007) states that good services will help those with LD develop relationships, including those of a physical and sexual nature. Emotional and sexual needs should be given the same recognition as housing, employment and general health. However, when issues arise the focus tends to be more on the presenting behaviour than on exploring sexual identity (Abbott and Howarth, 2007).

How do we promote development of relationships? Some support workers believe that it is intrusive and inappropriate to discuss sex and relationships unless the individual with an LD has raised the subject (Abbott and Howarth, 2007). Given that many people with an LD have limited communication skills, this is unlikely. This also reinforces the view that people with an LD are considered to not want sexual relationships.

Research summary

Abbott (2016) suggests that there is a legacy of people with an LD having their relationships controlled and regulated. He also discusses depictions of people with an LD being in need of protection or conversely having dangerous sexual appetites. There are definite gaps between policy, law and individuals' rights and the experiences people have. It is questionable how often people are supported to develop and maintain relationships. Support workers are restricted in enabling individuals, partly because of their own views but also because organisations push the topic to one side. The reluctance to undertake work around relationships could be because of the potential reaction from parents and carers.

Case study 23.3

Anabel has been dating Bill for two years. Both are of similar ages and both have a mild LD. They meet at a day service once a week and at a supervised club once a week. Bill was found to be printing naked pictures of Anabel, taken at his home, on his home computer.

(Continued)

(Continued)

Bill's supported living provider felt taking and printing these photos was inappropriate. They also made it clear that Bill was not to bring Anabel back to the home when there was no supervision.

Anabel and Bill were consenting adults, but the question was raised as to where they could meet in privacy and safety if they were unable to go to Bill's home. Anabel and Bill then went on a group supervised holiday but were asked to leave the venue after engaging in a sexual act in a public place. Anabel and Bill were told to end their relationship by the support provider and family. They were not offered, or given, any relationship support.

- What are the key issues?
- What could have been done differently?
- Are there any positive outcomes?
- What are the main learning points?

Support workers interviewed by Abbott and Howarth (2007) felt that there was some confusion with individuals seeking any type of relationship, albeit with someone of the same or opposite sex. This suggests an issue in how people seeking relationships are viewed.

Social workers and others working with LD need to ensure that individuals know it is safe to talk about their feelings and ask for support. In the case study, Anabel and Bill could have been offered the opportunity to discuss their relationship. Organisations should promote opportunities for individuals to talk about relationships as staff have a responsibility in this area (Abbott and Howarth, 2007). Such work includes supporting people with same-sex relationships. Abbott's research (2015) found that when individuals with an LD tried to exercise their right to same-sex relationships they were faced with significant barriers, high levels of bullying and discrimination. Staff were also often reluctant to support individuals to access pubs, clubs and groups.

Mental capacity and informed consent are important considerations in this area. It is unlawful for anyone other than the individual to consent to sexual relationships or sexual activity (Sexual Offences Act 2003, s4). However, de Than (2015) suggests the Mental Capacity Act (2005) has been used to prevent individuals from forming relationships. Sex and relationships are a contentious area of social work practice which require sensitivity to balance risk, the right to make unwise decisions and the human right to have relationships.

Conclusion

Working within LD is a rewarding area of social work practice with real scope to improve the quality of people's lives through supporting development of skills and independence. However, this chapter highlights some of challenges that are faced by individuals with an LD and their carers. Health provisions for individuals with an LD need continued improvement, with a higher priority in service design and provision. In addition, training for staff to enable person-centred care and appropriate communication skills should decrease instances where lack of medical attention and death occurs.

Cuts to services caused by austerity measures create further challenges. Social workers need to work closely with individuals and families to meet outcomes in creative ways that ensure safety, independence and choice. Collaborative work is also key to successful transitions across stages of the life course. Transitions may not always be successful the first time, but with good communication, honesty and planning they can be a positive experience for individuals and families empowered to fully participate.

Recognition should be given to older carers alongside an awareness of the inter-dependent relationships with their son/daughter. Links between LD and older person's social work teams ensure the right provision is put into place for both. Empowering people with LD to develop relationships also requires further promotion by support providers. It is a human right for individuals to have relationships and we need to be proactive in this as opposed to being reactive and responding only to crises.

Mental capacity and consent are overarching themes across social work within LD and need to be determined in many pieces of work to ensure appropriate management of risk but also to ensure that the individual has choice. This chapter has highlighted evidence of positive change and improvement in the field of LD; however, additional change is both possible and necessary and should be championed to further improve the lives of those we support.

Key points summary

- LD affects people for their whole lives.
- Communication and advocacy are key considerations when working within LD.
- It is essential to acknowledge the role of carers given that most individuals with an LD live with parents.
- Relationships within LD should be more widely discussed and promoted; it is a human right to have relationships.

Suggested further reading

Atherton, H. et al. (2011) *Learning Disabilities: Towards Inclusion* (6th ed). London: Churchill Livingstone.

Higashida, N. (2014) *The Reason I Jump: One Boy's Voice from the Silence of Autism.* Translated from Japanese by D. Mitchell and K. Yoshida. London: Sceptre.

Jones, V. and Haydon-Laurelut, M. (2019) *Working with People with Learning Disabilities: Systemic Approaches.* London: Red Globe Press.

24

Social work, fostering and adoption (working with children and adults)

Lucille Allain and Sioban O'Farrell-Pearce

Chapter objectives

This chapter introduces you to:

- social work practice in fostering, adoption and special guardianship;
- key legislation in England and Wales, notably the Children Act 1989;
- the processes in relation to the assessment, support and supervision of foster carers, special guardians and adopters and how this interrelates with the needs of looked after children.

Introduction

The chapter focuses on fostering and adoption in the United Kingdom and includes special guardianship as it represents a model of family care which has steadily risen over the past ten years (Simmonds et al., 2019). Links are made to the Knowledge and Skills Framework for Children and Families (KSS) (Department for Education, 2014) as this provides an important framework for practice. Attachment and resilience theories are considered as they form a central core of assessing and supporting carers and understanding the needs and experiences of looked after children. These child development theories provide a context for helping practitioners to plan and support children's journeys through the care system and enhance awareness about the sort of parenting looked after children need, including the impact of separation on children's emotional wellbeing and development.

The chapter introduces key practice debates and issues including rising numbers of children coming into the care system; different placement types; the importance of promoting good outcomes for children; and how placement standards and outcomes for children in care are measured. An important aspect is what young people themselves say about their own experiences of being looked after and their experiences of the care system.

The care of vulnerable children is an area of social work practice which attracts a great deal of political and media scrutiny with contentious debates about who should care for children and whether children should remain in their families of origin or be placed elsewhere. In considering these debates it is important to refer to the ethical and value base governing practice; see 'The Code of Ethics for Social Work' (BASW, 2014).

In writing this chapter we have drawn on our research and practice experiences as independent members of a fostering and adoption panel and through undertaking specialist assessments in this area. Through our panel experiences, we have seen firsthand carers' commitment to making a difference to children's lives. In most cases the child/ren who need care are likely to be at risk of harm, have experienced neglect or are unaccompanied children from overseas who have no responsible adult to care for them (Kohli, 2007).

Research summary

Reading panel reports and hearing back from carers and social workers about the progress children make in new families highlights the very important job foster carers and adopters do. This involves making new bonds with children and helping them to feel part of the family through building new relationships. This was highlighted in research with care leavers where the young people reflected on how their foster carers had supported them and continued to do so through the leaving care process. They reported that their foster carers were very important in helping them to find jobs, progress in education and set up and decorate their new homes: 'Their [foster carer's] son helped me to decorate my flat. They told him they would give him something to do it, paint everything, the foster carer helped' (Allain, 2016, p135).

(Continued)

(Continued)

There was evidence of carers helping the young people with transitions to adult-hood, of them celebrating their successes and often continuing to welcome them into their homes for family meals as young adults. Promoting a 'sense of belonging' in foster care for looked after children is very important and is discussed by Biehal (2014) who presents findings from research involving children and their foster carers in relation to how looked after children can be cared for in a way which promotes a sense of belonging.

On terminology

Children looked after: children who have been placed by a local authority under section 20, 'accommodated'; section 31A, care order giving parental responsibility to a local authority; aS44, emergency protection order; 'accommodation' subsequent to police exercising their police powers of protection under s46 of the Children Act 1989; and a placement order under section 21 of the Adoption and Children Act 2002.

Foster care: care provided by adults who have been assessed and approved by a local authority fostering panel or independent agency, or private foster carers who are subject to separate regulations to approve their care of children.

Adoption: permanent care provided by adult adopters who have been assessed and approved to adopt children permanently into their families.

Kinship care: care provided by family members for children that has not involved a local authority arranging their care or taking responsibility for the children's ongoing care.

Special guardianship: permanent care usually provided by family members and connected persons to children who may be looked after or placed in an arrangement made by family members. Special guardianship orders are made under section 14a of the Children Act 1989.

Fostering and adoption practice

Fostering and adoption involves adults offering daily care for children who are not their birth children. Although in some types of care arrangements the carers may already know the child/ren, for example, a connected person or kinship carer or special guardian, all of whom are likely to be members of the child's extended family or friend network, often grandparents. For details of the role of grandparents and special guardianship, see Allain and Hingley-Jones (2019).

Foster carers, special guardians and adopters all undertake a very important role in coming forward to look after children and offer them protective, loving parenting. Foster care is the main placement type used for looked after children, although special guardianship, which offers a form of permanency, is increasing as a placement option. Sometimes foster care can be episodic and short term and is sometimes referred to as short-break or respite care, or it can be emergency or planned short-term foster care.

Alternatively, children may be fostered long-term. In the case of adoption, it is referred to as permanent care and the adopters become the child's 'forever family'. Definitions under the legislation and policy section of the chapter give further details.

Activity 24.1

If you were caring for a child in your home, what would you do to help them feel welcome?

Comment

It would be important to reflect on the age of the child or young person, as what may be needed for a baby or young child is going to be very different to the needs of an older child. Did you consider how you would show them round your home, show them their bedroom and bathroom, explain mealtimes and where they could find you if they felt frightened at night going to sleep (Fahlberg, 1994)? Did you remember to let them know the WiFi password? This is going to be very important for adolescents, alongside information about safety and controls in your home in relation to social media (Megele, 2018).

Legal and policy framework

Models of substitute care are practised the world over to provide parenting to vulnerable children who cannot be cared for by their parents. Fostering and adoption practice differs across the world in families and communities where family members or non-related carers come forward to care for children. The care may be informal, unpaid and unregulated, whereas in some countries it is formalised with weekly payments and legal structures with care standards closely monitored. For more details regarding models of substitute care across different countries see Kiraly et al. (2015) which focuses on kinship care in Australia with aboriginal children and McCartan et al. (2018) who discuss models of kinship care across the four UK nations. In addition, the International Foster Care Organisation (**https://www.ifco.info/**) provides details of different models of care.

When a child is fostered, they become a 'looked after' child, a term that was introduced with the Children Act 1989. Sometimes looked after children are also referred as being 'in care' or young people may refer to themselves in this way. In meetings you may hear children in care referred to as a 'LAC child'. Although this is an abbreviation used by professionals, it is a term that children and young people can find demeaning as it reduces their experiences to a child who lacks something rather than needs care. From this, you can see that the language we use in social work is important in promoting children's rights.

When a child is adopted or is cared for under a legal order called a 'Special Guardianship Order' they are no longer 'looked after'. For more details, see Chapter 2 in Cocker and Allain (2019). In terms of definitions, there are different placement types and models of care which include: foster care, connected person foster care, kinship care, special guardianship and adoption. Foster carers may be approved by a local authority or voluntary agency fostering panel, but all are subject to the Fostering Minimum Standards (Department for Education, 2011) and the Fostering Services Regulations.

Foster carers may be single carers or care together with a partner or family member, and may have children of their own. The way children's care needs are met is under a statutory framework contained in Part 3 of the Children Act 1989 and the Care Planning, Placement and Case Review Regulations 2010. These combine to set out what responsibilities local authorities have to looked after children whose care they are responsible for providing. These include: how often children are visited in the foster home, how their day-to-day care meets their needs, and detailed arrangements for their education and health care. Local authorities also have responsibility for children who leave their care in order to help them move forward into adult life. Foster carers may continue to care for children after the age of 18 in arrangements called Staying Put (Cocker and Allain, 2019, p259). This model recognises that not all young adults are ready to leave at 18 years old and that children looked after may need to stay with their foster carers whilst they are on their journey to adulthood and independent living.

Another model is private fostering, which is care provided for 28 days or more by carers selected by parents who place their children and pay for their care. The statutory framework which relates to this is Part 9 of the Children Act 1989, Children (Private Arrangements for Fostering) Regulations 2005 and the Minimum Standards for Private Fostering. Private foster carers do not have to be approved as local authority foster carers and children are not 'looked after' children. The vulnerability of children to abuse in such circumstances was illustrated in the death of Victoria Climbié (Laming, 2003) which led to the implementation of the Children (Private Arrangements for Fostering) Regulations 2005 and Minimum Standards for Private Fostering. It is the duty of a local authority to make ongoing scheduled checks on private fostering arrangements so that they can consider if the carers and the placement are suitable for the child. Some parents may be unaware of the regulatory requirements but there is a duty on all children's agencies to work together to safeguard children's welfare and safety. In circumstances where parents and carers do not make local authorities aware of private arrangements, schools, and health workers should alert them.

Kinship care is provided by family members that has not involved a local authority arranging it or taking ongoing responsibility for it. This arrangement is made between family members and therefore differs from private fostering. Carers might be grandparents or extended family. Kinship carers can receive services in the same way as other families when the children they care for are children in need under section 17 of the Children Act 1989 but is subject to an assessment. Research by McCartan et al. (2018) discusses how kinship care can provide positive outcomes as children remain in their family networks but there can be multiple deprivation as carers and children do not always receive the financial, emotional and practical support they need. The care of children within kinship networks can be formalised when a court grants a Special Guardianship Order which is made under section 14A of the Children Act 1989. Special guardian carers have access to help and support under legislation called the Special Guardian Regulations 2005 (as amended by the Special Guardianship (Amendment) Regulations 2016). Despite this, research involving grandparent carers demonstrates that grandparents, although willing to care for their grandchildren, can struggle with managing aspects of daily care including contact arrangements (Hingley-Jones et al., 2020).

Special Guardianship is a form of permanent care which does not result in complete severing of parental legal rights in the way adoption does. Like adoption, special guardianship is increasingly used as the best option at the end of care proceedings, particularly for older children who have pre-existing relationships with the special guardians. It is used to provide legal security for permanent care arrangements. Legislation allows for a range of different people (excluding their birth parents) to be special guardians. Special guardian carers can access additional financial support from local authorities and since 2016 they have been able to access the Adoption Support Fund which can be used to pay for therapeutic input for children.

In common with adoption, children cease to be looked after once a Special Guardianship Order is made. The role of a special guardian who is a family member has much in common with the role of family members who provide foster care for children and have been approved. Both go through a rigorous assessment and in the case of special guardianship this is set out in a report scrutinised by the court to ensure that special guardians are suitable to meet the child's needs. However, special guardians do not receive the same levels of practical and financial support as connected persons foster carers, whose role is linked with local authority statutory responsibilities to looked after children. The task of providing safe care, building children's resilience, and promoting contact, often with parents who may have caused or be likely to cause significant harm to a child, can be a challenging one. Research in this area by Hingley-Jones et al. (2020) suggests that there is variation in the way that special guardians are supported.

Connected persons foster care is care provided by a friend/family member defined under section 105 of the Children Act 1989, who has been assessed and approved to care for a looked after child. Children who are cared for by connected persons foster carers are looked after children and local authorities have the same duties to them as they would have to any other looked after child. In these circumstances, children might have become looked after as a result of care proceedings, under section 31 of the Children Act 1989. Connected persons foster carers come forward to care for children they know and have a relationship with to avoid disruption and to promote the child's existing family links and identity. This often involves a process called a 'family group conference' where family members come together to agree the best option for family care of a child who cannot remain in the care of their parents. For more information about Family Group Conferences, please visit the website for the Family Rights Group (**www.frg.org.uk/ involving-families/family-group-conferences**).

Sometimes connected persons carers are asked to care for a child in their family network without advance plans being made, and have to be assessed and approved at short notice before a child is placed. The regulatory framework for relatives and connected persons allows for this whilst the assessment proceeds under regulation 24 of the Care Planning, Placement and Case Review Regulations 2010. Connected person foster carers, like other foster carers, receive support from local authorities after they are approved; this includes a Supervising Social Worker, training and an allowance.

Adoption is when permanent care is provided by adult adopters who have been assessed and approved to adopt children permanently into their families. Adopters are not usually known to the children placed with them, who come from a range of diverse backgrounds. All adopters undergo a rigorous approval process that closely reviews their capacity to parent children before children are placed with them. The National Standards for Adoption 2014, Minimum Standards for Adoption and Adoption Regulations under the Care Standards Act 2000 form the framework for the approval and support of adopters and organisation of adoption agencies. Children are placed for adoption under section 21 of the Adoption and Children Act 2002, following legal proceedings under the Children Act 1989. Local authorities cannot place a child for adoption without either the parents' consent or a section 21 Placement Order. Unlike children who are fostered, adoption results in children having a new permanent family 'as if they were born into that family' and they leave the care of local authorities and are not considered looked after children.

Adoption is used by local authorities to make sure that young children especially are given a secure and loving permanent home. Adopters have a vital role in providing a secure and loving relationship to children and sometimes this role means caring for children who have a complex history and a need for ongoing help which may have financial consequences. In recognition that their material circumstances should not discount them from providing permanent care the Adoption Support Services (Local Authorities) (England) Regulations 2003 set out the arrangements for supporting adopted children and adopters. This may include provision of an allowance for children with extra care needs and specialist therapeutic services through the Adoption Fund.

Needs of looked after children

Numbers of looked after children are steadily rising every year, with 72,650 children looked after on 31 March 2017 (DfE, 2017) which means there were 7,150 more children looked after compared to the same date in 2016 (Cocker and Allain, 2019, p5).

Activity 24.2

Why do you think the numbers of children coming into the care system continue to rise?

This question is discussed in Cocker and Allain (2019, p6) where links are made with research examining the impact of poverty and inequality on family stress and socio-economic disadvantage. Links are also made to improvements and developments in social work practice with more intensive support and intervention when children are at risk.

Looked after children require therapeutic and supportive parenting as they often come into care due to previous experiences of child abuse and neglect, making them a vulnerable group at risk of disadvantage. Effective practice with looked after children entails carers understanding how to build attachment bonds and provide a stable, nurturing and playful family environment. Carers and social workers know the importance of empathy, promoting resilience and being aware of discrimination and disadvantage. Children thrive when they are accepted for who they are, with carers building their resilience by encouraging and celebrating successes, however small.

Independent Reviewing Officer (IRO) role

Caring for children who are looked after is an area of social work which is highly regulated through legislation to make sure that children are properly cared for and supported. There are distinctions between children who have been placed by local authorities and children whose parents have placed them without local authority involvement even though local authorities have a duty to safeguard and protect children in need in their area. Children who have been placed by a local authority, often under sections 20 or 31 of the Children Act 1989, are called 'looked after children' and they have to have a care plan which covers how the different aspects of their needs will be met as they grow up away from their parents. The child's care plan is kept under review by a social worker appointed under section 25A of the Children Act 1989 who is called an 'Independent Reviewing Officer' (IRO). Their role includes reading reports about the care plan from the child's social worker and their foster carer, and most importantly talking to the child about their care as part of their review. Changes in children's care plans are designed to promote their care and their stability and this part of the care plan is carefully considered when the care options described above are decided.

Children might be placed by a local authority as a result of their parents or family members not being able to care for them for a variety of different reasons; some may need short-term care to cover for a few days' hospital admission, others might need a longer term placement when their parents' care of them has deteriorated to the point that they are at risk of significant harm. There is not one set way of caring for children who cannot be cared for by their parents; however, some care options may be prioritised as they are regarded as providing the best outcomes for children. When children are placed with carers, local authorities aim to place them with their wider family or connected persons they know and have a relationship with, as long as it is safe to do so and the child's needs will be met.

Caring for babies and mothers

Different arrangements may apply for babies in terms of substitute care; for example, approved adopters may also be approved to foster so that they can care for babies during care proceedings and then either work towards rehabilitating the baby home or adopt the baby if they cannot be returned to their parents' care. Some foster carers will foster a mother, sometimes who may be a looked after child herself, and her baby in order to keep the family together and offer them support. This could be in circumstances where the mother needs support in her own right as a young person without any concerns about her care of her baby, or circumstances when an assessment needs to be completed of her parenting because there are concerns about possible harm to the child. This type of fostering may be used during care proceedings.

Routes into care and care plans

Each type of looked after care option provides a means of providing a child with parenting, and how this is carried out is formalised in the written care plan which every looked after child must have. The child's care plan reflects what they need in terms of their basic care, health, education, their return home, special help from other professionals, and the arrangements made for them to see their parents, relatives and other people who are important to them. Children whose parents ask for them to be looked after because they cannot look after them are often called 'accommodated' and this refers to section 20 of the Children Act 1989. This is a voluntary arrangement which is usually short-term and parents can take their child back home any time. Unlike other looked after situations, local authorities do not have rights in decision making related to the child and these are limited to decisions about the child's more immediate welfare needs. Their care plan should strongly reflect the child's and their parents' wishes and feelings to ensure that their needs are known and acted on.

Children who are looked after because their care has deteriorated to the point that the local authority needs to step in and has obtained a court order are cared for under section 31 of the Children Act 1989. In these circumstances, there are stringent rules about removing children from their parents and families. Courts only grant orders for children to be removed after examination of evidence presented to it by all parties including representatives of the child (Children's Guardian) about risk of significant harm and their future care, when it is in children's best interests to remove them from their parents and provide them with alternative care. Children may also be placed with carers when they are considered to be at risk of imminent significant harm and need to be in a safe place. This can be done under section 46 of the Children Act 1989 by a police officer who may be called to investigate a situation and finds a child in circumstances in which they have reasonable cause to suspect a situation may place them at risk of significant harm. Or this can be done by a social worker who has reasonable cause to suspect significant harm; this then involves obtaining a court order to remove the child and take them to foster carers under section 44 of the Children Act 1989. This is often referred to by social workers as an 'emergency protection order'.

Both the police power and the court order last for short periods of time to enable the local authority to place the child in a safe place, usually with emergency foster carers, whilst the circumstances of the child's care are investigated, and decisions made about their safe return. The local authority can make decisions about the child's care in a way that ensures their welfare needs are met.

Case study 24.1

Sarah, aged six, and Rochelle, aged four, are half siblings who have been cared for by their maternal grandmother Marion in a kinship care arrangement for the past three years. Marion took over the children's care from her daughter Lynda but did not want to enter into a formal arrangement. She hoped Lynda would be able to care for her children once she had stopped using illicit drugs, and Rochelle's father had left, as he was abusive to Lynda and the children. Marion has managed to make sure that Sarah and Rochelle see their mother regularly but sometimes had to be very firm with her daughter when she demanded having the children to stay with her. Marion has called the police on some occasions because Rochelle's father has threatened her. Sarah finds this very upsetting and she says she wants to stay with her grandmother. Rochelle does not know what is happening but becomes very unsettled when she sees her mother. Sometimes Marion found it difficult to cope financially and asked for help from relatives and from her local authority. Marion is now finding it very difficult to know what to do as she needs to go into hospital for an operation and have time to recover afterwards which is anticipated to be about four weeks. Her daughter Lynda says she will be able to care for the children but Marion does not think that she will be able to, as she is still taking drugs. Marion's sister, Gloria, has said she could care for the children; she is a school escort for disabled children and Sarah and Rochelle enjoy visiting her. Marion asks for help from the local authority to help make the arrangements as she'd prefer her sister Gloria to be the carer.

How might you advise her and support the children?

Comment

It is important that the children are in a safe placement whilst their grandmother is in hospital; although their mother wants to care for them, her continued drug use makes this unsafe. Having a family meeting, called a 'family group conference', would help to plan and agree the arrangements plus contact with the children's mother. This would support Gloria in her care of the children.

Assessment, support and supervision

Social workers who work in fostering and adoption are referred to as 'supervising social workers', family placement social workers or adoption social workers. As well as working with foster carers and adopters, they also work closely with child and family social workers for looked after children. Their role is to assess and support foster carers, special guardians and prospective adopters, complete regular reviews and present cases to the relevant fostering and adoption panels, with changes underway currently to create regional adoption panels.

Social workers in fostering services ensure that foster carers are thoroughly assessed, supervised and are trained to make sure that they care for children in a way that meets the child's needs and is in line with the child's care plan. The social workers are involved in complex assessments and draw on theories of life course development, attachment theory, adult attachment style measures, parenting styles and models, plus carers' capacity to provide empathic, child centred care. They explore carers' emotional and practical care skills and bring awareness of diverse parenting styles as they recruit carers from all communities and a range of cultural backgrounds with different models of family care.

Foster carers may be provided by local authorities, or by private or voluntary organisations, some of whom provide specialist carers for children with specific needs that might be outside the experience of families ordinarily caring for children. All local authorities have to provide sufficient numbers of foster carers to meet the needs of the children living in its area. This means that local authorities recruit, assess and approve carers who can meet the needs of those children and work with private and voluntary agencies to ensure that when a child needs to be looked after they have a carer for them. This is an ongoing and challenging process as there is a shortage of foster carers in some regions. Alongside meeting their statutory obligations to children, local authorities organise services in different ways to ensure sufficiency and manage resources. This is based on research into the numbers of children in their area who might need to be cared for and what research says about how best outcomes for children who are looked after are achieved.

Key points summary

- Foster care is subject to a legal framework that determines how children are looked after by local authorities when they cannot be cared for by their parents.
- Children looked after come into the care of local authorities in a variety of ways, but all have a written care plan which their foster carers contribute to by providing them with day-to-day practical physical care and emotional nurture.
- Whilst the aim is always to try to return children home to their parents, sometimes this is not possible or safe to do, and children need to be found permanent homes with adopters or adults they already know often under a special guardian arrangement.
- Looked after children are supported by local authorities when they leave care to go home, or are adopted or have special guardians, and special rules apply to young people who have been in care to help them become independent adults.

Suggested further reading

Cocker, C. and Allain, L. (2019) *Social Work with Looked After Children* (3rd ed). London: Sage/ Learning Matters.
Cosis-Brown, H. (2014) *Social Work and Foster Care*. London: Sage/Learning Matters.

25

Social work with refugees and asylum seekers

Kim Robinson

Chapter objectives

By the end of this chapter you should be able to:

- describe the field of forced migration;
- consider social work in the context of the diversity of experiences of refugees and asylum seekers;
- be mindful of intersectionality (Romero, 2017), critical multicultural practice (Nipperess and Williams, 2019) and to hold a position of what Freire called 'critical curiosity' (1990);
- critically reflect on the social work role by challenging assumptions and dominant discourses that may contribute to marginalisation and social exclusion.

Introduction

I have witnessed many deaths, suicides, and self harm over the past five years. I have a profound understand of the suffering experienced by the people on Manus and Nauru and how they have been damaged mentally and physically. It's more than darkness and cruelty. I know many people who are separated from their families and children, others have children that have spent their whole lives inside a prison camp, and I know many young people who have lost their dreams and wasted their skills.

(Boochani, 2018b)

We are seeing displaced people throughout the world on an unprecedented scale. The United Nations High Commission for Refugees (UNHCR) estimates there are currently 68.5 million forcibly displaced people worldwide. There is currently an urgent humanitarian refugee situation in Australia and it is occurring off two previously little known islands called Manus and Nauru. The Australian Government has held refugees for over five years involuntarily, and there are women, children and men who have no hope of repatriation under the current immigration policies. Refugees are enduring extreme conditions and suffering poor physical and mental health. UNHCR is calling this 'health crisis' urgent and demanding the Australian Government close its offshore detention centres (Zhou, 2018). The doctors from the international non-governmental organisation (INGO) Médicin Sans Frontières (MSF) have been forced to leave the islands (MSF, 2018), and a significant reduction in services to refugees has occurred, with Amnesty International Australia (AIA) and the Refugee Council of Australia (RCOA) documenting alarming evidence (2019). MSF has published a report documenting the impact of 'offshore processing' and indefinite detention on the mental health of refugees, 79 per cent of whom are confirmed as such by UNHCR (MSF, 2018; AIA and RCOA, 2018). Blowing the whistle on poor conditions and challenging the government for ignoring medical advice has resulted in Australian doctors being denied visas and sacked (Koziol, 2018; Doherty, 2019). Social workers along with others have been subject to the Border Protection Act 2015, which prevents them from disclosing conditions and concerns about the refugees they work with in these offshore facilities. Despite international conventions and resolutions developed to protect the rights of refugees and asylum seekers, many lack access to health and legal services, and financial protection to access them (World Health Organization (WHO), 2018, p3).

This chapter considers the current challenges facing social workers who work with refugees in the context of *settlement*. While it does not focus on working with those in Australia, these issues of detention along with statelessness, internal displacement and increasing border controls resonate in the current international political environment (Briskman and Ife, 2018). Social workers are a key feature in settlement services, advocating and supporting new arrivals, addressing social justice issues and promoting social cohesion via education and employment, and facilitating community development to address racism and exclusion (Allweiss and Hilado, 2018). The role of social workers in INGOs, non-governmental organisations (NGOs), community settings, statutory services, health, education and housing providers, to name but a few, is both challenging and complex.

This chapter recommends two models to consider progressing the conceptual thinking for social work in this context. The first is an established model developed by

Ager and Strang (2008) called 'A Conceptual Framework Defining Core Domains of Integration', and the second is by Williams and Graham (2016) called 'Towards embedded transformatory practice'. Before considering the social work role specifically, I wish to provide some background to forced migration.

Forced migration

The response of the developed world to forced migration is both a politically fraught and challenging area of public policy at national and international levels. Humanitarian migrants face increasing barriers to settlement that are rooted in what Crock et al. (2017, p2) refer to as 'economic uncertainty, rising xenophobia and increased economic migration'. While most migration is safe, orderly and regular, UNHCR, (2018a) reports that global displacement is at a record high, affecting some 68.5 million people, with 85 per cent of them living in developing countries, increasingly called low and middle income countries (LMICs). Of the 25.4 million refugees, 3.1 million are claiming protection as asylum seekers, and of these only 102,800 refugees are resettled (UNHCR, 2018a). There are also 10 million stateless people who lack a nationality and access to basic rights such as education, healthcare, employment and freedom of movement.

It is internationally accepted that all countries adhering to the United Nations Universal Declaration of Human Rights (UDHR, 1948) respond to the arrival of refugees at their borders. Aristide Zolberg predicted 30 years ago that there would be a global increase in the numbers of refugees due to 'the formation of new states and confrontations over the social order in both old and new states' (Zolberg, 1989, p416). The international response to refugees, as articulated by UNHCR, continues to rest with two main strategies: the provision of aid to those in the LMICs and the implementation of strict policy guidelines for admission to countries offering settlement. These policies are influenced by political, economic and demographic factors for recipients such as age, class, gender, ability and health:

Decision making about eligibility for exit, transit, entry and stay is dominated by regulatory and classification systems, both implicit and explicit, which reflect assumptions about legitimacy, vulnerability and desirability related to these demographic characteristics.

(Bhabha, 2007, p16)

Research summary

The circumstances and challenges affecting the health and wellbeing of asylum seekers and refugees is specific to each phase of the migration cycle (pre-departure, departure, transit, arrival, settlement and potential return) (Allweiss and Hilado, 2018). Social work

(Continued)

(Continued)

can bring an awareness and understanding of the intersections of cultural backgrounds and migration journeys (Marlowe, 2018). There are key areas of practice social workers need to address, including the impact of destitution, detention, working with unaccompanied children, the long term effects of temporary protection visas, settlement and deportation (Briskman et al., 2012; Robinson and Gifford, 2019; Fozdar and Banki, 2017).

Understanding and becoming informed about the types of trauma and loss that can accompany forced migration, particularly exposure to war and violence, is vital to working in partnership with communities, families and children (Allan and Hess, 2010; Quiros and Berger, 2015). Refugees and migrants can be among societies' most vulnerable members but they also bring a range of skills and talents. A trauma-informed approach must balance knowledge of the complexity of trauma while maintaining a critical lens that keeps in focus the exposure to disadvantage and structural inequality that is present for many people with refugee backgrounds (Garrett, 2015). Social workers can play a vital role in settlement by supporting children in education, improving access to health services and housing, employment and training, and tackling broader issues such as racism, bullying and discrimination.

There are restrictions on gaining access to Australia to claim asylum, as with other high income countries, including stringent border controls, the use of mandatory detention and blanket interdiction or removal. These measures, described by Grewcock (2010) as 'state crime', have positioned the refugee as 'deviant' for seeking access to safety. Briskman and Fiske (2016) describe the practice of politicians successfully vilifying asylum seekers as illegal and 'creating criminals'. These strategies comprise a hostile approach by the state towards refugees and have alienated, criminalised and abused unauthorised migrants (Grewcock, 2010). This process of social control is referred to by Welch (2012) as 'crimmigration', and contributes to perpetuating myths and stereotypes that 'other' asylum seekers and refugees. The previous President of the Australian Human Rights Commission (AHRC), Professor Gillian Triggs, a strong advocate for refugees and asylum seekers, clearly states that 'the right to seek asylum is enshrined in the Universal Declaration of Human Rights' (Triggs, 2018, p207). The work of the Commission has consistently challenged and exposed the myths perpetuated against those seeking sanctuary from war and persecution, particularly in relation to the detention of children (HREOC, 2004; AHRC, 2014).

Activity 25.1

Search the internet for some of the headline stories about asylum seekers arriving in your country. What do you notice about the ways in which they are framed and the issues they focus on? Now look at the Refugee Council 'myths and facts sheet' site and contrast the way they address these same issues.

Key thinkers and theorists

Below is a list of key thinkers and theorists to familiarise yourself with:

- Jacqueline Bhabha – human rights of children, women
- Linda Briskman – critical social work, detention, human rights
- Stephen Castles – international migration
- Ignacio Correa-Velez – settlement of refugees, community development, men
- Mary Crock – human rights, unaccompanied minors
- Suman Fernando – mental health, refugees and minority ethnic groups
- Sandra Gifford – migration, young people, settlement
- Jim Ife – social work, globalisation, human rights
- Fethi Mansouri – migration, refugees
- Peter Mares – migration movements, detention regimes
- Klaus Neumann – refugee policy, settlement policy
- Louise Newman – children, mental health
- Robyn Sampson – alternatives to detention
- Derek Silove – asylum seekers and refugees, mental health
- Charlotte Williams – critical social work, transformative practice.

Social work in a range of contexts

Social work draws on a number of disciplines, including sociology, social theory, history, politics and psychology to make sense of the complexity facing individuals, families, communities and society with the aim to be transformative in people's lives (Fook, 2016). In drawing on the critical theoretical traditions, critical social work aims to disrupt and question dominant discourses and structures that oppress and marginalise (Morley et al., 2019; Parker and Ashencaen Crabtree, 2018). A broad new literature of critical social work highlights how intersectionality is essential to inform the ways in which we work across various axes including ethnicity, age, gender, ability, sexuality and class (Romero, 2017). It demands that social workers step up to challenge inequality and promote social justice (Marlowe, 2018; Williams and Graham, 2016; Nipperess and Williams, 2019).

Social work is a socially constructed activity and as such is both exposed to and shaped by dominant discourses and social workers can play a key role in challenging oppressive discourses by utilising a human rights framework (Briskman and Ife, 2018). Advocating for equitable social policy to meet the needs of asylum seekers and refugees can include direct practice, one-to-one support and advocacy, research, and community development to support newly arrived groups in addressing exclusion and marginalisation. Social workers have a responsibility to be prepared when working in this ethically fraught political and legislative area, by keeping up to date with rapidly changing laws and social policy (Parker and Ashencaen Crabtree, 2018; Briskman and Ife, 2018). They are well-placed to work collaboratively across sectors, and to support and educate other disciplines about anti-oppressive practice (Baines, 2017; Williams and Graham, 2016; Morley et al., 2019).

Refugee Councils and local refugee support groups play an essential role in providing support, and are vital in developing partnerships with service users. There are tensions for social workers working in statutory and voluntary services or INGOs/NGOs, regarding the issues of care and control, and not colluding with or perpetuating stereotypes about a victim status or removing agency (Robinson and Masocha, 2016). There is, however, an emphasis on interagency collaboration and multi-agency working in the refugee sector, with UNHCR emphasising the importance of partnership working with governments, other UN agencies, NGOs, the private sector and the refugee community (2018b, p186).

Activity 25.2

What legislation and policy do you think you will need to know to work in this area? Make a list of what you know, and then highlight areas you need to find out more about.

Models of practice

I want to highlight two models that might assist in framing the work of social workers who work with refugees and asylum seekers in health and social welfare settings. First is Ager and Strang's (2008) model that was developed to examine integration of people of refugee background into the United Kingdom.

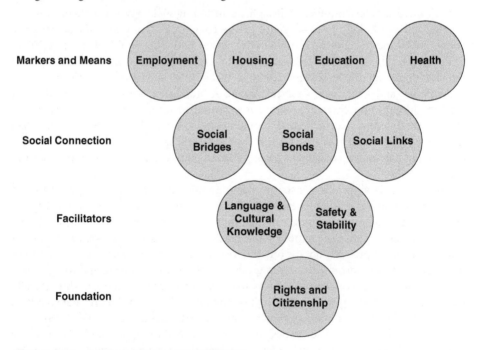

Figure 25.1 Ager and Strang Model (2008)

Ager, A. and Strang, A. (2008) Understanding integration: a conceptual framework, *Journal of Refugee Studies*, 21(2): 166–191, by permission of Oxford University Press.

The four domains refer to both a measurement of achievement and access to successful integration. For example, if someone has a job, a place to live, is studying or has had good education and has good physical and mental health, then they are likely to be doing well settling into a new country. If one of these Markers and Means are not progressing, it generally has a detrimental effect on settlement and success. Ager and Strang (2008) use the term social bridges to describe the connections with people from other communities and groups that widen opportunities and networks, and include a variety of community groups, including religious or sporting groups or women's or parents' groups. Social bonds describe the connections with family and friends, and trusted others. People from refugee backgrounds may have lost their family and social bonds through the refugee experience and they often access information and support from other more established newly arrived communities. Social connections stress the importance of relationships to the integration process. Social bridges help people to access social links and these are the services and systems that assist in establishing communities, such as financial supports, community health centres, education advice, English language classes and so on.

This model helps us to understand the foundations underpinning successful settlement into a new community, which are rights and citizenship. It is very difficult for someone to settle if they have no, or limited, rights or access to citizenship, as safety and stability are critical to a sense of belonging (Marlowe, 2018). Racial discrimination and exclusion impact negatively on all of these fields and in turn affect a community's ability to become established (Williams and Graham, 2016).

Activity 25.3

Consider working with someone from a refugee background and try to map out their lived experience using this model. How might they meet the Markers and Means? What about their Social Connection? Where are they located in relation to the other Facilitators and Foundation?

The second model is called 'Towards embedded transformatory practice' and was developed by Williams and Graham (2016, p14) specifically to look at issues of race and ethnicity. The focus of this model is underpinned by values principles contributing to social work practice that can be applied to a range of contexts and service user groups. First, 'critical reflexive interrogation' has long been part of the critical social work lexicon (Fook, 2016), with this practice being central to understanding the ways in which power operates across systems and structures. The brief summary of forced migration above highlights the importance of being informed about the powerful dominant discourses operating in this space of settlement and 'crimmigration'. Exploring the positionality of the self in relation to locality, nation, culture, historical context and place is part of working with all service user groups (Beresford, 2012) and is the basis of what Freire called 'critical curiosity' (1990). However, in relation to working with asylum seekers and refugees, social workers can engage with all these elements and be proactive in decolonising practice to ensure inclusivity and genuine

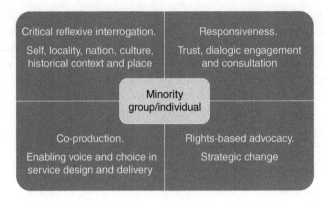

Figure 25.2 Towards embedded transformatory practice

Adapted from Williams and Graham, 2016: 14.

mutual engagement. In the second domain, 'responsiveness, trust, dialogic engagement and consultation' form the basis of the anti-oppressive practice skill set that
critical social work promotes and facilitates. These elements are essential when working with newly arrived communities, and there is considerable literature about
insider-outsider research and community development that genuinely engages with
service users' lived experience (Parker and Ashencaen Crabtree, 2018; Kenny and
Connors, 2016; Carling et al., 2014). Resisting narratives that remove agency and
assign a victim status to refugees is one way of promoting trust and engagement.

The third area is 'co-production, enabling voice and choice in service design and
delivery', which is challenging in an increasingly neo-liberal context (Garrett, 2016,
p1919). In services there is an increased emphasis on procedures, routines, surveillance and compliance with operational standards to ensure objectivity and certainty
predominate and form what Foucault describes as tools of governmentality (Foucault,
1991). These processes often exclude the voice of the service user, so activism and
facilitating co-production is core to ensuring services are not paternalistic and irrelevant (Nipperess and Williams, 2019). The final area is 'rights-based advocacy'
which for refugees and asylum seekers, many of whom have been denied rights, is
ensuring that practice takes account of power and resistance. Challenging the practices of workers and community members seen to be patronising and infantilising of
refugees and asylum seekers across all sectors is also part of this remit (Lange et al.,
2007, p39). Respecting diversity and human rights, and valuing human dignity in
partnership and collaboration, is the focus of critical social work practice (Ife, 2012;
Morley et al., 2019).

Activity 25.4

Please read the following case study and consider the four domains of the model above
in answering the following reflective questions.

- How do you position yourself in relation to the women in this group?
- How might you best establish yourself as the social worker in this group, and how would you go about building trust and engagement?
- How might you consider including the voice of these women in a community response to the issues they have raised?
- How would you go about advocating for their rights, and identify opportunities for strategic change?

Case study 25.1

Social work in the community

I've run some women's groups, with the mothers, and in particular Muslim women, I ran a very interesting project in the X area of Melbourne (Australia). It was around mental health, and the women get to talk about their experiences of mental health and how they access services. However, what I went in there to do didn't happen really, because when we got to talking about what affects your mental health in Australia one woman in the group put up her hand and said racism. But she didn't say racism, she said, 'The people next door to us, they come out every day and they abuse us. They squash all their fruit on our car.' And then it was of course like there were 14 women in that room, including the interpreter, and the school multicultural worker – and we spent the next two and a half hours of each and every one of those women talking about daily experiences of racism.

(Interview 9: Social Worker)

Conclusions and challenges facing social workers

This chapter highlights the context facing social workers who work with newly arrived asylum seekers and refugees. The models offer us ways of thinking about how we might engage with communities, and provide us with tools to reflect on our practice and push back on the dominant discourses of 'crimmigration' (Welch, 2012). I have highlighted for the reader the need to consider the global phenomena of forced migration, and how these issues are related beyond our nation state borders. I have also suggested we consider the ways in which social work can work with individuals and communities who come from refugee backgrounds.

A key element of liberal governmentality is the ability of individuals to engage in practices that oppose the government in legitimate ways. Activism with regard to refugees has been prominent in Australia and internationally, and social work has played a role in facilitating debate about human rights (Briskman and Goddard, 2007; Fraser, 2013). Engaging with the political, economic and social issues embedded in debates on immigration is essential to good practice for all social workers. Researchers have suggested that educators engage with these issues using Foucault's notion of ethics and fearless speech (*parrhesia*) (Christie and Sidhu, 2006, p460), and social workers too can stand in solidarity, resistance and partnership in this field. Key to doing this is to practise critical reflection and engage with how power is exercised. This is challenging when faced with the narratives of those with lived experience of human rights abuses, such as Boochani, whom I cite at the start of this chapter. Working with those who have lost part of their lives, loved ones and human dignity is confronting work. For Nick Martin, the doctor who lost his job on Nauru for exposing substandard conditions and highlighting how the Australian Government border force was ignoring medical advice, some acknowledgement has been forthcoming. He recently won the Blueprint for Free Speech award, a UK prize given to whistleblowers who expose serious corruption or wrongdoing in the public interest (Doherty, 2019). While not vindicated, as still the refugees are living on the islands, it is recognition of speaking truth to power. Social workers have a unique position to work in this sector, bringing hope and humanity to a global issue affecting us all.

Key points summary

- Social workers work across a range of services that engage with people from refugee backgrounds. It is important that we have an understanding of the complexities of forced migration globally and how these impact at national and local levels.
- There are a range of models and theoretical frameworks that can assist us in our practice in social work, and it is vital that we keep a focus on human rights, social transformation and critical social work.
- Co-production and working in collaboration with people from refugee backgrounds is key to developing responsive and respectful services, and ensuring that social work continues to challenge practice, policy and research in this increasingly politicised space.

Suggested further reading

Boochani, B. (2018) *No Friend but the Mountains: Writing From Manus Prison*. Sydney: Pan Macmillan.

Nipperess, S. and Williams, C. (eds) (2019) *Critical Multicultural Practice in Social Work: New Perspectives and Practices*. Sydney: Allen and Unwin.

Marlowe, J. M. (2018) *Belonging and Transnational Refugee Settlement: Unsettling the Everyday and the Extraordinary*. London: Routledge.

Morley, C., Ablett, P. and Macfarlane, S. (2019) *Engaging with Social Work*. Cambridge: Cambridge University Press.

Williams, C. and Graham, M. (eds) (2016) *Social Work in a Diverse Society: Transformative Practice with Black and Minority Ethnic Individuals and Communities*. Bristol: Policy Press.

26

Social work and substance use

Orlanda Harvey

Chapter objectives

By the end of this chapter you should be able to:

- give a brief overview of social work and substance use within the UK including highlighting relevant legislation and policies;
- outline several key theories and models relating to substance use;
- explore some of the challenges that social workers experience when working with people who use substances.

Introduction

This chapter begins by identifying four main classes of drug, highlighting relevant legislation and policies that govern drug use and outlining several key theories.

To be effective in this field and elsewhere, social workers should have an awareness of the implications and potential treatments of substance use, as social workers can find themselves supporting people with substance-related problems (Parrish, 2014). Fifteen of the 54 overview reports of serious case reviews, significant case reviews or multi-agency child practice reviews published in 2017 highlighted drug use or misuse as a factor (NSPCC, 2018). Therefore, the chapter will also discuss some of the challenges that social workers face when working in this area.

Drugs

The four main classes of drugs used recreationally (some legal, some illegal) are listed in Table 26.1.

Table 26.1   Main classes of drugs

Drug	Types	Positive effects	Negative effects
Opioids	Opium, heroin, methadone, buprenorphine, codeine	Can create a dreamy sense of wellbeing	Can be highly addictive, and lead to physical dependence. Powerful withdrawal symptoms
Stimulants	Cocaine, amphetamine, methamphetamine, caffeine, steroids, khat, mephedrone, tobacco	Release noradrenaline and dopamine, which triggers the 'flight or fight' response, making you feel alert, full of energy, not needing sleep or food	Can overstimulate the nervous system, put strain on the heart and be highly addictive
Depressants	Alcohol, gamma hydroxybutyrate (GHB), benzodiazepines	Can decrease anxiety and relieve insomnia and pain	Each substance can cause different physical harms, e.g. alcohol and liver damage, and create dependency
Psychedelics	LSD (Lysergic acid diethylamide), mushrooms, ibogaine, DMT (Dimethyltryptamine), mescaline	Create strong pro-social feelings of openness and talkativeness, and create intense visual and transcendental experiences	Least likely to be dependence inducing, whilst taking them they make it difficult to undertake everyday activities

Adapted from Nutt (2012)

Some drugs such as cannabis can cause effects that cross a number of classes, and other substances misused include: painkillers, tranquillisers, sedatives and human enhancement drugs (Nutt, 2012), all of which can cause harm. People may take a combination of drugs to enhance effects or combat side effects. Some drugs can be gateways into other types of drug, e.g. cannabis into heroin (Taylor et al., 2017).

Policy and legislation

Key legislation, criminal and policy law, relating to the use of substances is found in Table 26.2.

Table 26.2   Legislation and drug use (direct legislation in bold)

Legislation	Relevance to substance use
Misuse of Drugs Act 1971	**The main law regulating drug control in the UK.** The first UK legislation to control the personal use of substances was passed as emergency restrictions under the Defence of the Realm Act in 1916, regulation 40B, making non-medical possession an offence and requiring a doctor's prescription for cocaine. This was in response to fears about the drug use by soldiers (Berridge, 1978, 2014; BMA Board of Science, 2013). The Dangerous Drugs Act came into force in 1920 and forms the basis of current legislation.
Drug Trafficking Act 1994	**Defines drug trafficking as transporting or storing, importing or exporting, manufacturing or supplying drugs covered by the Misuse of Drugs Act 1971.**
The Psychoactive Substances Act 2016	**Criminalises the production, supply or possession with intent to supply of any psychoactive substance knowing that it is to be used for its psychoactive effects.**
The Care Act 2014	Provision of adult social care services includes support for people who are dependent on substances.
The Mental Capacity Act 2005	Provides a legal framework for acting and making decisions on behalf of adults who lack the capacity to make particular decisions for themselves (at that point in time). Defends people's right to make unwise decisions.
The Children's Act 1989	Allocates duties to local authorities, parents, and other agencies in the UK, to ensure children are safeguarded and their welfare is promoted.

Drug classification

Drug classifications in the UK fall under the Misuse of Drugs Act 1971, dividing substances into three classes (A, B and C). This provides a basis for attributing penalties for offences. Under the Act, it is not drug use per se that constitutes the offence but the possession of the drug. Possession offences range from on-the-spot fines to jail sentences. Supply and production offences can lead to a life sentence. The government can temporarily ban new drugs for one year while deciding on a classification, which is broadly based on the harms caused to the individual or society when misused. However, arguments exist suggesting that these classifications should be reviewed and classification based on scientific evidence of a broader base of harms (Nutt, 2012).

The UK drug strategies

The Government's Drug Strategy 2017, *Reducing Demand, Restricting Supply, Building Recovery* (UK Home Office, 2017), has two overarching aims:

(i)   reduce all illicit and other harmful drug use; and
(ii)   increase the rate of individuals recovering from their dependence.

Wales, Scotland and Northern Ireland each have their own strategies:

- Working Together to Reduce Harm: The Substance Misuse Strategy for Wales 2008–18 (Welsh Assembly Government, 2008)
- Rights, Respect and Recovery: Alcohol and Drug Treatment Strategy (The Scottish Government, 2018)
- New Strategic Direction for Alcohol and Drugs Phase 2: 2011–16: (Reviewed 2018) (Department of Health Social Services and Public Safety Northern Ireland, 2011)

Prevalence and treatment UK snapshot: drugs and alcohol

Drug-induced death is the fifth most common cause of preventable death among 15–49-year-olds in the UK; the majority of deaths included heroin use (European Monitoring Centre for Drugs and Drug Addiction (EMCDDA), 2017). Opioids (mainly heroin) were the most commonly reported primary substances among those seeking treatment for drug use problems. There has been an increase in the use of human enhancement drugs, e.g. 'muscle drugs'; weight-loss drugs; image enhancing drugs; and sexual, cognitive and mood enhancers (Evans-Brown et al., 2012).

In 2017, there were 7,697 alcohol-specific deaths in the UK (Office for National Statistics, 2018). Since 2001 rates of alcohol-specific deaths among males have more than doubled compared with females, and in England there are significantly higher death rates for those in the most deprived local areas when compared with the least deprived local areas. It was estimated that 595,000 people in England are dependent on alcohol and in need of specialist support, yet only around 108,000 were receiving treatment for their alcohol dependency (Alcohol Research UK, 2018).

Key theories and models

There are a range of theories that attempt to explain substance use. They can be summarised under three areas:

- Neurobiological: focusing on the effects of drugs, explaining drug dependence in biological terms.
- Psychological: concentrating on behavioural models and individual differences.
- Socio-cultural: considering the cultural and environmental factors.

Two important socio-cultural theories are Deviance and Social Learning Theory.

Deviance is used to describe behaviours that violate social norms and can differ between cultures, religions and societies. Sociologist Emile Durkheim argued that deviant behaviours were a normal and necessary part of society, which could lead to social change and push society's moral boundaries (Clinard and Meier, 1992). Two recent examples include:

1. *The perception of premarital sex*: in the past, unmarried, pregnant women were sent away to 'asylums'. Now sex before marriage is deemed unremarkable within UK culture.
2. *Gay sex*: for men a criminal activity until 1969, yet by 2014 same-sex marriage was legalised in Wales, England and Scotland, although some religious groups still see the behaviour as deviant.

Activity 26.1

It can be useful to understand a range of views. Seek out three people who may have a different perspective to you, e.g. someone older, or from a different religious or cultural background.
   Discuss with them which behaviours they might consider deviant today, or which behaviours they believe were once thought of as deviant are now socially accepted.

Deviance can be a way of asserting an identity, a way to rebel against group norms and show allegiance to a subculture. Deviant behaviours linked to drug use will depend on standards created by the society the person lives in (Clinard and Meier, 1992).

Chemsex: people use drugs to have sex, which can make them feel uninhibited; it is associated with gay communities (Glyde, 2015). It typically involves crystal methamphetamine, GHB or mephedrone. Risks include spreading of sexually transmitted diseases and blood borne viruses (BBVs) and sexual assault.

Activity 26.2

Consider the following statement:

   Cannabis use is not deviant. Engaging in chemsex is deviant behaviour.

*   Do you think this statement is true or false?
*   What has influenced your answers to the statement?

Neutralisation theory (Matza, 1964) explains how people with deviant behaviour justify or rationalise their behaviours by providing reasons for their actions, e.g. condemnation of the condemners, or denying responsibility. Another way of self-rationalising drug use is through the self-medication hypothesis, where substances are used to control a range of negative feelings (Khantzian, 1997).

Social Learning Theory: the theory of social learning (Baer and Bandura, 1963) incorporated the behaviourist learning theories of conditioning, adding two key ideas:

1. That mediating processes occur between stimuli and responses.
2. That behaviour is learned from the environment via observational learning.

Children learn from the people around them and actions are not traits people are born with but learned behaviour (Enaker, 2014). Behaviour can be acquired through imitation of adults and this can apply to attitudes towards and use of drugs (Moos, 2007), and learned behaviours can be strengthened by direct reinforcement (Baer and Bandura, 1963). Associations built from social learning come when people see others doing something in tandem with something else, e.g. physical training and anabolic androgenic steroid use. They perceive the positive effects (e.g. gain in muscle or getting positive comments) from the combination of the two activities and this acts as a reinforcement. If they then engage in the two activities and see positive benefits, this provides further reinforcement. This conditioning could be a possible explanation for dependent use (Rudd, 2014).

Activity 26.3

List five behaviours that you have learned through social conditioning.

When considering problematic substance use, Paylor et al. (2012) outline four different approaches:

- The disease model: seeing dependency on substances as an incurable disease.
- The cognitive behavioural model: using psychological theory and methods to approach substance problems.
- The medical model: focusing on treating the physiological effects of substance misuse.
- The biopsychosocial approach: incorporating elements of all three approaches.

Social workers should be encouraged to take a biopsychosocial approach to substance use (Parrish, 2014). There are a range of biopsychosocial methods that can help support people who misuse substances, including the Transtheoretical Model (Table 26.3), developed by Prochaska and DiClemente (1986), which was designed to help understand behavioural change processes. This model acknowledges the role of denial, which allows people to set aside realities such as the implications or consequences of their behaviour (Parrish, 2014).

Table 26.3   The Change Model: working with people who use substances

Stage	Description
Pre-contemplation	Resistance to change, often denying there is a problem
Contemplation	The user considers the pros and cons of change and can experience self-doubt and conflict between their values and behaviours

Preparation	Intention to change is explicit and small actions may be taken
Action	Deliberate strategies are in place to change their behaviour
Maintenance	Change has taken place, but the user may still feel the urge to return to using, so vigilance is needed to prevent relapse

Adapted from Barber (2002) and Teater (2014)

Motivational interviewing is a tool that can help people to move through the change cycle. It utilises a specific questioning technique designed to help people 'talk themselves into change, based on their own values and interests' (Miller and Rollnick, 2013, p4). It can help enhance self-esteem and self-efficacy (Dehghani et al., 2013); however, the provision of practical help with practical issues such as housing and parenting is also needed (Holland et al., 2014).

Systems theory, developed by Ludwig von Bertalanffy, considers the service user in their environment, and helps social workers to consider multiple areas for support (Parrish, 2014). The impact on family members and friends can be great (Klostermann and O'Farrell, 2013) and systems theory provides a wider picture of the circumstances for the person being supported to identify potential support networks. Application of this theory could help a social worker identify risks to initiating use or consider reasons for choices made, such as peer pressure.

The strengths-based approach was developed in response to the more traditional problem-based approach by such academics as Dennis Saleebey, Charles Rapp and Ann Weick. Rather than focusing on deficits and problems, the worker instead helps the service user to identify and consider strengths and abilities to help them undertake change (Karoll, 2010). This approach can help service users 'to creatively draw upon their own strengths and community resources to cope in ways that promote self-efficacy and community integration' (Karoll, 2010, p267) and is a contrast to models of substance use recovery such as the 12 steps model, with the idea of accepting a powerlessness over the substance and the need to gain strength from a 'higher power' (Sandoz, 2014).

Impact of using substances

Recognising and acknowledging the benefits or desired effects from drug use can help to understand the challenges faced by users around stopping use (Parrish, 2014).

Table 26.4 gives specific examples to highlight the perceived and actual benefits to users.

The misuse of substances can cause negative health effects, including changes in brain chemistry, psychological effects, respiratory disorders, damage to the body's major organs and even psychosis or death (Barber, 2002; Heanue and Lawton, 2012). There are particular harms associated with alcohol dependence, such as an increased risk of cancer, strokes, and liver disease which can adversely affect people of low economic status (Jones et al., 2015).

The neurobiological consequences of problematic substance use have differential impacts during different stages of life: perinatal, childhood, adolescence, adult and elderly (Azmitia, 2001). Substance misuse can negatively impact all aspects of life including: legal and financial problems, risky or criminal behaviours, inability to hold down employment, drive or self-care (Heanue and Lawton, 2012). Social workers need to be

Table 26.4 Ascribed psychological benefits of drugs (service user perspective)

Improving depth and clarity of thought	It inspires people to creativity. It gives you energy, makes you think clearer. It just makes you feel good all round. (F, 51)
Improving empathy toward others	When you're high, it just sort of connects you to that emotion quicker and on the same level. If you're all messed up you sort of really, really feel the gravity of the situation, like you'll get as upset as them. If someone's really amped then you'll sort of get really amped as well. (M, 25)
Enhancing confidence	Cocaine is more of a confidence thing so when you're out and about you've got the liquid courage and you want a bit more you can have a bit more cocaine, you seem to talk to a bit better with girls. (M, 26)
Elevating mood	Life can be quite stressful and it's nice to have that time of just feeling free, not caring … Just being able to let loose … You will laugh like you've never laughed with your friends or you'll cry with your friends. (F, 37)

Mey et al. (2018) What's the attraction? The role of performance enhancement as a driver of recreational drug use. *Journal of Substance Use*, 23(3). Reprinted by permission of the publisher (Taylor & Francis Ltd, http://www.tandfonline.com).

aware of the risk factors for the onset of substance use, including: child abuse, having family members with substance use problems, poor attachment, low educational achievements, exclusion, crime.

Research summary

Galvani (2015) suggests that social workers have three roles aligned to working with problematic substance use:

1. Engaging with the topic to support service users.
2. Motivating people to consider changing their behaviours.
3. Supporting people in maintaining the changes.

Support provision

A key challenge faced by social workers is to recognise the difference between substance use and 'problematic' substance use as this can impact on the ability to access some support services. Problematic substance use can be described as (Heanue and Lawton, 2012):

*   having caused a physical or psychological dependency;
*   affecting the physical or psychological health of the person;
*   causing harm to other people;
*   affecting the person's ability to function in a social environment.

The UK Care Act 2014 classes people as vulnerable adults, eligible for support, if their substance use affects their ability to manage everyday living (SCIE, 2015b).

In the UK, there are a range of services provided to support people who have problems with substance use including: prescription synthetic opiates; free injecting equipment provision and testing; referral to drug treatment; treatment for BBVs; and provision of take-home naloxone (EMCDDA, 2017). In return for the provision of opiate substitutes, support services often require service users to engage in group support to help manage their recovery. This can be challenging for people dependent on substances, as by the very nature of the condition they often lead chaotic lives (Lloyd, 1998). Moreover, substitutive practice is criticised as it raises the question of substituting one substance for another and there is a trend indicating a steady increase in the age of users seeking treatment for opioid substitutes. Some charities have set principles as part of their support for people who misuse substances, e.g. programmes based on the 12 steps. Such programmes require participants to work towards total abstinence and ask the individual to see themselves as essentially powerless over their substance use. They have been supported and criticised (Kurtz and Fisher, 2003; Rodriguez-Morales, 2017; Segal, 2017), but can be effective to help some people on the road to recovery. Social workers should be aware of how such organisations work, as this support may suit some, but others may struggle with the prescriptive approach and principles.

It is important to recognise the multi-layered nature of stress and mixed feelings that family members will bear due to the competing needs and obligations towards a family member with a misuse problem, and offer support (Orford et al., 2010). For instance, one case study reports a mother who attempted suicide in a cry for help, after finding it difficult to deal with her son's behaviour as a result of his substance use (Groenewald, 2018).

Substance use may often hide underlying mental health issues, and dual diagnosis can lead to challenges for social workers as people often fall between services (Parrish, 2014) or can be denied access to mental health services until they have stopped using. Resourcing issues may mean people experience long waiting times to access specialist services (such as residential rehabilitation) and a significant amount of justification from the professional supporting them may be needed, including guarantees of client commitment. Social workers have a role to support people to maintain engagement with services, as often the services offered may not seem necessary to the service user, yet sustained engagement in treatment services can depend on levels of motivation and the services' ability to increase service user autonomy (Tiquet, 2017).

Parenting and substance use

'Parental problem drug use can and often does compromise children's health and development at every stage from conception onwards' (Advisory Council on the Misuse of Drugs, 2003, p10) and can put children at risk of suffering significant harm (Kroll and Taylor, 2008). The misuse of substances can have the potential to undermine parenting capacity and have a negative impact on children's health through neglect, which can affect their emotional and physical development (Horgan, 2011). Several health harming behaviours – early sexual initiation, unintended teenage pregnancy, smoking, binge drinking, drug use, violence victimisation, violence perpetration, incarceration, poor diet and low levels of physical exercise – have been connected with parental drug misuse (Bellis et al., 2014); however, causality was not established in the study. Parents can be ambivalent about getting help, as they perceive enormous challenges in giving up their use (Kroll and Taylor, 2008) and often feel that providing they do not use around the children they are not causing them any harm:

> They always came first, dressed, fed, going to school … it didn't affect me with the kids at all, I always looked after them first, I didn't want them taken off me.

> (Drug-using mother of ten-year-old boy, Ireland) (Hogan and Higgins, 1997)

Parental substance misuse often coexists with a range of other issues, such as poverty, isolation, mental health issues and stigma (Horgan, 2011), and effective support should consider the impact on the whole family (Lander et al., 2013):

> They do love you but they have to put that (drugs) first … it's an illness really … it's number one, the drug is – definitely. That's something I've definitely had to accept to understand anything.

> (Young person, aged 20) (Kroll and Taylor, 2008)

While children of parents who misuse substances may not themselves misuse substances, there is evidence to suggest an increased risk (Li et al., 2002).

In 2008, the Family Drug and Alcohol Court (FDAC) was set up as an alternative to the traditional family court in England and Wales. The Department of Health recognised that many families coming into care proceedings had at least one parent with a substance use problem and needed a more specialised service. The FDAC works within the framework of care proceedings and has three distinct features:

- a problem-solving therapeutic approach, where judges speak directly to parents and social workers;
- a specialist multi-disciplinary team, experts and doctors to carry out assessments, to enable parents to stay engaged with services;
- judicial continuity; parents come up before the court every fortnight, seeing the same judge every time (FDAC National Unit, 2015).

FDAC was deemed to be effective as an evaluation found that a higher proportion of FDAC parents than comparison parents had ceased misusing by the end of proceedings than traditional family courts (Harwin et al., 2014). Moreover, the study found that parents in FDAC cases were offered more services than comparison parents for substance misuse, family services and other problems. However, the authors did raise questions about the need for support after families had been reunited in order to prevent relapse. A report that evaluated Innovative Children's Social Care Projects found that specific approaches and interventions such as family group conferencing, restorative practice and Signs of Safety could be effective in supporting people to bring about positive change in their lives (Sebba et al., 2017).

Case study 26.1

Dorothy is 49 years old, and has a diagnosis of Bipolar Disorder and self-declared Personality Disorder. She is currently on 80ml methadone daily and has been in treatment with the Addiction Service Community Team for eight years. She suffers with depression, has an eating disorder and has poor physical health. She has a childhood history of physical and sexual abuse and has experienced domestic abuse. She struggles with being around people, goes to bed mid-afternoon, wakes up at midnight, and walks her dogs in the park at dawn. Dorothy says her dogs are the only reason for her to keep living. One of her dogs recently died. She is seen once a month by her keyworker as part of the shared clinic scheme; they meet at a health centre five minutes' walk from her home. Dorothy collects her weekly prescription from the pharmacy, and does not attend support group meetings, as these terrify her. Dorothy sees her GP for a double appointment once a month and has refused help from the Community Mental Health Team. She phones her keyworker every week to talk about her health issues and suicidal ideation.

Recent government policy changes mean that there is a focus on recovery over harm reduction. Moreover, the shared clinic service is being phased out due to resourcing issues.

You are working with Dorothy to develop her new support plan. The plan includes both:

- Dorothy visiting the Support Centre for her meetings (four miles from her home), like all the other service users;
- helping Dorothy to reduce her current methadone prescription to less than 20ml within six months, as future changes to the planned service would not provide methadone for people who were not actively reducing and engaging with weekly group meetings.

Questions for reflection

- How might Dorothy feel about the changes proposed?
- What might Dorothy's aims be?
- How do you think Dorothy sees herself compared to the other users of the service?
- What difficulties do you think this change might place on Dorothy?
- What additional support might she need?

Reflections on case study

The organisation's aims of the intervention were: to work with Dorothy to plan a reduction; to help her accept the change of the location and frequency of her key-working sessions; and encourage her to accept specialist support for her mental health issues. No doubt Dorothy could be left distressed by the changes proposed. This case highlights the way an agency is affected by policy changes, shows the need for agencies to work together, and highlights how different policies can impact negatively on the lives of individuals, often leaving them feeling disempowered and oppressed.

Contemporary social work challenges

Normalisation of some types of recreational drug use

Recreational drug culture became normalised in the 1990s (Parker et al., 1995). This normalisation potentially means that more people might use and share drugs whilst downplaying or ignoring the potential consequences, e.g. the recent popularity of novel psychoactive substances or 'legal highs', which come with an additional level of harm as concentrations are varied and many of the side effects are unknown (Barnard et al., 2017). In 2017, cannabis was reported as the most commonly used illicit drug in the UK, with the most common form of cannabis used in the UK having potency rates measured from between 0.9 per cent–26 per cent THC[1] (Independent Drug Monitoring Unit, 2018). Daily use of high potency cannabis can lead to increased risk of psychosis (Di Forti et al., 2014), yet cannabis is widely perceived to be 'safe' (Duff and Erickson, 2014). This normalisation of use could be influenced by: past normalised, recreational use of low potency, unadulterated cannabis by the baby boomer generation; the impact of medicinal use; the legalisation of cannabis in some countries.

Political agendas

There are differing perspectives when considering substance use, e.g. public health organisations would consider such issues as the spreading of BBVs and hence focus on harm minimisation, whereas local authorities may be concerned with links to criminal activity. Currently, in the UK, liberal or left-leaning politicians take a harm minimisation perspective, whereas those on the political right take a preventative and/or abstinence perspective (Tharoor, 2017). These differences often mean that a change in government sees a change in policy and funding priorities. For example, in 2018, a report by Alcohol Concern highlighted how funding cuts, rapid re-tendering cycles, loss of qualified staff and lack of political support had impacted some of the most vulnerable people in society (Alcohol Research UK, 2018) and services often face uncertainty about their futures regardless of proven outcomes for people, e.g. FDAC was saved by funding from a group of private backers and philanthropists (LexisNexis, 2019).

Labelling and stigma

Much of the harm of drug use is linked with stigmatisation and criminalisation, and society should be responsive to vulnerability (Ben-Ishai, 2012). We live in a world of media hype, and language is a powerful tool in influencing the public's opinion on groups of people, which can be detrimental. Deviant behaviours can be a reason why society in general might perceive it as acceptable to stereotype these groups and use derogatory language. People who use substances are often described using derogatory terms such as 'junkies', 'roid-head', 'crackwhore'. Stigma can be a barrier for people accepting and engaging with services (Kroll and Taylor, 2008) and can bring about social exclusion which can contribute to health inequalities (Radley et al., 2017). Stigma and shame are associated with accessing treatment services and people feel infantilised (Radley et al., 2017). This highlights the important impact that the approach of the social worker can have on a service user and the importance of working with compassion and empathy. It is also important to accept that the stigma does not just affect the service user but also their families, for example:

I don't know. I'd just rather she [mother] drank … Because people wouldn't call her a junkie.

(18-year-old boy, UK) (Bancroft, 2007)

Social workers are influenced by social norms and media stereotypes, and one challenge when working with people is to be non-judgemental of actions that may suggest the service user is putting their own needs above those of others, e.g. a mother who appears to put her need to take heroin over the needs of her baby, whilst not compromising on the need to safeguard the child. Pitfalls in judgements for social workers include selective stereotyping and labelling (Milner and O'Byrne, 2009) as 'the reduction of individual situations to a set of problems and causes may suggest that there are clear "right and wrong" actions' (Parker, 2017, p6). Social workers need to consider the potential for personal biases to compromise good practice (Parrish, 2014), and supervision provides a useful platform to explore such perceptions and challenge assumptions. Social workers should advocate for their service users and challenge the perceptions of other profession-als, e.g. healthcare professionals can often be perceived to discriminate against people who use substances (Harling, 2017).

Conclusion

Social workers need to consider substance use as part of their everyday practice. The implications and risks of harms from substance misuse can be wide-ranging and have potentially negative long-term physical and social implications for both users and those they care for. The holistic, values-led, ethical and ecological approach that is part of social work practice means that social workers are well placed to support people with substance use problems (Galvani, 2015). Social workers need to appreciate the benefits to people from using substances and be non-judgemental, empathetic and realistic in their practice when considering risk assessment and support plans.

Key points summary

- Social workers need to have knowledge of the physical and social benefits, harms and risks associated with substance misuse.
- Substance use can often be a symptom of underlying psychological harm or mental health issues.
- Substance use needs to be considered in its wider cultural and social context.

(Continued)

(Continued)

- A psychosocial approach should be taken when assessing risks and developing support plans for people who misuse substances.
- Substance misuse is a complex issue and is not something that can be quickly and easily resolved.
- Support for people who misuse substances needs to be holistic, long-term and non-judgemental.

Suggested further reading

Galvani, S. (2015) *Alcohol and Other Drug Use: The Roles and Capabilities of Social Workers*. Public Health England and Manchester Metropolitan University. Available at: **http://cdn.basw.co.uk/upload/basw_25925-3.pdf**

Heanue, K. and Lawton, C. (2012) *Working with Substance Users*. Maidenhead: McGraw-Hill/ Open University Press.

Nutt, D. (2012) *Drugs – Without the Hot Air: Minimizing the Harms of Legal and Illegal Drugs*. Cambridge: UIT Cambridge.

27

Social work with older people

Ann Anka

Chapter objectives

By the end of the chapter you should be able to:

- understand the context of social work practice with older people including key issues, aspects of work, skills and values required to effectively practice with older people;
- know about demographic challenges and opportunities;
- have an awareness of three new emerging ways of working;
- apply the knowledge gained to support older people.

Introduction

The chapter considers social work practice with older people, including key issues affecting them, aspects of work and emerging new ways of working, namely: social navigation, social prescribing, and 'the three conversations'. It contextualises the discussion within the United Kingdom but the chapter draws from the broad literature and research in the UK and internationally. The key issues affecting older people discussed within the chapter have universal application. Social work students and practitioners outside the UK can adapt the content, taking into consideration their national and local policies, law and indigenous knowledge and values when working with older people. The chapter begins by looking at what old age means.

Definitional issues: what is old age?

Old age is difficult to define because it means different things to different people. There is also no single agreed definition of who exactly 'older people' are. Different societies and cultures have different interpretations of what constitutes old age and individuals from different social and cultural backgrounds may experience old age differently. The term 'older people' is also often used interchangeably with 'elderly people' and 'older adult' by both lay people and professionals.

The academic literature delineates three broad categories for defining old age to include: biological age, chronology and political economy (people's place within societal structures). For further reading see McDonald (2010) and Payne (2012). Traditional universalistic theories which offer some understanding on ageing include disengagement theory (older people are seen to withdraw from society and society to withdraw from them); activity theory (views old age as a period of activity and participation in different life pursuits) and Erikson's stage theory of psychosocial development, the eighth and final stages: integrity versus despair, which relates to reflecting on one's life and feeling satisfied and happy with the life lived (integrity) or having a deep sense of regret (despair) (Llewellyn et al., 2015). Although these theories provide a useful lens for understanding ageing, critics argue that they fail to adequately address the diversity of experiences in old age.

Ageism, which relates to prejudicial treatment of older people just because they are old, is of particular concern in social work with older people. Structural age discrimination exists in allocation and delivery of health and social care resources and these often intersect with other dimensions of social inequalities such as race, gender, sexuality, disabilities, religion and belief, which some of the traditional universalistic theories have been accused of failing to consider. (See the box below for an extract from the literature on ageism – concepts and origins.)

Key thinkers and theorists on ageism

Human ageing is not solely the biological process of senescence – the gradual deterioration of bodily functions that increases the risk for morbidity and mortality after maturation. Human ageing is embedded in social contexts and is shaped by social factors. We grow old within a social network of partners, family members, and friends. In many countries, we count on old age pensions as well as health and social care services. And we have explicit and implicit assumptions about older people (as a social group), growing old (as a developmental process), and being old (as part of the life course). These assumptions, expectations and beliefs shape human ageing as well. We often speak about older people in general (and not about different individuals), about 'the' process of ageing (and not about the multiple, unique courses which exist), and about old age as a uniform stage at the end of life (and not about the diverse and heterogeneous living situations of older people). As soon as we neglect the differences between individuals, we over-generalise and treat older people, ageing, and old age in a stereotypical manner. This stereotypical construction of older people, ageing, and old age is called 'ageism.'

(Ayalon and Tesch-Römer, 2018, p1)

Activity 27.1

Can you think of examples of the stereotypical construction of older people in medical, economic and social discourses?

What do social workers do?

Social workers are uniquely placed to challenge structural age discrimination. The IFSW (2018, 3.1) stipulates that:

Social workers challenge discrimination, which includes but is not limited to age, capacity, civil status, class, culture, ethnicity, gender, gender identity, language, nationality (or lack thereof), opinions, other physical characteristics, physical or mental abilities, political beliefs, poverty, race, relationship status, religion, sex, sexual orientation, socioeconomic status, spiritual beliefs, or family structure.

Most older people would not require social work input as old age itself is not a problem or an indication of need. However, for those requiring social work support, some of the most common factors which lead older people to social work may include physical or mental illness, impairment, frailty and disability; poverty, isolation, loneliness or carer support. Some older people may seek social work support to manage living with long-term chronic illnesses such as dementia, cancer, stroke, falls and end of life care resulting in the inability to look after oneself. Others may seek support with housing and accommodation or moving into residential care (McDonald, 2010). Some older people may have abused alcohol or other substances when they were younger and may have developed problems in their old age (Lynch, 2014; Payne, 2012). Most agencies that work with older people use an age cut off point of 65 to frame the design and delivery of care and support services for older people, except for those in prison where the age threshold is 50, both in the UK and internationally. Older people are not homogeneous within these groups; there are diversities of experiences and vulnerabilities and individual needs and circumstances differ.

Social work plays a vital role in contributing to the achievement of goals, aspirations and outcomes for older people and their carers through participatory and empowerment practices that build on older people's capabilities, strengths and resilience. Social work practice with older people involves direct work with people with either short or long-term chronic illness and may involve providing home care support to enable an older person to remain in their own home, involvement in discharge planning from hospitals to re-ablement services, residential care following an acute illness or other life transitions. Social work practice with older people includes safeguarding and risk enablement work and end of life care (which may include bereavement counselling); help with accessing welfare benefit (social security) and information and advice. These may, but not always, involve the facilitation of multi-disciplinary and inter-agency work.

In the UK, social work practice with older people takes place across both statutory and voluntary sectors and the core tasks include assessments of needs that identify and address interconnected physical, social, economic, psychological and emotional needs of older people. In statutory settings, social workers also have key roles in determining eligibility for care and support, writing care and support plans and implementations of various interventions with older people. Social workers also monitor and review various interventions implemented, though research focusing on monitoring and reviews is limited. In contrast, social work practice with older people in the voluntary sector varies. The UK has various small non-profit organisations alongside social enterprises and bigger voluntary organisations such as Age UK and the Salvation Army, who offer various support services to older people. Similarly to the UK, in Europe social work practice with older people takes place in the statutory sector (e.g. Department of Social Security), in the non-profit and voluntary organisations and the private sector (Carvalho, 2014). In North America, as well as participation in health care delivery and interdisciplinary practice, social workers are employed in care homes and engage in various practices including advocacy and monitoring the quality of care of older people (Milne et al., 2013). What follows considers some of the challenges and opportunities in social work practice with older people.

Case study 27.1

Mrs Pat Smith is 72 years old. She describes herself as an Irish-born Catholic. She lives in a two-bedroom owner-occupied flat with her partner Mr Michael Smith, who is 69. Mrs Smith was recently admitted to hospital, due to a fall at her home where she sustained an injury to her hip. Whilst in hospital, she became very unwell; further tests revealed that she has terminal cancer and has less than six months to live. An assessment revealed that Mrs Smith was born a man and was known as Mr Patrick O'Connor. He was previously married to a Mrs Nancy O'Connor and had two children with her but had gender reassignment surgery about ten years ago. During the assessment she mentioned that she didn't want her family and friends to know where she lived after the surgery, but Michael had encouraged her to maintain contact with the family. The family are now in contact with each other and are very concerned about her health. Mrs Smith maintains that the doctors have got the cancer diagnosis wrong because she has been a good person all her life and cannot understand why this is happening to her.

Activity 27.2

What are the key issues covered in the case study and how would you address these?

Skills and attributes

Social work practice with older people requires effective communication skills such as the ability to listen and communicate at the right pace with people affected by life limiting illnesses. Practitioners require the ability to cope with and manage strong emotions relating to end of life care (helping older people and their carers come to terms with the life-threatening illness). Practitioners also need practical skills in securing and coordinating resources, and negotiating contracts with service providers (e.g. home care or residential care). Other practice skills needed include administrative skills, critical judgement, making difficult decisions; managing conflicts within families and/or among different professionals. Social workers also require attributes such as empathy (including anticipatory empathy), warmth and congruence; thoughtfulness, kindness, resilience and the ability to build trust and form relationships over time (both short and long-term relationships) (Egan, 2014). Whilst these skills and attributes are important, possessing these alone is not enough. Asking older people about what their needs are and involving them in identifying what matters to them and what they would like to be put into place to support them is more effective in effecting change.

Research tells us that later life is characterised by various life transitions in social identities; roles; relationships; status and participation (Milne et al., 2013). The case study (Mrs Smith) draws attention to the fact that older people's experiences are shaped by a number of factors as health, sexual identity and religion. Social work with older people therefore requires a deeper understanding of various life transitions and how they shape and affect individuals differently in the context of their lived experiences as well as how different aspects of life and social identities intersect and affect individuals differently.

A study by Tanner et al. (2015) tells us that understanding life transitions can help social workers to improve older people's experiences of moving into and between health care services. Citing Chick and Meleis (1986, p239–240), Tanner et al. (2015, p2059) define transition as

> *A passage from one life phase, condition, or status to another ... transition refers to both the process and the outcome of complex person – environment interactions. It may involve more than one person and is embedded in the context and the situation. Defining characteristics of transition include process, disconnectedness, perception and patterns and response.*

In their research, Tanner et al. (2015) found that social work discharge planning of older people from hospital often fails to consider the psychological and emotional needs of older people by mainly focusing on their physical needs. The authors draw from Van Gannep's (1960, cited in Tanner et al., 2015, p2058) three stage transitions theory which consists of initial separation from one's social situations to a place of limbo and to where one can take up a new social status, to urge social workers to consider psychological and emotional needs of older people in assessments and interventions plans. Research by Mowat and O'Neill (2013) on spirituality and ageing suggest supporting older people to come to terms with what life was, what it is now and how it would look in the future is important. Religious care should be given 'in the context of shared religious beliefs, values, liturgies and lifestyle of a faith community' (Mowat and O'Neill, 2013, p5). In the case study, it is suggested that Mrs Smith previously had gender reassignment surgery and she did not want her family knowing about the surgery. Research suggests that accepting social norms inhibits older people's sexual expressions and engagement in new relationships (Gewirtz-Meydan et al., 2018b). As with meeting her spiritual and religious needs, social work practice with older people includes talking about sex and sexuality. Social workers would be expected to work with Mrs Smith and the whole family to help them to come to terms with Mrs Smith's acquired gender identity. Below is an extract from Gewirtz-Meydan et al.'s (2018b) work on ageism and sexuality that may help you to reflect on your engagement with older people.

Key thinkers and theorists: ageism and sexuality

Some other main issues and key myths that have been conceptualized in relation to older people's sexuality include: a lack of sexual desire that accompanies ageing; the physical unattractiveness and undesirability of older people, which is particularly evident in relation to gender; the idea that it is shameful and perverse for older people to engage in sexual activity; the invisibility of the older Lesbian, Gay, Bisexual, Transgender, Queer and Intersex (LGBTQ&I) community, and individuals who may need to return to the 'closet' in later life (Hafford-Letchfield, 2008).

(Gewirtz-Meydan et al., 2018b, p150)

The authors posit in a different paper which looked at sexuality and accepting social norms in older people that 'by including physical contact, such as hugging, kissing, cuddling and holding hands in the equation, many older people experienced a satisfactory sense of sexuality' (Gewirtz-Meydan et al., 2018a, p10). Support for those from more vulnerable groups will be needed when discussing sexuality and meeting the sexual needs of older people. Evidence remains that individuals from the transgender community experience discrimination when accessing health and social care and their needs are often ignored in policy and practice (House of Commons Women and Equalities Committee, 2015). Taking positive action to counter discrimination includes examining institutional practices, policies, procedures and how institutions engage with and address the sexual needs of older people from all communities.

Demographic context

Data on population ageing suggests that there is a rise in the number of people aged 65 and above both in the UK and internationally (United Nations, 2017). The demographic context presents a number of challenges and opportunities for policy makers, commis-sioners and social workers. Kingston et al. (2018) project that two-thirds or more of the gain in years of life at age 65 will be years spent with four or more long-term conditions or complex multi-morbidity, and this is set to double by 2035. Public Health England (2018) suggests there are some 850,000 people living with dementia in the UK and it is estimated that over one million people will have dementia by 2025. This is set to exceed two million by 2050 (Public Health England, 2018). The prevalence of dementia increases as people become older. It is reported that one in 14 of those aged 65 have dementia and this rises to one in six over the age of 80 (Public Health England, 2018). The World Health Organization (WHO, 2017) reported that there are an estimated 47 million people living with dementia worldwide; this is set to increase to 75 million by 2030 and more than triple by 2050. Social workers provide vital support to people living with dementia and their carers, to cope with the challenges and transitions associated with dementia (for further reading on dementia see Downs and Bowers, 2014).

Case study 27.2

Peter is aged 98 and lives in an owner-occupied bungalow with his wife Margaret, aged 88. Peter is known to wander on occasions, easily getting lost at home and when out-side. He was diagnosed as having dementia some five years ago. As a result of the dementia, he tends to be on the move more frequently throughout the day, sitting for no more than 30 minutes at a time. He occasionally wanders at night and has been returned home by the police on several occasions. The couple live near a busy high street. Margaret is having difficulty in containing him.

Activity 27.3

Should we use global positioning systems (GPS) to monitor and determine the location of older people with dementia who get lost?

Advances in technology, compounded with an ageing population, would probably result in the use of different technological devices as a substitute for care. The current policy agenda in the care of older people in the UK and internationally focuses on early intervention and prevention, achieved through joined up working, integration, collabo-ration and co-production of service development and delivery (The King's Fund, 2018). Policy also requires that older people are first supported to remain in their own home. Emphasis is placed on harnessing support from carers, the community and neighbours to meet the needs of older people (DHSC, 2018). It is now not uncommon to use assistive technology such as GPS tracking devices to monitor and track older people, particularly those diagnosed with dementia who get lost. A study by White and Montgomery (2014) with carers (n = 10) of persons with dementia who have used GPS devices to monitor, track and locate their relatives justified the motivation to do so on safety rather than on liberty and autonomy. Vandemeulebroucke et al. (2018) advise that those using assistive technology give all stakeholders a voice in the ethical debates concerning their use, especially older people who are recipients of care. Whilst it is acknowledged that this may not always be possible, as some older people may lack capacity, it is nonetheless important to work co-productively with older people in order to plan how they would like their voices to be included in their health and social care through advanced decisions or living wills in which they name a person to make decisions on their behalf when they are unable to do so.

In what follows, new emerging ways of working built on traditional social work practice methods are discussed.

New emerging ways of practice

Three new emerging ways of working gaining recognition in social work with older people are social navigation, social prescribing and the 'three conversations'. They are built on traditional ways of working such as social work casework, community work, and individual care planning which involved utilisation of traditional social work skills of coordinating existing services and liaising with other agencies to support the needs of older people (McDonald, 2010), particularly those with limited networks of support, by connecting older people to resources within their social networks and community (for further reading, see Healy, 2012).

Social navigation

Research suggests older people with complex health and social care needs and their families and carers find navigating through different health and social care systems confusing and challenging (Carter et al., 2018; Humphries et al., 2016). Built on traditional social work approaches, system navigation practice has emerged in some health and social care settings to support older people to navigate in and between different systems. In system navigation practice, navigators are deployed to secure resources and coordinate care on behalf of older people and their carers. A systematic review conducted by Carter et al. (2018) on existing system navigation models in North America and the UK found that navigators most often communicated with various health, social care and community-based organisations on behalf of people they worked with to facilitate or coordinate access to health and social care service. Navigators provide various types of support and these included arranging various health care appointments or support with transitioning from and/or between services.

Social prescribing

Another practice approach built on traditional social work methods emerging in health and social care settings, aimed at providing early intervention and preventative support for older people, is social prescribing practice. Social prescribing acknowledges that a range of social, economic and environmental factors affect an individual's health and wellbeing. Social prescribing practice is therefore aimed at addressing mitigating social and economic factors, which are likely to impact on the health and wellbeing of older people by linking them to community and neighbourhood support services.

Different models of social prescribing practice exist in the UK (Dayson and Bennett 2016; Kimberlee, 2013). The most common practice comprises three components involving a referral of the person requiring assistance from a healthcare professional to a link worker. The central task of the link worker is to consult with the person requiring assistance to identify their needs and outcomes. Both the link worker and the individual requiring assistance work together to identify what is needed to meet the individual's needs and outcomes using resources within the community and or through statutory services (Alderwick et al., 2015). The emerging literature in this area suggests that most social prescription activities consist of supporting individuals to access green spaces through walking clubs; gardening or art activities; transport to attend social events or participate in physical activity. These activities are aimed at supporting those who regularly use health services and are dependent on emergency services (Alderwick et al., 2015).

The 'three conversations'

Similarly, the 'three-conversation' approach developed by Newman at Partners4Change (SCIE, 2017) is gaining recognition in adult social care assessments and interventions with older people in England. The approach is structured around three distinct processes of conversation aimed at exploring individuals' needs and harnessing people's strengths and assets using social navigations principles of liaising, coordinating and connecting people to personal, family and community-based resources. These include, for example, charitable organisations, various social enterprises and local pubs to meet the needs of older people (for more information on applying the 'three-conversation' approach see SCIE, 2017).

Utilisation of community-based resource and neighbour support is premised on notions of social capital. Bourdieu (1986) contends that social capital relates to networks and social connections that individuals have. Social capital resides in individuals through their investments in others. Social capital is seen as a precursor to social support. (See the box below on Bourdieu's conceptualisation of social capital.)

Key thinkers and theorists: Pierre Bourdieu – social capital

Social capital is the aggregate of the actual or potential resources which are linked to possession of a durable network of more or less institutionalized relationships of mutual acquaintance and recognition – or in other words, to membership in a group which provides each of its members with the backing of the collectively owned capital, a 'credential' which entitles them to credit, in the various senses of the word. These relationships may exist only in the practical state, in material and/or symbolic exchanges which help to maintain them.

(Bourdieu, 1986, p4)

Although the new ways of working are not fully researched, they draw on previous strengths of traditional social work ways of practice, which view the individual and their community as assets.

Conclusion

This chapter considered key issues affecting older people and the context of social work practice with older people including aspects of work; what social workers do, including skills and attributes needed to work effectively with older people. It also looked at demographic challenges; the use of assistive technological devices such as GPS to track and monitor older people with dementia who get lost and their implications for practice. The chapter included discussions of theories and research drawn from the UK and internationally, to help our understanding of issues affecting older people. The chapter also discussed three distinct emerging new ways of practice built on traditional social work methods.

Key points summary

Older people are not homogeneous; when applying the content in this chapter it is hoped you will:

- draw from individual needs, narratives, goals and aspirations;
- build on older people's strengths and capabilities; and
- learn with and from older people when engaging with them.

Suggested further reading

Downs, M. and Bowers, B. (2014) *Excellence in Dementia Care: Research Into Practice*. Berkshire: Open University Press. Offers insights into dementia care. The authors draw from research, practice and the experience of those affected with dementia.

Healy, K. (2012) *Social Work Methods and Skills: The Essential Foundations of Practice*. Basingstoke: Palgrave Macmillan. Discusses different social work methods and practice approaches including traditional social work methods of practice.

Llewellyn, A., Agu, L. and Mercer, D. (2015) *Sociology for Social Workers* (2nd ed). Cambridge: Policy Press. Provides different theoretical perspectives on ageing.

McDonald, A. (2010) *Social Work with Older People*. Cambridge: Polity Press.

Payne, M. (2012) *Citizenship Social Work with Older People*. Bristol: Policy Press.

Both offer accessible perspectives on working with older people in different settings.

28

Social work at the end of life: death, dying, bereavement and loss

Sue Taplin

Chapter objectives

After reading this chapter you should be able to:

- understand the centrality of loss in people's lives, and particularly loss through death;
- understand the role of social work in helping people who are facing death, bereavement and loss;
- explore some of the models and theories available to social workers in helping people to understand death, dying, bereavement and loss.

Introduction

The main aim of this chapter is to introduce and explore the role of social work in death, dying, bereavement and loss. We shall do this by first of all theorising what we know about dying before turning to consider how the process is managed, conceptualised and coped with by individuals. The chapter finishes by considering social work practice with people living with life-threatening illness and their families.

Theorising dying

According to Holloway (2007, p37):

Death, dying and bereavement have been the subject of considerable interest to scholars since the middle of the twentieth century, despite the message that we are a 'death-denying' society.

The work of sociologists in the study of death, dying and bereavement dates back to the 1960s in the United States, when the first, still influential, empirical observational studies looking at the care of people who were dying were conducted in hospitals (Glaser and Strauss, 1965, 1968; Strauss and Glaser, 1970). Such research fundamentally changed the way people thought about the management of dying, and brought the experiences of those dying (in this case, in a hospital environment) very much into public awareness.

Research summary

Studies in Britain have also explored the management of death and dying, both within the acute hospital setting and within the hospice movement (Field, 1989; Seale, 1989). The development of the hospice movement and that of palliative care as a specialism are interesting in this context, as these did much to bring the needs of dying people, and particularly those dying from cancer, to public consciousness. The work of Dame Cicely Saunders in developing services for people who were dying outwith the mainstream acute hospital setting was formative in establishing a particular framework for the care of people with 'terminal' illnesses, and this seemed to many to be above reproach. However, the studies of British medical sociologists (mentioned above) sought to challenge some of the taken-for-granted assumptions of palliative care, which, although uncomfortable for many, has at least opened up the debate about what palliative care can and does achieve (Exley, 2004). James and Field (1992), for example, suggested that the provision of palliative care within hospices, far from being individualised and holistic as it purports to be (in contrast to the care provided in the hospital setting) is, in fact, becoming increasingly 'routinised' and bureaucratic as it develops its own mores and standards of care, which could be seen as another way of defining a 'good' death which does not allow for individual choice or preference. Another example is Lawton's (2000) ethnographic study of the care provided within an NHS hospice. This work has been particularly influential in challenging the way in which people who are in receipt of palliative care services are actually viewed. According to Exley (2004, p113):

The public image of hospices facilitating dignified or 'good' deaths was challenged as she sought to examine what happens when people's bodies fail them in the most socially unacceptable of ways, leaving them devoid of personal identity and unable to engage any longer on any meaningful level with significant others because their physical bodies have failed them so badly.

Managing dying

According to Holloway:

Twentieth century developments in the care of people who are dying emerged out of a deep concern about the attitudes and practices prevalent in the western world and entrenched in its hospitals and healthcare systems, and the additional and unnecessary suffering this caused to dying people and their families. Thus, the hospice and palliative care movement has been underpinned by a valuing of the individual and has developed a philosophy of care which places their comfort and dignity at the centre … However, that which grew out of the transforming influence of the hospice movement has been in danger of turning into the opposite – a restrictive template which pathologises those whose dying does not conform.

(2007, p115)

In common with Holloway, I recognise the need to understand how 'dying well' means different things to each individual, and that a careful process of negotiation is necessary to ensure that the support given to someone living with a life-threatening illness is personally acceptable and that the social circumstances of the individual are recognised and taken into consideration.

Walters refers to this as 'dying with panache', which may include 'raging into the night', to paraphrase Dylan Thomas's poem about his father's death, if this is how that person has lived their life and would be congruent and authentic in death (Walters, 2004, p408). In this chapter, I am seeking to explore how possible it is to *live* with panache and to be as 'individual' in facing death as one may have been before life-threatening illness was diagnosed, and what might be the contribution of social work in facilitating this individualised approach to care.

Conceptualising dying

A significant area in the literature on death and dying is the development of theory concerning the processes and course of dying. In 'Time for Dying' (1968), Glaser and Strauss described what they called 'dying trajectories'. In essence, such trajectories are defined by 'duration' (the chronological *time* between the onset of dying and the arrival of death) and 'shape' (the characteristic *course* of the dying process). Illnesses that have a relatively short dying trajectory tend to move more or less directly to death, while those with a longer, more extended dying trajectory may involve either a fairly consistent decline or one that is more variable and ambiguous.

Research summary

Glaser and Strauss (1968) observed a subjective element in the concept of dying trajec-tories, since they noted an attempt on the part of professional care providers to predict the course that the disease would follow. In other words, when confronted by an ill person, Glaser and Strauss noted that professionals often make fairly rapid estimations about whether (or not) and how a person may die. They observed that professionals organise their work on the basis of these estimates, and that people who are living with life-threatening illnesses are therefore treated in differentiated ways. Thus dying trajec-tories involve both disease processes which are peculiar to the individuals who are ill and also important elements of assessment, communication and interaction between dying persons and their care providers.

Coping with dying

A second area of conceptual development in the literature has involved coping with dying, although it has not always been explicitly framed in this language. This focus was evident in the work of Pattison (1977) who, as previously mentioned, deliberately sought to represent many variables in the dying process. These variables included differences associated with temporal and developmental aspects of dying, dissimilarities in expecta-tions about dying, disparate social and familial contents for dying, diverse ways in which individuals cope with dying, and the many personal ramifications of dying (see also Corr et al., 1999).

Perhaps the most widely known, and possibly the most misrepresented, work in this area is that of Kübler-Ross (1969), which was published in her seminal book *On Death and Dying*. This approach postulated a sequence of five stages in response to awareness of impending death: denial, anger, bargaining, depression and acceptance. The stages themselves were described in various ways by Kübler-Ross: as 'reactions' or 'responses', as 'defence' mechanisms and as 'coping' strategies (Corr et al., 1999). While Kübler-Ross noted that 'the one thing that usually persists through all these stages is hope' (p138), popular attention has focused mainly on the so-called 'stages' and the progress (or otherwise) of an individual through them, and far less on hope and its implications.

Although all stage theories are inherently sequential and directional (one is seen to move forwards or backwards in a process of progression or regression, toward or away from some 'baseline'), Kübler-Ross herself suggested that dying people and others who were coping with dying could 'jump around' from one stage, or psychosocial reaction, to another and that various stages could sometimes exist simultaneously. That tends to undercut the most widespread interpretation of her work which emphasises the intrinsic interconnectedness and linearity inherent in the basic concept of stages.

The fundamental merit of this theoretical framework and what I would see as its most salutary feature is the emphasis placed by Kübler-Ross on the dying individual's responses to what is happening. With this in mind, Corr (1992) proposed three lessons to be drawn from her work: (1) that dying people are *still alive* and may have important things they need or want to do; (2) prospective helpers cannot expect to provide effective care for dying people unless they *actively listen* to such individuals and determine with them the priorities that should govern such care; and (3) there is much that all human beings can *learn from* dying people about our common mortality and ways of responding to imminent death.

His constructive understanding of coping led Weisman (1972) to confirm the importance of hope in experiences of dying and to advance the concept of an 'appropriate death' (as against an 'appropriated death'). Perhaps unconsciously alluding to Kübler-Ross's fundamental tenets, Weisman (1972, p21) observed that

hope and acceptance of death are basic concepts because they insist that mortality is a dimension of living, not merely a negation or an endpoint that cancels out everything. Hope is, indeed, the basic assumption in living and dying.

Activity 28.1

Think about your own knowledge and experience of death and dying.

* What is your approach to questions about death and dying and where do you think this may have originated from?
* How do you think this may influence your practice as a social worker with people facing such issues?

Practice interventions: models and methods

Working independently, Corr (1992) and Doka (1993) emphasised ways in which dying people cope with the knowledge of their own mortality. Both found *task-centred approaches* to be valuable in understanding the issues that people face as they cope with the awareness of their own impending death. For this, Corr identified four dimensions of task work that need to be included in a holistic account of coping with dying: physical, psychological, social and spiritual. Physical tasks centre on the satisfaction of bodily needs and the minimisation of physical distress; psychological tasks typically emphasise security and autonomy; social tasks involve interpersonal attachments to particular individuals and social groups; and spiritual tasks are based on concepts such as meaningfulness, connectedness and hope. This would seem to accord with the increasing emphasis on a holistic and multi-disciplinary approach to care for individuals with life-threatening illnesses, incorporating health and social care in equal measure (Holloway and Moss, 2010).

The concept of tasks implies an element of influence which individuals can exert in an effort to manage what is happening to them. This is consistent with other task-based models relating to mourning after a death (Attig, 1991, 1996; Corr and Doka, 1994; Worden, 2008). Task work also provides room for variation in the ways in which individuals choose to focus on the many potential tasks that may confront them at any given time, and how they may address the tasks that they select for emphasis.

Task theory is vulnerable to criticism insofar as it expresses a cultural bias towards work and achievement. It is possible that it could be subject to criticism in a similar way as are stage-based theories, in that individuals may feel pressurised by caregivers – both formal and informal – to regard their final phase of life as a series of coping tasks. As with any approach, it would be seem to be essential to use theory as a guide rather than expecting people to act in a certain prescribed way.

Arising from a different standpoint, Rando's (1993) work on anticipatory grief offers some complementary ideas to this discussion of coping with dying. Rando expanded the original concept of anticipatory grief to include not only an individual's reactions to possible impending death, but also to the numerous changes and transitions which are generally experienced throughout the course of a long illness. This helped her to draw attention to a broad variety of losses, including, at any given point in the dying trajectory, past losses, present or ongoing losses and future losses, that is, the awareness of those which have yet to occur. Rando (1993) concluded that it is misleading to speak of 'anticipatory' grief when in fact grief reactions are not limited solely to expectations of future losses. Rando also drew attention to the wide range of reactions and strategies involved in coping with pre-death losses, again emphasising the importance of individuality in behaviour and the need for an individualised response (Corr et al., 1999).

Meaning-making

In her study of individuals living with cancer, Armstrong-Coster found that

Confrontation with a potentially fatal disease can focus the mind; it provides the opportunity for values to be reassessed, priorities to be examined and commitments and relationships to be re-evaluated.

(Armstrong-Coster, 2004, p1)

Kellehear (1996, p157) notes that

in the period during and after the crisis, one's whole way of understanding life may need revision because a major part is found wanting. The meaning and value of one's life may be called into question.

This questioning becomes part of a new cancer identity whereby the sufferer tries to make sense not just of his or her illness, but also of life (Mathieson and Stam, 1995, p284).

Learning from others

Over the last few decades, facing death from cancer and other illnesses has become a focus of interest, with personal stories of the experience now occupying a prominent place within contemporary culture. This is particularly evident in literature, magazines, on the Internet, in newspapers, books and television, film and radio drama.

(Bingley et al., 2006)

From the 1950s, when relatively little was written about facing death from a personal perspective, there has been a steady rise in the number of published narratives describing the personal experience of life-threatening illness. In the last decade, with the creation of the Internet, there has been an exponential increase in unpublished, web-based writings (Pitts, 2004). More people seem to want to share their stories of the process involved in facing, and wherever possible, 'fighting' or 'coming to terms with' their illness. During the past half century, narratives written by those facing death from cancer and other diseases reflect a major sociological and perceptual shift, in particular towards higher expectations of medical provision as treatments and survival rates improve and end-of-life care services develop. Narratives specifically about dying from cancer are a recent phenomenon, only starting to emerge as a distinct genre in the 1970s. It would seem that a resurgence in academic interest has also been prompted by the volume of 'illness narratives' in the public domain.

(Bingley et al., 2006)

I contend that these narratives provide a rich source of evidence of the experience of living with cancer, from which we can begin to deduce a more coherent theoretical framework to aid our understanding of what the experience of cancer might mean for individuals.

This method of developing understanding in respect to the experience of living with dying is not new. According to Dame Cicely Saunders, 'We have helped people to listen to dying people and to hear what they're saying, and the challenge for the future is to keep on listening' (interview, cited in Walter, 1994, p67). For Saunders, it was important to give people who were living with life-threatening illness the opportunity to tell their stories, in order to increase public awareness of issues of death and dying, to improve public understanding and reduce fear and ultimately to improve the care and support that people in this situation receive.

Kübler-Ross in America in the 1970s also told people's stories, and these stories also had an emotional effect on people. As a result, things did change – the impersonal nature of hospital care was exposed by the very personal stories of the patients who suffered within them. If the premise of contemporary health and social care is that the patient (or service user) should come first, then it is vital to let the person (him or herself) speak, not only as has often been the case through the mouthpieces of professionals and academics such as Dame Cicely and Kübler-Ross, but also through the many printed case studies, biographies and autobiographies (Walter, 1994).

For health and social care professionals to truly understand an illness from inside an individual's experience necessarily requires taking a longitudinal view of issues like when the illness began, how the person understands their illness, how it affects them, what adaptations they have made, in other words, listening to their stories. The individual meanings given to living with a chronic illness are shaped in part by relationships with other people and the expectations shared in those relationships (Kleinman, 1988). While each person's story will be highly individual, Frank (1995) suggests that the activity of telling the story is in itself empowering and can contribute to collective knowledge as it provides an opportunity for healing, creates empathetic bonds between the teller and the listener and thus widens the 'circle of shared experience' (pxii). The gathering of these stories of individual experience, as opposed to seeking one common and dominant cultural experience, may assist others in understanding the 'illness journey'.

How, then, can this 'collective experience' help us as practitioners to respond to the changing nature of life-threatening illness in Western society, and what models are available to us to help us develop practice with people who are confronting death?

The role and responsibility of social work to people living with life-threatening illness

According to Small (2001, p961), 'there are close links between the philosophy and practice of palliative care and that of social work', and social work has a particular contribution to make to the care of people who are living with life-threatening illness in three main respects: that social work has always been concerned with responding to loss; that social work brings a 'whole system' approach, putting individual experience into a wider context and social work is concerned with helping people to ameliorate the practical impact of change. What characterises social work in the context of life-threatening illness is its ability to recognise the holistic needs of individuals and families, and how, despite recent trends towards care management in mainstream social work (Lloyd, 1997; Lloyd, 2002), palliative care social work as practised in hospices and other specialist settings has, by and large, managed to retain its traditional casework approach.

In my experience as a palliative care social worker from 1995 to 2004, the role of the social worker complemented that of the multi-disciplinary team by ensuring that a psychosocial model of care was offered to patients and families alongside the medical model, and that service users were encouraged to identify and achieve self-defined goals, to fulfil their potential and to live their lives for as long as was possible – essentially an individualised approach to care was provided, which counteracted some of the more restrictive aspects of the medical interventions which service users would often have to undergo.

Intrinsic to this approach is a recognition of the spiritual needs of service users who require palliative care services; according to Everard (2005, p129):

In focusing on the needs and wishes of their clients, in using their skills and experience to facilitate the expression of spiritual and emotional pain, and in being willing to enter at some level into the search for meaning in, and some resolution of, the suffering that patients and their families experience, social workers in palliative care settings make an important contribution to the meeting of the spiritual needs of their clients.

Despite this, however, Clausen et al. (2005, p283) found that, although many patients and carers had clearly expressed psychosocial needs, which could clearly be met by social workers, few, if any, were found to have had any social work involvement. This was partly attributed to a lack of understanding on the part of the wider team about the roles and tasks of social work, and a reluctance on the part of potential service users to request a social work assessment, fearing the social stigma associated with this.

In 2007, Beresford et al. reported on the first major research study into service users' perspectives on specialist palliative care social work in the UK. Beresford et al.'s (2007) research determined that what palliative care service users who did receive social work intervention desired from and valued about the service they received was the ability and willingness of the worker to 'journey' with them, providing continuity of care and acting as a guide into the unknown (Beresford et al., 2007; also Miller, 1990; Clausen, 2005; Reith and Payne, 2009). Specifically, Beresford et al. (2007) found that palliative care service users and those receiving bereavement support from a social worker valued:

1. the importance of the relationship and the preparedness of the worker to be committed to the individual and their family's own definition of their needs;
2. reliability and clarity about what the social worker could do;
3. a friendly and approachable manner;
4. an emphasis on holistic care.

Case study 28.1

Lorna is a 40-year-old woman who has been diagnosed with advanced stage breast cancer. She has a seven-year-old son, Carl, who lives with her and visits his birth father every other weekend.

Lorna has spoken to you of her desire to keep life as 'normal' as possible for herself and Carl for as long as possible. She is aware that she is dying, but she doesn't want to 'give up' before she has to. She has asked you to apply for funding to enable her and Carl to spend a week on the east coast in a caravan at the beginning of the summer holiday, which is in three weeks' time.

She has also spoken to you of her concern that her 'cancer nurse' is cross with her, as she has not completed the task the nurse set her of making a memory box for Carl for when she is no longer there.

In the light of your reading of this chapter, consider the following questions. Thinking about the importance of 'care and control' – the need to balance patient choice and an individualised approach to care with assessment of risk – what is your responsibility to Lorna and to Carl? How might your response as a social worker differ to that of the health professional? How might you work in partnership with Lorna and her nurse to find the best solution?

Conclusion

The challenge for contemporary social work practice would seem to be for organisations and policy-makers to recognise the importance of an individualised approach to care and to enable social workers to reach out to those who are living with, as well as dying from, life-threatening illness, recognising that the need for psychosocial intervention and support is ongoing and that the same skills that are valued by those who are dying may be equally as applicable to those who are surviving.

Key points summary

- All social work is concerned with loss and change, and there is a clear role for social work practitioners in the care of people living with life-threatening illness.
- Social work brings a whole system approach to death and dying, thus ensuring an individualised approach to care while recognising the importance of societal and cultural perspectives.

Suggested further reading

Beresford, P., Adshead, P. and Croft, S. (2007) *Palliative Care, Social Work and Service Users: Making Life Possible*. London: Jessica Kingsley Publishers.

Holloway, M. (2007) *Negotiating Death in Contemporary Health and Social Care*. Bristol: Policy Press.

Payne, M. and Taplin, S. (2014) Social work in healthcare settings, in Teater, B. (ed) *Contemporary Social Work Practice: A Handbook for Students*. Maidenhead: Open University Press.

29

Working with communities
Keith Popple

Chapter objectives

By the end of this chapter you should be able to:

- provide a better understanding of what we mean by the term community;
- highlight the community perspective in the evolution of social work;
- discuss why community is important to social work;
- note the impact of economic policies on poor communities;
- consider the role social workers can adopt when working in communities.

Introduction

This chapter will cover areas relating to working in communities which are relevant for practising social workers and social work students. We start by asking the question of what we mean by the term 'community'. Then we consider how the state and social work have over many years intervened at the locality level. We then discuss why community is important to social work and refer to the international definition of social work which broadly interprets the notion whereas in the UK it tends to be peripheral to individually focused work. This leads us to consider the role social workers can adopt when working in communities, before emphasising that work in communities should be seen as a central and complementing feature of social work.

What do we mean by the term community?

Activity 29.1

What does community mean to you? List and briefly comment on the communities that you consider yourself to be a member of. Then read the following section and compare your notes to it.

There are few discussions among sociologists and geographers that attract as much debate and disagreement as that which relates to defining the term community. There is, for example, debate as to whether when we use the term community we mean locality or perhaps we mean neighbourhood. There are also explorations of communities that concern people's culture, religion, 'race', nationality, sexuality, disability, or class – so we talk of the black community, the Asian community, white working class communities, the Jewish community, the gay community, and so on. The term can therefore refer to relationships that are defined within a geographical area or to relationships that are not locally based but are present at a more intangible or ideological level, or refer to an identity.

Research summary

Over the years there has been a whole genre of study devoted to community studies. One of the most well-known in the UK is the study undertaken by Young and Willmott (1957) who investigated the impact of post-war changes on Bethnal Green in East London. When the authors began their research they expected to discover a community suffering from major changes in employment, housing and personal relationships, but instead found a neighbourhood that had retained its sense of community with strong extended kinship networks where women were important in sustaining bonds of solidarity.

Since the publication of this classic study there has been some criticism of it, relating to what a number of researchers consider was a romantic view of a working class community. For example, both Wilson (1980) and Cornwell (1984) claim the study represents a rather starry-eyed view of community life which fails to present the more contentious aspects of people living in close proximity with each other. In fact, Cornwell's study of the same community undertaken 25 years later found a different sort of area with a noticeable degree of hostility from white residents towards the black and Asian residents that lived there.

In recent years there has been increasing evidence coming from the fields of sociology and social policy of rising individualism and declining social capital (or social connections and knowledge that helps people to achieve their ambitions and goals). The political scientist and professor of public policy Robert Putnam (2000) has argued that this has led to a diminishing of involvement in civic and community affairs. Putnam's ground-breaking research was undertaken in the USA and we need to ask whether this trend has been replicated in the UK. Certainly the use of digital technologies has increased and, whilst there is evidence that people may spend less time in daily face-to-face contact, Chambers (2006) and Kraut et al. (2006) argue that the new technologies have increased digital traffic between people and in turn have formed dynamic different online communities such as Twitter and Facebook.

What these and the many other studies published in the last 30 or so years point to is the need for a greater understanding of what we mean by the term community which is constantly changing and evolving. So, in considering working in communities, we should be aware that definitions of community in the twenty-first century remain elusive, imprecise, contradictory and controversial. We need therefore to continue to look out for well researched and documented community studies that capture the different experiences of people, often at a time of social dislocation and change.

The state intervenes in community life

Since the end of the Second World War, the British state has increasingly intervened in communities, usually to assist social cohesion, encourage economic regeneration and development, and to monitor and regulate the lives of those living in poor neighbourhoods. In the early stages, many of these forms of intervention were headed up by policies of urban regeneration. Between 1955 and 1974, 3.1 million people were rehoused and 1.2 million dwellings were demolished through slum clearance schemes. These substantial development schemes revealed people living in poverty and communities experiencing racial tension which led successive governments to introduce different forms of intervention other than those primarily focused on physical regeneration (Atkinson and Moon, 2010; Couch, 2010). Thus, in the 1960s, the Urban Programme and Community Development Projects were created to provide area-based coordination that focused on addressing community tensions and deprivation and the need for better services delivered at a local level. The complexity of the issues facing communities due to structural causes including economic deficit was further recognised as the state introduced inner city partnerships which were intended to establish links between central and local government, and community groups to address urban decline and help stimulate wealth creating businesses (Loney, 1983).

In the 1970s state led schemes were complemented by those from the market with the wealthy moving into increasingly gentrified urban areas leading to substantial rises in property prices and pushing out poor residents (Cochrane, 2007; Parkinson, 2010). The emphasis now is on stimulating economic growth and job creation, with numerous initiatives which include partnerships combining local authorities, business and third sectors, and civil society (Couch et al., 2011). However, with reduced support from central government, local authorities are looking for alternative forms of finance including public-private partnerships (PPP). These involve a long-term contract between two or more public and private sectors to finance and deliver social and public infrastructure schemes such as schools, hospitals and transport systems (Wettenhall, 2019).

The changing role of social work in communities

Social work has played its part in addressing the economic and social changes that have impacted on communities. In fact, social work has a long history of engaging with communities which pre-dates the modern era. Social work evolved from divergent charitable roots during the late nineteenth and early twentieth centuries with the work of the Charity Organisation Society (COS) and the Settlement Movement (see Chapter 1). The advocates of the COS, which focused on individual case work with families and individuals, argued that whilst the Industrial Revolution brought with it enormous social problems, especially in the rapidly expanding urban areas, many of the problems in communities were due to the poor behaviour and attitudes of people who lived there. Those involved in the Settlement Movement, which provided neighbourhood services including day-care, education, and healthcare to the poorest, argued, however, that it was the inequalities inherent in the capitalist system that created the poverty that led to major social problems. The outcome was that the COS promoted and delivered an individual service to the 'deserving' poor; the Settlement Movement, meanwhile, provided a collective community based response to social need (Payne, 2005).

The notion of a community located social work response surfaced again in the 1950s when the report by Dr Eileen Younghusband on the role of social workers in local authority services identified community work as one of the three key constituents of social work. The two other approaches were identified as case work and group work (Younghusband, 1959).

A decade later the influential Seebohm Report (1968), which recommended the establishment of 'generic' local authority social work services in England and Wales, contained an entire chapter entitled 'community'. This watershed report, which was to overhaul the delivery and financing of social work, was intended to

provide a more co-ordinated and comprehensive approach to the problems of individuals, families and communities.

(Seebohm Report, 1968, para. 9)

Case study 29.1

A year after the publication of the Seebohm Report, the government launched the National Community Development Project, which was developed out of growing concern that certain sections of the population were failing to successfully respond to the changing social and economic circumstances. Funded by a combination of local and central government finance, the 12 neighbourhood Community Development Projects (CDPs) located in 'deprived areas' started from the premise that disadvantaged communities failed to compete in the marketplace because of internal community or personal problems. However, the workers and researchers employed by the local CDPs soon rejected the conservative explanations of poverty and instead produced a radical critique that demonstrated the structural basis of poverty which was created and perpetuated by the unequal distribution of resources and power throughout society. As expected, successive governments found this analysis uncomfortable and this ground-breaking project had its central funding withdrawn by the end of the 1970s (Popple, 2011).

The Barclay Committee (1982) re-emphasised the case for an approach to social work based upon local, neighbourhood, decentralised strategies. The report advocated social workers practising as close as possible to service users in what came to known as 'patch' based work or community social work (CSW). Whilst the Barclay Report recommended that CSW should become an essential feature of social services provision, with social workers seeking to integrate formal services with informal networks of support, there was scant evidence this recommendation was taken much further. What Abrams et al. (1989) and Oakley and Rajan (1991) discovered was that the communities that most needed CSW had limited social networks and few if any support networks. Nevertheless, both the Seebohm and Barclay Reports saw community as a key source of mutual support and assistance.

The Seebohm and Barclay Reports were followed by the Wagner Report (1988) and the Griffiths Report (1988), both of which encouraged more appropriate social care in the community.

We have further confirmation of the view that now is the time to again take seriously community in the organisation and delivery of social work. This view is argued by a number of writers and practitioners including Jordan (2007), Stepney and Popple (2008), Jordan and Drakeford (2012), Turbett (2014), Hatton (2016), and by the Social Work Action Network (see **www.socialworkfuture.org**).

Why community is important for social work

In many countries, working in communities is recognised as having a more prominent role to play in social work than we come across in the UK. For example, if we look at the International Federation of Social Workers' (IFSW, 2014) definition of social work we find it recognises the role social work plays in 'engaging people and structure to address life challenges and enhance wellbeing'.

Similarly if we read the 2014 IFSW statement on social work practice (**www.ifsw.org**) there is the following statement:

Social work practice spans a range of activities including various forms of therapy and coun-selling, group work, and community work; policy formulation and analysis, and advocacy and political interventions ... this definition supports social work strategies aimed at increasing people's hope, self-esteem and creative potential to confront and challenge oppressive power dynamics and structural sources of injustices, thus incorporating into a coherent whole the micro-macro, personal-political dimension of intervention.

There is a strong case that working in communities is more essential now than ever. We see in our communities, both in the UK and internationally, major economic, social and political change and challenge. The neo-liberal globalised finance capitalism that has driven economies everywhere since the early 1980s is presently undergoing reassessment by leading economists and writers as to its credibility to satisfactorily deliver for millions if not billions of people (Hall et al., 2013; Srnicek, 2016). For the last four decades neo-liberal policies have led the push to 'roll back the state' with the argument from the economists and politicians that advocated such policies that the free market economy is best placed to increase prosperity and deliver full employment (Friedman, 1962, 1993; Hayek, 1978). These policies have led to lower personal taxation rates and reduced state funding, particularly in the areas of welfare, housing and education.

The tight squeeze on public finances was to be accompanied by the impact of the international financial crash of 2008 which had a massive influence on the world econ-omy. The result was investment banks in the UK, Ireland and France being taken into government ownership to avoid them from imploding (Mason, 2009). Oxfam (2013) has estimated that the bailout of banks cost the UK government £141 billion. As a result of the financial crash, governments in many countries introduced 'austerity measures' which led to millions of people globally experiencing stagnant wages, rising living costs and greater job insecurity. The situation in the UK was no different, as successive gov-ernments made draconian cuts to public services which have put individuals, families and communities under increasing pressure.

The financial crash of 2008, the imposition of austerity and the resultant central and local government massive reductions in support for welfare has increased the pressure on those pursuing the neo-liberal ideology to change and adjust. One of the major criti-cisms of neo-liberalism has been the growth in income and wealth inequality. If we look at economic inequality in the UK, we find disturbing figures, with the country having a higher level of inequality compared to other developed countries.

Research summary

According to the Equality Trust, households in the bottom earning 10 per cent of the population have a disposable income below £10,000 a year, which is nine times less than those in the top 10 per cent of earners. Further, the top 1 per cent of income earners enjoy a substantially higher income than the rest of those in the top 10 per cent, with a yearly amount of over a quarter of a million pounds. Figures show too that those in the top 0.1 per cent have incomes around a million pounds a year (**www.equalitytrust.org.uk**). It is an indictment on British society that according to the Trussell Trust food banks gave out 1.3 million three-day emergency supplies in 2018. The introduction of Universal Credit by the government has further added to food hunger as claimants now have to wait five weeks after making their first claim till they receive payment (**www.trusselltrust.org**). As Jordan and Drakeford (2012, p37) point out,

> Deregulated free markets failed to create the spontaneous order which their supporters claimed. Instead, it produced inherent inequality and instability on a massive scale. In the process, the share of national wealth taken by workers, and those without work, has fallen as have their real incomes.

Nevertheless, inequality is not inevitable. Research by Dorling (2015, 2017a, 2017b) shows how steps can be taken to reduce the impact of inequality and argues that by doing this we can move towards greater equality for individuals and communities. Wilkinson and Pickett (2010) make a similar argument, with extensive evidence drawn from a range of international sources. They state that greater equality is possible and would create a 'qualitatively better and more sociable society for all' (2010, p272).

What role can social workers adopt when working in communities?

Activity 29.2

Before reading this next section consider the following question. What can you do in your social work practice to ensure that community is more fully considered? Write down your thoughts and refer to them as you read through this part of the chapter.

We now have a clearer understanding of a number of issues relating to working in communities. First, we have been made aware of the complexities and difficulties when trying to define what we mean by the term community; we have noted that the state has a long record of intervening in communities for both economic and social reasons; we have seen how community has proved to be an important notion in the evolution of social work and the moves to deliver services that are based in the locality; finally, we have been presented with evidence of the impact of economic policies on poor communities. It is people living in these communities who tend to be the ones most likely to be in receipt of social work services (Ferguson, 2008; Ferguson, 2011).

In order to specifically focus on working in communities, let us refer to the view of Jordan and Drakeford (2012, p107) who call for the social work profession to lose its *myopic focus on individuals and mechanistic methods of intervention that it acquired in the previous 30 years. In that period, it became largely detached from community work ... and lost many of its capacities to understand individuals in their cultural contexts.*

Recognition of this state of affairs has to be a prerequisite for any effective work in the community. The modern welfare state emerged after the Second World War as part of an integral package of measures to provide the country with security for its citizens. An aspect of this was the creation of the personal social services which, as we have noted, has at different times addressed the need for social work to be located closer to communities. However, particularly since the 1980s, we have seen demands for social work specialisms, the introduction of public service managerialism and the drive for cost efficiency all of which has led to social work being seen through a prism of individualism, and a mechanistic approach to outcomes and standards (Rogowski, 2010). We now have 'inspections' and league tables which have stripped away the unique relationship social workers once had with their clients, and in its place a relationship that is based on the power of the state being exercised through the agency of the social work services and the social worker (Clarke, 2004). This in no way diminishes the tremendous work of thousands of social workers doing a difficult and demanding job despite the circumstances they have to work in.

It is for these reasons that we need to seriously consider how we can work more effectively in communities and in ways that challenge the notion that the present way of delivering social work is necessarily the best. To achieve this there are certain steps social workers can take to move the profession and the organisation of social work in a direction that is closer to those it is meant to serve. Because of the complexity and breadth of what we mean by community I am principally considering social work at the neighbourhood level. So, what can we do to assist the shift in the focus of social work from the individual to the community?

There are three ways that can be initiated to facilitate better working in communities. These are:

a)   *Strengthen the teaching of social policy on social work courses*

A study of social policy should be central in the training and education of social workers. Although social policy is difficult to precisely define, fundamentally it is an interdisciplinary and applied subject that involves the economic, political, sociological examination of the ways in which state policies affect individuals and communities. Its importance to social work is that it helps to contextualise the professional activity within social values, social theories and welfare ideologies. A failure to understand how social policy emerges and is contested can hinder effective practice. Social policy underpins the legislative framework that social workers operate within and provides a clear understanding of the need for the collective response to social problems. It offers a perspective that makes clearer the connection between economic factors such as employment, income and wealth, and spending on welfare, education and health; and social factors such as the impact from poverty and inequality. Further, it shines a light into areas of discrimination such as sexism and racism.

Importantly, a critical understanding of social policy during this period of massive change in the public sector will assist social workers to engage more effectively with the new and emerging relationship between the local state, voluntary organisations and local communities.

There are a number of useful texts on social policy and social work which can assist students and professionals as they seek a better understanding of the forces that shape working in communities. These texts include those by Green and Clarke (2016), and Cunningham and Cunningham (2017).

b) *Community profiling*

Social workers who are committed to working in communities need to ensure they have up-to-date and relevant information about the locality they are working in. Whilst the collection of this information is an on-going task, it is possible to carry out some of this groundwork during the early stages of intervening. One of the best ways of identifying community issues and attitudes, and assessing economic and social conditions, is to carry out a community profile. Such a profile can be updated as more data is collected.

It is possible to do this by collecting information from both primary and secondary sources. Primary source collection can be achieved through interviews, listening to the concerns being voiced by local people, attending meetings of residents in the areas, undertaking surveys, and meeting with other professionals in the community. Secondary source collection can involve researching the demography of the local population and the projected growth trends; identifying local labour force figures and major employers and industries; asking what the sort of housing and tenancies exist in the community; finding out the what community and cultural facilities and resources exist; discovering where children attend schools; and locating the medical facilities in the area.

If community profiles already exist, it may be possible to amalgamate data and information from your own investigations. Finally, there may be accessible documented histories relating to the community, and there is the possibility that oral histories exist that can be retrieved.

To assist in developing a community profile, probably the most useful text on the subject is Hawtin and Percy-Smith (2007).

c) *Networking*

In order for social workers to work effectively in communities, they need to engage in the networks within the locality they are working. Like social policy, learning how to network should be a key theme of social work training and education, something that already happens in the training of community development workers.

Networking involves making and using contacts and developing networks as structures and communication systems. Gilchrist (2009) has provided one of the best guides to the practice and policy of how networks contribute to the wellbeing of community life and civil society. In an earlier publication, Gilchrist (1995, p2) describes networking as

the process by which relationships and contacts between people or organisations are established, nurtured and utilised for mutual benefit … Informal links between individuals and organisations provide an important means by which people gain access to ideas, information, opinions, resources and expertise which would not otherwise be directly available.

To a large extent, networking and developing networks is an organic approach. Unlike the present drive to record and deploy surveillance of people and operations, it challenges the different barriers that exist between organisations and those it is meant to work for. Networking involves collaborative working, sharing resources, and creating and promoting networking opportunities. It requires skill and commitment and has a central place in working in communities.

When networking, recognition needs to be made of the extensive and varied work undertaken by voluntary organisations, community groups and community action groups. It is these groups that social workers need to successfully network with.

Other than the excellent text by Alison Gilchrist referred to above, the role of networking and networking skills for social workers are also considered in Stepney and Popple (2008) and Trevithick (2012).

Conclusion

This chapter has highlighted the benefits of social workers having a perspective and practice of working in communities. We have noted that organisations including those in the voluntary and statutory social work sectors have a history of intervening in communities. The state has, for example, been responsible for the delivery of major rebuilding programmes, but there have been many other forms of interventions which are more tangential but as important such as social work services.

The case has been made here to consider social work being conceptualised and delivered in a manner that is focused on engaging with the collective rather than focused on the individual. One of the major benefits of effective working in communities is that it can provide the greater participation of service users in the delivery of the services they benefit from. Working in this way too will challenge the power dynamic of managers and bureaucrats who benefit from the circumstances in which social work is presently delivered. This is not to say that there isn't a place for working in ways which focus on the individual. Rather working in communities should be seen as complementing these one-to-one approaches.

The successful outcome of working in communities will be a strengthening of civil society, something that is much needed at a time when the credibility of neo-liberal economic and social policies are under scrutiny, with millions in the UK living in neighbourhoods that are experiencing growing inequality and insecurity.

Key points summary

This chapter has:

- outlined how community has proved to be important in the evolution of social work;
- noted ways that facilitate better working in communities;

- considered the impact of economic policies on poor communities, the very neighbourhoods which tend to be most likely to be in receipt of social work services;
- made the case to consider social work being conceptualised and delivered in a manner that is focused on engaging with the collective rather than focused on the individual.

Suggested further reading

Gilchrist, A. and Taylor, M. (2016) *The Short Guide to Community* Development (2nd ed). Bristol: Policy Press.

Popple, K. (2015) *Analysing Community Work: Theory and Practice* (2nd ed). Maidenhead: Open University Press.

Teater, B. and Baldwin, M. (2012) *Social Work in the Community: Making a Difference*. Bristol: Policy Press.

Appendix 1

Professional Capabilities Framework

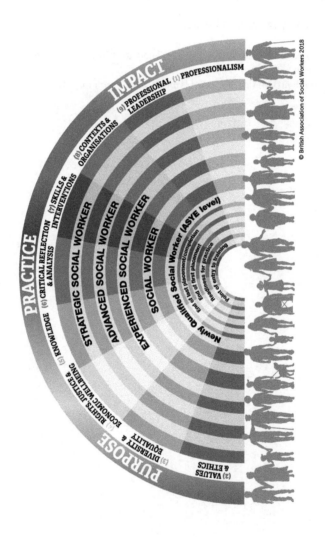

The 9 Domains

1. PROFESSIONALISM – Identify and behave as a professional social worker, committed to professional development.
2. VALUES AND ETHICS – Apply social work ethical principles and value to guide professional practices
3. DIVERSITY AND EQUALITY – Recognise diversity and apply anti-discriminatory and anti-oppressive principles in practice.
4. RIGHTS, JUSTICE AND ECONOMIC WELLBEING – Advance human rights and promote social justice and economic wellbeing.
5. KNOWLEDGE – Develop and apply relevant knowledge from social work practice and research, social sciences, law, other professional and relevant fields, and from the experience of people who use services.
6. CRITICAL REFLECTION AND ANALYSIS – Apply critical reflection and analysis to inform and provide a rationale for professional decision-making.
7. SKILLS AND INTERVENTIONS – Use judgement, knowledge and authority to intervene with individuals, families and communities to promote independence, provide support, prevent harm and enable progress.
8. CONTEXTS AND ORGANISATIONS – Engage with, inform, and adapt to changing organisational contexts, and the social and policy environments that shape practice. Operate effectively within and contribute to the development of organisations and services, including multi-agency and inter-professional settings.
9. PROFESSIONAL LEADERSHIP – Promote the profession and good social work practice. Take responsibility for the professional learning and development of others. Develop personal influence and be part of the collective leadership and impact of the profession.

Published with kind permission of BASW – **www.basw.co.uk**

See also the country specific occupational standards:

Northern Ireland Social Care Council, National Occupational Standards for Social Work https://niscc.info/storage/resources/nos_-_social_work.pdf

Scottish Social Services Council, National Occupational Standards for Social Services Scotland https://learn.sssc.uk.com/nos/index.html

Social Care Wales/Gofal Cymdeithasol Cymru, National Occupational Standards for Social Work https://socialcare.wales/nos-areas/social-work

Appendix 2

Subject benchmark for social work

5 Knowledge, understanding and skills

Subject knowledge and understanding

5.1 During their qualifying degree studies in social work, students acquire, critically evaluate, apply and integrate knowledge and understanding in the following five core areas of study.

5.2 Social work theory, which includes:

    i.   critical explanations from social work theory and other subjects which contribute to the knowledge base of social work

    ii.   an understanding of social work's rich and contested history from both a UK and comparative perspective

    iii.   the relevance of sociological and applied psychological perspectives to understanding societal and structural influences on human behaviour at individual, group and community levels, and the relevance of sociological theorisation to a deeper understanding of adaptation and change

    iv.   the relevance of psychological, physical and physiological perspectives to understanding human, personal and social development, well-being and risk

    v.   social science theories explaining and exploring group and organisational behaviour

    vi.   the range of theories and research-informed evidence that informs understanding of the child, adult, family or community and of the range of assessment and interventions which can be used

    vii.   the theory, models and methods of assessment, factors underpinning the selection and testing of relevant information, knowledge and critical appraisal of relevant social science and other research and evaluation methodologies, and the evidence base for social work

    viii.   the nature of analysis and professional judgement and the processes of risk assessment and decision-making, including the theory of risk-informed decisions and the balance of choice and control, rights and protection in decision-making

    ix.   approaches, methods and theories of intervention in working with a diverse population within a wide range of settings, including factors guiding the choice and critical evaluation of these, and user-led perspectives.

5.3   Values and ethics, which include:

    i.   the nature, historical evolution, political context and application of professional social work values, informed by national and international definitions and ethical statements, and their relation to personal values, identities, influences and ideologies

    ii.   the ethical concepts of rights, responsibility, freedom, authority and power inherent in the practice of social workers as agents with statutory powers in different situations

    iii.   aspects of philosophical ethics relevant to the understanding and resolution of value dilemmas and conflicts in both interpersonal and professional context

    iv.   understanding of, and adherence to, the ethical foundations of empirical and conceptual research, as both consumers and producers of social science research

    v.   the relationship between human rights enshrined in law and the moral and ethical rights determined theoretically, philosophically and by contemporary society

    vi.   the complex relationships between justice, care and control in social welfare and the practical and ethical implications of these, including their expression in roles as statutory agents in diverse practice settings and in upholding the law in respect of challenging discrimination and inequalities

    vii.   the conceptual links between codes defining ethical practice and the regulation of professional conduct

    viii.   the professional and ethical management of potential conflicts generated by codes of practice held by different professional groups

    ix.   the ethical management of professional dilemmas and conflicts in balancing the perspectives of individuals who need care and support and professional decision-making at points of risk, care and protection

    x.   the constructive challenging of individuals and organisations where there may be conflicts with social work values, ethics and codes of practice

    xi.   the professional responsibility to be open and honest if things go wrong (the duty of candour about own practice) and to act on concerns about poor or unlawful practice by any person or organisation

    xii.   continuous professional development as a reflective, informed and skilled practitioner, including the constructive use of professional supervision.

5.4   Service users and carers, which include:

    i.   the factors which contribute to the health and well-being of individuals, families and communities, including promoting dignity, choice and independence for people who need care and support

    ii.   the underpinning perspectives that determine explanations of the characteristics and circumstances of people who need care and support, with critical evaluation drawing on research, practice experience and the experience and expertise of people who use services

    iii.   the social and psychological processes associated with, for example, poverty, migration, unemployment, trauma, poor health, disability, lack of education and other sources of disadvantage and how they affect well-being, how they interact and may lead to marginalisation, isolation and exclusion, and demand for social work services

    iv.   explanations of the links between the factors contributing to social differences and identities (for example, social class, gender, ethnic differences, age, sexuality and religious belief) and the structural consequences of inequality and differential need faced by service users

    v.   the nature and function of social work in a diverse and increasingly global society (with particular reference to prejudice, interpersonal relations, discrimination, empowerment and anti-discriminatory practices).

5.5   The nature of social work practice, in the UK and more widely, which includes:

    i.   the place of theoretical perspectives and evidence from European and international research in assessment and decision-making processes

    ii.   the integration of theoretical perspectives and evidence from European and international research into the design and implementation of effective social work intervention with a wide range of service users, carers and communities

    iii.   the knowledge and skills which underpin effective practice, with a range of service users and in a variety of settings

    iv.   the processes that facilitate and support service user and citizen rights, choice, co-production, self-governance, well-being and independence

    v.   the importance of interventions that promote social justice, human rights, social cohesion, collective responsibility and respect for diversity and that tackle inequalities

    vi.   its delivery in a range of community-based and organisational settings spanning the statutory, voluntary and private sectors, and the changing nature of these service contexts

    vii.   the factors and processes that facilitate effective interdisciplinary, interprofessional and interagency collaboration and partnership across a plurality of settings and disciplines

    viii.   the importance of social work's contribution to intervention across service user groups, settings and levels in terms of the profession's focus on social justice, human rights, social cohesion, collective responsibility and respect for diversities

    ix.   the processes of reflection and reflexivity as well as approaches for evaluating service and welfare outcomes for vulnerable people, and their significance for the development of practice and the practitioner.

5.6   The leadership, organisation and delivery of social work services, which includes:

    i.   the location of contemporary social work within historical, comparative and global perspectives, including in the devolved nations of the UK and wider European and international contexts

    ii.   how the service delivery context is portrayed to service users, carers, families and communities

    iii.   the changing demography and cultures of communities, including European and international contexts, in which social workers practise

    iv.   the complex relationships between public, private, social and political philosophies, policies and priorities and the organisation and practice of social work, including the contested nature of these

    v.   the issues and trends in modern public and social policy and their relationship to contemporary practice, service delivery and leadership in social work

    vi.   the significance of legislative and legal frameworks and service delivery standards, including on core social work values and ethics in the delivery of services which support, enable and empower

    vii.   the current range and appropriateness of statutory, voluntary and private agencies providing services and the organisational systems inherent within these

    viii.   development of new ways of working and delivery, for example the development of social enterprises, integrated multi-professional teams and independent social work provision

    ix.   the significance of professional and organisational relationships with other related services, including housing, health, education, police, employment, fire, income maintenance and criminal justice

x.   the importance and complexities of the way agencies work together to provide care, the relationships between agency policies, legal requirements and professional boundaries in shaping the nature of services provided in integrated and interdisciplinary contexts

xi.   the contribution of different approaches to management and leadership within different settings, and the impact on professional practice and on quality of care management and leadership in public and human services

xii.   the development of person-centred services, personalised care, individual budgets and direct payments all focusing upon the human and legal rights of the service user for control, power and self-determination

xiii.   the implications of modern information and communications technology for both the provision and receipt of services, use of technologically enabled support and the use of social media as a process and forum for vulnerable people, families and communities, and communities of professional practice.

Subject-specific skills and other skills

5.7   The range of skills required by a qualified social worker reflects the complex and demanding context in which they work. Many of these skills may be of value in many situations, for example, analytical thinking, building relationships, working as a member of an organisation, intervention, evaluation, and reflection. What defines the specific nature of these skills as developed by social work students is:

i.   the context in which they are applied and assessed (for example, communication skills in practice with people with sensory impairments or assessment skills in an interprofessional setting)

ii.   the relative weighting given to such skills within social work practice (for example, the central importance of problem-solving skills within complex human situations)

iii.   the specific purpose of skill development (for example, the acquisition of research skills in order to build a repertoire of research-based practice)

iv.   a requirement to integrate a range of skills (that is, not simply to demonstrate these in an isolated and incremental manner).

5.8   All social work graduates demonstrate the ability to reflect on and learn from the exercise of their skills, in order to build their professional identity. They understand the significance of the concepts of continuing professional development and lifelong learning, and accept responsibility for their own continuing development.

5.9   Social work students acquire and integrate skills in the following five core areas.

Problem-solving skills

5.10 These are subdivided into four areas.

5.11 Managing problem-solving activities: graduates in social work are able to:

i.   think logically, systematically, creatively, critically and reflectively, in order to carry out a holistic assessment

ii.   apply ethical principles and practices critically in planning problem-solving activities

iii.   plan a sequence of actions to achieve specified objectives, making use of research, theory and other forms of evidence

iv.   manage processes of change, drawing on research, theory and other forms of evidence.

5.12 Gathering information: graduates in social work are able to:

    i.   demonstrate persistence in gathering information from a wide range of sources and using a variety of methods, for a range of purposes. These methods include electronic searches, reviews of relevant literature, policy and procedures, face-to-face interviews, and written and telephone contact with individuals and groups

    ii.   take into account differences of viewpoint in gathering information and critically assess the reliability and relevance of the information gathered

    iii.   assimilate and disseminate relevant information in reports and case records.

5.13 Analysis and synthesis: graduates in social work are able to analyse and synthesise knowledge gathered for problem-solving purposes, in order to:

    i.   assess human situations, taking into account a variety of factors (including the views of participants, theoretical concepts, research evidence, legislation and organisational policies and procedures)

    ii.   analyse and synthesise information gathered, weighing competing evidence and modifying their viewpoint in the light of new information, then relate this information to a particular task, situation or problem

    iii.   balance specific factors relevant to social work practice (such as risk, rights, cultural differences and language needs and preferences, responsibilities to protect vulnerable individuals and legal obligations)

    iv.   assess the merits of contrasting theories, explanations, research, policies and procedures and use the information to develop and sustain reasoned arguments

    v.   employ a critical understanding of factors that support or inhibit problem-solving, including societal, organisational and community issues as well as individual relationships

    vi.   critically analyse and take account of the impact of inequality and discrimination in working with people who use social work services.

5.14 Intervention and evaluation: graduates in social work are able to use their knowledge of a range of interventions and evaluation processes creatively and selectively to:

    i.   build and sustain purposeful relationships with people and organisations in communities and interprofessional contexts

    ii.   make decisions based on evidence, set goals and construct specific plans to achieve outcomes, taking into account relevant information, including ethical guidelines

    iii.   negotiate goals and plans with others, analysing and addressing in a creative and flexible manner individual, cultural and structural impediments to change

    iv.   implement plans through a variety of systematic processes that include working in partnership

    v.   practice in a manner that promotes well-being, protects safety and resolves conflict

    vi.   act as a navigator, advocate and support to assist people who need care and support to take decisions and access services

    vii.   manage the complex dynamics of dependency and, in some settings, provide direct care and personal support to assist people in their everyday lives

    viii.   meet deadlines and comply with external requirements of a task

    ix.   plan, implement and critically monitor and review processes and outcomes

    x.   bring work to an effective conclusion, taking into account the implications for all involved

    xi.   use and evaluate methods of intervention critically and reflectively.

Communication skills

5.15 Graduates in social work are able to communicate clearly, sensitively and effectively (using appropriate methods which may include working with interpreters) with individuals and groups of different ages and abilities in a range of formal and informal situations, in order to:

i.   engage individuals and organisations, who may be unwilling, by verbal, paper-based and electronic means to achieve a range of objectives, including changing behaviour

ii.   use verbal and non-verbal cues to guide and inform conversations and interpretation of information

iii.   negotiate and, where necessary, redefine the purpose of interactions with individuals and organisations and the boundaries of their involvement

iv.   listen actively and empathetically to others, taking into account their specific needs and life experiences

v.   engage appropriately with the life experiences of service users, to understand accurately their viewpoint, overcome personal prejudices and respond appropriately to a range of complex personal and interpersonal situations

vi.   make evidence-informed arguments drawing from theory, research and practice wisdom, including the viewpoints of service users and/or others

vii.   write accurately and clearly in styles adapted to the audience, purpose and context of the communication

viii. use advocacy skills to promote others' rights, interests and needs

ix.   present conclusions verbally and on paper, in a structured form, appropriate to the audience for which these have been prepared

x.   make effective preparation for, and lead, meetings in a productive way.

Skills in working with others

5.16 Graduates in social work are able to build relationships and work effectively with others, in order to:

i.   involve users of social work services in ways that increase their resources, capacity and power to influence factors affecting their lives

ii.   engage service users and carers and wider community networks in active consultation

iii.   respect and manage differences such as organisational and professional boundaries and differences of identity and/or language

iv.   develop effective helping relationships and partnerships that facilitate change for individuals, groups and organisations while maintaining appropriate personal and professional boundaries

v.   demonstrate interpersonal skills and emotional intelligence that creates and develops relationships based on openness, transparency and empathy

vi.   increase social justice by identifying and responding to prejudice, institutional discrimination and structural inequality

vii.   operate within a framework of multiple accountability (for example, to agencies, the public, service users, carers and others)

viii. observe the limits of professional and organisational responsibility, using supervision appropriately and referring to others when required

ix.   provide reasoned, informed arguments to challenge others as necessary, in ways that are most likely to produce positive outcomes.

Skills in personal and professional development

5.17 Graduates in social work are able to:

    i.   work at all times in accordance with codes of professional conduct and ethics

    ii.   advance their own learning and understanding with a degree of independence and use supervision as a tool to aid professional development

    iii.   develop their professional identity, recognise their own professional limitations and accountability, and know how and when to seek advice from a range of sources, including professional supervision

    iv.   use support networks and professional supervision to manage uncertainty, change and stress in work situations while maintaining resilience in self and others

    v.   handle conflict between others and internally when personal views may conflict with a course of action necessitated by the social work role

    vi.   provide reasoned, informed arguments to challenge unacceptable practices in a responsible manner and raise concerns about wrongdoing in the workplace

    vii.   be open and honest with people if things go wrong

    viii. understand the difference between theory, research, evidence and expertise and the role of professional judgement.

Use of technology and numerical skills

5.18 Graduates in social work are able to use information and communication technology effectively and appropriately for:

    i.   professional communication, data storage and retrieval and information searching

    ii.   accessing and assimilating information to inform working with people who use services

    iii.   data analysis to enable effective use of research in practice

    iv.   enhancing skills in problem-solving

    v.   applying numerical skills to financial and budgetary responsibilities

    vi.   understanding the social impact of technology, including the constraints of confidentiality and an awareness of the impact of the 'digital divide'.

References

Abbott, D. (2015) Love in a cold climate: changes in the fortunes of LGBT men and women with learning disabilities? *British Journal of Learning Disabilities*, 43: 100–105.

Abbott, D. (2016) Sexuality and relationships in the lives of people with intellectual disabilities: standing in my shoes. *Disability & Society*, 3(9): 1306–1307.

Abbott, D. and Howarth, J. (2007) Still off-limits? Staff views on supporting gay, lesbian and bisexual people with intellectual disabilities to develop sexual and intimate relationships. *Journal of Applied Research in Intellectual Disabilities*, 20: 116–126.

Abrams, P., Abrams, S., Humphrey, R. and Snaith, R. (1989) *Neighbourhood Care and Social Policy*. London: HMSO.

Adams, R. (2008) *Empowerment, Participation and Social Work* (4th ed). Basingstoke: Palgrave.

Adams, R., Dominelli, L. and Payne, M. (2002) *Social Work: Themes, Issues and Critical Debates* (2nd ed). Basingstoke: Palgrave.

Advisory Council on the Misuse of Drugs (2003) Hidden harm: responding to the needs of children of problem drug users. *Home Office*. Available at: www.gov.uk/government/uploads/system/uploads/attachment_data/file/120620/hidden-harm-full.pdf

Agazarian, Y. M. (2004) *Systems-Centred Psychotherapy for Groups*. London: Karnac.

Agazarian, Y. M. and Gantt, S. P. (2005) The systems perspective, in Wheelan, S. (ed) *The Handbook of Group Research and Practice*. London: Sage.

Ager, A. and Strang, A. (2008) Understanding integration: a conceptual framework. *Journal of Refugee Studies*, 21(2): 166–191.

Agnew, A., Manktelow, R., Taylor, B. J. and Jones, L. (2010) Bereavement needs assessment in specialist palliative care settings: a review of the literature. *Palliative Medicine*, 24(1): 46–59.

Alcohol Research UK (2018) The hardest hit: addressing the crisis in alcohol treatment services. Available at: www.alcoholconcern.org.uk/Handlers/Download.ashx?IDMF=56d6e255-ccad-4171-ac86-8a15059ffdda

Alderwick, H., Ham, C. and Buck, D. (2015) *Population Health Systems: Going Beyond Integrated Care*. London: The King's Fund.

Ali, A., Hall, I., Blickwedel, J. and Hassiotis, A. (2015) Behavioural and cognitive-behavioural interventions for outwardly-directed aggressive behaviour in people with intellectual disabilities. *Cochrane Database of Systematic Reviews*, 4: CD003406.

Allain, L. (2016) *The Involvement of Young People Leaving Care in Social Work Education and Practice* (DProf thesis). London: Middlesex University.

Allain, L. and Hingley-Jones, H. (2019) Exploring the experiences of Special Guardians and the professionals who work with them. Available at: www.grandparentsplus.org.uk/kinship-care-professionals-group-meeting-notes

Allan, J. and Hess, L. (2010) The nexus between material circumstances, cultural context and experiences of loss, grief and trauma: complexities in working with refugees in the early phases of settlement. *Grief Matters: The Australian Journal of Grief and Bereavement*, 13(3): 76–80.

Allen, G. (2011) *Early Intervention: The Next Steps*. London: HMSO.

Allensworth Hawkins, C. and Knox, K. (2014) Educating for international social work: human rights leadership. *International Social Work*, 57(3): 248–257.

Allweiss, S. and Hilado, A. (2018) The context of migration: pre-arrival, migration, and resettlement experiences, in Hilado, A. and Lundy, M. (eds) *Models for Practice with Immigrants and Refugees: Collaboration, Cultural Awareness, and Integrative Theory*. Thousand Oaks, CA: Sage.

Archer, J., Bower, P., Gilbody, S., Lovell, K., Richards, D., Gask, L., Dickens, C. and Coventry, P. (2012) Collaborative care for depression and anxiety problems. *Cochrane Database of Systematic Reviews*, 10: CD006525.

Armstrong, D. (2004) A risky business? Research, policy, governmentality and youth offending. *Youth Justice*, 4(2): 100–116.

Armstrong-Coster, A. (2004) *Living and Dying with Cancer*. Cambridge: Cambridge University Press.

Association of Directors of Children's Services (2015) Age Assessment Guidance: Guidance to Assist Social Workers and Their Managers in Undertaking Age Assessments in England: ADCS. London: DfE, Home Office.

Association of Directors of Children's Services (2018) National Transfer Scheme Protocol for Unaccompanied Asylum Seeking Children Version 2.0. London: DfE, Home Office.

Atkinson, R. and Moon, G. (2010) Post-war urban problems and the rediscovery of urban poverty. In Tallon, A. (ed) *Urban Regeneration and Renewal*. London: Routledge.

Attig, T. (1991) The importance of conceiving of grief as an active process. *Death Studies*, 15(4): 385–393.

Attig, T. (1996) *How We Grieve: Relearning the World*. Oxford: Oxford University Press.

Australian Human Rights Commission (AHRC) (2014) The forgotten children: national inquiry into children in immigration detention. Available at: www.humanrights.gov.au/our-work/asylum-seekers-and-refugees/national-inquiry-children-immigration-detention-2014

Ayalon, L. and Tesch-Römer, C. (2018) Introduction to the section: ageism – concept and origins. In Ayalon, L. and Tesch-Römer, C. (eds) *Contemporary Perspectives on Ageism*. Switzerland: Springer Open.

Azmitia, E. C. (2001) Impact of drugs and alcohol on the brain through the life cycle: knowledge for social workers. *Journal of Social Work Practice in the Addictions*, 1(3): 41–63.

Badham, B. (2004) Participation – for a change: disabled young people lead the way. *Children and Society*, 18(2): 143–154.

Baer, P. and Bandura, A. (1963) Behavior theory and identificatory learning. *American Journal of Orthopsychiatry*, 33(4): 591–601.

Baines, D. (ed) (2017) *Doing Anti-Oppressive Practice: Building Transformative Politicized Social Work* (3rd ed). Halifax, Canada: Fernwood Publishing.

Ballan, M. and Freyer, M. (2017) Trauma-informed social work practice with women with disabilities: working with survivors of intimate partner violence. *Violence Advances in Social Work*, 18(1): 131–144.

Baltes, P. (1987) Theoretical propositions of life-span developmental psychology: on the dynamics between growth and decline. *Developmental Psychology*, 23(5): 611–626.

Bancroft, A. (2007) Parental drug and alcohol misuse: resilience and transition among young people. *Joseph Rowntree Foundation*. Available at: www.jrf.org.uk/sites/default/files/jrf/migrated/files/1859352499.pdf

Banks, S. (2012) *Ethics and Values in Social Work* (4th ed). Basingstoke: Palgrave.

Barber, J. (2002) *Social Work with Addictions* (2nd ed). London: Red Globe Press.

Barclay Committee (1982) *Social Workers: Their Roles and Tasks*. London: National Institute for Social Work/Bedford Square Press.

Barker, R. L. (2003) *The Social Work Dictionary* (5th ed). Washington DC: NASW Press.

Barlow, J., Smailagic, N., Huband, N., Roloff, V. and Bennett, C. (2014) Group-based parent training programmes for improving parental psychosocial health. *Cochrane Database of Systematic Reviews*, 5: CD002020.

Barnard, M., Russell, C., McKeganey, N. and Hamilton-Barclay, T. (2017) The highs and lows of NPS / 'Legal High' use: qualitative views from a UK online survey. *Drugs: Education, Prevention and Policy*, 24(1): 96–102.

Bass, B. M. (1990) *Handbook of Leadership: A Survey of Theory and Research*. New York: Free Press.

BASW (2014) Code of Ethics for Social Work. Available at: www.basw.co.uk/about-basw/code-ethics

BASW (2015) Position Statement: Age Assessment. Available at: www.basw.co.uk/system/files/resources/basw_114345-7_0.pdf

BASW (2018) Professional Capabilities Framework. Available at: www.basw.co.uk/system/files/resources/Detailed%20level%20descriptors%20for%20all%20domains%20wi%20digital%20aug8.pdf

Batchelor, S. and McNeill, F. (2005) The young person-worker relationship, in Bateman, T. and Pitts, J. (eds) *The RHP Companion to Youth Justice*. Lyme Regis: Russell House Publishing. 166–71.

Bateman, T. (2017) *The State of Youth Justice 2017*. London: NAYJ.

Bates, J., Best, P., McQuilkin, J. and Taylor, B. J. (2017) Will web search engines replace bibliographic databases in the systematic identification of research? *Journal of Academic Librarianship*, 43(1): 8–17.

BBC (2016) Dentists Condemn Call for Child Migrants' Teeth to be Tested. Available at: www.bbc.co.uk/news/uk-37700074

BBC (2018) Channel Migrants: Home Secretary declares a major incident. Available at: www.bbc.co.uk/news/uk-46705128

BBC (2019) Newsnight. Asylum Seekers: 'They didn't believe I was a child'. Available at: https://www.bbc.co.uk/news/uk-48750708

Beckett, C. and Horner, N. (2016) *Essential Theory for Social Work Practice* (2nd ed). London: Sage.

Beckett, C., Maynard, A. and Jordan, P. (2017) *Values and Ethics in Social Work* (3rd ed). London: Sage.

Beckett, J. (2018) The changing nature of social work. *International Social Work*, 61(6): 968–973.

Beddoe, L. (2010) Surveillance or reflection: professional supervision in 'the risk society'. *British Journal of Social Work*, 40(4): 1279–1296.

Bedford, A. (2015) *Serious Case Review into Child Sexual Exploitation in Oxfordshire: from the experiences of Children A, B, C, D, E, and F*. Oxford: Oxford Safeguarding Board.

Beirens, H., Hughes, N., Hek, R. and Spicer, N. (2007) Preventing social exclusion of refugee and asylum seeking children: building new networks. *Social Policy and Society*, 6(2): 219–229.

Bellfield, C. R., Noves, M. and Barrett, W. S. (2006) *High/Scope Perry Pre-School Program: Cost Benefit Analysis using data from the age 40 year follow up*. New Brunswick, NJ: NIEER.

Bellis, M. A., Hughes, K., Leckenby, N., Perkins, C. and Lowey, H. (2014) National household survey of adverse childhood experiences and their relationship with resilience to health-harming behaviours in England. *BMC Medicine*, 12(1): doi:10.1186/1741-7015-12-72.

Ben-Ishai, E. (2012) Responding to vulnerability: the case of injection drug use. *International Journal of Feminist Approaches to Bioethics*, 5(2): 39.

Bengtson, V. L., Elder, G. H. and Putney, N. M. (2012) The life course perspective on ageing: linked lives, timing and history, in Katz, J., Pearce, S. and Spurr, S. (eds) *Adult Lives: A Life Course Perspective*. Bristol: Policy Press.

Bennis, W. and Shepard, H. (1956) A theory of group development. *Human Relations*, 9(4): 415–437.

Beresford, P. (2012) The theory and philosophy behind user involvement, in Beresford, P. and Carr, S. (eds) *Social Care, Service Users and User Involvement*. London: Jessica Kingsley Publishers.

Beresford, P. (2013) *Personalisation*. Bristol: Policy Press.

Beresford, P., Adshead, P. and Croft, S. (2007) *Palliative Care, Social Work and Service Users: Making Life Possible*. London: Jessica Kingsley Publishers.

Berger, P. L. and Luckmann, T. (1966) *The Social Construction of Reality*. Garden City, NY: Doubleday.

Berman-Rossi, T. (1993) The tasks and skills of the social worker across stages of group develop-ment, in Ephross, P. H., Vassil, T. V. and Varghese, R. K. (eds) *Social Work with Groups: Expanding Horizons*. Binghamton: The Haworth Press.

Berman-Rossi, T. (ed) (1994) *Social Work: The Collected Writings of William Schwartz*. Itasca, IL: F. E. Peacock Publishers, Inc.

Bernard, C. and Greenwood, T. (2019) 'We're giving you the sack': social workers' perspectives of intervening in affluent families when there are concerns about child neglect. *The British Journal of Social Work*, 49(8): 2266–2282.

Berridge, V. (2014) Drugs, alcohol, and the First World War. *The Lancet*, 384(9957): 1840–1841.

Best, P., Manktelow, R. and Taylor, B. J. (2014) Online communication, social networking and adolescent wellbeing: a systematic narrative review. *Children and Youth Services Review*, 41: 27–36.

Bhabha, J. (2007) Border rights and rites: generalisations, stereotypes and gendered migration, in van Walsum, S. and Spijkerboer, T. (eds) *Women and Immigration Law: New Variations of Classical Feminist Themes*. Oxon: Routledge-Cavendish.

Biehal, N. (2014) A sense of belonging: meaning of family and home in long-term foster care. *British Journal of Social Work*, 44: 955–971.

Bion, W. R. (1959) *Experiences in Groups*. New York: Ballantine Books.

Blom, B. and Morén, S. (2010) Explaining social work practice: the CAIMeR theory. *Journal of Social Work Practice*, 10(1): 98–119.

Bloy, M. (2002) The principle of less eligibility. Available at: www.victorianweb.org/history/poor law/eligible.html

Boal, A. (1979) *Theatre of the Oppressed*. London: Pluto Press.

Boetto, H. (2017) A transformative eco-social model: challenging modernist assumptions in social work. *The British Journal of Social Work*, 47(1): 48–67.

Bolt D. (2018) An inspection of how the Home Office considers the 'best interests' of unaccompa-nied asylum-seeking children: August–December 2017, Independent Chief Inspector of Borders and Immigration. Available at: https://assets.publishing.service.gov.uk/government/uploads/system/uploads/attachment_data/file/695310/An_inspection_of_the_best_interests_of_unaccompanied_asylum_seeking_children_March_2018.pdf

Boochani, B. (2018a) *No Friend but the Mountains: Writing From Manus Prison*. Sydney: Pan Macmillan Australia.

Boochani, B. (2018b) Statement in support of the Academics for Refugees National Day of Action, 17 October 2018. Available at: https://academicsforrefugees.wordpress.com/nda-public-read-ins/

Bools, C. (2008) *Fabricated or Induced Illness in a Child by a Carer*. Abingdon: Radcliffe Publishing.

Bostock, L., Bairstow, S., Fish, S. and Mcleod, F. (2005) Managing risks and minimising mistakes in services to children and families. SCIE Report no. 6. London: Social Care Institute for Excellence.

Bourdieu, P. (1986) The forms of capital, in Richardson, J. (ed) *Handbook of Theory and Research for the Sociology of Education*. Westport, CT: Greenwood.

Bournemouth, Poole and Dorset (2017) Bournemouth, Poole and Dorset Multi Agency Risk Management (MARM) Principles and Guidance for Agencies. Available at: www.dorsetforyou.gov.uk/care-and-support-for-adults/information-for-professionals/dorset-safeguarding-adults-board/dorset-safeguarding-adults-board-pdfs/multi-agency-risk-management-marm-guidance.pdf

Bovarnick, S., Scott, S. and Pearce, J. (2017) *Direct Work with Sexually Exploited and At Risk Children and Young People: A Rapid Evidence Assessment*. Bedford: University of Bedford/DMSS/Barnardo's.

Bower, P., Knowles, S., Coventry, P. A. and Rowland, N. (2011) Counselling for mental health and psychosocial problems in primary care. *Cochrane Database of Systematic Reviews*, 9: CD001025.

Bowlby, J. (1980) *Attachment and Loss: Vol 3: Loss, Sadness and Depression*. New York: Basic Books.

Bowlby, J. (1988) *A Secure Base: Clinical Application of Attachment Theory*. London: Routledge.

Bowles, W., Boetto, H., Jones, P. and McKinnon, J. (2018) Is social work really greening? Exploring the place of sustainability and environment in social work codes of ethics. *International Social Work*, 61(4): 503–517.

Bowyer, S. and Wilkinson, J. (2013) *Evidence Scope: Models of Adolescent Care Provision*. Dartington: Research in Practice.

Braye, S. and Preston-Shoot, M. (2016) *Practising Social Work Law* (4th ed). Basingstoke: Red Globe Press.

Brent, M. (2016) Personalisation, in Evans, T. and Keating, F. (eds) *Policy and Social Work Practice*. London: Sage.

Briant, E., Watson, N. and Philo, G. (2013) Reporting disability in the age of austerity: the changing face of media representation of disability and disabled people in the United Kingdom and the creation of new 'folk devils'. *Disability & Society*, 28(6): 874–889.

Bride, B. E. (2007) Prevalence of secondary traumatic stress among social workers. *Social Work*, 52(1): 63–70.

Briggs, D. (2013) Conceptualising risk and need: the rise of actuarialism and the death of welfare? Practitioner assessment and intervention in the Youth Offending Service. *Youth Justice*, 13(1): 17–30.

Brilliant, E. (1986) Social work leadership: a missing ingredient? *Social Work*, 30: 325–331.

Briskman, L. and Fiske, L. (2016) Creating criminals: Australia's response to asylum seekers and refugees, in Furman, R., Lamphear, G. and Epps, D. (eds) *The Immigrant Other: Lived Experiences in a Transnational World*. New York: Columbia University Press.

Briskman, L. and Goddard, C. (2007) Not in my name: the people's inquiry into immigration detention, in Lusher, D. and Haslam, N. (eds) *Yearning to Breathe Free*. Sydney: The Federation Press.

Briskman, L. and Ife, J. (2018) Extending beyond the legal: social work and human rights, in Rice, S., Day, A. and Briskman, L. (eds) *Social Work in the Shadow of the Law*. Sydney: The Federation Press.

Briskman, L., Zion, D. and Loff, B. (2012) Care or collusion in asylum seeker detention. *Ethics and Social Welfare*, 6(1): 37–55.

British Institute of Learning Disabilities (2019) Information about learning disabilities. Available at: www.bild.org.uk/resources/faqs/#What-is-the-difference-between-the-terms-learning-disabilities-learning-difficulties-and-intellectual-disabilities

British Library Online Archive (date unknown) Synopsis of the Forster Education Act 1870. Available from: www.bl.uk/collection-items/synopsis-of-the-forster-education-act-1870

Broach, S., Clements, L. and Read, J. (2010) *Disabled Children: A Legal Handbook*. London: LAG Education Services Trust Limited.

Broadhurst, K., Hall, C., Wastell, D., White, S. and Pithouse, A. (2010a) Risk, instrumentalism and the humane project in social work: Identifying the informal logics of risk management in children's statutory services. *British Journal of Social Work*, 40(4): 1046–1064.

Broadhurst, K., Wastell, D., White, S., Hall, C., Peckover, S., Thompson, K., Pithouse, A. and Davey, D. (2010b) Performing 'initial assessment': identifying the latent conditions for error at the front door of local authority children's services. *British Journal of Social Work*, 40(2): 352–370.

Broadhurst, K., Alrouh, B., Yeend, E., Harwin, J., Shaw, M., Pilling, M., Mason, C. and Kershaw, S. (2015) Connecting events in time to identify a hidden population: birth mothers and their children in recurrent care proceedings in England. *British Journal of Social Work*, 45(8): 2241–2260.

Bronfenbrenner, U. (1979) *The Ecology of Human Development: Experiments by Nature and Design*. Cambridge, MA: Harvard University Press.

Brookfield, S. (1997) *Developing Critical Thinkers*. Buckingham: Open University.

Brookfield, S. (2009) The concept of critical reflection: promises and contradictions. *European Journal of Social Work*, 12(3): 293–304.

Brown, R. and Ward, H. (2012) *Decision Making within a Child's Timeframe*. London: Department of Health.

Burrell, G. and Morgan, G. (1985) *Sociological Paradigms and Organisational Analysis*. Aldershot: Gower.

Burton, M. (2014) Self-harm: working with vulnerable adolescents. *Practice Nursing*, 25(5): 245–251.

Butler-Sloss, E. (1988) Report of the Inquiry into Child Abuse in Cleveland 1987. London: HMSO.

Butterworth, S., Singh, Swaran P., Birchwood, M., Islam, Z., Munro, E R., Vostanis, P., Paul, M., Khan, A. and Simkiss, D. (2017) Transitioning care-leavers with mental health needs: 'they set you up to fail!' *Child and Adolescent Mental Health*, 22(3): 138–147.

Byrne, B. and Brooks, K. (2015) 'Post-YOT Youth Justice': Howard League for Penal Reform. Available at: http://socialwelfare.bl.uk/subject-areas/services-client-groups/youngoffenders/howardleagueforpenalreform/174662HLWP_19_2015.pdf

Bywaters, P. (2013) Inequalities in child welfare: towards a new policy, research and action agenda. *British Journal of Social Work*, 45(1): 6–23.

Bywaters, P., Brady, G., Sparks, T. and Bos, E. (2016) Child welfare inequalities: new evidence, further questions. *Child & Family Social Work*, 21: 369–380.

Campbell, A., Taylor, B. J. and McGlade, A. (2016) *Research Design in Social Work*. London: Sage.

Canavan, J., Pinkerton, J. and Dolan, P. (2016) *Understanding Family Support: Policy, Practice and Theory*. London: Jessica Kingsley Publishers.

Canton, R. (2011) *Probation: Working with Offenders*. Abingdon: Routledge.

Caplan, G. (1964) *Principles of Preventive Psychiatry*. New York: Basic Books.

Carling, J., Erdal, M. B. and Ezzati, R. (2014) Beyond the insider–outsider divide in migration research. *Migration Studies*, 2(1): 36–54.

Carr, S., Hafford-Letchfield, T., Faulkner, A., Megele, C., Gould, D., Khisa, C., Cohen, R. and Holley, J. (2019) 'Keeping control': a user-led exploratory study of mental health service user experiences of targeted violence and abuse in the context of adult safeguarding in England. *Health and Social Care in the Community*, 27(5): e781–e792.

Carter, N., Valaitis, R. K., Lam, A., Feather, J., Nicholl, J. and Cleghorn, L. (2018) Navigation delivery models and roles of navigators in primary care: a scoping literature review. *British Medical Council Health Services Research*, 18(1): 96.

Carter, R. (2017) 'Decisions are being taken out of our hands': social workers on care cuts. Available at: www.communitycare.co.uk/2017/09/19/decisions-taken-hands-social-workers-care-cuts/

Carvalho, M. I. (2014) Social work and intervention with older people in Portugal: a critical point of view. *European Journal of Social Work*, 17(3): 336–352.

Carver, C. S., Scheier, M. F. and Weintraub, J. K. (1989) Assessing coping strategies: a theoretically based approach. *Journal of Personality and Social Psychology*, 56: 267–283.

Case, S. (2018) *Youth Justice: A Critical Introduction*. Abingdon: Routledge.

Case, S. P. and Haines, K. R. (2009) *Understanding Youth Offending: Risk Factor Research, Policy and Practice*. Cullompton: Willan Publishing.

Castillo, H. and Ramon, S. (2017) 'Work with me': service users' perspectives on shared decision making in mental health. *Mental Health Review*, 22(3): 166–178.

Cemlyn, S. J. and Nye, M. (2012) Asylum seeker young people: social work value conflicts in negotiating age assessment in the UK. *International Social Work*, 55(5): 675–688.

Chambers, D. (2006) *New Social Ties: Contemporary Connections in a Fragmented Society*. Basingstoke: Palgrave.

Charlesworth, L. (2010) *Welfare's Forgotten Past: A Socio-legal History of the Poor Law*. Abingdon: Routledge.

Chase, E. (2010) In Search of Security: Young People's Experiences of Seeking Asylum Alone in the UK. PhD thesis. University of London, Institute of Education.

Chase, E. (2013) Security and subjective wellbeing: the experiences of unaccompanied young people seeking asylum in the UK. *Sociology of Health & Illness*, 35(6): 858–872.

Chase, E. (2017) Health and Wellbeing: Becoming Adult Research Brief 5. London: UCL.

Chase, E. and Sigona, N. (2017) Forced Returns and Protracted Displacement: Becoming Adult Research Brief 7. London: UCL.

Cherry, M. (2013) Freedom of Thought 2013: A Global Report on the Rights, Legal Status, and Discrimination Against Humanists, Atheists, and the Non-religious. Amsterdam: International Humanist and Ethical Union.

Chick, N. and Meleis, A. I. (1986) Transitions: a nursing concern, in Chinn, P. L. (ed) *Nursing Research Methodology*. Boulder, CO: Aspen Publishers.

Chrestman, K. R (1999) Secondary exposure to trauma and self-reported distress amongst therapists, in Stamm, B. H. (ed) *Secondary Traumatic Stress: Self Care Issues for Clinicians, Researchers and Educators* (2nd ed). Lutherville, MD: Sidran Press.

Christie, P. and Sidhu, R. (2006) Governmentality and 'fearless speech': framing the education of asylum seeker and refugee children in Australia. *Oxford Review of Education*, 32(4): 449–465.

CIPD (2019) Health and well-being at work. Available at: www.cipd.co.uk/Images/health-and-well-being-2019-public-sector-summary_tcm18-55945.pdf

Clarke, J. (2004) *Changing Welfare, Changing States: New Directions in Social Policy*. London: Sage.

Clausen, H., Kendall, M., Murray, S., Worth, A., Boyd, K. and Benton, F. (2005) Would palliative care patients benefit from social workers retaining the traditional 'casework' role rather than working as care managers? A prospective serial qualitative interview study. *British Journal of Social Work*, 35: 277–285.

Clinard, M. B. and Meier, R. F. (1992) *Sociology of Deviant Behavior*. Fort Worth: Harcourt Brace College Publishers.

Clyde, J. (1992) Inquiry into the Removal of Children from Orkney in February 1991. Edinburgh: HMSO.

Cochrane, A. (2007) *Understanding Urban Policy: A Critical Approach*. Oxford: Blackwell.

Cocker, C. and Allain, L. (2019) *Social Work with Looked After Children* (3rd ed). London: Sage/ Learning Matters.

Cohen, S. (1994) Perceived Stress Scale. USA: Mind Garden. Available at: www.mindgarden.com/ documents/PerceivedStressScale.pdf

Colby Peters, S. (2018) Defining social work leadership: a theoretical and conceptual review and analysis. *Journal of Social Work Practice*, 32(1): 31–44.

Collier, K. and Boucher, S. (2019) *50 Acts of Professional Self Care for Social Workers*. Litchfield: Kirwin Maclean Associates and Self Care Psychology.

Collings, J. A. and Murray, P. J. (1996) Predictors of stress amongst social workers: an empirical study. *British Journal of Social Work*, 26: 375–387.

Collins, S. (2008) Statutory social workers: stress, job satisfaction, coping, social support and individual differences. *British Journal of Social Work*, 38: 1173–1193.

Colton, M., Drakeford, M., Roberts, S., Scholte, E., Casas, F. and Williams, M. (1997) Social workers, parents and stigma. *Child & Family Social Work*, 2: 247–257.

Cooper, A. (2018) *Conjunctions: Social Work, Psychoanalysis and Society*. Abingdon: Routledge.

Cooper, A. and Lousada, J. (2005) *Borderline Welfare: Feeling and Fear of Feeling in Modern Welfare*. London: Karnac.

Coppock, V. and Dunn, B. (2010) *Understanding Social Work Practice in Mental Health*. London: Sage.

Coram Children's Legal Centre (2017) National Referral Mechanism Factsheet. London: Coram Children's Legal Centre.

Coram Children's Legal Centre (2017) Leaving Care Support for Migrant Children and Young People. London: Coram Children's Legal Centre.

Coren, E., Hutchfield, J., Thomae, M. and Gustafsson, C. (2010) Parent training support for intellectually disabled parents. *Campbell Systematic Reviews*, 6(1): 1–60.

Corless, I. B., Limbo, R., Bousso, R. S., Wrenn, R. L., Head, D., Lickiss, N. and Wass, H. (2014) Languages of grief: a model for understanding the expressions of the bereaved. *Health Psychology and Behavioral Medicine*, 2(1): 132–143.

Cornwall Adult Protection Committee (2007) Steven Hoskins Serious Case Review. Cornwall: Cornwall Adult Protection Committee.

Cornwell, J. (1984) *Hard-Earned Lives: Accounts of Health and Illness from East London*. London: Unwin Hyman.

Corr, C. A. (1992) A task-based approach to coping with dying. *Omega: The Journal of Death and Dying*, 24(1): 81–94.

Corr, C. A. and Doka, K. J. (1994) Current models of death, dying and bereavement. *Critical Care Nursing of North America*, 6(3): 545–552.

Corr, C. A., Doka, K. J. and Kastenbaum, R. (1999) Dying and its interpreters: a review of selected literature and some comments on the state of the field. *Omega: The Journal of Death and Dying*, 39(2): 239–259.

Couch, C. (2010) Aspects of the historical development of urban renewal, in Tallon, A. (ed) *Urban Regeneration and Renewal*. London: Routledge.

Couch, C., Sykes, O. and Borstinghaus, W. (2011) Thirty years of urban regeneration in Britain, Germany and France: the importance of context and path dependency. *Progress in Planning*, 75(1): 1–52.

Cournoyer, B. (2011) *The Social Work Skills Workbook*. Belmont, CA: Cengage.

Coventry Safeguarding Board (2013) Daniel Pelka Serious Case Review. Coventry: Coventry Safeguarding Board.

Coyle, D., Edwards, D., Hannigan, B., Fothergill, A. and Burnard, P. (2005) A systematic review of stress among mental health social workers. *International Social Work*, 48(2): 201–211.

Crain, W. (2011) *Theories of Development: Concepts and Applications* (6th ed). New York: Taylor & Francis.

Crawley, H. (2010) Chance Or Choice? Understanding Why Asylum Seekers Come to the UK. London: Refugee Council.

Crawley, H. (2016) Unravelling the Mediterranean Migration Crisis (SoundCloud Podcast, February 2016).

Crawley, H. and Rowlands, S. (2007) When is a Child Not a Child? Asylum, Age Disputes and the Process of Age Assessment. London: ILPA.

Creaney, S. (2018) Children's voices – are we listening? Progressing peer mentoring in the youth justice system. *Child Care in Practice*, 26(1): 22–37.

Creaney, S. and Smith, R. (2014) Youth justice back at the crossroads. *Safer Communities*, 13(2): 83–87.

Crisp, B. R., Anderson, M. T., Orme, J. and Lister, P. G. (2005) *Knowledge Review 08: Learning and Teaching in Social Work Education: Textbooks and Frameworks on Assessment*. London: Social Care Institute for Excellence.

Croisdale-Appleby, D. (2014) Revisioning Social Work Education: An Independent Review. London: Department of Health.

Crome, I., Chambers, P., Frisher, M., Bloor, R. and Roberts, D. (2009) The relationship between dual diagnosis: substance misuse and dealing with mental health issues. Available at: www.scie.org

Cunningham, J. and Cunningham, S. (2014) *Sociology and Social Work* (2nd ed). London: Sage.

Currer, C. (2001) *Responding to Grief: Dying, Bereavement and Social Care*. Basingstoke: Palgrave Macmillan.

Damasio, A. (1994) *Decartes' Error: Emotion, Reason and the Human Brain*. New York: HarperCollins.

Davey, V., Fernández, J. L., Knapp, M., Vick, N., Jolly, D., Swift, P., Tobin, R., Mercer, G. and Priestley, M. (2007) *Direct Payments: A National Survey of Direct Payments Policy and Practice*. Canterbury: Personal Social Services Research Unit.

Davies, M. (1994) *The Essential Social Worker* (3rd ed). London: Routledge.

Day, L. and Yallop, J. J. G. (2009) Learning, teaching, and researching through poetry. *Creative Approaches to Research*, 2(2): 46–57.

Dayson, C. and Bennett, E. (2016) Evaluation of the Rotherham Mental Health Social Prescribing Pilot. Rotherham: Rotherham Clinical Commissioning Group

de Than, C. (2015) Sex, disability and human rights, in Owens, T. (ed) *Supporting Disabled People with Their Sexual Lives*. London: Jessica Kingsley Publishers.

Dean, J. (2014) Drawing what homelessness looks like: using creative visual methods as a tool of critical pedagogy. *Sociological Research Online* 20(1): 2. Available at: www.socresonline.org.uk/20/1/2.html

Dehghani, S., Ghasemi, H., Safari, S., Akbar Ebrahimi, A. and Etemadi, O. (2013) The effectiveness of group motivational interviewing sessions on enhancing of addicted women's self-esteem and self efficacy. *Research on Addiction*, 7(26): 145–158.

Delalibera, M., Presa, J., Coelho, A., Barbosa, A. and Pereira Franco, M. H. (2015) Family dynamics during the grieving process: a systematic literature review. *Revista Ciencia & Saude Coletiva* [online] 20(4).

DeLamater, J. D. and Collett, J. L. (2019) *Social Psychology* (9th ed). New York: Taylor & Francis.

Department for Education (2011) Fostering services: national minimum standards. London: DfE.

Department for Education (2014) Knowledge and Skills Statements for Children (KSS). Available at: https://assets.publishing.service.gov.uk/government/uploads/system/uploads/attachment_data/file/338718/140730_Knowledge_and_skills_statement_final_version_AS_RHChecked.pdf

Department for Education (September 2014) Young person's guide to the Children and Families Act 2014. Available at: https://assets.publishing.service.gov.uk/government/uploads/system/uploads/attachment_data/file/359681/Young_Person_s_Guide_to_the_Children_and_Families_Act.pdf

Department for Education (January 2015) The Children Act 1989 Guidance and Regulations Volume 3: Planning Transition to Adulthood for Care Leavers. London: DfE.

Department for Education (June 2015) The Children Act 1989 Guidance and Regulations. Volume 2: Care Planning, Placement and Case Review. London: DfE.

Department for Education (2017) Children looked after in England (including adoption), year ending 31 March 2017. Available at: www.gov.uk/government/statistics/children-looked-after-in-england-including-adoption-2016-to-2017

Department for Education (February 2017) Child sexual exploitation: definition and guide for practitioners. London: DfE.

Department for Education (November 2017) Care of Unaccompanied Migration Children and Child Victims of Modern Slavery. London: DfE.

Department for Education (November 2017) Characteristics of children in need: 2016 to 2017. Available at: https://assets.publishing.service.gov.uk/government/uploads/system/uploads/attachment_data/file/656395/SFR61-2017_Main_text.pdf

Department for Education (February 2018) Extending Personal Adviser Support to all Care Leavers to Age 25: Statutory Guidance for Local Authorities. London: DfE.

Department for Education (March 2018) Children in need of help and protection: data and analysis. Available at: https://assets.publishing.service.gov.uk/government/uploads/system/uploads/attachment_data/file/690999/Children_in_Need_of_help_and_protection_Data_and_analysis.pdf

Department for Education (August 2018) Working Together to Safeguard Children: A guide to inter-agency working to safeguard and promote the welfare of children. Available at: https://assets.publishing.service.gov.uk/government/uploads/system/uploads/attachment_data/file/729914/Working_Together_to_Safeguard_Children-2018.pdf

Department for Education (April 2019) Children looked after by local authorities in England – Guide to the SSDA903 collection, 1 April 2018 to 31 March 2019, version 1.2, October 2018. Available at: https://assets.publishing.service.gov.uk/government/uploads/system/uploads/attachment_data/file/746510/CLA_SSDA903_2018-19_Guide_Version_1.2.pdf

Department for Education (2015, updated October 2019) Keeping Children Safe in Education: Statutory guidance for schools and colleges on safeguarding children and safer recruitment. London: DfE.

Department of Health (2000) Framework for the Assessment of Children in Need and Their Families. London: DoH.

Department of Health (2001) Valuing People: A New Strategy for Learning Disability for the 21st Century [online]. London: DoH. Available at: https://assets.publishing.service.gov.uk/government/uploads/system/uploads/attachment_data/file/250877/5086.pdf

Department of Health (2005) Building and nurturing an improvement culture: Improvement Leader's Guides 3. London: DoH.

Department of Health (2011) No Health without Mental Health. London: DoH.

Department of Health and Social Care (2014) Care Act 2014: statutory guidance for implementation. London: DHSC.

Department of Health and Social Care (2018) Care and Support Statutory Guidance Issued under the Care Act 2014. Available from: www.gov.uk/guidance/care-and-support-statutory-guidance

Department of Health and Social Security (1974) Committee of Inquiry into the Care and Supervision Provided in Relation to Maria Colwell. London: DHSS.

Department of Health, Social Services and Public Safety Northern Ireland (2011) New Strategic Direction for Alcohol and Drugs Phase 2 2011–2016: A Framework for Reducing Alcohol and Drug Related Harm in Northern Ireland. Available at: www.health-ni.gov.uk/sites/default/files/publications/health/alcohol-and-drug-new-strategic-direction-phase-2-2011-16.pdf

Derluyn, I. (2018) A critical analysis of the creation of separated care structures for unaccompanied refugee minors. Children and Youth Services Review, 92: 22–29.

Devenney, K. (2017) Pathway planning with unaccompanied young people leaving care: biographical narratives of past, present, and future. Child & Family Social Work, 22(3): 1313–1321.

Dewey, J. (1910) How We Think. New York: D. C. Heath & Co.

Di Forti, M. et al. (2014) Daily use, especially of high-potency cannabis, drives the earlier onset of psychosis in cannabis users. Schizophrenia Bulletin, 40(6): 1509–1517.

Dickens, J. (2016) Social Work and Social Policy: An Introduction (2nd ed). Abingdon: Routledge.

Dickens, J. (2017) Social work values, the law and the courts, in Critical Issues in Social Work Law. Basingstoke: Palgrave.

Didion, J. (2005) The Year of Magical Thinking. New York: A. A. Knopf.

Doel, M. (2005) Using Groupwork. Abingdon: Routledge/Community Care.

Doel, M. and Kelly, T. B. (2014) A–Z of Groups and Groupwork. Basingstoke: Palgrave Macmillan.

Doherty, B. (2019) Nauru doctor wins global free speech award for speaking out on offshore immigration. The Guardian, 17 January. Available at: www.theguardian.com/australia-news/2019/jan/17/nauru-doctor-wins-global-free-speech-award-for-speaking-out-on-offshore-immigration

Doka, K. J. (1993) Living with Life-Threatening Illness. Lexington, MA: Lexington Books.

Doka, K. J. (ed) (2002) Disenfranchised Grief: New Directions, Challenges and Strategies for Practice. Champaign: Research Press.

Dominelli, L. (2002) Anti-Oppressive Social Work Theory and Practice. New York: Palgrave.

Dorling, D. (2015) Injustice: Why Social Inequality Persists. Bristol: Policy Press.

Dorling, D. (2017a) The Equality Effect: Improving Life for Everyone. Oxford: New Internationalist.

Dorling, D. (2017b) Do We Need Economic Inequality? Cambridge: Polity Press.

Dorling, K. (2013) Happy Birthday? Disputing the Age of Children in the Immigration System. London: Coram Children's Legal Centre.

Dougall, D., Lewis, M. and Ross, S. (2018) Transformational Change in Health and Care: Reports from the Field. London: The King's Fund.

Downs, M. and Bowers, M. (2014) Excellence in Dementia Care: Research Into Practice. Berkshire: Open University Press.

Drew, P. and Heritage, J. (1992) Analyzing talk at work, in P. Drew and J. Heritage (eds) *Talk At Work*. Cambridge: Cambridge University Press.

Duff, C. and Erickson, P. (2014) Cannabis, risk and normalisation: evidence from a Canadian study of socially integrated, adult cannabis users. *Health, Risk & Society*, 16(3): 210–226.

Duffy, F. (2016) A social work perspective on how ageist language, discourses and understandings negatively frame older people and why taking a critical social work stance is essential. *British Journal of Social Work*, 47(7): 2068–2085.

Dyke, C. (2016) *Writing Analytical Assessments in Social Work*. Northwich: Critical Publishing Ltd.

Earle, S., Komaromy, C. and Bartholomew, C. (2009) *Death and Dying: A Reader*. Milton Keynes: The Open University.

Easton, C., Gee, G., Durbin, B. and Teeman, D. (2011) Early intervention, using the CAF process, and its cost effectiveness: Findings from LARC 3. Slough: NFER.

Eekelaar, J. and Maclean, M. (2013) *Family Justice: The Work of Family Judges in Uncertain Times*. Oxford and Portland, Oregon: Hart Publishing.

Egan, G. (2014) *The Skilled Helper* (10th ed). Belmont, CA: Brooks/Cole, Cengage Learning.

Elliott, M. and Scourfield, J. (2017) Identifying and understanding inequalities in child welfare intervention rates: comparative studies in four UK countries. London: The Nuffield Foundation.

Ellis, A. (1957) Rational psychotherapy and individual psychology. *Journal of Individual Psychology*, 13: 38–44.

Enaker, V. (2014) Using the theory of planned behaviour to predict nonmedical anabolic steroid use in young adults. *American Journal of Health Studies*, 29(2): 178–181.

Englander, D. (1998) *Poverty and Poor Law Reform in Nineteenth-Century Britain: 1834–1914: From Chadwick to Booth*. London: Routledge.

European Monitoring Centre for Drugs and Drug Addiction (2017) United Kingdom, Country Drug Report 2017. Luxembourg: EMCDDA.

Evans-Brown, M., McVeigh, J., Perkins, C. and Bellis, M. (2012) *Human Enhancement Drugs: The Emerging Challenges to Public Health*. Liverpool: North West Public Health Observatory, Liverpool John Moores University.

Everard, S. (2005) Spirituality and social work in palliative care, in Parker, J. (ed) *Aspects of Social Work and Palliative Care*. London: Quay.

Exley, C. (2004) Review article: the sociology of death, dying and bereavement. *Sociology of Health and Illness*, 26(1): 110–122.

Fahlberg, V. (1994) *A Child's Journey through Placement*. London: BAAF.

Falconer, K., Sachsenweger, M., Gibson, K. and Norman, H. (2011) Grieving in the internet age. *New Zealand Journal of Psychology*, 30(3): 79–88.

Farmbrough, J. (2014) Factors that Contribute to the Emotional Wellbeing, Educational Success and Social Connectedness of those Arriving in One Local Authority as Unaccompanied Asylum Seeking Children. D.Ed.Psych. thesis. Birmingham: University of Birmingham.

Farrington, D. P., Coid, J. W., Harnett, L., Joliffe, D., Soteriou, N., Turner, R. and West, D. J. (2006) Criminal careers and life success: new findings from the Cambridge Study in Delinquent Development. London: Home Office.

Featherstone, B., Morris, K. and White, S. (2014) *Re-imagining Child Protection: Towards Humane Social Work with Families*. Bristol: Policy Press.

Featherstone, B., Morris, K. and Daniel, B., Bywaters, P., Brady, G., Bunting, L., Mason, W. and Mirza, N. (2017) Poverty, inequality, child abuse and neglect: Changing the conversation across the UK in child protection? *Children and Youth Services Review*, 97: 127–133.

Fenge, L-A., Cutts, W. and Seagrave, J. (2018) Understanding homelessness through poetic inquiry: looking into the shadows. *Social Work & Social Sciences Review*, 19(3): 119–133.

Fenge, L-A., Hodges, C. and Cutts, W. (2011) Seen but seldom heard: creative participatory methods in a study of youth at risk. *International Journal of Qualitative Methods*, 10(1): 418–430.

Fenton, J. (2014) An analysis of 'ethical stress' in criminal justice social work in Scotland: the place of values. *British Journal of Social Work*, 45(5): 1415–1432.

Ferguson, H. (2011) *Child Protection Practice*. Basingstoke: Palgrave Macmillan.

Ferguson, H. (2016) Making home visits: creativity and the embodied practices of home visiting in social work and child protection. *Qualitative Social Work*, 17(1): 65–80.

Ferguson, H. (2017) How children become invisible in child protection work: findings from research into day-to-day social work practice. *British Journal of Social Work*, 47: 1007–1023.

Ferguson, H. (2018) How social workers reflect in action and when and why they don't: the possibilities and limits to reflective practice in social work. *Social Work Education*, 37(4): 412–427.

Ferguson, I. (2008) *Reclaiming Social Work*. London: Sage.

Ferguson, I. (2011) Why class (still) matters, in Lavalette, M. (ed) *Radical Social Work Today: Social Work at the Crossroads*. Bristol: Policy Press.

Field, D. (1989) *Nursing the Dying*. London: Routledge.

Field, P., Jasper, C. and Littler, L. (2016) *Practice Education in Social Work: Achieving Professional Standards* (2nd ed). St Albans: Critical Publishing.

Figley, C. R. (1995) Compassion fatigue as secondary traumatic stress disorder: an overview. In Figley, C. R. (ed) *Compassion Fatigue: Coping with Secondary Traumatic Stress Disorder in Those Who Treat the Traumatized*. New York: Brunner-Routledge, pp1–20.

Finch, J. (2020) Emotions and the importance of personality in development, in Parker, J. and Ashencaen Crabtree, S. (eds) *Human Growth and Development in Children and Young People: Theoretical and Practice Perspectives – Volume 1*. Bristol: Policy Press.

Finch, J. and Schaub, J. (2015) Projective identification as an unconscious defence: social work, practice education and the fear of failure, in Armstrong, D. and Rustin, M. (eds) *Social Defences against Anxiety: Explorations in the Paradigm*. London: Karnac.

Firmin, C., Warrington, C. and Pearce, J. (2016) Sexual exploitation and its impact on developing sexualities and sexual relationships: the need for contextual social work interventions. *British Journal of Social Work*, 46: 2318–2337.

Fischer, J. (2009) *Toward Evidence-Based Practice: Variations on a Theme*. Chicago, IL: Lyceum.

Folgheraiter, F. (2007) Relational social work: principles and practice. *Social Policy and Society*, 6(2): 265–274.

Fook, J. (2016) *Critical Social Work* (3rd ed). London: Sage.

Fook, J. and Askeland, G. (2006) The 'critical' in critical reflection, in White, S., Fook, J. and Gardner, F. (eds) *Critical Reflection in Health and Welfare*. Maidenhead: Open University Press.

Fook, J. and Gardner, F. (2013) *Critical Reflection in Context: Applications in Health and Social Care*. Abingdon: Routledge.

Foote, W. (2013) Threshold theory and social work education. *Social Work Education*, 32(4): 424–438.

Ford, J. and Lawler, J. (2007) Blending existentialist and constructionist approaches in leadership studies: an exploratory account. *Leadership & Organisational Development Journal*, 28(5): 409–425.

Forrester, D., Lynch, A., Bostock, L., Newlands, F., Preston, B. and Cary, A. (2017) Family Safeguarding Hertfordshire. Children's Social Care Innovation Programme Evaluation Report 55. London: DfE.

Forrester, D., Westlake, D., Killian, M., Antonopolou, V., McCann, M., Thurnham, A., Thomas, R., Waits, C., Whittaker, C. and Hutchison, D. (2019) What is the relationship between worker skills and outcomes for families in child and family social work? *British Journal of Social Work*, 49(8): 2148–2167.

Fothergill, A. (2002) The stigma of charity: gender, class, and disaster assistance. *The Sociological Quarterly*, 44(4): 659–680.

Foucault, M. (1991) Governmentality, in Burchell, G., Gordon, C. and Miller, P. (eds) *The Foucault Effect: Studies in Governmentality*. Hemel Hempstead: Harvester Wheatsheaf.

Fozdar, F. and Banki, S. (2017) Settling refugees in Australia: achievements and challenges. *International Journal of Migration and Border Studies*, 3(1): 43–66.

Frampton, M. (2019) *European and International Social Work: Ein Lehrbuch*. Basel: Beltz Juventa.

France, A., Bottrell, D. and Armstrong, D. (2012) *A Political Ecology of Youth and Crime*. Basingstoke: Palgrave Macmillan.

France, A. P. (2015) Theorising and researching the youth crime nexus: habitus, reflexivity and the political ecology of social practice, in Costa, C. and Murphy, M. (eds) *Bourdieu, Habitus and Social Research: The Art of Application*. London: Palgrave Macmillan.

Francis, R. (2013) Report of the Mid Staffordshire NHS Foundation Trust Public Inquiry. London: HMSO.

Frank, A. W. (1995) *The Wounded Storyteller: Body, Illness and Ethics*. Chicago: Chicago University Press.

Fraser, H. (2013) Designing advocacy and social action curriculum: reflections from the classroom, in Noble, C., Henrickson, M. and Han, I. Y. (eds) *Social Work Education: Voices from the Asian Pacific* (2nd ed). Sydney: Sydney University Press.

Freed, A. F. and Ehrlich, S. (2010) The function of questions in institutional discourse, in Freed, A. F. and Ehrlich, S. (eds) *'Why do You Ask?' The Function of Questions in Institutional Discourse*. Oxford: Oxford University Press.

Freire, P. (1990) A critical understanding of social work. *Journal of Progressive Human Services*, 1(1): 3–9.

French, C. H. and Bell, W. L. (1997) *Organization Development: Behavioural Science Interventions for Organization Improvement* (6th ed). London: Pearsons.

French, S. and Swain, J. (2000) Personal perspectives on the experience of exclusion, in Moore, M. (ed) *Insider Perspectives on Inclusion: Raising Voices, Raising Issues*. Sheffield: Phillip Armstrong.

Friedman, M. (1962) *Capitalism and Freedom*. Chicago: University of Chicago.

Friedman, M. (1993) *Why Government is the Problem*. Stanford, CA: Hoover Institution Press.

Frost, N. and Elmer, S. (2008) An Evaluation of the Family Group Conference Service in South Leeds. Leeds: Leeds Metropolitan University.

Frost, N., Abram, F. and Burgess, H. (2013a) Family Group Conferences: evidence, outcomes and future research. *Child & Family Social Work*, 19(4): 501–507.

Frost, N., Abram, F. and Burgess, H. (2013b) Family Group Conferences: context, process and way forward. *Child & Family Social Work*, 19(4): 480–490.

Frost, N., Abbott, S. and Race, T. (2015) *Family Support: Prevention, Early Intervention and Early Help*. Cambridge: Polity.

Furedi, F. (2011) *Changing Societal Attitudes and Regulatory Responses to Risk Taking in Adult Care*. York: Joseph Rowntree Foundation.

Gallop, L. and Hafford-Letchfield, T. (2012) *How to Become a Better Manager in Social Work and Social Care*. London: Jessica Kingsley Publishers.

Galvani, S. (2015) Alcohol and other drug use: the roles and capabilities of social workers. Public Health England and Manchester Metropolitan University. Available at: http://cdn.basw.co.uk/upload/basw_25925-3.pdf

Galvin, K. and Todres, K. (2011) Research based empathic knowledge for nursing: a translational strategy for disseminating phenomenological research findings to provide evidence for caring practice. *International Journal of Nursing Studies*, 48(4): 522–530.

Gant, V. and Bates, C. (2017) Retrospect and prospect: what are the future possibilities in the Care Act (2014) for older parent-carers of adults with learning disabilities? A discussion paper. *Journal of Health and Social Care Improvement*, 1(2), 15–26.

Garland, J., Johnes, H. and Kolodny, R. (1965) A model for stages of development in social work groups, in Bernstein, S. (ed) *Explorations in Group Work: Essays in Theory and Practice*. Boston, MA: Boston University School of Social Work.

Garrett, M. P. (2015) Questioning tales of 'ordinary magic': 'resilience' and neo-liberal reasoning. *British Journal of Social Work*, 46(7): 1909–1925.

Gearing, T. and Dant, B. (1990) Doing biographical research, in Pearce, S. M. (ed) *Researching Social Gerontology: Concepts, Methods and Issues*. London: Sage.

Gewirtz-Meydan, A., Hafford-Letchfield, T., Ayalon, L., Benyamini, Y., Biermann, V., Coffey, A., Jackson, J., Phelan, A., Voß, P., Geiger Zeman, M. and Zeman, Z. (2018a) How do older people discuss their own sexuality? A systematic review of qualitative research studies. *Culture, Health & Sexuality*, 4: 1–4.

Gewirtz-Meydan, A., Hafford-Letchfield, T., Benyamini, Y., Phelan, A., Jackson, J. and Ayalon, L. (2018b) Ageism and sexuality, in Ayalon, L. and Tesch-Römer, C. (eds) *Contemporary Perspectives on Ageism*. Switzerland: Springer Open.

Gibbard, A. (1990) *Wise Choices, Apt Feelings*. Cambridge, MA: Harvard University Press.

Gibbs, G. (1988) *Learning by Doing*. Oxford: Oxford Brookes University.

Gibbs, L. (2003) *Evidence-based Practice for the Helping Professions: A Practical Guide with Integrated Multimedia*. Pacific Grove, CA: Brooks/Cole.

Gibson, F., McGrath, A. and Reid, N. (1989) Occupational stress in social work. *British Journal of Social Work*, 19: 1–16.

Giele, J. Z. and Elder, G. H. (1998) Life course research: development of a field, in Giele, J. Z. and Elder, G. H. (eds) *Methods of Life Course Research: Qualitative and Quantitative Approaches*. Thousand Oaks, CA: Sage.

Gilchrist, A. (1995) *Community Development and Networking*. London: Community Development Foundation.

Gilchrist, A. (2009) *The Well Connected Community: A Networking Approach to Community Development* (2nd ed). Bristol: Policy Press.

Gillespie, D. (2014) Service evaluation of the positive living programmes in day centres. Dissertation (MSc Professional Development in Social Work). Coleraine, Northern Ireland: Ulster University.

Gilligan, C. F. (1982) *In a Different Voice: Psychological Theory and Women's Development*. Cambridge, MA: Harvard University Press.

Gilligan, R. (2006) Creating a warm place where children can blossom. *Social Policy Journal of New Zealand*, 28: 36–45.

Gitlin, A. (2008) Cultivating the qualitative research borderlands: educational poetics and the politics of inclusivity. *International Journal of Qualitative Studies in Education*, 21(6): 627–645.

Gitterman, A. and Germain, C. B. (2008) *The Life Model of Social Work Practice: Advances in Theory and Practice* (3rd ed). New York: Columbia University Press.

Gitterman, A. and Shulman, L. (2005) *Mutual Aid Groups, Vulnerable and Resilient Populations, and the Life Cycle* (3rd ed). New York: Columbia University Press.

Glasby, J. and Tew, J. (2015) *Mental Health Policy and Practice* (3rd ed). London: Palgrave Macmillan.

Glaser, B. G. and Strauss, A. L. (1968) *Time for Dying*. Chicago: Aldine.

Glover, A. S., Long, M., Hendron, J. and Taylor, B. J. (2018) Understanding carer resilience in Duchenne Muscular Dystrophy: a systematic narrative review. *Chronic Illness* [online].

Glyde, T. (2015) Chemsex exposed. *The Lancet*, 386(10010): 2243–2244.

Godar, R. (2013) *Commissioning Early Help*. Dartington: Research in Practice.

Goldberg, D. (1978) *Manual of the General Health Questionnaire*. Windsor: NFER Nelson.

Goldson, B. and Yates, J. (2008) Youth justice policy and practice: reclaiming applied criminology as critical intervention, in Stout, B. and Yates, J. (eds) *Applied Criminology*. London: Sage.

Goleman, D. (1996) *Emotional Intelligence*. London: Bloomsbury.

Golightly, M. and Goemans, R. (2017) *Social Work and Mental Health* (6th ed). London: Sage/Learning Matters.

Gollins, T., Fox, A., Walker, B., Romeo, L., Thomas, J. and Woodham, G. (2015) *Developing a Wellbeing and Strengths-Based Approach to Social Work Practice: Changing Culture*. London: Think Local Act Personal.

Goodman, A. and Gregg, P. (2010) *Poorer children's educational attainment: how important are attitudes and behaviour?* York: JRF.

Görlich, A. (2016) Poetic inquiry: understanding youth on the margins of education. *International Journal of Qualitative Studies in Education*, 29(4): 520–535.

Graham, M. and Schiele, J. H. (2010) Equality-of-oppressions and anti-discriminatory models in social work: reflections from the USA and UK. *European Journal of Social Work*, 13(2): 231–244.

Grant, G. and Kinman, G. (2012) Enhancing well being in social work students: building resilience in the next generation. *Social Work Education*, 31(5): 605–621.

Grant, L., Kinman, G. and Baker, S. (2015) 'Put on your own oxygen mask before assisting others': social work educators perspectives on an emotional curriculum. *British Journal of Social Work*, 45: 2351–2367.

Gray, M. and Webb, S. (2010) *Ethics and Value Perspectives in Social Work*. Basingstoke: Palgrave Macmillan.

Green, L. (2017) *Understanding the Life Course: Sociological and Psychological Perspectives* (2nd ed). Cambridge: Polity Press.

Green, L. and Clarke, K. (2016) *Social Policy for Social Work*. Bristol: Policy Press.

Greening, T. (2006) Five basic postulates of humanistic psychology. *Journal of Humanistic Psychology*, 46: 239.

Griffiths Report (1988) *Community Care: Agenda for Action*. London: HMSO.

Groenewald, C. (2018) A mother's reflections of living with an adolescent drug abuser: a case report. *Journal of Substance Use*, 23(6): 667–669.

Gupta, A. and Blumhardt, H. (2016) Giving poverty a voice: families' experiences of social work practice in a risk-averse system. *Families, Relationships and Societies*, 5(1): 163–172.

Hadfield, M. and Haw, K. (2001) 'Voice', young people and action research. *Educational Action Research*, 9(3): 485–502.

Hafford-Letchfield, T. (2008) What's love got to do with it? Developing supportive practices for the expression of sexuality, sexual identity and the intimacy needs of older people. *Journal of Care Services Management*, 2(4): 389–405.

Hafford-Letchfield, T. (2009) *Management and Organisations in Social Work* (2nd ed). Exeter: Learning Matters.

Hafford-Letchfield, T., Lambley, S., Spolander, G. and Cocker, C. (2014) *Inclusive Leadership in Social Work and Social Care: Making a Difference*. Bristol: Policy Press.

Hagan, R., Manktelow, R., Mallett, J. and Taylor, B. J. (2014) Reducing loneliness amongst older people: systematic search and narrative review. *Aging and Mental Health*, 18(6): 683–693.

Häggman-Laitila, A., Salokekkilä, P. and Karki, S. (2018) Transition to adult life of young people leaving foster care: a qualitative systematic review. *Children and Youth Services Review*, 95: 134–143.

Hahn, H. (1984) Reconceptualizing disability: a political science perspective. *Rehabilitation Literature*, 45(11–12): 362–374.

Haines, K. R. and Case, S. P. (2015) *Positive Youth Justice: Children First, Offenders Second*. Bristol: Policy Press.

Hall, C. (2011) Beyond Kübler-Ross: recent developments in our understanding of grief and bereavement. *In Psych*, 33(6) [online].

Hall, C., Slembrouck, S. and Sarangi, S. (2010) *Language Practices in Social Work: Categorization and Accountability in Child Welfare*. Abingdon: Routledge.

Hall, C., Juhila, K., Matarese, M. and Van Nijnatten, C. (2014) *Analysing Social Work Communication: Discourse in Practice*. Abingdon: Routledge.

Hall, S., Massey, D. and Rustin, M. (2013) After neoliberalism: analysing the future. *Soundings*, 53: 8–25.

Hamilton, D., Taylor, B. J., Killick, C. and Bickerstaff, D. (2015) Suicidal ideation and behaviour among young people leaving care: case file survey. *Child Care in Practice*, 21(2): 160–176.

Hamilton, R. (2018) Work-based learning in social work education: the challenges and opportunities for the identities of work-based learners on university-based programs. *Social Work Education*, 38(6): 766–778.

Hammond, S. P. and Cooper, N. J. (2013) *Digital Life Story Work: Using Technology to Help Young People Make Sense of Their Experiences*. London: CoramBAAF.

Hampson, K. (2017) Desistance approaches in youth justice: the next passing fad or a sea change for the positive? *Youth Justice Journal*, December 2017 [online].

Hardiker, P., Exton, K. and Barker, M. (1991) *Policies and Practices in Preventive Child Care*. Gower: Aldershot.

Hardy, E. and Tilly, L. (2012) *An Introduction to Supporting People with a Learning Disability*. Birmingham: British Institute of Learning Disabilities.

Haringey Safeguarding Board (2009) Peter Connelly Serious Case Review. London: London Borough of Haringey.

Harling, M. (2017) Comparisons between the attitudes of student nurses and other health and social care students toward illicit drug use: an attitudinal survey. *Nurse Education Today*, 48: 153–159.

Harrow Council (2011) Good Practice Guidance for Trafficked Children in Care. London: Harrow Council.

Hart, D. and Thompson, C. (2009) Young people's participation in the youth justice system. London: National Children's Bureau.

Harwin, J., Alrouh, B., Ryan, M. and Tunnard, T. (2014) *Changing Lifestyles, Keeping Children Safe: an evaluation of the first Family Drug and Alcohol Court (FDAC) in care proceedings*. London: Brunel University.

Hatton, K. (2015) *New Directions in Social Work Practice*. London: Sage/Learning Matters.

Hawtin, M. and Percy-Smith, J. (2007) *Community Profiling* (2nd ed). Maidenhead: Open University Press.

Hawton, K., Witt, K. G., Taylor Salisbury, T. L., Arensman, E., Gunnell, D., Townsend, E., van Heeringen, K. and Hazell, P. (2015) Interventions for self-harm in children and adolescents. *Cochrane Database of Systematic Reviews*, 12: CD012013.

Hayek, F. A. (1944) *The Road to Serfdom*. London: Routledge.

Hayek, F. A. (1948) *Individualism and Economic Order*. London: Routledge.

Hayek, F. A. (1978) *Law, Legislation and Liberty*. Chicago: University of Chicago

Hayes, H., Buckland, S. and Tarpey, M. (2012) Briefing notes for researchers: public involvement in NHS, public health and social care research. London: Involve Coordinating Centre at the National Institute for Health Research.

Hayward, K. (2008) Cultural criminology, in Goldson, B. (ed) *The Dictionary of Youth Justice*. Cullompton: Willan.

Health and Care Professions Council (2016) Standards of Conduct, Performance and Ethics. London: HCPC.

Health and Social Care Board (2015) Social Work Research and Continuous Improvement Strategy 2015–2020: In Pursuit of Excellence. Belfast: HSCB.

Healy, K. (2002) Managing human services in a market environment: what role for social workers? *British Journal of Social Work*, 32(5): 527–540.

Healy, K. (2005) *Social Work Theories in Context*. Basingstoke: Palgrave Macmillan.

Healy, K. (2008) *International Social Work: Professional Action in an Interdependent World* (2nd ed). New York: Oxford University Press.

Healy, K. (2012) *Social Work Methods and Skills: The Essential Foundations of Practice*. Basingstoke: Palgrave Macmillan.

Healy, K. (2014) *Social Work Theories in Context* (2nd ed). Basingstoke: Palgrave Macmillan.

Healy, K. and Mulholland, J. (2007) *Professional Writing for Social Work*. London: Sage.

Heanue, K. and Lawton, C. (2012) *Working with Substance Users*. Maidenhead: McGraw-Hill/Open University Press.

Heffernan, K. (2006) Social work, new public management and the language of 'service user'. *The British Journal of Social Work*, 36(1): 139–147.

Hek, R., Hughes, N. and Ozman, R. (2012) Safeguarding the needs of children and young people seeking asylum in the UK: addressing past failings and meeting future challenges. *Child Abuse Review*, 21(5): 335–348.

Helen Sanderson Associates (2019a) Person Centred Practices [online]. Available at: http://helen sandersonassociates.co.uk/person-centred-practice/

Helen Sanderson Associates (2019b) Care and Support Planning [online]. Available at: http:// helensandersonassociates.co.uk/person-centred-practice/care-support-planning/

Her Majesty's Inspectorate of Probation (2016) Desistance and young people: an inspection by HM Inspectorate of Probation. Available at: www.justiceinspectorates.gov.uk/hmiprobation/wp-content/uploads/sites/5/2016/05/Desistance_and_young_people.pdf

Heritage, J. and Sefi, S. (1992) Dilemma of advice: aspects of the delivery and reception of advice in interactions between Health Visitors and first-time mothers, in Drew, P. and Heritage, J. (eds) *Talk at Work: Interaction in Institutional Settings*. Cambridge: Cambridge University Press.

Heritage, J., Robinson, J. D., Elliot, M. N., Beckett, M. and Wilkes, M. (2007) Reducing patients' unmet concerns in primary care: the difference one word can make. *Journal of General Internal Medicine*, 22(10): 1429–1433.

Heslop, P. and Abbott, D. (2008) Help to move on – but to what? Young people with learning difficulties moving on from out-of-area residential schools or colleges. *British Journal of Learning Disabilities*, 37: 12–20.

Heywood, A. (2007) *Political Ideologies: An Introduction* (4th ed). Basingstoke: Palgrave Macmillan.

Higgins, M. (2018) Getting started, in Mantell, A. and Scragg, T. (2018) *Reflective Practice in Social Work*. London: Sage/Learning Matters.

Hill, A. (2018) Migration: how many people are on the move around the world? Available at: https://www.theguardian.com/news/2018/sep/10/migration-how-many-people-are-on-the-move-around-the-world

Hill, D., Agu, L. and Mercer, D. (2019) *Exploring and Locating Social Work: A Foundation for Practice*. London: Red Globe Press Ltd.

Hill, M., Davis, J., Prout, A. and Tisdall, K. (2004) Moving the participation agenda forward. *Children and Society*, 18(2): 77–96.

Hingley-Jones, H., Allain, L., Gleeson, H. and Twumasi, B. (2020) 'Roll back the years': a study of grandparent special guardians' experiences and implications for social work policy and practice in England. *Child & Family Social Work*, in press.

HMG (2003) Every Child Matters. Available at: www.gov.uk/government/publications/every-child-matters

Hodes, M., Jagdev, D., Chandra, N. and Cunniff, A. (2008) Risk and resilience for psychological distress amongst unaccompanied asylum seeking adolescents. *Journal of Child Psychology and Psychiatry*, 49(7): 723–732.

Hodges, C. E. M., Fenge, L-A. and Cutts, W. (2014) Challenging perceptions of disability through performance poetry methods: the 'Seen but Seldom Heard' project. *Disability & Society*, 29(7): 1090–1103.

Hogan, D. and Higgins, L. (1997) When parents use drugs: key findings from a study of children in the care of drug-using parents. Available at: www.drugsandalcohol.ie/5061/1/322-022When-Parents.pdf

Hogeveen, B. (2006) Unsettling youth justice and cultural norms: the youth restorative action project. *Journal of Youth Studies*, 9(1): 47–66.

Holland, S., Forrester, D., Williams, A. and Copello, A. (2014) Parenting and substance misuse: understanding accounts and realities in child protection contexts. *British Journal of Social Work*, 44(6): 1491–1507.

Hollingsworth, K. (2019) Children and juvenile justice law: the possibilities of a relational-rights approach, in Dwyer, J. (ed) *The Oxford Handbook of Children and the Law*. Oxford: Oxford University Press.

Holloway, M. (2007) *Negotiating Death in Contemporary Health and Social Care*. Bristol: Policy Press.

Holloway, M. and Moss, B. (2010) *Spirituality and Social Work*. Basingstoke: Palgrave Macmillan.

Holloway, M. and Taplin, S. (2013) 'Editorial' to Death and Social Work – 21st Century Challenges. *British Journal of Social Work*, 43(2): 203–215.

Holt, K. and Kelly, N. (2018) Limits to partnership working: developing relationship based approaches with children and their families. *Journal of Social Welfare & Family Law*, 40(2): 147–163.

Holt, K. and Kelly, N. (2019) Care in crisis, is there a solution? Reflections on the Care Crisis Review 2018. *Child & Family Social Work*, 25(1): 1–7.

Home Office (2018) Assessing Age, Version 2.0. Available at: https://assets.publishing.service. gov.uk/government/uploads/system/uploads/attachment_data/file/746532/assessing-age-v2.0ext.pdf

Hoong Sin, C., Hedges, A., Cook, C., Mguni, N. and Comber, N. (2011) Adult protection and effective action in tackling violence and hostility against disabled people: some tensions and challenges. *The Journal of Adult Protection*, 13(2): 63–74.

Horgan, J. (2011) Parental substance misuse: addressing its impact on children. Dublin: Stationery Office.

Horner, N. (2003) *What is Social Work?* Exeter: Learning Matters.

Horner, N. (2006) *What is Social Work?* (2nd ed). Exeter: Learning Matters.

Horner, N. (2012) *What is Social Work?* (4th ed). Exeter: Learning Matters.

Horner, N. (2019) The beginnings of social work: 'the comfort of strangers', in *What Is Social Work?* (5th ed). London: Sage.

House of Commons Women and Equalities Committee (2015) Transgender Equality, First Report of Session 2015–16. London: HMSO.

Houston, S. (2010) Further reflections on Habermas's contribution to discourse in child protection: an examination of power in social life. *British Journal of Social Work*, 40(6): 1736–1753.

Howard, K. and Brooks-Gunn, J. (2009) The role of home-visiting programs in preventing child abuse and neglect. *Future of Children*, 19(2): 119–146.

Howe, D. (2009) *A Brief Introduction to Social Work Theory*. Basingstoke: Palgrave Macmillan.

Howe, D. (2008) *An Introduction to Social Work Theory* (revised ed). Farnham: Ashgate.

Howe, D. (2011) *Attachment Across the Lifecourse*. Basingstoke: Palgrave Macmillan.

Hugman, R. (2010) *Understanding International Social Work: A Critical Analysis*. Basingstoke: Palgrave Macmillan.

Human Rights and Equal Opportunity Commission (2004) A last resort? National inquiry into children in immigration detention. Available at: www.humanrights.gov.au/sites/default/files/document/publication/alr_complete.pdf

Humphries, R., Thorlby, R., Holder, H., Hall, P. and Charles, A. (2016) *Social Care for Older People: Home Truths*. London: The King's Fund.

Hursthouse, R. (1999) *On Virtue Ethics*. Oxford: Oxford University Press.

Hylton, J. (2014) Acknowledging desistance: a practitioner response to 'A view from the inside out'. *Probation Journal*, 61(3): 286–291.

Ibbetson, K. (2013) Child F – Serious Case Review. London: Tower Hamlets Safeguarding Children Board.

Ife, J. (2012) *Human Rights and Social Work: Towards Rights-Based Practice*. Cambridge: Cambridge University Press.

Independent Drug Monitoring Unit (2018) Types of Cannabis Available in the UK. Available at: www.idmu.co.uk/can.htm

Intellectual Disability and Health (2019) Transition for Children with Intellectual Disabilities. Available at: www.intellectualdisability.info/life-stages/articles/transition-for-children-with-intellectual-disabilities

James, N. and Field, D. (1992) The routinization of hospice: charisma and bureaucratization. *Social Science and Medicine*, 34(12): 1363–1375.

Jasper, M. (2013) *Beginning Reflective Practice*. Andover: Cengage Learning EMEA.

Jay, A. (2014) Independent Inquiry into Child Sexual Exploitation in Rotherham 1997–2013. Rotherham: Rotherham Metropolitan Borough Council.

Johns, C. (2017) *Becoming a Reflective Practitioner* (5th ed). Oxford: Blackwell.

Johns, R. (2017) *Using the Law in Social Work* (7th ed). London: Sage.

Johnson, M. (1976) That was your life: a biographical approach to later life, in Munnichs, J. M. A. and van den Heuvel, W. M. J. (eds) *Dependency or Interdependency in Old Age*. The Hague: Martinus Nijhoff.

Johnstone, J. and Dallos, R. (2013) *Formulation in Psychology and Psychotherapy* (2nd ed). Abingdon: Routledge.

Jones, C., Hacker, D., Cormac, I., Meaden, A. and Irving, C. B. (2012) Cognitive behavioural therapy versus other psychosocial treatments for schizophrenia. *Cochrane Database of Systematic Reviews*, 4: CD008712.

Jones, K., Cooper, B. and Ferguson, H. (2008) *Best Practice in Social Work: Critical Perspectives*. Basingstoke: Palgrave Macmillan.

Jones, L., Bates, G., McCoy, E. and Bellis, M. A. (2015) Relationship between alcohol-attributable disease and socioeconomic status, and the role of alcohol consumption in this relationship: a systematic review and meta-analysis. *BMC Public Health*, 15(1): 400.

Jordan, B. (2007) *Social Work and Well-Being*. Lyme Regis: Russell House Publishing.

Jordan, B. and Drakeford, M. (2012) *Social Work and Social Policy under Austerity*. Basingstoke: Palgrave Macmillan.

Jordan, L. (2012) The legal foundations of family support work, in Davies, M. (ed) *Social Work with Children and Families*. Basingstoke: Palgrave Macmillan.

Joseph Rowntree Analysis Unit (2018) UK Poverty 2018. York: JRF.

Kadushin, A. and Kadushin, G. (2013) *The Social Work Interview: A Guide for Human Service Professionals* (5th ed). New York: Columbia University Press.

Kant, I. ([1785] 1976) Groundwork of the metaphysic of morals, in Paton, H. J. (ed) *The Moral Law*. London: Routledge.

Kapoulitsas, M. and Corcoran, T. (2015) Compassion fatigue and resilience: a qualitative analysis of social work practice. *Qualitative Social Work*, 14(1): 86–101.

Karoll, B. R. (2010) Applying social work approaches, harm reduction, and practice wisdom to better serve those with alcohol and drug use disorders. *Journal of Social Work*, 10(3): 263–281.

Kellehear, A. (1996) *Experiences Near Death: Beyond Medicine and Religion*. Oxford: Oxford University Press.

Kelly, P. J. (2003) Growing up as risky business? Risks, surveillance and the institutionalized mistrust of youth. *Journal of Youth Studies*, 6(2): 165–180.

Kelly, T. B. and Berman-Rossi, T. (1999) Advancing stages of group development theory: the case of institutionalized older persons. *Social Work with Groups*, 22(2/3): 119–138.

Kelly, T. B., Lowndes, A. and Tolson, D. (2005) Advancing stages of group development: the case of a virtual nursing community of practice groups. *Groupwork*, 15(2): 17–38.

Kelly, T. B., Schofield, I., Booth, J. and Tolson, D. (2006) The use of online groups to involve older people in influencing nursing care guidance. *Groupwork*, 16(1): 69–94.

Kennedy, P. (2013) *Key Themes in Social Policy*. London: Routledge.

Kenny, A. (2011) *The Eudemian Ethics*. Oxford: Oxford University Press.

Kenny, S. and Connors, P. (2016) *Developing Communities for the Future* (5th ed). Sydney: Cengage AU.

Khantzian, E. J. (1997) The self-medication hypothesis of substance use disorders: a reconsideration and recent applications. *Harvard Review of Psychiatry*, 4(5): 231–244.

Killick, C. and Taylor, B. J. (2009) Professional decision making on elder abuse: systematic narrative review. *Journal of Elder Abuse and Neglect*, 21: 211–238.

Killick, C., Taylor, B. J., Begley, E., Anand, J. C. and O'Brien, M. (2015) Older people's conceptualization of abuse: systematic narrative review. *Journal of Elder Abuse and Neglect*, 27(2): 100–120.

Kimberlee, R. H. (2013) *Developing a Social Prescribing Approach for Bristol*. Bristol: University of the West of England.

Kingston, K., Robinson, L., Booth, H., Knapp, M. and Jagger, C. (2018) Projections of multimorbidity in the older population in England to 2035: estimates from the Population Ageing and Care Simulation (PACSim) model. *Age and Ageing*, 47(3): 374–380.

Kiraly, M., James, J. and Humphreys, C. (2015) 'It's a family responsibility': family and cultural connection for Aboriginal children in kinship care. *Children Australia*, 40(1): 23–32.

Kirk, C. A., Killick, C., McAllister, A. and Taylor, B. J. (2019) Social workers perceptions of restorative approaches with families in cases of elder abuse: a qualitative study. *Journal of Adult Protection*, 21(3): 190–200.

Kleinman, A. (1988) *The Illness Narratives: Suffering, Healing, and the Human Condition*. New York: Basic Books.

Klostermann, K. and O'Farrell, T. J. (2013) Treating substance abuse: partner and family approaches. *Social Work in Public Health*, 28(3/4): 234–247.

Knott, C. and Scragg, T. (2013) *Reflective Practice in Social Work*. London: Sage/Learning Matters.

Kohli, R. K. S. (2006a) The sound of silence: listening to what unaccompanied asylum-seeking children say and do not say. *The British Journal of Social Work*, 36(5): 707–721.

Kohli, R. K. S. (2006b) The comfort of strangers: social work practice with unaccompanied asylum-seeking children and young people in the UK. *Child & Family Social Work*, 11(1): 1–10.

Kohli, R. K. S. (2007) *Social Work with Unaccompanied Asylum-Seeking Children*. Basingstoke: Palgrave Macmillan.

Kolb, D. (1984) *Experiential Learning: Experience as the Source of Learning and Development*. Englewood Cliffs, NJ: Prentice Hall.

Koprowska, J. (2014) *Communication and Interpersonal Skills in Social Work* (4th ed). London: Sage/Learning Matters.

Koprowska, J. (2017) The problem of participation in child protection conferences: an interactional analysis. *International Journal of Child and Family Welfare*, Special Issue 1–2: 105–122.

Koprowska, J. (2020) *Communication and Interpersonal Skills in Social Work* (5th ed). London: Sage/Learning Matters.

Koziol, M. (2018) Australia's chief medical officer on Nauru deported amid health policy crisis. *Sydney Morning Herald*, 17 October. Available at: www.smh.com.au/politics/federal/australia-s-chief-medical-officer-on-nauru-deported-amid-health-policy-crisis-20181017-p50a3r.html

Kraut, R., Bryin, M. and Kielser, S. (eds) (2006) *Computers, Phones and the Internet: Domesticating Internet Technology*. Buckingham: Open University Press.

Kroll, B. and Taylor, A. (2008) Interventions for children and families where there is parental drug misuse. Available at: www.drugsandalcohol.ie/11478/1/Krollsummary.pdf

Kübler-Ross, E. (1969) *On Death and Dying*. New York: Macmillan

Kuppers, P. (2006) Disability Culture Poetry: The Sound of the Bones – A Literary Essay. *Disability Studies Quarterly*, 26(4) [online].

Kurland, R. (2005) Planning: the neglected component of group development, in Malekoff, A. and Roselle, K. (eds) *A Quarter Century of Classics (1978–2004): Capturing the Theory, Practice and Spirit of Social Work with Groups*. Binghamton: The Haworth Press.

Kurtz, K. (2009) *The Evidence Base to Guide Development of Tier 4 CAMHS*. London: DH.

Kurtz, L. F. and Fisher, M. (2003) Participation in community life by AA and NA members, *Contemporary Drug Problems: An Interdisciplinary Quarterly*, 30(4): 875–904.

Laing, R. D. (1965) *The Divided Self: An Existential Study in Sanity and Madness*. London: Penguin.

Lamb, B. (2009) Lamb enquiry: special needs and parental confidence. Available at: www.dcfs.gov.uk/lambenquiry

Lambert, K. (2016) 'Capturing' queer lives and the poetics of social change. *Continuum: Journal of Media and Cultural Studies*, 30(5): 576–586.

Lambley, S. (2011) Managers: are they really to blame for what's happening to social work? *Social Science and Social Services Review*, 14(2): 6–20.

Laming, W. H. (2009) The protection of children in England: action plan. London: DfE.

Laming, W. H. (2003) The Victoria Climbié Inquiry Report. London: DfE.

Lammy, D. (2017) Lammy Review: an independent review into the treatment of, and outcomes for, Black, Asian and Minority Ethnic individuals in the Criminal Justice System. Available at:

https://assets.publishing.service.gov.uk/government/uploads/system/uploads/attachment_data/file/643001/lammy-review-final-report.pdf

Lander, L., Howsare, J. and Byrne, M. (2013) The impact of substance use disorders on families and children: from theory to practice. *Social Work in Public Health*, 28(3–4): 194–205.

Lange, C., Kamalkhani, Z. and Baldassar, L. (2007) Afghan Hazara refugees in Australia: constructing Australian citizens. *Social Identities*, 13(1): 31–50.

Langer, E. (1983) *Psychology of Control.* Thousand Oaks, CA: Sage.

Lavalette, M. (2019) Austerity and the context of social work today, in Lavalette, M. (ed) *What is the Future of Social Work?* Bristol: Policy Press.

Lawler, J. (2005) The essence of leadership? Existentialism and leadership. *Leadership*, 1(2): 215–31.

Lawler, J. and Bilson, A. (2010) *Social Work Management and Leadership: Managing Complexity with Creativity.* Abingdon: Routledge.

Lawton, J. (2000) *The Dying Process: Patients' Experiences of Palliative Care.* London: Routledge.

Lazarus, R. S. and Folkman, S. (1984) *Stress, Appraisal and Coping.* New York: McGraw-Hill.

Lea, M. R. and Stierer, B. (eds) (2000) *Student Writing in Higher Education: New Contexts.* Milton Keynes, UK/Philadelphia, USA: Open University Press/Society for Research into Higher Education.

Leavy, P. (2010) A/r/t: a poetic montage. *Qualitative Inquiry*, 16(4): 240–243.

Leeson, C. (2007) My life in care: experiences of non-participation in decision-making processes. *Child & Family Social Work*, 12(3): 268–277.

Lepper, J. (2017) Councils Face £25,000 Per Child Shortfall Under Refugee Scheme. Available at: www.cypnow.co.uk/cyp/news/2004075/councils-face-gbp25-000-per-child-shortfall-under-refugee-scheme

Levenson (2012) An Inquiry into the Culture, Practice and Ethics of the Press, Executive Summary and Recommendations. Available at: https://assets.publishing.service.gov.uk/government/uploads/system/uploads/attachment_data/file/229039/0779.pdf

Levinson, D. (1978) *The Seasons of a Man's Life.* New York: Knopf.

Lewis-Brooke, S. and Bradley, N. (2011) Family Intervention Projects: a holistic approach to working with families with multiple problems, in Cocker, C. and Allain, L. (eds) *Advanced Social Work with Children and Families.* London: Sage/Learning Matters.

LexisNexis (2019) Plan agreed to revive central support for pioneering FDAC. Available at: www.familylaw.co.uk/news_and_comment/private-donors-raise-280k-to-fund-fdacs

Lillis, T., Leedham, M. and Twiner, A. (2020) 'If it's not written down it didn't happen': contemporary social work as a writing intensive profession. *Journal of Applied Linguistics and Professional Practice* (in press).

Lishman, J. (2009) *Communication in Social Work* (2nd ed). Basingstoke: Palgrave Macmillan.

Llewellyn, A., Agu, L. and Mercer, D. (2015) *Sociology for Social Workers* (2nd ed). Cambridge: Polity Press.

Lloyd, C. (1998) Risk factors for problem drug use: identifying vulnerable groups. *Drugs: Education, Prevention and Policy*, 5(3): 217–232.

Lloyd, C., King, R. and Chenoweth, L. (2002) Social work, stress and burnout: a review. *Journal of Mental Health*, 11(3): 255–265.

Lloyd, M. (1997) Dying and bereavement: spirituality and social work in a mixed economy of welfare. *British Journal of Social Work*, 27(2): 175–190.

Lloyd, M. (2000) A framework for working with loss, in Thompson, N. (ed) *Loss and Grief: a Guide for Human Service Practitioners.* London: Palgrave.

London Safeguarding Children's Board (2011) London Safeguarding Trafficked Children Toolkit. London: London Safeguarding Children's Board.

Loney, M. (1983) *Community Against Government: The British Community Development Project 1968–78.* London: Heinemann Educational Books.

Lovell, J. (2017) *Self-Disclosure in Mental Health Services.* PhD thesis. York: University of York.

Lushey, C., Hyde Dryden, G., Holmes, L. and Blackmore, J. (2017) No Wrong Door – an example of good practice with adolescents. Children's Social Care Innovation Programme Evaluation Report 51.

Lymbery, M. (2005) *Social Work with Older People: Context, Policy and Practice*. London: Sage.

Lymbery, M. (2013) Reconciling radicalism, relationship and role: priorities for social work with adults in England. *Critical and Radical Social Work*, 1(2): 201–215.

Lynch, R. (2014) *Social Work Practice with Older People: A Positive Person-Centred Approach*. London: Sage.

Lyons, K., Manion, K. and Carlsen, M. (2006) *International Perspectives on Social Work: Global Conditions and Local Practice*. Basingstoke: Palgrave Macmillan.

Macdonald, G., Higgins, J. P. T., Ramchandani, P., Valentine, J. C., Bronger, L. P., Klein, P., O'Daniel, R., Pickering, M., Rademaker, B., Richardson, G. and Taylor, M. (2014) Cognitive-behavioural interventions for children who have been sexually abused: systematic review. *Campbell Systematic Reviews*, 8(1): 1–111.

Machin, L. (2011) *Working with Loss and Grief: A New Model for Practitioners*. London: Sage.

Maciejewski, P. K., Zhang, B., Block, S. D. and Prigerson, H. G. (2007) An empirical examination of the stage theory of grief. *JAMA*, 297(7): 716–723.

MacLaughlin, H. (2012) *Understanding Social Work Research* (2nd ed). London: Sage.

Maclean, S., Finch, J. and Tedam, P. (2018) *SHARE: A New Model of Social Work*. Litchfield: Kirwin Maclean Associates.

Macneil, C. A., Hasty, M. K., Conus, P. and Berk, M. (2010) Is diagnosis enough to guide interventions in mental health? Using case formulation in clinical practice. *BMC Medicine*, 10: 111.

Mairs, N. (1986) On Being a Cripple [online]. Available from: http://thelamedame.tumblr.com/post/30938417648/on-being-a-cripple

Mandelstam, M. (2017) *Care Act 2014: An A-Z of Law and Practice*. London: Jessica Kingsley Publishers.

Mantell, A. and Scragg, T. (2018) *Reflective Practice in Social Work*. London: Sage/Learning Matters.

Mares, S. (2016) Fifteen years of detaining children who seek asylum in Australia: evidence and consequences. *Australasian Psychiatry*, 24(1): 11–14.

Marlowe, J. M. (2018) *Belonging and Transnational Refugee Settlement: Unsettling the Everyday and the Extraordinary*. London: Routledge.

Martell, J. (2016) Opening a dialogue in mental health [online]. Available at: https://blogs.bmj.com/bmj/2016/10/18/opening-a-dialogue-in-mental-health/

Maslach, C. and Jackson, S. (1981) The measurement of experienced burnout. *Journal of Occupational Behaviour*, 2: 99–113.

Maslach, C. and Leiter, M. P. (1997) *The Truth About Burnout: How Organizations Cause Personal Stress and What To Do About It*. San Francisco, CA: Jossey-Bass.

Maslach, C., Jackson, S. and Leiter, M. (1996) *Maslach Burnout Inventory Manual*. Palo Alto, CA: Consulting Psychological Press.

Mason, P. (2009) *Meltdown: The End of the Age of Greed*. London: Verso.

Mason, P. and Prior, D. (2008) Engaging young people who offend: source document. London: Youth Justice Board.

Mason, P., Ferguson, H., Morris, K., Munton, T. and Sen, R. (2017) *Leeds Family Valued: Evaluation Report*. Children's Social Care Innovation Programme Evaluation Report 4.

Mathias, J. (2015) Thinking like a social worker: examining the meaning of critical thinking in social work. *Journal of Social Work Education*, 51(3): 457–474.

Mathieson, C. M. and Stam, H. K. (1995) Renegotiating identity: cancer narratives. *Sociology of Health and Illness*, 17(3): 282–306.

Matthews, A. (2014) 'What's Going to Happen Tomorrow?': Unaccompanied Children Refused Asylum. London: Office of the Children's Commissioner.

Matthews, A. (2018) Literature review on how the Home Office ensures it acts in the best interests of the child when conducting its immigration, asylum and nationality functions, specifically how it determines, reviews and secures the child's best interests. London: Independent Chief Inspector of Borders and Immigration.

Matthews, H. (2003) Children and regeneration: setting an agenda for community participation and integration. *Children and Society*, 17(4): 264–276.

Matza, D. (1964) *Delinquency and Drift*. New York: Wiley.

Mayer, J. E. and Timms, N. (1970) *The Client Speaks: Working Class Impressions of Casework*. London: Routledge and Kegan Paul.

Mayhew, H. (1851) Of a neglected child, a street seller, in *London Labour and the London Poor*. London: George Woodfall and Son. Available from: https://web.archive.org/web/20030127023543/http://etext.lib.virginia.edu/etcbin/toccer-new2?id=MayLond.sgm&images=images/modeng&data=/texts/english/modeng/parsed&tag=public&part=305&division=div2

McDougall, T. and Cotgrove, G. (2014) *Specialist Mental Healthcare for Children and Adolescents: Hospital, Intensive Community, and Home Based Services*. Abingdon: Routledge.

McAra, L. and McVie, S. (2007) Youth justice? The impact of system contact on patterns of desistance from offending. *European Journal of Criminology*, 4(3): 315–345.

McAra, L. and McVie, S. (2010) Youth crime and justice: key messages from the Edinburgh Study of Youth Transitions and Crime. *Criminology and Criminal Justice*, 10(2): 179–209.

McCartan, C., Bunting, L., Bywaters, P., Davidson, G., Elliott, M. and Hooper, J. (2018) A four-nation comparison of kinship care in the UK: the relationship between formal kinship care and deprivation. *Social Policy and Society*, 17(4): 619–635.

McDonald, A. (2006) *Understanding Community Care: A Guide for Social Workers* (2nd ed). Basingstoke: Palgrave Macmillan.

McDonald, A. (2010) *Social Work with Older People*. Cambridge: Polity Press.

McEwen, B. S. (2008) Central effects of stress hormones in health and disease: understanding the protective and damaging effects of stress and stress mediators. *European Journal of Pharmacology*, 583: 174–185.

McFadden, P., Campbell, A. and Taylor, B. J. (2015) Resilience and burnout in child protection social work: individual and organizational themes from a systematic literature review. *British Journal of Social Work*, 45(5): 1546–1563.

McFarlane, D. (2017) We need to engage and motivate social workers – let's get creative. *The Guardian*, 25 January. Available at: www.theguardian.com/social-care-network/social-life-blog/2017/jan/25/we-need-to-engage-and-motivate-social-workers-lets-get-creative

McGinn, A. H., McColgan, M. and Taylor, B. J. (2020) Male IPV perpetrators' perspectives on intervention and change: a systematic synthesis of qualitative studies. *Trauma, Violence & Abuse*, 21(1): 97–112.

Médecins Sans Frontières (2018) Indefinite despair: the tragic mental health consequences of off-shore processing on Nauru (MSF mental health project, Nauru). Available at: www.msf.org.au/sites/default/files/attachments/indefinite_despair_3.pdf

Medway Improvement Board (2016) Final Report of the Board's Advice to Secretary of State for Justice. Available at: https://assets.publishing.service.gov.uk/government/uploads/system/uploads/attachment_data/file/523167/medway-report.pdf

Megele, C. (2015) *Psychosocial and Relationship Based Practice*. St Albans: Critical Publishing.

Megele, C. (2018) *Safeguarding Children and Young People Online: A Guide for Practitioners*. Bristol: Policy Press.

Meloni, F. and Chase, E. (2017) Transitions into Institutional Adulthood: Becoming Adult Research Brief 4. London: UCL.

Meloni, F., Chase, E. and Haile, S. (eds) (2017) *Walking a Tightrope: Unaccompanied Migrant Young People, Transitions and Futures*. London: UCL.

Melzak, S. (2005) *On New Ground: Supporting Unaccompanied Asylum Seeking Children and Young People*. Dartington: Research in Practice.

Mencap (2018a) What is a Learning Disability? [online]. Available at: www.mencap.org.uk/learning-disability-explained/what-learning-disability

Mencap (2018b) Advocacy [online]. Available at: www.mencap.org.uk/advice-and-support/services-you-can-count/advocacy

Mental Health Foundation (2018) Stress [online]. Available at: www.mentalhealth.org.uk/a-to-z/s/stress

Mey, A., Plummer, D., Anoopkumar-Dukie, S. and Domberelli, A. (2018) What's the attraction? The role of performance enhancement as a driver of recreational drug use. *Journal of Substance Use*, 23(3): 294–299.

Mill, J. S. (1861 [1970]) Utilitarianism, in Warnock, M. (ed) *Utilitarianism*. London: Fontana.

Miller, D. (1979) *Social Justice*. Oxford: Oxford University Press.

Miller, S., Maguire, L. K. and Macdonald, G. (2011) Home-based child development interventions for preschool children from socially disadvantaged families. *Cochrane Database of Systematic Reviews*, 12: CD008131.

Miller, W. and Rollnick, S. (2013) *Motivational Interviewing: Helping People Change* (3rd ed). New York: Guilford Press.

Milne, A., Sullivan, M. P., Tanner, D., Richards, S., Ray, M., Lloyd, L., Beech, C. and Phillips, J. (2013) *Social Work with Older People: A Vision for the Future*. London: The College of Social Work.

Mind (2012) Health and Social Care Reform: Making it Work for Mental Health. Available at: www.mind.org.uk/media/552972/APPGMH-Report-Health-and-Social-Care-Reform-Making-it-work-for-Mental-Health.pdf

Minnis, H., Everett, K., Pelosi, A. J., Dunn, J. and Knapp, M. (2006) Children in foster care: mental health, service use and costs. *European Child & Adolescent Psychiatry*, 15(2): 63–70.

Monroe, B. and Oliviere, D. (eds) (2007) *Resilience in Palliative Care: Achievement in Adversity*. Oxford: Oxford University Press.

Moos, R. (2007) Theory-based active ingredients of effective treatments for substance use disorders. *Drug & Alcohol Dependence*, 88(2/3): 109–121.

Morley, C., Ablett, P. and Macfarlane, S., (2019) *Engaging with Social Work: A Critical Introduction*. Port Melbourne: Cambridge University Press.

Morris, J. (2001) Impairment and disability: ethic of care promoting human rights. *Hypatia*, 16(4): 1–32.

Morrison, J. (2019) *Scroungers: Moral Panics and Media Myths*. London: Zed Books.

Morrison, T. (2007) Emotional intelligence, emotion and social work: context, characteristics, complications and contribution. *British Journal of Social Work*, 37: 245–263.

Mowat, H. and O'Neil, M. (2013) *Spirituality and ageing: Implications for the care and support of older people, Insight 19*. Glasgow: The Institute for Research and Innovation in Social Services (IRISS).

Mullender, A. (2013) *Empowerment in Action: Self-directed Groupwork*. Basingstoke: Palgrave Macmillan.

Munby, J. (2013) View from the President's Chambers: the process of reform; the revised PLO and the local authority. *Family Law*, 680.

Muncie, J. (2006) Governing young people: coherence and contradiction in contemporary youth justice. *Critical Social Policy*, 26(4): 770–793.

Muncie, J. and Hughes, G. (2002) Modes of youth governance: political rationalities, criminalisation and resistance, in Muncie, J., Hughes, G. and McLaughlin, E. (eds) *Youth Justice: Critical Readings*. London: Sage.

Munro, E. (2010a) The Munro Review of Child Protection Services. *Part One: A Systems Analysis*. London: DfE.

Munro, E. (2010b) Learning to reduce risk in child protection. *British Journal of Social Work*, 40: 1135–1151.

Munro, E. (2011) The Munro Review of Child Protection: Final Report: A Child Centred System. DfE.

Musson, P. (2011) *Effective Writing Skills for Social Work Students*. London: Sage.

NACRO (2008) Principles of Participation for Youth Justice (Youth Crime Briefing). London: NACRO.

Narey, M. (2014) Making the Education of Social Workers Consistently Effective. London: DoH.

National Education Union and Child Poverty Action Group (2018) Child poverty and education: a survey of experiences. London: CPAG.

National Institute for Health and Care Excellence (2004) Guidance on Cancer Services: Improving Supportive and Palliative Care for Adults with Cancer. The Manual. London: NICE.

Needham, C. and Carr, S. (2009) Co-production: an emerging evidence base for adult social care transformation. Research briefing 31. London: Social Care Institute for Excellence.

Neimeyer, R. A. (ed) (2001) *Meaning Reconstruction and the Experience of Loss.* Washington: American Psychological Association.

Nelson, D., Price, E. and Zubrzycki, J. (2017) Critical social work with unaccompanied asylum-seeking young people: restoring hope, agency and meaning for the client and worker. *International Social Work*, 60(3): 601–613.

Newell, J. M and MacNeil, G. A. (2010) Professional burnout, vicarious trauma, secondary stress trauma and compassion fatigue: a review of theoretical terms, risk factors and preventative methods for clinicians and researchers. *Best Practice in Mental Health*, 6(2): 57–68.

NHS (2018a) Overview: Learning Disabilities [online]. Available at: www.nhs.uk/conditions/learning-disabilities/

NHS (2018b) NHS continuing healthcare [online]. Available at: www.nhs.uk/conditions/social-care-and-support-guide/money-work-and-benefits/nhs-continuing-healthcare/

NHS England (2017) Learning Disabilities Mortality Review (LeDeR) Programme: Annual Report 2017 [online]. Available at: www.hqip.org.uk/wp-content/uploads/2018/05/LeDeR-annual-report-2016-2017-Final-6.pdf

NHS Health Advisory Service (1995) Together We Stand: Commissioning, Role and Management of Child and Adolescent Mental Health Services. London: HMSO.

Ní Raghallaigh, M. and Thornton, L. (2017) Vulnerable childhood, vulnerable adulthood: direct provision as aftercare for aged-out separated children seeking asylum in Ireland. *Critical Social Policy*, 37(3): 386–404.

Nipperess, S. and Williams, C. (eds) (2019) *Critical Multicultural Practice in Social Work: New Perspectives and Practices.* Sydney: Allen and Unwin.

Northen, H. and Kurland, R. (2001) *Social Work with Groups* (3rd ed). New York: Columbia University Press.

Northouse, P. G. (2011) *Introduction to Leadership Concepts and Practice* (2nd ed). London: Sage.

Nozick, R. (1974) *Anarchy, State and Utopia.* New York: Basic Books.

NSPCC (2018) Recently published case reviews, NSPCC Learning. Available at: learning.nspcc.org.uk/case-reviews/recently-published-case-reviews/

Nuffield Trust (2018) Striking increase in mental health conditions in children and young people [online]. Available at: www.nuffieldtrust.org.uk/news-item/striking-increase-in-mental-health-conditions-in-children-and-young-people

Nutt, D. (2012) *Drugs – Without the Hot Air: Minimizing the Harms of Legal and Illegal Drugs.* Cambridge: UIT Cambridge.

O'Higgins, A. (2018) Analysis of care and education pathways of refugee and asylum-seeking children in care in England: implications for social work. *International Journal of Social Welfare*, 28(1): 53–62.

O'Higgins, A., Ott, E. M. and Shea, M. W. (2018) What is the impact of placement type on educational and health outcomes of unaccompanied refugee minors? A systematic review of the evidence. *Clinical Child and Family Psychology Review*, 21: 354–365.

O'Reilly, D. and Reed, M. (2010) 'Leaderism': an evolution of managerialism in UK public services reform. *Public Administration*, 88(4): 903–1145.

Oakley, A. (2019) *Women, Peace and Welfare: A Suppressed History of Social Reform, 1880–1920.* Bristol: Policy Press.

Oakley, A. and Rajan, L. (1991) Social class and social support: the same or different? *Sociology*, 25(1): 31–59.

O'Donnell, R. and Kanics, J. (2016) Separated and unaccompanied children in the EU. *Forced Migration Review*, 51: 73–75.

Office for National Statistics (2018) Alcohol-specific deaths in the UK: registered in 2017 [online]. Available at: www.ons.gov.uk/peoplepopulationandcommunity/healthandsocialcare/causesofdeath/bulletins/alcoholrelateddeathsintheunitedkingdom/registeredin2017

Office for National Statistics and Department for Work and Pensions (2018) Family Resources Survey 2016/17 [online]. Available at: https://assets.publishing.service.gov.uk/government/uploads/system/uploads/attachment_data/file/692771/family-resources-survey-2016-17.pdf

Ogborn, C. (2019) Social workers are a bit like artists. *Professional Social Work Online.* Available at: www.basw.co.uk/resources/psw-magazine/psw-online/social-workers-are-bit-artists

Oliver, M. (1990) *The Politics of Disablement.* Basingstoke: Macmillan.

Oliver, M. (2013) The social model of disability: thirty years on. *Disability & Society,* 28(7): 1024–1026.

Oliver, M., Sapey, B. and Thomas, P. (2012) *Social Work with Disabled People* (4th ed). Basingstoke: Macmillan.

Oliviere, D., Monroe, B. and Payne, S. (eds) (2011) *Death, Dying and Social Differences* (2nd ed). Oxford: Oxford University Press.

Orford, J., Velleman, R., Copello, A., Templeton, L. and Ibanga, A. (2010) The experiences of affected family members: a summary of two decades of qualitative research. *Drugs: Education, Prevention and Policy,* 17(1): 44–62.

Owton, H. (2017) *Doing Poetic Inquiry.* Basingstoke: Palgrave Macmillan.

Owusu-Bempah, K. (2014) *Children and Separation: Socio-Genealogical Connectedness Perspective.* Abingdon: Routledge.

Oxfam (2013) *Truth and Lies about Poverty: Ending Comfortable Myths about Poverty.* Cardiff: Oxfam Cymru.

Oxford University Press (2019) *English Oxford Living Dictionaries* [online]. Available at: https://en.oxforddictionaries.com/

Palinkas, L. A. and Soydan, H. (2012) *Translation and Implementation of Evidence-Based Practice.* Oxford: Oxford University Press.

Parker, C. (2018) School reports boy, 15, to Home Office over fears he's 30-year-old asylum seeker after Snapchat picture spread by classmates. *The Sun,* 2 November. Available at: www.thesun.co.uk/news/7642364/stoke-high-school-snapchat-age-30-ipswich/

Parker, H., Measham, F. and Aldridge, J. (1995) Drugs futures: changing patterns of drug use amongst English youth. London: Institute for the Study of Drug Dependence.

Parker, J. (2007) Social work, disadvantage by association and anti-oppressive practice, in Burke, P. and Parker, J. (eds) *Social Work and Disadvantage: Addressing the Roots of Stigma through Association.* London: Jessica Kingsley Publishers.

Parker, J. (2015) Single shared assessments in social work, in Wright, J. D. (ed) *The International Encyclopedia of Social and Behavioral Sciences* (2nd ed). London: Elsevier.

Parker, J. (2017) *Social Work Practice: Assessment, Planning, Intervention and Review* (5th ed). London: Sage.

Parker, J. (2018) Social work, precarity and sacrifice as radical action for hope. *International Journal of Social Work and Human Services Practice,* 6(2): 46–55.

Parker, J. (2019a) Descent or dissent? A future of social work education in the UK post-Brexit. *European Journal of Social Work,* published online 12 Feb.

Parker, J. (2019b) The convergence of the isomorphs: poetic inquiry as resistance and heterodoxy in contemporary higher education. Keynote paper presented at ASCOPET Symposium on Higher Education Learning Through Performance Practices EPFL, Lausanne, Switzerland, 13 June.

Parker, J. (2020) Critical perspectives on human growth and development, in Parker, J. and Ashencaen Crabtree, S. (eds) *Human Growth and Development in Children and Young People: Theoretical and Practice Perspectives: Volume 1.* Bristol: Policy Press.

Parker, J. and Ashencaen Crabtree, S. (2018) *Social Work with Disadvantaged and Marginalised People.* London: Sage.

Parker, J., Ashencaen Crabtree, S., Azman, A., Nikku, B. R. and Nguyen, Y. (2017) A comparative study of social work assessment in Malaysia, Nepal, Vietnam and the United Kingdom: towards an understanding of meaning. *Social Work and Society Online International Journal*, 15(2): 1–17.

Parkes, C. M. and Weiss, R. S. (1983) *Recovery from Bereavement*. New York: Basic Books.

Parkinson, M. (2010) The Thatcher government's urban policy, 1979–1989, in Tallon, A. (ed) *Urban Regeneration and Renewal*. London: Routledge.

Parrish, M. (2014) *Social Work Perspectives on Human Behaviour* (2nd ed). London: Open University Press.

Parton, N. (2008) Changes in the form of knowledge in social work: from the 'social' to the 'informational'? *British Journal of Social Work*, 38(2): 253–269.

Passarlay, G. and Ghouri, N. (2015) *The Lightless Sky: My Journey to Safety as a Child Refugee*. London: Atlantic Books.

Pattison, E. M. (1977) *The Experience of Dying*. Englewood Cliffs, NJ: Prentice Hall.

Pawson, R. and Tilley, N. (1997) *Realistic Evaluation*. Thousand Oaks, CA: Sage.

Paylor, I., Wilson, A. and Measham, F. (2012) *Social Work and Drug Use*. Maidenhead: McGraw-Hill Education.

Payne, M. (1997) *Modern Social Work Theory*. Basingstoke: Palgrave Macmillan.

Payne, M. (2005) *The Origins of Social Work: Continuity and Change*. Basingstoke: Palgrave Macmillan.

Payne, M. (2012) *Citizenship Social Work with Older People*. Bristol: Policy Press.

Payne, M. (2020) *How to Use Social Work Theory in Practice: An Essential Guide*. Bristol: Policy Press.

Payne, M. and Taplin, S. (2014) Social work in healthcare settings, in Teater, B. (ed) *Contemporary Social Work Practice: A Handbook for Students*. Maidenhead: Open University Press.

Peer Power (2018) Getting it Right: Young People's Vision for Liaison and Diversion Services. London: Peer Power and Young Minds.

Pellissery, S., Lødemel, I. and Gubrium, E. K. (2014) Shame and shaming in policy processes, in Gubrium, K., Pellissery, S. and Lødemel, I. (eds) *The Shame of It: Global Perspectives on Anti-Poverty Policies*. Bristol: Policy Press.

Penhale, B. and Young, J. (2015) Review of the Literature Concerning what the Public and Users of Social Work Services in England Think about the Conduct and Competence of Social Workers. Norwich: UEA Consulting Limited. Available at: www.professionalstandards.org.uk/docs/default-source/publications/research-paper/what-the-public-think-about-the-conduct-and-competence-of-social-workers-2015.pdf?sfvrsn=71c47f20_6

Pharoah, F., Mari, J. J., Rathbone, J. and Wong, W. (2010) Family intervention for schizophrenia. *Cochrane Database of Systematic Reviews*, 12: CD000088.

Phillips, H. U. (1957) *Essentials of Social Group Work Skill*. New York: Association Press.

Phillips, J. (2017) A comparison of Coalition and Labour government asylum policies in Australia since 2001. 2 February. Available at: http://www.aph.gov.au/About_Parliament/Parliamentary_Departments/Parliamentary_Library/pubs/rp/rp1617/AsylumPolicies

Pilgrim, D. (2014) *Key Concepts in Mental Health* (3rd ed). London: Sage.

Pillay, D., Pithouse-Morgan, K. and Naicker, I. (2017) Self-knowledge creation through collective poetic inquiry: cultivating productive resistance as university academics. *Cultural Studies/Critical Methodologies*, 17(3): 262–265.

Pinkerton, J. and Katz, I. (2003) Perspective through international comparison in the evaluation of family support, in Katz, I. and Pinkerton, J. (eds) *Evaluating Family Support: Thinking Internationally, Thinking Critically*. London: Wiley.

Podrazik, D., Shackford, S., Becker, L. and Heckert, T. (2000) The death of a pet: implications for loss and bereavement across the lifespan. *Journal of Personal and Interpersonal Loss*, 5(4): 361–395.

Polkinghorne, D. (2004) *Practice and the Human Sciences: The Case for a Judgment-Based Practice of Care*. Albany, NY: SUNY.

Popple, K. (2011) Rise and fall of the National Community Development Projects 1968–1978: lessons to learn?, in Gilchrist, R. Hodgson, T., Jeffs, T., Spence, J., Stanton, N. and Walker, J. (eds) *Reflecting in the Past: Essays in the History of Youth and Community Work*. Lyme Regis: Russell House Publishing.

Prendergast, M., Gouzouasis, P., Leggo, C. and Irwiin, R. (2009) A haiku suite: the importance of music in the lives of secondary school students. *Music Education Research*, 11(3): 303–317.

Prigerson, H. G. and Maciejewski, P. K. (2008) Grief and acceptance as opposite sides of the same coin: setting a research agenda to study peaceful acceptance of loss. *British Journal of Psychiatry*, 193(6): 435–437.

Prochaska, J. and DiClemente, C. (1986) Toward a comprehensive model of change, in Heather, N. and Miller, W. R. (eds) *Treating Addictive Behaviors*. Boston, MA: Springer US.

Public Health England (2016) People with learning disabilities in England 2015: Main report [online]. Available at: https://assets.publishing.service.gov.uk/government/uploads/system/uploads/attachment_data/file/613182/PWLDIE_2015_main_report_NB090517.pdf

Public Health England (2018) Guidance Dementia: applying All Our Health. London: Public Health England. Available at: https://www.gov.uk/government/publications/dementia-applying-all-our-health/dementia-applying-all-our-health

Puffett, N. (2017) Youth reoffending rises to highest level on record. *Children & Young People Now*. Available at: www.cypnow.co.uk/cyp/news/2003562/youth-reoffending-rises-to-highest-level-on-record

Pullen-Sansfaon, A. (2012) *The Ethical Foundations of Social Work*. Harlow: Pearson.

Putnam, R. (2000) *Bowling Alone: The Collapse and Revival of American Community*. New York: Simon and Schuster.

Quarmby, C. (2011) *Scapegoat: Why We are Failing Disabled People*. London: Portobello Books.

Quiros, L. and Berger, R. (2015) Responding to the sociopolitical complexity of trauma: an integration of theory and practice. *Journal of Loss and Trauma: International Perspectives on Stress and Coping*, 20(2): 149–159.

Radley, A., Melville, K., Easton, P., Williams, B. and Dillon, J. F. (2017) 'Standing outside the junkie door': service users' experiences of using community pharmacies to access treatment for opioid dependency. *Journal of Public Health*, 39(4): 846–855.

Rae, M., Holman, R. and Nethery, A. (2018) Self-represented witnessing: the use of social media by asylum seekers in Australia's offshore immigration detention centres. *Media, Culture and Society*, 40(4): 479–495.

Rai, L. (2011) Reflections on writing in social work education and practice, in Seden, J., Matthews, S., McCormick, M. and Morgan, A. (eds) *Professional Development in Social Work: Complex Issues in Practice*. London: Routledge.

Rai, L. (2014) *Effective Writing for Social Work*. Bristol: Policy Press.

Rai, L. and Lillis, T. (2011) A case study of a research-based collaboration around writing in social work. *Across the Disciplines*, 8(3).

Rai, L. and Lillis, T. (2013) 'Getting it write' in social work: exploring the value of writing in academia to writing for professional practice. *Teaching in Higher Education*, 18(4): 352–364.

Rando, T. A. (1993) *Treatment of Complicated Mourning*. Champaign, IL: Research Press.

Ravalier, J. M. (2018) Psycho-social working conditions and stress in UK social workers. *British Journal of Social Work*, 49(2): 371–390.

Rawls, J. (1999) *A Theory of Justice* (2nd ed). Oxford: Oxford University Press.

Raymond, G. (2010) Grammar and social relations: alternative forms of yes/no-type initiating actions in health visitor interactions, in Freed, A. F. and Ehrlich, S. (eds) *'Why do You Ask?' The Function of Questions in Institutional Discourse*. Oxford: Oxford University Press.

Refugee Children's Consortium (2017) Briefing on the National Transfer Scheme. Available at: https://www.basw.co.uk/resources/briefing-national-transfer-scheme-august-2017

Refugee Council (2017) Tell it like it is: the truth about refugees and asylum. Available at: www.refugeecouncil.org.uk/assets/0004/0315/Ref_C_TILII_APRIL_2017_FINAL.pdf

Refugee Council of Australia (2017) Recent changes in Australian refugee policy. Updated 7 July 2018. Available at: www.refugeecouncil.org.au/publications/recent-changes-australian-refugee-policy/

Refugee Support Network (2018) Education for refugee and asylum seeking children. Available at: www.refugeesupportnetwork.org/resources/16-education-for-refugee-and-asylum-seeking-children

Reith, M. and Payne, M. (2009) *Social Work in End-of-Life and Palliative Care*. Bristol: Policy Press.

Ridley, J. (2002) *The Tudor Age* (3rd ed). London: Constable and Robinson.

Roberts, R. (1990) *Lessons from the Past: Issues for Social Work Theory*. London: Tavistock/Routledge.

Robinson, D. D. (2010) Charity in Islamic societies. *Digest of Middle East Studies*, 19(1): 117.

Robinson, K. and Gifford, S. (2019) Life (forever) on hold: unaccompanied asylum seeking minors in Australia, in Clayton, S., Gupta, A. and Willis, K. (eds) *Unaccompanied Young Migrants: Identity, Care and Justice*. Bristol: Policy Press.

Robinson, K. and Masocha, S. (2016) Divergent practices in statutory and voluntary-sector settings? Social work with asylum seekers. *British Journal of Social Work*, 47: 1517–1533.

Robinson, K. and Williams, L. (2015) Leaving care: unaccompanied asylum-seeking young Afghans facing return. *Refuge*, 31(2): 85–94.

Rochester, C., Campbell Gosling, G., Penn, A. and Zimmeck, M. (2011) *Understanding the Roots of Voluntary Action: Historical Perspectives on Current Social Policy*. Brighton: Sussex Academic Press.

Rodger, J. Woolger, A., Cutmore, M. and Wilkinson, L. (2017) *Creating Strong Communities in North East Lincolnshire*. Children's Social Care Innovation report, July.

Rodriguez-Morales, L. (2017) In your own skin: the experience of early recovery from alcohol-use disorder in 12-step fellowships. *Alcoholism Treatment Quarterly*, 35(4): 372–394.

Roets, G., Roose, R., De Wilde, L. and Vanobbergen, B. (2017) Framing the 'child at risk' in social work reports: truth-telling or storytelling? *Journal of Social Work*, 17(4): 453–469.

Rogers, C. R. (1959) A theory of therapy, personality, and interpersonal relationships as developed in the client-centered framework, in Koch, S. (ed) *Psychology: A Study of Science: Formulations of the Person and the Social Context*. New York: McGraw-Hill.

Rogowski, S. (2010) *Social Work: The Rise and Fall of a Profession?* Bristol: Policy Press.

Romero, M. (2017) *Introducing Intersectionality*. Bristol: Policy Press.

Royal College of Occupational Therapists (2018) *Assessment of Motor and Process Skills Course* [online]. Available at: www.rcot.co.uk/events/assessment-motor-and-process-skills-course-amps-0

Ruch, G., Turney, D. and Ward, A. (2010) *Relationship Based Social Work: Getting to the Heart of Practice*. London: Jessica Kingsley Publishers.

Ruch, G., Turney, D. and Ward, A. (2018) *Relationship Based Social Work: Getting to the Heart of Practice* (2nd ed). London: Jessica Kingsley Publishers.

Rudd, B. (2014) *Introducing Psychopathology*. London: Sage.

Rutter, J. (2006) *Refugee Children in the UK*. London: McGraw-Hill Education.

Rutter, M. (1999) *Bright Futures: Promoting Children and Children's Mental Health*. London: Mental Health Foundation.

Ryan, T. and Walker, R. (2016) *Life Story Work: Why, What, How and When*. London: CoramBAAF.

Sacks, H. (1987) On the preferences for agreement and contiguity in sequences in conversation, in Button, G. and Lee, J. R. E. (eds) *Talk and Social Organisation*. Clevedon: Multilingual Matters.

Sadler, K., Vizard, T., Ford, T., Marchaselli, F., Pearce, N., Dhriti, M., Davis, J., Brodie, E., Forbes, N., Goodman, A., Goodman, R., McManus, S. and Collinson, D. (2017) Mental Health of Children and Young People in England 2017, Health and Social Care Information Centre. Available at: https://files.digital.nhs.uk/F6/A5706C/MHCYP%202017%20Summary.pdf

Sandoz, J. (2014) Finding God through the spirituality of the 12 Steps of Alcoholics Anonymous. *Religions*, 5(4): 948–960.

Sapin, K. (2008) *Essential Skills for Youth Work Practice*. London: Sage.

Satir, V. (1964) *Conjoint Family Therapy*. Palo Alto, CA: Science and Behavior Books.

Sauer, P. J. J., Nicholson, A. and Neubauer, D. (2016) Age determination in asylum seekers: physicians should not be implicated. *European Journal of Paediatrics*, 175(3), 299–303.

Schiller, L. Y. (1997) Rethinking stages of group development in women's groups: implications for practice. *Social Work with Groups*, 20(3): 3–19.

Schön, D. (1983) *The Reflective Practitioner*. London: Basic Books.

Schoone, A. (2017) Joy, grace and transformation: the pedagogy of tutors in New Zealand's alternative education centres. *International Journal of Inclusive Education*, 21(8): 808–821.

Schut, H. and Stroebe, M. (2010) Effects of support, counselling and therapy before and after the loss: can we really help bereaved people? *Psychologica Belgica*, 50(1/2): 89–102.

Schwartz, W. (1971 [1994]) On the use of groups in social work practice, in Berman-Rossi, T. (ed) *Social Work: The Collected Writings of William Schwartz*. Itasca, IL: F. E. Peacock Publishers, Inc.

Scope (2014) 'Priced out': households below average income [online]. Available at: www.scope.org.uk/media/disability-facts-figures#q0sysoXv4rZtpysJ.99

Scottish Recovery Network (2012) What is recovery? Available at: www.scottishrecovery.net/resource/mental-health-recovery-and-the-assets-based-approach/

Scragg, T. (2018) Reflective practice on placement, in Mantell, A. and Scragg, T. (eds) *Reflective Practice in Social Work*. London: Sage/Learning Matters.

Scull, A. T. (1979) *Museums of Madness: The Social Organization of Insanity in 19th Century England*. New York: St. Martin's Press.

Seale, C. (1989) *Constructing Death: The Sociology of Dying and Bereavement*. Cambridge: Cambridge University Press.

Sebba, J., Luke, N., McNeish, D. and Rees, A. (2017) Children's Social Care Innovation Programme: final evaluation report. Available at: https://assets.publishing.service.gov.uk/government/uploads/system/uploads/attachment_data/file/659110/Children_s_Social_Care_Innovation_Programme_-_Final_evaluation_report.pdf.

Secker, J., Hill, R., Villeneau, L. and Parkman, S. (2003) Promoting independence: but promoting what and how? *Ageing and Society*, 23: 375–391.

Sedan, J. and Reynolds, J. (2003) *Managing Care in Practice*. London: Routledge.

Seebohm Report (1968) *Report of the Committee on Local Authority and Allied Personal Social Services*. Cmnd 3703. London: HMSO.

Segal, G. (2017) How an addict's power of choice is lost and can be regained, in Heather, N. and Segal, G. (eds) *Addiction and Choice: Rethinking the Relationship*. New York: Oxford University Press.

Selye, H. (1955) Stress and disease. *Science*, 122(3171): 625–631.

Selye, H. (1975) Confusion and controversy in the stress field. *Journal of Human Stress*, 1: 37–44.

Seymour, C. and Seymour, R. (2011) *Courtroom and Report Writing Skills for Social Workers*. London: Sage.

Shannon, M. (2019) *Family Support for Social Care Practitioners*. London: Red Globe Press.

Sharf, R. S. (2016) *Theories of Psychotherapy and Counseling: Concepts and Cases* (6th ed). Boston, MA: Cengage Learning.

Shear, M. K., Ghesquiere, A. and Glickman, K. (2013) Bereavement and complicated grief. *Current Psychiatry Reports*, 15: 406.

Shemmings, D. (2016) *Attachment in Children and Young People*. Dartington: Research in Practice.

Shulman, L. (1984) *The Skills of Helping Individuals and Groups*. Itasca, IL: F. E. Peacock Publishers.

Shulman, L. (2015) *The Skills of Helping Individuals, Families, Groups and Communities* (8th ed). Boston, MA: Cengage Learning.

Simcock, P. and Castle, R. (2016) *Social Work and Disability*. Cambridge: Polity Press.

Simmonds, J., Harwin, J., Brown, R. and Broadhurst, K. (2019) Special guardianship: a review of the evidence. Summary report. Available at: www.nuffieldfjo.org.uk/files/documents/NuffieldFJO-Special-Guardianship-190731-WEB-final.pdf

Simpson, G. and Connor, S. (2011) *Social Policy for Social Welfare Professionals: Tools for Understanding, Analysis and Engagement.* Bristol: Policy Press.

Sinclair, R. (2004) Participation in practice: making it meaningful, effective and sustainable. *Children and Society,* 18(2): 106–118.

Sirriyeh, A. and Ní Raghallaigh, M. (2018) Foster care, recognition and transitions to adulthood for unaccompanied asylum seeking young people in England and Ireland. *Children and Youth Services Review,* 92: 89–97.

Slack, P. (1990) *The English Poor Law, 1531–1782.* Cambridge: Cambridge University Press.

Small, J. (2000) Ethnicity and placement: beginning the debate. *Adoption and Fostering,* 24(1): 9–14.

Small, N. (2001) Social work and palliative care. *British Journal of Social Work,* 31: 961–971.

Smith, M. and Nursten, J. (1998) Social workers' experience of distress: moving towards change? *British Journal of Social Work,* 28(3): 351–368.

Smith, R. (2008) Interventions: responsibility, rights or reconciliation?, in Stout, B., Yates, J. and Williams, B. (eds) *Applied Criminology.* London: Sage.

Smith, R. (2014a) *Youth Justice: Ideas, Policy, Practice* (3rd ed). Abingdon: Routledge.

Smith, R. (2014b) Towards a 'welfare + rights' model in youth justice. *Critical and Radical Social Work,* 2(3): 287–303.

Smith, R. and Gray, P. (2018) The changing shape of youth justice: models of practice. *Criminology & Criminal Justice,* 19(5): 554–571.

Social Care Institute for Excellence (2012) People not processes: the future of personalisation and independent living [online]. London: SCIE. Available at: www.scie.org.uk/publications/reports/report55/

Social Care Institute for Excellence (2015a) Care Act 2014: Adult safeguarding practice questions [online]. Available at: http://www.scie.org.uk/care-act-2014/safeguarding-adults/adult-safe-guarding-practice-questions

Social Care Institute for Excellence (2015b) Care Act guidance on strengths-based approaches [online]. London: SCIE. Available at: www.scie.org.uk/strengths-based-approaches/guidance

Social Care Institute of Excellence (2017) Model: improve mental health support for our children and young people. Available at: www.scie.org.uk/files/children/care/mental-health/practice/ewg-model.pdf

Social Care Online (2017) Asset-based places: a model for development [online]. London: SCIE.

Spicker, P. (2013) *Principles of Social Welfare: An Introduction to Thinking about the Welfare State* (2nd ed). London: Routledge.

Srnicek, N. (2016) 'What comes after neoliberalism?': film of a talk at the launch of Economic and Social Research Aotearoa. Available at: www.esra.nz/what-comes-after-neoliberalism

Stacey, J. (1997) *Teratologies: A Cultural Study of Cancer.* London: Routledge.

Stamm, B. H. (2010) The concise ProQOL manual (2nd ed) [online]. *Pocatello.* Available at: ProQOL.org

Stephenson, M., Giller, H. and Brown S. (2007) *Effective Practice in Youth Justice.* Cullompton: Willan Publishing.

Stepney, P. and Popple, K. (2008) *Social Work and the Community: A Critical Context for Practice.* Basingstoke: Palgrave Macmillan.

Stevenson, J. (2014) Leading the well-being of early years teams, in Manning-Morton, J. (ed) *Exploring Well-Being in the Early Years.* Maidenhead: Open University Press.

Stevenson, M. and Taylor, B. J. (2017) Risk communication in dementia care: professional perspectives on consequences, likelihood, words and numbers. *British Journal of Social Work,* 47(7): 1940–1958.

Stevenson, M. and Taylor, B. J. (2019) Involving individuals with dementia as co-researchers in analysis of findings from a qualitative study. *Dementia: The International Journal of Social Research and Practice,* 18(2): 701–712.

Stevenson, M., Taylor, B. J. and Knox, J. (2016) Risk in dementia care: searching for the evidence. *Health, Risk and Society,* 18(1/2): 4–20.

Stevenson, M., McDowell, M. E. and Taylor, B. J. (2018) Concepts for communication about risk in dementia care: a review of the literature. *Dementia: The International Journal of Social Research and Practice*, 17(3): 359–390.

Strauss, A. and Glaser, B. (1970) *Anguish: A Case History of a Dying Trajectory*. Mill Valley, CA: Sociology Press.

Stroebe, M. S. and Schut, H. (1999) The dual process model of coping with bereavement: rationale and description. *Death Studies*, 23(3): 197–224.

Stroebe, M. S., Schut, H. and Boerner, K. (2017) Cautioning health-care professionals: bereaved persons are misguided through the stages of grief. *OMEGA*, 74(4): 455–473.

Sung, K. T. and Dunkle, R. E. (2009) How social workers demonstrate respect for elderly clients. *Journal of Gerontological Social Work*, 52(3), 250–260.

Swain, J., French, S. and Cameron, C. (2003) *Controversial Issues in a Disabling Society*. Buckingham: Open University Press.

Swain, J., French, S., Barnes, C. and Thomas, C. (2014) *Disabling Barriers: Enabling Environments* (3rd ed). London: Sage.

Szasz, T. S. (1972) *The Myth of Mental Illness*. London: Paladin.

Tafvelin, S., Hyvönen, U. and Westerberg, K. (2014) Transformational leadership in the social work context: the importance of leader continuity and co-worker support. *British Journal of Social Work*, 44(4), 886–904.

Tanner, D., Glasby, J. and McIver, S. (2015) Understanding and improving older people's experiences of service transitions: implications for social work. *British Journal of Social Work*, 45: 2056–2071.

Taplin, S. (2016) 'Living to tell the tale': narratives of surviving cancer and the social work response. *Journal of Social Work Practice*, 30(2): 155–168.

Taylor, B. J. (2006) Risk management paradigms in health and social services for professional decision making on the long-term care of older people. *British Journal of Social Work*, 36(8): 1411–1429.

Taylor, B. J. (2012) Intervention research, in Gray, M., Midgley, J. and Webb, S. (eds) *Social Work Handbook*. New York: Sage.

Taylor, B. J. (2016) Heuristics in professional judgement: a psycho-social rationality model. *British Journal of Social Work*, 4(1): 1043–1060.

Taylor, B. J. (2017) *Decision Making, Assessment and Risk in Social Work* (3rd ed). London: Sage.

Taylor, B. J., Killick, C., O'Brien, M., Begley, E. and Carter-Anand, J. (2014) Older people's conceptualisation of elder abuse and neglect. *Journal of Elder Abuse and Neglect*, 26(3): 223–243.

Taylor, B. J., Killick, C. and McGlade, A. (2015) *Understanding and Using Research in Social Work*. London: Sage.

Taylor, B. J., Stevenson, M. and McDowell, M. (2018) Communicating risk in dementia care: survey of health and social care professionals. *Health and Social Care in the Community*, 26(2): 291–303.

Taylor, M., Collin, S. M., Munafò, M. R., MacLeod, J., Hickman, M. and Heron, J. (2017) Patterns of cannabis use during adolescence and their association with harmful substance use behaviour: findings from a UK birth cohort. *Journal of Epidemiology and Community Health*, 71(8): 764–770.

Teater, B. (2014) *An Introduction to Applying Social Work Theories and Methods* (2nd ed). Maidenhead: Open University Press.

Teater, B. (2015) Social work theories, in Wright, J. (ed) *International Encyclopedia of Social and Behavioral Sciences* (2nd ed). Oxford: Elsevier Science Ltd.

Teater, B. (2020) *An Introduction to Applying Social Work Theories and Methods* (3rd ed). London: Open University Press.

Tedam, P. (2012) The MANDELA model of practice learning: an old present in new wrapping? *Journal of Practice Teaching and Learning*, 11(2): 60–76.

Tew, J. (2011) *Social Approaches to Mental Distress*. London: Palgrave Macmillan.

Tew, J., Ramon, R., Slade, M., Bird, V. and Melton, M. (2012) Social factors and recovery from mental health difficulties: a review of the evidence. *British Journal of Social Work*, 42(3): 443–460.

Tharoor, A. (2017) UK General Election 2017: Drug Policies of the Main Parties, TalkingDrugs [online]. Available at: www.talkingdrugs.org/general-election-2017-drug-policies-of-the-main-parties

The Children's Commission on Poverty (2014) *At What Cost? Exposing the Impact of Poverty on School Life*. London: The Children's Society.

The Children's Society (2015) *Leaving Poverty Outside the School Gates*. London: The Children's Society.

The King's Fund (2011) The future of leadership and management in the NHS. No more heroes. Report from the King's Fund Commission on Leadership and Management in the NHS, edited by Edwina Rowling. London: The King's Fund.

The King's Fund (2018) *Key Challenges Facing the Adult Social Care Sector in England*. London: The King's Fund.

The Policy, Ethics and Human Rights Committee (2014) The Code of Ethics for Social Work. London: BASW.

The Scottish Government (2018) Rights, Respect and Recovery. Available at: www.gov.scot/binaries/content/documents/govscot/publications/strategy-plan/2018/11/rights-respect-recovery/documents/00543437-pdf/00543437-pdf/govscot%3Adocument/00543437.pdf

The World Health Organization (2017) *Global action plan on the public health response to dementia 2017–2025*. Switzerland: WHO.

Thomas, N. (2007) Towards a theory of children's participation. *International Journal of Children's Rights*, 15(2): 199–218.

Thompson, N. (2002) *Loss and Grief: A Guide for Human Services Practitioners*. Basingstoke: Palgrave Macmillan.

Thompson, N. (2015) *Understanding Social Work: Preparing for Practice* (4th ed). Houndsmill: Palgrave Macmillan.

Thompson, N. (2016) *Anti-Discriminatory Practice* (6th ed). London: Palgrave Macmillan.

Thompson, N., Stradling, S., Murphy, M. and O'Neill, P. (1996) Stress and organisational culture. *British Journal of Social Work*, 26(1): 57–63.

Thompson, S. and Thompson, N. (2018) *The Critically Reflective Practitioner*. London: Palgrave Macmillan.

Timms, N. (1983) *Social Work Values: An Enquiry*. London: Routledge and Kegan Paul.

Tiquet, M.-E. (2017) Coercion, drug treatment and the criminal justice system: a service user perspective. Doctoral thesis. Portsmouth: University of Portsmouth.

Tisdall, K. and Davis, J. (2004) Making a difference? Bringing children's and young people's views into policy-making. *Children and Society*, 18(2): 131–142.

Townsend, R. (2018) *PTSD Understanding and Recovery*. Lewes: Pomegranate Press.

Treisman, K. (2017) *Working with Relational and Developmental Trauma in Children and Adolescents*. London: Routledge

Trevithick, P. (2000) *Social Work Skills: A Practice Handbook*. Maidenhead: Open University Press.

Trevithick, P. (2012) *Social Work Skills and Knowledge: A Practice Handbook* (3rd ed). Maidenhead: Open University Press.

Trevithick, P. (2014) Humanising managerialism: reclaiming emotional reasoning, intuition, the relationship and knowledge and skills in social work. *Journal of Social Work Practice: Psychotherapeutic Approaches in Health, Welfare and the Community*, 28(3): 287–311.

Triggs, G. (2018) *Speaking Up*. Melbourne: Melbourne University Press.

Tuckman, B. (1965) Developmental sequence in small groups. *Psychological Bulletin*, 63: 384–399.

Tuckman, B. and Jensen, M. C. (1977) Stages of small group development revisited. *Group and Organizational Studies*, 2: 419–427.

Turbett, C. (2014) *Doing Radical Social Work*. Basingstoke: Palgrave Macmillan.

Turnbull, G. and Spence, J. (2011) What's the risk? The proliferation of risk across child and youth policy in England. *Journal of Youth Studies*, 14: 939–959.

Turner, S. and Bernard, C. (2014) Supporting older people with learning disabilities: a toolkit for health and social care commissioners [online]. Available at: http://www.bild.org.uk/resources/ageingwell/resources/

Tyrrell, L., Duell-Piening, P., Morris, M. and Casey, S. (2016) Talking about health and experiences of using health services with people from refugee backgrounds. Melbourne: Victorian Refugee Health Network.

UK Home Office (2017) 2017 Drug Strategy. Available at: https://assets.publishing.service.gov.uk/government/uploads/system/uploads/attachment_data/file/628148/Drug_strategy_2017.pdf

Um, M-Y. and Harrison, D. (1998) Role stressors, burnout, mediators and job satisfaction: a stress stain outcome model and empirical test. *Social Work Research*, 22(2): 110–115.

UN Equality and Human Rights Commission (2017) *How well is the UK performing on disability rights?* Geneva: United Nations. Available at: www.equalityhumanrights.com/sites/default/files/ehrc_un_crpd_report.pdf

UN General Assembly (2006) Convention on the Rights of Persons with Disabilities: resolution adopted by the General Assembly, 24 January 2007 (A/RES/61/106). Available at: www.refworld.org/docid/45f973632.html

UNHCR (2017) Global Trends, Forced Displacement in 2017 [online]. Available at: www.unhcr.org/5b27be547.pdf

UNCHR (2018a) Figures at a Glance [online]. Updated 19 June 2018. Available at: http://www.unhcr.org/en-au/figures-at-a-glance.html

UNHCR (2018b) Expanding Partnership Report 2017 [online]. Available at http://www.unhcr.org/en-au/publications/fundraising/5b30bbe67/unhcr-global-report-2017-expanding-partnerships.html

UNICEF (2015) *Family and Parenting Support*. Florence: UNICEF.

United Nations (2015) *Universal Declaration of Human Rights*. New York: United Nations.

United Nations (2017) *World Population Prospects: The 2017 Revision: Key Findings and Advance Tables*. New York: United Nations.

Valentine, C. (ed) (2018) *Families Bereaved by Alcohol or Drugs: Research on Experiences, Coping and Support*. Abingdon: Routledge.

van Kooy, J. and Bowman, D. (2018) 'Surrounded with so much uncertainty': asylum seekers and manufactured precarity in Australia. *Journal of Ethnic and Migration Studies*, 45(5): 1–18.

Vandemeulebrouckea, T., Dierckx de Casterléb, B. and Gastmansa, C. (2018) The use of care robots in aged care: a systematic review of argument-based ethics literature. *Archives of Gerontology and Geriatrics*, 74: 15–25.

Venning, H. and Ramsden, D. (2016) *Clare in the Community*. Series 11, Episode 2, 'Hell on Wheels'. First broadcast: 22 November 2016.

Vostanis, P. (2007) *Mental Health Interventions and Services for Vulnerable Children and Young People*. London: Jessica Kingsley Publishers.

Wade, B. E. (2007) Prevalence of secondary traumatic stress among social workers. *Social Work*, 52(1): 63–70.

Wade, J. (2011) Preparation and transition planning for unaccompanied asylum-seeking and refugee young people: a review of evidence in England. *Children & Youth Services Review*, 33(12): 2424–2243.

Wade, J., Sirriyeh, A., Kohli, R. and Simmonds, J. (2012) *Fostering Unaccompanied Asylum-Seeking Young People: Creating a Family Life Across a World of Difference*. London: BAAF Adoption & Fostering.

Wagaman, M. A., Geiger, J. M., Shockley, C. and Segal, E. A. (2015) The role of empathy in burnout, compassion satisfaction and secondary traumatic stress among social workers. *Social Work*, 60(3): 201–208.

Wagner, G. (1988) *Residential Care: A Positive Choice*. London: HMSO.

Walker, S. (2011) *The Social Worker's Guide to Child and Adolescent Mental Health*. London: Jessica Kingsley Publishers.

Wallcraft, J. (2005) The place of recovery, in Ramon, S. and Williams, J. E. (eds) *Mental Health at the Crossroads*. Abingdon: Routledge.

Walter, T. (1994) *The Revival of Death*. London: Routledge.

Walters, G. (2004) Is there such a thing as a good death? *Palliative Medicine*, 18(5): 404–408.

Wang, C-W., Chan, C. L. W. and Chow, A. Y. M. (2018) Social workers' involvement in advance care planning: a systematic narrative review. *BMC Palliative Care*, 17(1): 5.

Watt, J. (2013) *Report Writing for Social Workers*. London: Sage.

Watzlawick, P., Beavin, J. H. and Jackson, D. D. (1967) *Pragmatics of Human Communication*. New York: W.W. Norton & Company.

Weems, M. E., White, C. J., McHatton, P. A., Shelley, C., Bond, T., Brown, R. N., Melina, L., Scheidt, L. A., Goode, J., De Carteret, P. and Wyatt, J. (2009) Heartbeats: exploring the power of qualitative research expressed as autoethnographic performance texts. *Qualitative Inquiry*, 15(5): 843–858.

Weinstein, J. (2008) *Working with Loss, Death and Bereavement: A Guide for Social Workers*. London: Sage.

Weisman, A. D. (1972) *On Dying and Denying: A Psychiatric Study of Terminality*. New York: Behavioral Publications.

Weisman, D. and Zornado, J. (2012) *Professional Writing for Social Work Practice*. New York: Springer.

Weiss, H. B. (2003) Foreword, in Katz, I. and Pinkerton, J. (eds) *Evaluating Family Support: Thinking Internationally, Thinking Critically*. Chichester: Wiley.

Welch, M. (2012) The sonics of crimmigration in Australia: wall of noise and quiet manoeuvring. *The British Journal of Criminology*, 52(2): 324–344.

Welsh Assembly (2008) Working together to reduce harm: the substance misuse strategy for Wales 2008–2018. Available at: http://www2.nphs.wales.nhs.uk:8080/SubstanceMisuseDocs.nsf

Wendell, S. (1996) *The Rejected Body*. London: Routledge.

Werner, E. E. (1989) High-risk children in young adulthood: a longitudinal study from birth to 32 years. *American Journal of Orthopsychiatry*, 59(1): 72–81.

Westwell, G. (2015) Experiential therapy, in Wilkins, P. (ed) *Person-Centred and Experiential Therapies: Contemporary Approaches and Issues in Practice*. London: Sage.

Westwood, J. (2014) *Children in Need of Support*. Basingstoke: Palgrave Macmillan.

Wettenhall, R. (2019) The public-private interface: surveying the history, in Hodge, G. and Greve, C. (eds) *The Challenge of Public-Private Partnerships: Learning from International Experience*. Cheltenham: Edward Elgar.

White, E. B. and Montgomery, P. (2014) Electronic tracking for people with dementia: an exploratory study of the ethical issues experienced by carers in making decisions about usage. *Dementia*, 13(2): 216–232.

White, S. (2013) Practising reflexivity: nurturing humane practice, in Parker, J. and Doel, M. (eds) *Professional Social Work*. London: Sage/Learning Matters.

Whyte, B. (2009) *Youth Justice in Practice: Making a Difference*. Bristol: Policy Press.

Wilkins, A., Khan, M., Stabler, L. Newlands, F. and Mcdonnell, J. (2018) Evaluating the quality of social work supervision in UK children's services: comparing self-report and independent observations. *Clinical Social Work Journal*, 46(4): 350–360.

Wilkins, D. (2017) Writing Court Reports [online]. Available at: www.ccinform.co.uk/practice-guidance/writing-court-reports/

Wilkinson, R. and Pickett, K. (2010) *The Spirit Level: Why Equality is Better for Everyone*. London: Penguin.

Williams, C. and Graham, M. (2016) Building transformative practice: what does the theory say?, in Williams, C. and Graham, M. (eds) *Social Work in a Diverse Society: Transformative Practice with Black and Minority Ethnic Individuals and Communities*. Bristol: Policy Press.

Willis, P., Almack, K., Hafford-Letchfield, T., Simpson, P., Billings, B. and Mall, N. (2018) Turning the co-production corner: methodological reflections from an action research project to promote LGBT inclusion in care homes for older people. *International Journal of Economic Research and Public Health*, 15(4): 695.

Wilson, D. and Rees, G. (2006) *Just Justice: A Study into Black Young People's Experiences of the Youth Justice System*. London: Children's Society.

Wilson, E. (1980) *Only Halfway to Paradise: Women in Post-War Britain 1945–1968*. London: Tavistock.

Winnicott, D. W. (1971) *Playing and Reality*. London: Tavistock.

Wood, J. and Kemshall, H. (2008) Risk management, accountability and partnerships in criminal justice, in Stout, B., Yates, J. and Williams, B. (eds) *Applied Criminology*. London: Sage.

Woods, B., Aguirre, E., Spector, A. E. and Orrell, M. (2012) Cognitive stimulation to improve cognitive functioning in people with dementia. *Cochrane Database of Systematic Reviews*, 2: CD005562.

Worden, J. W. (2008) *Grief Counselling and Grief Therapy: A Handbook for the Mental Health Practitioner* (4th ed). New York: Springer.

World Health Organization (2011) World Report on Disability: Summary, 2011, WHO/NMH/VIP/11.01. Available at: www.refworld.org/docid/50854a322.html

World Health Organization (2018) Draft Global Action Plan to Promote the Health of Refugees and Migrants. Available at: http://www.who.int/migrants/Global_Action_Plan_for_migration.pdf

Worsley, A., McLaughlin, K. and Leigh, J. (2017) A subject of concern: the experiences of social workers referred to the Health and Care Professions Council. *The British Journal of Social Work*, 47(8): 2421–2437.

Wright, P., Turner, C., Cley, D., Mills, H. (2006) *Participation of Children and Young People in Developing Social Care* (Practice Guide 2006). London: SCIE.

Young Minds (2018) New figures show a rise in young people's mental health problems since 2004 [online]. Available at: https://youngminds.org.uk/blog/new-figures-show-a-rise-in-young-peoples-mental-health-problems-since-2004/

Young, I. (2005) Five faces of oppression, in Cudd, A. E. and Andreasen, R. O. (eds) *Feminist Theory: A Philosophical Anthology*. Malden, MA: Blackwell Publishing.

Young, I. M. (1990) *Justice and the Politics of Difference*. Princeton, NJ: Princeton University Press.

Young, M. and Willmott, P. (1957) *Family and Kinship in East London*. London: Routledge and Kegan Paul.

Younghusband, E. L. (1959) *Report of the Working Party on Social Workers in the Local Authority Health and Welfare Services*. London: HMSO.

Youth Justice Board (2008) *Assessment, Planning Interventions and Supervision: Key Elements of Effective Practice*. London: YJB.

Youth Justice Board (2014) *AssetPlus: Assessment and Planning in the Youth Justice System*. London: YJB.

Youth Justice Board (2016) *Participation Strategy: Giving Young People a Voice in Youth Justice*. London: YJB.

Yuill, C. and Gibson, A. (eds) (2011) *Sociology for Social Work*. London: Sage.

Zabern, A. and Bouteyre, E. (2018) Leading protective factors for children living out of home: a literature review. *Child & Family Social Work*, 23: 324–335.

Zastrow, C. (2009) *Introduction to Social Work and Social Welfare: Empowering People* (10th ed). Belmont, CA: Brooks/Cole.

Zetter, R. (2007) More labels, fewer refugees: remaking the refugee label in an era of globalization. *Journal of Refugee Studies*, 20(2): 172–192.

Zhou, N. (2018) UN: 'health crisis' demands closure of Australia's offshore detention centres. *The Guardian*, 13 October. Available at: www.theguardian.com/australia-news/2018/oct/13/un-health-crisis-demands-closure-of-australias-offshore-detention-centres

Zolberg, A. R. (1989) The next waves: migration theory for a changing world. *International Migration Review*, 23(3): 403–430.

Court cases

Bolitho v City and Hackney Health Authority (1998) House of Lords AC232.

Gough v United Kingdom S (2014) ECHR 317. 49327/11.

Whitehouse v Lemon (1979) Whitehouse v Lemon; Whitehouse v Gay News Ltd: 2 WLR 281 [1979]. HL 21 Feb 1979.

Y (Autism-Care Proceedings-Deprivation of Liberty) Re (2018) EWHC B63 (23 Apr 2018)

Legislation

Australian Border Force Act (2015): www.legislation.gov.au/Details/C2017C00354

Care Act (2014): www.legislation.gov.uk/ukpga/2014/23/contents/enacted

Children Act (1989): www.legislation.gov.uk/ukpga/1989/41/contents

Children and Families Act (2014): www.legislation.gov.uk/ukpga/2014/6/contents/enacted

Community Care (Direct Payments) Act (1996): www.legislation.gov.uk/ukpga/1996/30/contents

European Convention on Human Rights (2013). Council of Europe: https://www.echr.coe.int/Documents/Convention_ENG.pdf

Equality Act (2010): www.legislation.gov.uk/ukpga/2010/15/contents

Factory Act (1833): www.nationalarchives.gov.uk/education/resources/1833-factory-act

Human Rights Act (1998): www.legislation.gov.uk/ukpga/1998/42/contents

Mental Capacity Act (2005): www.legislation.gov.uk/ukpga/2005/9/contents

Mental Health Act (2007): www.legislation.gov.uk/ukpga/2007/12/contents

Sexual Offences Act (2003): www.legislation.gov.uk/ukpga/2003/42/contents

Resources

Child Law Advice: Childlawaadvice.org.uk

Diagnostic and Statistical Manual of Mental Disorders (DSM): www.psychiatry.org/psychiatrists/practice/dsm

Disability Rights UK: https://www.disabilityrightsuk.org

Family Drug and Alcohol Court: https://fdac.org.uk

Family Rights Group: www.frg.org.uk/involving-families/family-group-conferences

Health and Safety Executive (a) – Management Standards: www.hse.gov.uk/stress/standards

Health and Safety Executive (b) – Stress management competency indicator tool: www.hse.gov.uk/stress/mcit.pdf

Safety resources – managing stress: https://safetyresourcesblog.files.wordpress.com/2014/10/managing-the-causes-of-work-related-stress-a-step-by-step-approach-using-management-standards.pdf

International Classification of Diseases and Related Problems (1992): www.who.int/classifications/icd/en

International Federation of Social Workers (2012): http://ifsw.org/policies/definition-of-social-work

International Foster Care Association: www.ifco.info

Mental Health Foundation – Fundamental Facts about Mental Health (2016): www.mentalhealth.org.uk/publications/fundamental-facts-about-mental-health-2016

National Association of Social Workers – code of ethics: https://www.socialworkers.org/About/Ethics/Code-of-Ethics

CAMHS Four-Tier Strategic Framework: webarchive.nationalarchives.gov.uk/20100202120904/
http://www.dcsf.gov.uk/everychildmatters/healthandwellbeing/mentalhealthissues/camhs/
fourtierstrategicframework/fourtierstrategicframework

IFSW Statement of Ethical Principles: www.ifsw.org/global-social-work-statement-of-ethical-
principles

The Independent Inquiry into Child Sexual Abuse in the UK (IICSA) or Westminster Inquiry:
www.iicsa.org.uk

The Scottish Child Abuse Inquiry: www.childabuseinquiry.scot

The Universal Declaration of Human Rights (1948): http://www.un.org/en/universal-declaration-
human-rights/index.html

Wechsler Intelligence Test (2019): wechslertest.com/about-wechsler-intelligence-test

Wellness Recovery Action Plan (WRAP) (2019): http://mentalhealthrecovery.com/wrap-isLigenimus
pos eos re exerunt que et aut alit, eturi dolupta ssimentur?

Index